Extraordinary acclaim for Brad Gooch's

PUBLIC LIBRAR
Ooch Street
MURRAY, KY 42071

P9-DHT-187

FLANNERY

A LIFE

OF

FLANNERY O'CONNOR

Selected as one of the best books of the year by *Chicago Tribune, The Atlantic, The New Yorker, Boston Globe, Booklist, Time Out New York, Tin House, Pittsburgh Post-Gazette, Minneapolis Star Tribune, Atlanta, Washington Times,* and *Palm Beach Post*

"The author of some of the most brilliant fiction in American literature, Flannery O'Connor was, according to Brad Gooch's new biography, in many ways like her work: tough-minded, God-haunted, fiercely original, and take-no-prisoners funny. . . . *Flannery* is full of information that will come as news to the writer's fans (how amazing that O'Connor, famous for her grotesque, comical characters, originally wanted to be a cartoonist! How astonishing that, as a child, she appeared in a newsreel with a chicken she'd taught to walk backward!). Enlivening the book is Gooch's keen eye for the many real-life inspirations that this literary master transformed into art."

— Francine Prose, *O, The Oprah Magazine*

"Rich, intimate. . . . A finely layered portrait of this utterly singular woman. . . . Gooch warmly reconstructs how the taciturn O'Connor, with her sharp wit and self-described 'thirteenth-century' religious sensibility, attracted a range of lifelong friends. . . . Gooch does a brilliant job of resurrecting on the page this major American writer."

— David McFadden, Associated Press

DEC 87 2011

"O'Connor emerges once again, as quirky, passionate, and tart-tongued as ever."   — Tina Jordan, *Entertainment Weekly*

"Flannery O'Connor's work (like that of Sylvia Plath, a contemporary) is hard for a reader to approach without being dazzled by a high beam of personal myths — the reclusiveness, the lupus, the pathetically short lifespan. Now we have Brad Gooch's *Flannery,* its subject's first major biography and a more controlled illumination of the background to O'Connor's two novels and two story collections. . . . As Gooch shows, many of her stories' outlandish elements were inspired by actual events."
          — Joseph O'Neill, *The Atlantic*

"Excellent. . . . Mr. Gooch is patient and tactful with the publicity-shy and dauntingly complex O'Connor. His book is a welcome introduction to the quiet, narrow life of a fiercely funny and unnervingly powerful writer."
          — Adam Begley, *New York Observer*

"In his engaging, sympathetic, and yet intellectually scrupulous biography of O'Connor, Brad Gooch provides the ideal biographical commentary: his voice is never obtrusive, yet we feel his judgment throughout; his allegiance to his subject is never in doubt, yet we sense his critical detachment, especially in his tracing of the ways in which 'Flannery' — as Gooch calls O'Connor — seems to have mapped out a strategy of survival for herself."
          — Joyce Carol Oates, *New York Review of Books*

"Brad Gooch's rapt, authoritative *Flannery* is the first major biography of a writer who died forty-four years ago. . . . What makes *Flannery* so valuable is the degree of intimacy with which it captures O'Connor's sensibility."   — Janet Maslin, *New York Times*

"Excellent. . . . Likely to be the definitive life of Flannery O'Connor for this generation of readers. . . . Gooch has done a splendid job of catching up the observations, memories, and speculations of O'Connor's contemporaries."

— Angeline Goreau, *American Scholar*

"One of the strengths of Brad Gooch's biography is its elegant pooh-poohing of her claim that 'experience is the greatest deterrent to fiction.'"

— *Economist*

"O'Connor has become, as Brad Gooch points out in *Flannery,* 'a one-woman academic industry,' an industry wherein Gooch labors and thrives by producing that big, calm, gentlemanly biography. . . . Gooch is a professional, and a gracious and determined one."

— Joy Williams, *New York Times Book Review*

"The details of the chapter on her time [at the Iowa Writers' Workshop] is one of the best in *Flannery* and one of the best accounts of a writer's development in recent literary biography. . . . *Flannery* sweeps away myriad myths that have built up around O'Connor's life."

— Allen Barra, Salon.com

"The story Gooch tells is amply shaded and evocatively detailed. . . . It is a poignant, inspiring story of one brave, dedicated, brilliant writer."

— Floyd Skloot, *Boston Globe*

"Mr. Gooch has crafted the first serious biography of the distinguished Georgia writer. . . . Admirers of Flannery O'Connor will welcome Mr. Gooch's thorough and informative biography of one of the most fascinating and rewarding writers in twentieth-century American literature."

— James E. Person Jr., *Washington Times*

"It's incredible that this is the first biography of the great Southern writer Flannery O'Connor. . . . As Brad Gooch shows, her life was as dark and rich and dense with meaning as her fiction is.

— Lev Grossman, *Time*

"Impressive. . . . Gooch's account is meticulous." — *The New Yorker*

"This gentlemanly biography reminds us that every now and then we need to renew our acquaintance with this thrilling writer. . . . Gooch makes us feel the vitality of O'Connor's literary creations all over again." — Susan Larson, *New Orleans Times-Picayune*

"Brad Gooch illuminates the short, tragic life of Flannery O'Connor, the Southern-gothic genius whose fiction, occasional prose, and correspondence are as dazzling as the exotic peacocks that roamed her Georgia homestead." — Lisa Shea, *Elle*

"This is one of those rare biographies that makes the writer almost as fascinating as what she wrote."

— Charles Matthews, *Houston Chronicle*

"The South runs through Brad Gooch's new biography of Flannery O'Connor as it runs through her fierce and funny stories. . . . A must-read for any fan." — Clyde Edgerton, *Garden and Gun*

"O'Connor lives and breathes — and spits fire — in Brad Gooch's portrait of the too-short life of the peacock-loving writer who dealt in the dark grotesqueries of human nature."

— Elissa Schappell, *Vanity Fair*

"*Flannery* is attractively written, thorough but not obtrusively detailed, and — most important — wholly to the point. . . . It is the work of a biographer whose goal is not to advocate or justify but simply to tell the story of O'Connor's too-short life and (insofar as possible) show how it was mirrored in her fiction."

— Terry Teachout, *Commentary*

"Lucidly written. . . . Brad Gooch has done an earnest, respectful, but mercifully not hagiographic job."

— Jonathan Yardley, *Washington Post*

"Gooch comfortably traces Flannery O'Connor's fiction to its real-life roots in a meticulous yet seemingly effortless writing style, resulting in the definitive biography."   — *Booklist* (starred review)

"*Flannery* plumbs the private side of one of American literature's most original storytellers."   — *Vogue*

"In the first major biography of the short story master, Brad Gooch makes up for torrid romances and bad behavior — of which there were none in O'Connor's life — with detail and insight, undoing some popular myths along the way."   — *Atlanta*

"Gooch is brilliant on O'Connor's fiction, passionate and smart, able to contextualize both the individual pieces and the scope of the career."   — David L. Ulin, *Los Angeles Times*

"Brad Gooch's exquisite portrait of Flannery O'Connor is engaging and essential reading."   — Tim Davis, *BookLoons*

"Brad Gooch's *Flannery* sets a new standard. . . . It will give readers a new respect for O'Connor's accomplishments, a new admiration for the almost biblical power of her vision, her voice."

— Daniel Dyer, *Cleveland Plain Dealer*

"This welcome biography of Flannery O'Connor is crisply written, fully researched, and relatively brief. . . . Brad Gooch is a sympathetic critic of both O'Connor's life and writings."

— William H. Pritchard, *Chicago Tribune*

"Gooch's biography is a marvel of concision but skimps on nothing. . . . If a library is to have only one book on Flannery O'Connor, this should be it. Highly recommended."

— *Library Journal* (starred review)

"Gooch provides a glimpse into what it must have been like for Flannery O'Connor to face her far-too-short time on Earth looking 'down the barrel of the Misfit's shotgun.'"

— Charles Ealy, *Austin American-Statesman*

"As Brad Gooch's fine new biography of Flannery O'Connor details, her relations with the heavenly powers were never smooth or simple." — Algis Valiunas, *American Spectator*

"Gooch's well-researched, warm biography does many things, and not the least is dispelling those images of her as the 'reclusive Emily Dickinson of Milledgeville.' . . . Gooch writes movingly of O'Connor's stoic acceptance of her illness and fight to continue to write." — Colette Bancroft, *St. Petersburg Times*

"Brad Gooch's excellent biography explores the mystery of how this solitary, pampered Catholic girl from Georgia became an unequivocal moral thinker, an acerbic wit, and one of America's most astonishing writers. . . . Gooch is enough of an artist to understand that no amount of explanation can divest lightning of its surprise and magnificence."

— R. T. Smith, *Roanoke Times*

"So compelling is Flannery O'Connor that one almost forgets there's another writer at work in Brad Gooch's fascinating biography of the Southern short-story master. But this fact is a testament to just how well written and thoroughly researched *Flannery* is."
— Erin Wylie, *Time Out New York*

"Superb. . . .In Gooch, Flannery O'Connor has found her definitive biographer, a storyteller himself who reveals, as best anyone can, this mysterious personality."
— Cary Clack, *San Antonio Express-News*

"Gooch is respectful, allowing O'Connor's wit to handle whatever revelations she has to offer and leaving us to feel affection for a gifted writer who did her best with the time she had."
— Anne Stephenson, *Arizona Republic*

"In his excellent biography of Flannery O'Connor, Brad Gooch probes the relationship between O'Connor's life and her fiction as he highlights the various facets of O'Connor's complex personality."
— Patrick Samway, *America*

"Gooch presents a rousing tale of a quintessentially American artist, whose industry, fierce individualism, and boldness summoned into being an unlikely triumph."
— Shawn Macomber, *Weekly Standard*

"Gooch tenders a sensitive and nuanced examination of Flannery O'Connor's misfit status."   — Maud Newton, NPR.org

"Excellent. . . . Gooch, against heavy odds, brings the brilliant Catholic recluse to life."   — Jay McInerney, *Time*

"If you love Flannery O'Connor and her stories and want to know more about her so you can love her stories even more, Gooch's biography is a wonderful gift."

— William H. Willimon, *Christian Century*

"As Brad Gooch shows in this skillful, gentle biography, what it lacked in titillation O'Connor's short, poignant life made up for in intensity. . . . Rather than belaboring it, Gooch has the good sense to let her loneliness emerge between the lines, an ambient mood of exile, alienation, sadness."   — Sarah Churchwell, *Guardian*

"Gooch's rigorous attention to the 'felt life' creates context for each major text, offering a service which O'Connor studies currently needs crucially."

— Avis Hewitt, *Cheers! The Flannery O'Connor Society Newsletter*

"Much like a novelist, Gooch is able to take small, insignificant details and make them contribute to his portrait. . . . He presents O'Connor's flaws and contradictions with the relish and love she'd bestow on her own characters."   — Kelly Kerney, *Irish Echo*

"An impeccable narrative."

— Carl Rollyson, *Minneapolis Star Tribune*

"Gooch never doubts that a small life can be a big life in every way that counts."   — Catherine Holmes, *Charleston Post and Courier*

"Brad Gooch displays a novelist's insight. . . . He relates Flannery's writings to life at Andalusia with care and sensitivity. . . . It is a tribute to Gooch's fine book that we can see the author herself."

— Paul Binding, *Times Literary Supplement*

FLANNERY

A LIFE
OF
FLANNERY O'CONNOR

BRAD GOOCH

BACK BAY BOOKS
LITTLE, BROWN AND COMPANY
New York Boston London

Also by Brad Gooch

City Poet: The Life and Times of Frank O'Hara

Copyright © 2009 by Brad Gooch

All rights reserved. Except as permitted under the U.S. Copyright Act of 1976, no part of this publication may be reproduced, distributed, or transmitted in any form or by any means, or stored in a database or retrieval system, without the prior written permission of the publisher.

Back Bay Books / Little, Brown and Company
Hachette Book Group
237 Park Avenue, New York, NY 10017
www.hachettebookgroup.com

Originally published in hardcover by Little, Brown and Company, February 2009
First Back Bay paperback edition, March 2010

Back Bay Books is an imprint of Little, Brown and Company. The Back Bay Books name and logo are trademarks of Hachette Book Group, Inc.

The author wishes to thank the John Simon Guggenheim Memorial Foundation, the National Endowment for the Humanities, and Furthermore, a program of the J. M. Kaplan Fund, for their support during the writing of this book. Grateful acknowledgment is made to Farrar, Straus and Giroux and to Houghton Mifflin Harcourt for permission to reprint excerpts from Flannery O'Connor's work.

Copyright acknowledgments appear on page 385 and constitute a continuation of the copyright page.

Library of Congress Cataloging-in-Publication Data
Gooch, Brad.
    Flannery : a life of Flannery O'Connor / Brad Gooch. — 1st ed.
      p. cm.
    Includes bibliographical references and index.
    ISBN: 978-0-316-00066-6 (hc) / 978-0-316-01899-9 (pb)
  1. O'Connor, Flannery. 2. Authors, American — 20th century — Biography.
3. Milledgeville (Ga.) — Biography. I. Title.
    PS3565.C57Z6795 2008
    813'.54 — dc22
    [B]   2008028504

10 9 8 7 6 5 4 3 2 1

RRD-IN

Printed in the United States of America

For Paul Raushenbush

Contents

As for biographies, there won't be any biographies of me because, for only one reason, lives spent between the house and the chicken yard do not make exciting copy.

— Flannery O'Connor

FLANNERY

WALKING BACKWARD

✿

When Flannery O'Connor was five years old, the Pathe newsreel company dispatched a cameraman from its main offices in New York City to the backyard of the O'Connor family home in Savannah, Georgia. The event, as O'Connor wryly confessed in an essay in *Holiday* magazine in September 1961, almost three decades later, "marked me for life." Yet the purpose of the visit from "the New Yorker," as she labeled him, wasn't entirely to film her, outfitted as she was in her best double-breasted dark coat and light wool knit beret, but rather to record her buff Cochin bantam, the chicken she reputedly taught to walk backward.

How a Yankee photographer wound up for a memorable half day at the bottom of the O'Connors' steep back stairs isn't entirely clear. One rumor ascribes the connections of Katie Semmes, a well-to-do dowager cousin who lived in the grander house next door, and whose tall windows looked down on the yard where the filming took place. According to a girlhood playmate of O'Connor's, "Miss Katie brought them down here to do it." O'Connor simply credits an item on her celebrity chicken in the local papers: "Her fame had spread through the press and by the time she reached the attention of Pathé News, I suppose there was nowhere left for her to go — forward or backward. Shortly after that she died, as now seems fitting."

The shoot did not go smoothly. O'Connor was certainly prepared. Whenever the cumbersome camera on its tripod began to grind, she adopted a fierce, dignified expression — the one she used if she felt she was being watched. The problem was her uncooperative tan "frizzled" chicken, with its backward-growing feathers, spending hours scratching obliviously in the yard while the cameraman fidgeted. Finally, as the afternoon wore on, the bird began to back up. O'Connor, a natural mimic, jumped next to her and began to walk backward as well. The operator stuck his head under his tent. A few seconds later, the hen hit a bush and abruptly sat down. Exasperated, "the Pathé man" gathered his equipment and made a quick exit, refusing even to enjoy a dish of ice cream.

O'Connor's screen debut exists in all its fragility in a Pathé film archive. The brief stretch of scratchy footage opens with a title card announcing in italic script: "Odd fowl walks backward to go forward so she can look back to see where she went." For all of four seconds, O'Connor, a self-possessed little girl, is glimpsed in glaring afternoon light, a wisp of curls peeking from beneath her cap, calmly coping with three chickens fluttering in her face. In close-up, the biggest of her bantams then jerks backward a half-dozen times on a short stretch of pavement, supporting the skeptical theory of one relative that it was merely suffering from a cognitive skip. Some obvious gimmickry aids the brief stunt: with the help of a reverse-feed technique, the chicken as well as lines of barnyard cows, mares, and ducks comically parade backward. The End.

O'Connor never had the pleasure of seeing the tandem performance on-screen. The short never came to a Savannah movie theater, though "Unique Chicken Goes in Reverse" was released as a one-minute, twenty-seven-second, vignette in March 1932, a week shy of her seventh birthday. Its cute subject matter was the sort that appealed to Depression-era audiences in other lighthearted spoofs that played on seven-to-eight-minute reels along with current events and sports news before the main feature. Among other whimsical topics treated by Pathe that year in its animal "gag reels" were Florida sportsmen feeding crackers to turtles; Boston kids showing off their pet tabby cats; a girl at the Westminster Kennel Club Exhibition in New York City producing a tiny dog out of her satchel.

While O'Connor's star turn is brief, its afterimage still flickered in her mind years later. Even though she was not a woman, or author, overly given to delving into childhood memories to unlock her identity, something about that afternoon's performance stayed with her. Certainly the obdurate refusal of her bird to be easily seduced by the ambassador from klieg-lit culture kept her giggling. But so did its pratfall, and, by association, hers. O'Connor loved to make fun of her own diminutive stature in popular culture. When a friend accused her of "celebrity" after the publication of her first book of stories, *A Good Man Is Hard to Find,* she gleefully wrote back that her fame was "a comic distinction shared with Roy Rogers's horse and Miss Watermelon of 1955."

She also enjoyed the attention. O'Connor dates her lifelong passion for raising exotic birds to the rush she at least pretended to have gotten from the noisy movie camera. "From that day with the Pathé man I began to collect chickens," she writes in "The King of the Birds," her *Holiday* magazine article. As a Catholic schoolgirl trying to re-create her winning formula, she began to collect other birds with freakish traits: one green eye and one orange, an overly long neck, a comb askew. She searched in vain for a one of a kind with three legs or three wings, and pondered a picture in Robert Ripley's *Believe It or Not!* of a rooster that survived thirty days without its head. "Apparently Pathé News never heard of any of these other chickens of mine," O'Connor writes, with a stage sigh. "It never sent another photographer."

Yet the memory did not stop there. In the fall of 1948, O'Connor was a guest at the Yaddo artists' colony in upstate New York. Now a young woman of twenty-three, a budding writer, she had settled on fiction as her vocation after several years preparing for a career as a cartoonist by designing linoleum-cut cartoons for her women's college in Milledgeville, Georgia. Her artistic signature: the initials of her name arranged to resemble a bird with beak, though she eventually dropped the "M" for Mary, simply becoming "Flannery." At the Iowa Writers' Workshop, where she went for an MFA, her professors helped her win a residency in the prestigious colony for a few months. Another guest that fall was Robert Lowell, a thirty-one-year-old poet who had won a Pulitzer Prize the year before for his first book, *Lord Weary's Castle.*

Lowell needed no introduction, because she already knew his work. The two quickly developed a friendship based on mutual admiration; he would remain one of the rare souls for whom she felt a lifelong affection. But in her first walk-on appearance in his consciousness, in a letter Lowell writes to the poet Elizabeth Bishop on October 1, 1948, cataloging the crew he had met at dinner, O'Connor can be caught using the backward chicken as her comic calling card: "Now there are an introverted and an extroverted colored man; a boy of 23 who experiments with dope; a student of a former Kenyon class-mate of mine, who at the age of six was in a Pathe News Reel for having a chicken that walked backwards; and Malcolm Cowley, nice but a little slow."

That fall and winter at Yaddo, O'Connor was mostly holed up from breakfast until dinner in her tiny room in West House, a smaller version of the unheated main Mansion, closed to guests at the end of summer. There she worked on drafts of her first novel, *Wise Blood.* Lowell read and commented on the work in progress, begun in Iowa City two years earlier. The challenge of the novel was its protagonist, Haze Motes. Once she hit on his tone and stature, the novel began to cohere. In earlier drafts, he was a homesick

Southern boy. By the time she finished, he was a more extreme character, a high-contrast and highly contrary prophet. The phrase O'Connor used to nail his essence is put in his landlady's head in the novel's last few pages: "She saw him going backwards to Bethlehem and she had to laugh."

It's tempting to read Haze Motes as O'Connor's backward-walking hen, baptized by fire. "Backward" is surely the word for him. "Time goes forward, it don't go backward," his landlady warns him. He's the template for a number of memorable O'Connor creations who decide to operate their souls in reverse: The Misfit, snarling about a world thrown off balance, or O. E. Parker, who gets an image of God tattooed on his back. Maybe this first instinct to draw a line connecting Motes back to her stubborn Cochin bantam, which fittingly died, struck O'Connor as right. This time around the performance would be humorous, entertaining, weird, but religious as well. Maybe she snickered as she realized what she'd done, or maybe not. Perhaps their kinship was accidental rather than planned.

Where O'Connor literally went with the backward-walking chicken is spelled out in "The King of the Birds," first published under the title "Living with a Peacock": "My quest, whatever it was actually for, ended with peacocks." As a woman living with her mother on a farm in central Georgia for the rest of her adult writing life, after being diagnosed with lupus when she was twenty-six, O'Connor reverted to her childhood passion for collecting unusual birds — a one-eyed swan, a tribe of mallard ducks, three Japanese silkie bantams, two Polish crested bantams, a pen of pheasants, and a pen of quail. Yet the high-profile birds she first ordered from an ad in a Florida *Market Bulletin,* at sixty-five dollars a pair, were a peacock and a peahen, or as she usually called them, "peafowl."

These fantastic creatures, with tails that resembled maps of the solar system, are the birds most often associated with O'Connor. After she became a well-known author, many photographers visited, or wished to visit, her farm, Andalusia. As much as she cast her younger self as pixilated by the attention of the Pathe cameraman, as a woman she dreaded his kind. When she did allow *Time* magazine or one of the Atlanta papers to send a photographer, the results invariably featured her exotic birds. She wanted them to upstage her. In the most famous of these photographs, taken by Joe McTyre for the *Atlanta Journal* in 1962 and later used on the back cover of her collected letters, *The Habit of Being,* O'Connor is posed on aluminum crutches before a screen door, seemingly in dialogue with a peacock preening on the brick steps beside her.

O'Connor loved to play with patterns in her stories. The jalopy that Tom T. Shiftlet drives in "The Life You Save May Be Your Own" looks a lot like that of Haze Motes, last seen pushed over a cliff in *Wise Blood.* The big black valise the Bible salesman lugs in "Good Country People" might be the same one that the three little arsonists carry in "A Circle in the Fire." Most poignantly, "Judgment Day," a story O'Connor was working on during the last weeks of her life, was a retelling of her first published story, "The Geranium," remarkably closing her fictional circle. The separation between her life and her art was porous: a peacock comes walking off Andalusia onto the farm of "The Displaced Person." In "The King of the Birds," she reveals an eye for such patterns in her life as well. The emphasis is hers when she notes a line of pedigree from the unique chicken of her childhood to its artistic descendant, her unfurled peacock that will "dance forward *and backward.*"

The girl with the expression she recalled as exhibiting "dignified ferocity," recorded in the archival footage in "Unique Chicken Goes in Reverse," is instantly recognizable to us. Her features are clearly those discerned in anecdotes about her childhood in Savannah — contrary, a prankster, determined, funny, creative, and focused. And just as her Cochin bantam morphed into a peacock — a bird observed by the old priest in "The Displaced

Person" as "taking minute steps backward, his head against the spread tail" — so this clever child performer grew into the one-of-a-kind woman writer, "going backwards to Bethlehem," who freighted her acidly comic tales with moral and religious messages, running counter to so much trendy literary culture.

Part One

CALLOWAY COUNTY PUBLIC LIBRAR
710 Main Street
MURRAY, KY 42071

Chapter One

S AVANNAH

In the fall of 1963 Flannery O'Connor delivered her final public lecture. The occasion was the 175th anniversary celebration of Georgetown University, in Washington, DC, where she read prepared remarks through her prominent eyeglasses for about forty-five minutes from the proscenium stage of the ornate Gaston auditorium in historic Healy Hall. "The Catholic Novelist in the Protestant South" was the last of more than sixty such talks and readings she had given in the decade since the publication of her first novel, *Wise Blood,* enough for her to have confided about her "element of ham" to a friend: "I have a secret desire to rival Charles Dickens upon the stage."

Early in her speech that evening, she cast back to the beginnings of her creative life. "The things we see, hear, smell and touch affect us long before we believe anything at all," she said softly, in a flat, dry Georgia accent, while leaning on crutches. "The South impresses its image on the Southern writer from the moment he is able to distinguish one sound from another. He takes it in through his ears and hears it again in his own voice, and, by the time he is able to use his imagination for fiction, he finds that his senses respond irrevocably to a certain reality, and particularly to the sound of a certain reality. The Southern writer's greatest tie with the South is through his ear."

For O'Connor these sights and sounds had their origins in Savannah, where she was born Mary Flannery O'Connor on March 25, 1925, at St. Joseph's Hospital, and lived her first thirteen years, nearly a third of her life. The Savannah into which she was born was a classic Southern city, pungent in spring with blooming jasmine, though more sophisticated than other insular Georgia towns like Macon or Valdosta. No longer a booming nineteenth-century port, teeming with cotton brokers and shipping agents, the cosmopolitan center, with seventy-five thousand residents, still hosted a dozen or more foreign consulates; strangers with accents did not draw stares on the streets; and a cavalcade of steamers embarked daily from its harbor to ports in Germany, Britain, and Japan.

On the blustery spring day of her birth, the one-word weather forecast in the *Savannah Morning News* was dramatic enough: "unsettled." Savannahians awoke that morning to word of President Calvin Coolidge calling for a naval conference on the readiness of the American fleet. Most of the local talk concerned a girl evangelist from Fresno, California, packing crowds into the Municipal Auditorium with her message, "Sinner Must Be Reborn in Christ." Most auspicious for O'Connor's Irish Catholic parents, Edward and Regina, was the the date in the Roman Catholic calendar: it was the Feast of the Annunciation, marking the visit of the angel Gabriel to the infant's spiritual namesake, Mary, to announce her motherhood of Jesus.

O'Connor was born into a special corner of the life of Savannah simply by being born at St. Joseph's Hospital. The homey redbrick building, with big porches on its first and second floors, took up an entire city block at the corner of Habersham and East Taylor, just a few blocks south of the O'Connors' home. Known in the community as "old St. Joseph's," this intimate hospital, much trusted by Irish Catholics, was founded by Irish nuns, the Sisters of Mercy, who became local heroes in the summer of 1876 while caring for yellow fever victims crowded into the corridors of what was then Old Medical College. As their legacy, the founding sisters left behind, in the main entrance, a tall, stately statue of St. Joseph on a low pedestal that O'Connor's parents walked by often.

St. Joseph's was not only the hospital for the Irish Catholic community, but it was the O'Connors' family hospital, the one Cousin Katie Semmes presided over as prime benefactress. Her father, Captain John Flannery, a Confederate officer in the Jasper Greens, Savannah's Irish military corps, had parlayed his war record into success as a rich banker and a broker in the Savannah Cotton Exchange. When he died in 1910 he left all of his money, nearly a million dollars, to his only daughter, Katie, who used her inheritance to fund construction of a new adjoining east building, Flannery Memorial, in honor of Captain John and his wife, Mary Ellen Flannery. If O'Connor's parents wished to give thanks in prayer for the birth of their daughter — her name itself a memorial to Cousin Katie's mother — they stepped into the Flannery Memorial Chapel.

Named after the wife of a Civil War hero, the infant O'Connor was initiated at once into a social set haunted by the war still referred to in Savannah in the twenties and thirties as the "War Between the States" — a living memory for some, a single generation removed for others. The Catholic bishop of the Diocese of Savannah, Benjamin J. Keiley, retiring only two years before O'Connor's birth, served in the war as a Confederate drummer boy. Katie Semmes's deceased husband, Raphael Semmes, was the nephew of a famous Confederate admiral of the same name. Though O'Connor later swore, "I never was one to go over the Civil War in a big way," she grew up among a set of older women who were forever slipping on white gloves, and putting on big hats, to go off to chapter meetings of the Daughters of the Confederacy.

The Irish families using St. Joseph's Hospital had a double loyalty — to Confederate Memorial Day, and to St. Patrick's Day, with St. Patrick winning by a nose. The Irish pride parade in March just managed to overshadow the annual Confederate Day parade held each April 26. As O'Connor later wrote to a friend, "I was brought up in Savannah where there was a colony of the Over-Irish. They have the biggest St. Patrick's Day parade anywhere around and generally go nutty on the subject." She went on to exclaim incredulously that she had even heard her hometown compared to Dublin. Making up most Catholics in Savannah, the Irish were certainly a presence. In the year of her birth, two of the six city aldermen were Irish Catholics and so was the city attorney.

Yet the Irish Catholics of Savannah were given to a bunker mentality, with some justification. Catholics were expressly banned, along with rum, lawyers, and blacks, under the original Georgia Trust in 1733. While that law had long ago been overwritten, and waves of Irish immigrants arrived during the potato famines of the 1840s, an anti-Catholic law was still on the books at the time of O'Connor's birth: the Convent Inspection Bill became Georgia law in 1916. Under this weird legislation, grand juries were charged with inspecting Catholic convents, monasteries, and orphanages, to search for evidence of sexual immorality and to question all the "inmates," ensuring that they were not held involuntarily. Tom Watson, elected U.S. senator from Georgia in 1920, went so far as to accuse the bishop of Savannah of keeping "white slave pens" of missing girls.

With their ambiguous status, subdivided further into middle-class "lace curtain" and lower-class "shanty," the Irish could at least take comfort that legal segregation didn't apply to them as it did to the city's blacks. Jim Crow laws kept Savannah strictly divided by race. St. Joseph's Hospital was listed in the "White Department" rather than the "Colored" section of the *Savannah City Directory*.

The Catholic diocese ran seven churches — four for whites, three for blacks. Growing up, O'Connor saw blacks mainly in menial roles, usually maids slipping through the back doors of distressed antebellum homes. Her cousin Patricia Persse, who remembers her own family's electricity being turned off because of unpaid bills during the Depression, recalls, as well, "We had a black cook and nursemaid who came every day for fifty years, though she didn't live with us."

Edward and Regina O'Connor brought their newborn daughter home from the hospital to Lafayette Square, the epicenter of Roman Catholic life in Savannah, socially situated in the better half of the Irish ghetto, and one of twenty-one original squares put in place on a two-and-a-half-square-mile grid in an enlightened display of city planning. Settling the town in 1733, the English governor James Edward Oglethorpe had used as his model the design of a Roman military camp. A checkerboard of squares with allusive names such as Monterey, Chippewa, and Troup, Savannah was built from an inventory of architectural styles — Federal, Edwardian, Regency, Colonial, and Victorian — its tabby and cobblestone streets lined by live oaks hung with Spanish moss; chinaberry, Japanese maple, and Southern magnolia trees; and azalea and camellia bushes.

Each of the town's squares, many a bit worn by 1925, filled with dirt, or cut by streetcar tracks, had a distinctive neighborhood feel. Lafayette Square reflected the self-sufficiency of the Irish Catholics. Opposite the O'Connors' home, on the other side of the square, was the massive white-stucco French Gothic Cathedral of St. John the Baptist, occupying a full city block. Between the cathedral and their house was St. Vincent's Grammar School for Girls and, diagonally opposite St. Vincent's, its companion, Marist Brothers School for Boys. "I remember the square as a barren, sandy pile crawling with boys playing sports," says an ex-Marist pupil, Dan O'Leary. A

Presbyterian girl who lived across the street from the O'Connors has remarked, "It was so Catholic that I felt a bit like a fish out of water." During the school year, hundreds of Catholic children (together the schools enrolled about seven hundred students) marched back and forth across the square.

Built in 1856 of Savannah gray bricks, covered in light tan stucco, the O'Connors' three-story Georgian row house, its front door topped with a ruby etched-glass transom, was still joined, in 1925, with 209 East Charlton Street. Its twin, also a twenty-footer, was not torn down until three years later when Katie Semmes moved into 211 East Charlton and wanted an elevator attached to her sidewall. Mrs. O'Connor took pride in the modest elegance of her well-kept parlor floor with its small entrance foyer; attractive, dark green double living room with two black marble fireplaces, two chandeliers, and four eight-foot bay windows; large dining room with a heavy dark oak table, where the family would gather for formal meals; small kitchen; and back sunporch, where she kept her green plants. Upstairs, the parents' front bedroom was connected by a doorway to their daughter's back bedroom, both heated in winter by coal fireplaces.

The often-repeated Savannah comment that Flannery O'Connor "was conceived in the shadow of the cathedral" is not entirely rhetorical. Looming through her parents' bedroom windows were always its pale green twin spires, topped by gold crosses — visible, indeed, for miles around. Clearly audible was the tremulous booming of the big bells every morning, noon, and evening, signaling the praying of the Angelus, in honor of Mary. Like St. Joseph's Hospital, the cathedral — named St. John the Baptist, some said, to mollify a paranoid Protestant majority — was the handiwork of Captain John Flannery. A generous benefactor of the first cathedral, destroyed by fire in 1898, Captain Flannery then became chairman of the building committee for the present cathedral, dedicated in 1900. One of its three stained-glass windows, depicting a scene from the life of John the Baptist, was donated by him, "In Memory of Mary Ellen Flannery."

So when Mary Flannery O'Connor's parents carried her across the square for baptism at a four o'clock afternoon service on Easter Sunday, April 12, she wasn't just any little girl, though she was one of many babies and their gathered parents and godparents. Far from the promise "You count now," given by the Reverend Bevel Summers after he baptizes the young Harry in O'Connor's story "The River," was the Latin blessing pronounced that morning by the rector, Father T. A. Foley, as he marked the sign of the cross in water on her forehead: "Mary Flannery, ego te baptizo in nomine Patris et Filii et Spiritus Sancti." Listed on her baptismal certificate, as "first sponsor," was her father's brother, John Joseph O'Connor, a dentist in town. Her "second sponsor" was Mary Cline, her mother's oldest sister, who presided over the family's mansion in Milledgeville.

Early on, her parents brought the infant girl by the home of Katie Semmes, who was still living in an imposing 1852 redbrick Greek Revival at Bull and Taylor streets on Monterey Square. As Katherine Doyle Groves has recalled: "My first memories of her, we are third cousins, our great-grandmothers were sisters, was when she was an infant and they didn't have all this kind of equipment they have now for hauling babies. I remember a basket of some sort. We were visiting with my cousin, Mrs. Semmes. . . . We would go down, my mother and father, my sister and myself, in the evening to call on my cousin, and Ed and Regina, Flannery's parents, would be there with this baby in the basket on the floor." Groves has stressed that Flannery O'Connor actually bore no Flannery blood, as Captain Flannery was merely a cousin by marriage.

At home, the baby was rolled between the two second-floor

bedrooms — all the windows kept wide open for ventilation in spring and summer — and into the backyard, as well, in an elaborate crib. The contraption was common enough nursery furniture in the 1920s, especially in the South — a waist-high, flat, rectangular box, painted white, five feet in length, screened on the top and sides, and pushed on large metal wheels. Marketed as a "Kiddie-Koop Crib," with the insinuation of being a chicken coop for kids, the box doubled as a playpen, allowing a child to stand, or to be laid flat on a board through the middle, protected by its closed lid from the pesky flies and mosquitoes of coastal Georgia. As its successful 1923 ad slogan asked, "Danger or Safety — Which?"

When Mrs. O'Connor took her infant daughter for strolls around the perimeter of Lafayette Square, the child's conveyance was a bit more deluxe: a perambulator with oversized metal wheels and a padded interior lined with dark brown corduroy, given as a baby gift by Katie Semmes. Fashioned of wood, with a long swan's-neck metal handle and an adjustable protective hood of slatted wicker with portholes on either side, all painted in the same cream color, the elegant focal point was a monogram of the new baby's initials — "MFOC" — embossed in gold on the side. At rest in the hallway, the pushchair complemented the gilt picture-rail molding in the parlor, as well as Mrs. O'Connor's upholstered green brocade love seat, with gilded cabriole legs, and tea cart.

The word used over and over by friends to describe O'Connor's childhood is "protected," or, just as often, "overprotected." As a daughter in a Southern family with extended circles of relatives, especially unmarried female cousins and aunts, she was hardly overlooked. Thanks largely to her mother, she was kept as sealed during her early years as she was as a baby in her Kiddie-Koop — the brand name almost too neatly predicting her identification with fowl as her friends. Yet along with excessive control was entitlement and encouragement; the embossed initials on the perambulator predicted the heightened attention that would be paid, at least by the adults in the family, to each creative and sometimes downright peculiar gesture of this only child.

※

O'CONNOR WAS BORN into a clan of strong women, beginning with the family of her mother, the regally named Regina Lucille Cline. She was undoubtedly thinking of her mother's side of the family when writing to a friend of her relatives, "I don't think mine have ever been in a world they couldn't cope with because none of them that I know of have left the 19th century." Known around the region as "Old Catholic," both the Cline and Flannery families could be traced back to the Irish Treanors and Hartys, who settled, in the late eighteenth century, in old Locust Grove, in Taliaferro County, Georgia.

Flannery's great-grandfather Hugh Donnelly Treanor, who emigrated from county Tipperary in 1824, had a reputation for being well read. He developed a prosperous water-powered grist mill on the Oconee River in Milledgeville, in central Georgia, which became the family seat; as O'Connor later reported in a letter from Milledgeville, "Mass was first said here in my great-grandfather's hotel room, later in his home on the piano." After Hugh Treanor died, his widow, O'Connor's great-grandmother Johannah Harty Treanor, also Irish-born, settled with her family in the Locust Grove community. She donated the land on which Sacred Heart, the Catholic church at the corner of Hancock and Jefferson streets in Milledgeville, was built in 1874.

One of Hugh Treanor's daughters, Kate, married Peter J. Cline, a successful dry-goods store owner in Milledgeville, and when she died, her sister, Margaret Ida, married him, in turn. The two bore a total of sixteen children, with Regina, born in 1896, being the second-youngest daughter of the second family. Like Haze's father in a draft of *Wise Blood,* Peter Cline's father was a humble Latin scholar, a schoolteacher in Augusta. Peter's wealth sufficiently trumped his oddity as a small-town Irish Catholic to allow him to buy an antebellum mansion in Milledgeville soon after the Civil War, to be unanimously elected its mayor in 1889, and to have his every movement covered in the local paper: he set off "a grand py-rotechnic display" in front of his home on Christmas Eve 1890, and left town "for the northern markets" in March 1903.

As a young daughter of a first family in town, Regina was often sassy. One afternoon when she was walking with some girlfriends, a laborer rolling a wagon along the street called out to her, "Little girl, what you got in your bag?" She snapped her blond head about and startled her playmates by shouting back, "I've got the biscuits. Have you got the honey?" After elementary school, she went away to Mount St. Joseph Boarding and Day School for Girls, in Au-gusta, a convent school supported with funding from its alumna Katie Semmes, who paid for the school's own Flannery Hall, and whose aunt, Mother Gabriel, served as its Mother Superior. At her high school graduation, in May 1916, Regina recited a Latin poem, "Fortiter et Recte," while her younger sister, Agnes, graduating as well, played a piano selection from Wagner's *Die Meistersinger.*

Of a visit at age four to the school, O'Connor later wrote to her friend Father James McCown: "I don't know anybody in Augusta. I visited there once when I was four — at the convent where my cousin was Mother Superior and celebrating her something-or-other jubilee. They had ice cream for dessert in the shape of calla lilies. That was the only time I was ever tempted to join an or-der — I thought they ate that way every day."

This childhood visit impressed her enough for Mount St. Jo-seph to be echoed in the name Mount St. Scholastica in her story "A Temple of the Holy Ghost." The rest of the description of its fictional double resembled Sacred Heart Academy, located in downtown Augusta on Ellis Street. It was a redbrick house set back in a garden in the center of town, surrounded by a high black grillwork fence.

A protracted six years after graduation, Regina Cline met her future husband, Edward Francis O'Connor, Jr., at the wedding of her youngest brother, Herbert Aloysius Cline, to O'Connor's younger sister Anne Golden O'Connor. The simple ceremony at the Sacred Heart Chapel of the cathedral in Savannah, on July 18, 1922, was characterized in a newspaper announcement as an "interesting, quiet wedding . . . neither bride nor bridegroom having an attendant." As Regina Cline was twenty-six years old at the time, some of the older women in her family might have felt — like Lucynell Crater for her daughter in "The Life You Save May Be Your Own" — "ravenous" for a suitor. Apparently the pretty young woman with the heart-shaped face had once been disappointed in love when a Protestant family living in Pennsylvania convinced their son, who was working in Milledgeville, not to marry her on religious grounds.

Ed O'Connor, also twenty-six, and also on the rebound from an unhappy love affair, made a likely candidate. With a stage actor's good looks, direct pale blue eyes, and the flair of a mustache, he cut quite a figure in Irish circles about town. As his sister recalled, he loved to "put on his white linen suit, tilt his straw boater over his eye, and go out to Tybee Island dancing of a summer evening." The oldest of eight children, he was educated at Benedictine College, a military prep school in Savannah, and attended Mount St. Mary's College in Emmetsburg, Maryland, after failing to secure a spot at Annapolis because of a low math score — a lack of aptitude for numbers inherited by his daughter. Her friend Robert Fitzgerald recalled a photograph of him as "a robust, amused young man. . . . sitting like the hub of a wheel with his five gay younger brothers beside and behind him."

After college, Ed O'Connor served between May 1916 and August 1917 in the Georgia National Guard taking part in the "Mexican Expedition" led by General John J. Pershing to patrol the border of New Mexico against incursions by the rebel general of the Mexican Revolution, Pancho Villa, often vilified in the press as a bandit and horse thief. The "Expedition" included punitive invasions into Mexican territory. During World War I, O'Connor was deployed overseas, between April 1918 and May 1919, in the 325th Infantry of the 82nd Division of the American Expeditionary Force, the "All Americans" out of Camp Gordon, Georgia, with their famed "AA" shoulder patches. For helping rout the German Imperial Army from France, he was awarded, at the rank of second lieutenant, a World War I Victory Medal and Victory Button.

A nagging downside for Regina Cline, in choosing a husband, was Ed O'Connor's background — his family never achieved the social stature of the Clines of Milledgeville, or the Flannerys of Savannah, though they led comfortable middle-class lives. His grandfather Patrick O'Connor, a wheelwright, emigrated from Ireland with his brother Daniel in 1851, and established a livery stable on Broughton Street. His father, Edward Francis O'Connor, Sr., was a wholesale distributor of candies and tobacco; he was a prominent enough businessman, though, to have been president of the People's Bank, and a director of the Hibernia Bank. When Regina Cline met him, her future husband was living with his parents at 115 East Gwinnett Street, working as a salesman in his father's company, and hoping to make a start in the real estate business.

Their courtship was quick. Less than three months after they met, one of Regina Cline's older brothers, Dr. Bernard Cline, placed an engagement announcement in the *Savannah Morning News,* promising, "The wedding will take place at an early date." Just a week later, on Saturday, October 14, 1922, the couple was married at Sacred Heart Church, in Milledgeville, by the Reverend T. J. Morrow. The newlyweds then moved into a small set of rooms that the young husband could afford in the recently built

Graham Apartments, downtown, on Oglethorpe Square. In March 1923, Katie Semmes generously intervened with a favorable deal so that they could move into the pretty Charlton Street town house that she owned on Lafayette Square. Ed O'Connor agreed to pay a minimal monthly rental fee against a modest purchase price loan, basically a private mortgage, of forty-five hundred dollars, to be repaid when his real estate business took off.

During their first years on Charlton Street, Regina O'Connor's cool attitude toward her husband's family grew more pronounced. From conversations with family members, O'Connor's close friend, as well as editor and biographer, Sally Fitzgerald, later concluded, "There seems little doubt that there were little failures of kindness and tact on the young wife's part." One of the faux pas was the announcement of their child's impending birth, at an evening party. Small cards accompanying the refreshments declared the happy occasion, so the paternal grandmother-to-be learned the news along with the other casual guests. She was "wounded," and relations with her daughter-in-law grew more strained. Ed O'Connor insisted that his daughter be named after his mother, but since the name Mary could fit either Mary Elizabeth O'Connor or Mary Ellen Flannery, Regina did not find compliance terribly difficult.

Ed O'Connor's sense of being outvoted by the women in his wife's family may well have increased in late 1929 — four years after their daughter's birth — when Mrs. Semmes departed Monterey Square to move into her Greek Revival home at 211 East Charlton Street, adjacent to, and dwarfing, the O'Connors' house. With her, she brought not only lots of construction work, but also her unmarried cousin Annie Treanor, an aunt of Regina O'Connor. A few years later, she was joined by Miss M. C. Hynes and the widow Mrs. Fitzpatrick Forston. An early photograph of "Aunt Annie" shows a severe woman in wire-rim spectacles, her white hair gathered in a bun, wearing a long, dark skirt and sweater, dark stockings, and lace-up oxfords, evidently one of those family members that O'Connor felt had never "left the 19th century." A cousin recalled these Treanor aunts as having a penchant for the word "'umbled, omitting the 'h.' Humility was a great message in our family."

O'Connor's early childhood is captured in a collection of family photographs. In the earliest, a series of studio portraits taken for a family Christmas card, the little girl is smiling and charming, legs crossed on a stage prop of a bench, showing all the signs of being, as one family friend has recalled, "beautifully cared for" — in some she is hugging a doll; in others she is posed next to her mother, who reveals a sultry beauty as she stares quietly into the camera. In these staged portraits, mother and daughter look together into the camera. In pictures with her father, the girl turns her beaming face toward his, and he returns her smile. Both parents communicate fond doting in all the shots. A solo portrait of O'Connor, age two or three, sitting on an ottoman, brow furrowed, satin bow in hair, frowning with full concentration into the curled page of a book on her lap, reveals a remarkably self-possessed expression of adult intensity.

As a little girl, O'Connor's appearance favored her father. She bore his direct gaze and his clean, handsome features. This resemblance is striking in her confirmation portrait, taken at seven years old. In a dress trimmed in white lace, with her short, straight brown hair combed slickly to the side, she is the mirror image of her clear-eyed father. The adult Flannery O'Connor would become fascinated by the cloning of features between generations, considering them as a sign of some spiritual bond. In "A View of the Woods," the grandfather finds his granddaughter Mary Fortune's face "a small replica of the old man's," and feels "she was like him on the inside too." In "The Artificial Nigger," Mr. Head's ten-year-old nephew Nelson has a "face very much the same shape as the old man's." Calhoun is horrified in "The Partridge Festival" when his aunt Bessie reminds him, "You look very like Father."

The affinity between Ed O'Connor and his daughter was certainly "on the inside too." His pride in her could amount to infatuation. From 1927 until 1931, he included a separate listing for "Miss Mary Flannery O'Connor" in the *Savannah City Directory,* an unusual, whimsical gesture for a preschool child. Another fond touch shows up in a 1936 diocesan bulletin, "Roll of the Female Orphanage Society," crediting Mary Flannery O'Connor as a contributor rather than her parents. A coconspirator in her world of childhood fantasy, wishing sometimes to be a writer himself, he slipped her notes signed "King of Siam." In their games, she dubbed herself "Lord Flannery O'Connor." She would hide little poems or drawings under his breakfast plate, or tuck them into his napkin for him to discover when he sat down at the kitchen table. He liked to fold up these tokens of affection, stick them in his wallet, and show them off to friends during the day.

Her relationship with her mother was just as intimate, though more fraught. Regina told a friend of having to spank her six-year-old daughter to make her wear hose and a dress for her first piano recital. A cartoon that O'Connor drew when she was nine years old shows a child walking with her father and mother. In a balloon coming from the mother's mouth are the words: "Hold your head up, Mary Flannery, and you are just as bad, Ed." To which the girl, dragging along, snidely replies, "I was readin where someone died of holding up their head." As a family friend summed up the difference in attitude of the parents, "Ed would not have put the kind of pressure on her that Regina did. He liked her just as she was." Regina's devotion to her daughter often took the form of trying, unsuccessfully, to mold her into the perfect Southern-style little girl.

Yet there is no evidence that O'Connor's childhood was troubled. As far as pressuring went, she was quite capable of digging in her heels. Her self-confidence was clear in her bold act of calling her parents by their first names — they were "Regina" and "Ed" to her from early on. They were also her first audience. When the O'Connors went out for the evening, their little daughter, in the care of the babysitter, would write letters, or make drawings, to surprise them. One of these was done on a piece of white cardboard bent in half, with a red silk cord threaded through two holes at the fold. On one side, she traced her mother's initials "R.C.O'C.," pasting a cutout drawing, childishly hand-colored, of a pretty little girl on a bridge, watching ducks swimming in the stream below. On the flip side, for her father, "E.F.O'C.," she glued an illustration of an old clockmaker, peering intently through wire-rim glasses, tinkering at his worktable.

❋

AN EVENTFUL YEAR in Mary Flannery's life was 1931. Not only had she been filmed by Pathe News, but she took her first steps into an ever-so-slightly larger world by entering the first grade at St. Vincent's Grammar School for Girls. This parochial school was housed in the Gerard mansion, an early-nineteenth-century, three-story converted private home, with an iron lattice balcony across its second floor, and a low iron picket fence. Though St. Vincent's was located a mere forty yards from the O'Connors' door, each morning the child would make the brief walk to the front gate holding her mother's hand, taking part in a ritual in which, as one student recalls, "All the mothers walked the little girls to school."

Outside the stone walls of the elegant box-shaped school, with its eaves and pillared portico, Savannah, like much of America, was coping with the aftershocks of the stock market crash of 1929 and the deepening, worldwide Great Depression: real estate values were declining, businesses stagnating, property rapidly changing hands, grand town houses being cut into apartments renting for as little as eight dollars a month. The poorer population was moving downtown, where charity food lines were appearing for the first time since Sherman's occupation. An economic downshift was felt in middle-class homes as well. O'Connor later claimed that at the height of the Depression her family had eaten ground round steak and turnip greens for supper *"every day."*

O'Connor's father had invested all of his business hopes in the vulnerable real estate market. The year his daughter entered the first grade, the downward graph of Edward O'Connor's business career was already visible in the *Savannah City Directory*. In 1927, he had officially entered his new business for the first time, listing himself as manager of the Dixie Realty Company. In 1927 and 1928, the company's most successful years, he took out display ads pitching his company as buying, selling, renting, and insuring properties. In 1930, he added the Dixie Construction Company to the business entry, but by the next year the affiliated venture had disappeared. At the height of the economy, in 1928, Dixie Realty Company was one of a hundred companies placing such ads; by 1930, one year into the Depression, that number had already decreased to eighty-five.

Whatever tensions the girls entering St. Vincent's were sensing in their own homes, the school maintained a nearly medieval aura of Latinate order and spirituality. Run by the Sisters of Mercy, who also ran St. Joseph's Hospital, where Mary Flannery was born, St. Vincent's was an enclave of parochialism of the sort she would later label the "novena-rosary tradition." Each morning the "big girls" of grades five through eight, with their classes on the top floor, lined the long interior staircase, while the "little girls," including Mary Flannery during most of her years at the school, remained standing in their classrooms on the floor below, adding their high, quivering voices to sing the opening daily hymn, "Veni Creator Spiritus," or "Come, Holy Ghost." Prayers were then dutifully recited before classes, before and after lunch, and at the dismissal.

In preparation for a special "Communion Sunday" during the school year, the girls gathered before intricately carved, dark wood confessionals, with velvet drapes and sliding panels — two at the back, two at the transept at the front of the cathedral — to count their sins and rehearse the formula of the sacrament of penance: "Bless me, Father, for I have sinned." They fasted from midnight on the day before the Communion, and, like their parents and other family members, abstained from eating meat on Fridays. For a florid May Day procession, all the girls — 324 of them, taught by nine sisters the year she began — lined up in matching white dresses, clutching bouquets of spring flowers, and marched into the cathedral to recite the rosary and sing sentimental Marian hymns: "O Mary we crown thee with flowers today / Queen of the angels, queen of the May."

She caught glimpses, too, of the activities of boys — unfamiliar outsiders in her enclosed world. Mostly these were among the 340 pupils of Marist Brothers School, run, in 1931, by nine Brothers of Mary. Underlining the awkward divide between the two companion schools and genders, Dan O'Leary, enrolled at Marist while O'Connor was at St. Vincent's, recalls being enlisted to deliver a note to one of the nuns: "I delivered my message, and the sister said, 'Thank you, son.' I said, 'You're welcome, brother.' All the girls cracked up and I retreated with my ears burning." On Sundays, chosen Marist boys served as acolytes or altar boys, dressed in white surplices, with Buster Brown collars, swinging censers and reciting brief Latin responses at the Italianate marble high altar of the cathedral, or singing, as boy sopranos, at midnight mass.

In such a regulated and meticulously organized world within a world, O'Connor found herself a misfit from the start. In an autobiographical sketch for a Magazine Writing course at Iowa, she remembered herself as "a pidgeon-toed, only-child with a receding chin and a you-leave-me-alone-or-I'll-bite-you complex" that did little to reassure her parents of their good fortune. Showing her irascibility at St. Vincent's, she bragged of substituting

"St. Cecilia" for "Rover" in third-grade composition exercises such as "Throw the ball to Rover." A thinly disguised only child named "Mary Flemming" in a student story of O'Connor's wears orthopedic "Tarso-Supernator-ProperBuilt shoes" and needs to "take toe exercises every night and remember to walk on the outsides of her feet."

This bravado that O'Connor adopts on the page when telling tales of her childhood was not always the tone of the earliest memories of her classmates. Rather, Mary Flannery was usually pegged as quiet, painfully shy, self-reliant but remote, the introvert on the sidelines whose cousin remembers her wearing "some sort of corrective shoes, she had a distinctive kind of loping walk." On rare occasions when she went with other little girls to Broughton Street, the main shopping strip downtown, she clutched her pocketbook tightly in her hand. "If I took off with some of the other children to go through Colonial Cemetery, she'd stand on the side and watch," a girlfriend remembers of their shortcuts. "She would not go through the cemetery, no way." She was never seen at the playground two blocks from her home, though she did walk the eight or nine blocks to the movie theater, with a friend, and roller-skated around the block.

The six-year-old girl was much more likely to be found upstairs, secluded, in her small, pine-floored corner bedroom, with one east window facing Katie Semmes's home, and two rear windows looking down into the family's walled backyard and the Charlton Lane service alley behind. In this hideaway, sparsely furnished with two single, matching, unpainted, pine beds — camp cots of a Sears, Roebuck catalog style — a little green doll's bed, and a narrow closet full of clothes, many sewn for her by her mother, she kept the precious crayons and paper she preferred as gifts to candy and sweets. Removed from all the comings and goings downstairs, she spent most of her free time making drawings, usually of birds. As she later wrote of her sketches to her friend

Betty Hester, "I suppose my father toted around some of my early productions. I drew — mostly chickens, beginning at the tail, the same chicken over and over, beginning at the tail."

Sometime during 1931, she picked up a pencil and blue crayon and traced a jumble of capital letters from the alphabet she had been learning onto the thickly lined, pulpy page of a school tablet — an E, a backward D, other shaky letters at odd angles, while a steadier adult hand modeled letters on the same page. Next to the scattered alphabet, she attempted the unfinished form of a face with large, round eyes and dark, pronounced pupils. When she turned the page over, she completed, much more surely, an instantly recognizable turkey with featherless crown and wattle, its feet planted on the ground, and a smiling child in a tall, square hat gleefully flying overhead. Cut in the shape of a two-inch square, just the right size for her father's wallet, this joyful depiction of whimsical role reversal — grounded bird, soaring child — survives as her earliest cartoon.

Taught that first year by Sister Mary Consuela, O'Connor earned decent grades. She did well in Reading, 93, but her overall average, 88, was brought down by her worst grade, 81, in Arithmetic, lowered even further to a 70 her second year, when she was taught by Sister Mary Franzita. Her strongest showing was in Catechism, where she scored 96 her first year, and 98 her second. A graded class in Roman Catholic theology, Catechism was taught at the time in American parochial schools and churches using a pale blue hardcover edition of the *Baltimore Catechism*. The book was organized in a simple Q-and-A format, leading students to memorize rote answers to fundamental questions in a singsong litany with the nuns:

Q: Who made us?

A: God made us.

Q: Why did God make us?

*A: He made us to know him, to love him, to serve him in this
world and to be happy with him forever in the next.*

Q: From whom do we learn to know, love, and serve God?

*A: We learn to know, love, and serve God from Jesus Christ,
the Son of God, who teaches us through the Catholic
Church.*

O'Connor later revisited this set piece of her childhood in her story
"The Enduring Chill," when a large, red-faced country priest,
blind in one eye and introducing himself as "Fahther Finn — from
Purrgatory," examines Asbury, an arty intellectual who has been
living too long in Manhattan. To the primary question, "Who
made you?" Asbury replies, "Different people believe different
things about that," and to "Who is God?" he says, "God is an idea
created by man." Channeling some of the no-nonsense faith of the
priests and teaching nuns of St. Vincent's, Father Finn grumbles,
"You are a very ignorant boy."

A flash of the contrary girl O'Connor was on her way to becoming was revealed as early as the first grade. Each Sunday, a mandatory children's mass was held in the basement of the cathedral, and
the nuns devoted several minutes on Monday mornings to addressing their attendance records. With the support of her parents, she
always attended the later adult mass. Indeed, when the children's
mass was once shifted from eight to ten a.m., the O'Connor family
chose to switch to the earlier mass. Each Monday morning, Lanier Jones, another first-grader, whose family lived near a golf
course outside town, and Mary Flannery, who lived near the church
and had no such excuse, would be lined against the blackboard to
explain their absences. As Jones recalled of her bold classmate,
"She'd stand there and tell sister, 'The Catholic Church does not

dictate to my family what time I go to Mass.' I was five and she was six, and I knew she was different."

In the third and fifth grades, O'Connor was taught by Sister Mary Consolata, "just off the boat" from Ireland, and installed as a teacher while still very young. "When we were in the third grade, Sister Consolata used to give Mary Flannery a real hard time about her compositions," recalled a classmate who lived a few doors down at 302 East Charlton Street. "She said that she always wrote about ducks and chickens and she said she never wanted to hear about another duck or a chicken." Though discouraged by the nun in her obsessive fixation on birds, the young girl was getting lots of outside support, not only from Katie Semmes, a bird lover herself, but also from her uncle Dr. Bernard Cline, a bird-watcher, who was later profiled in the *Atlanta Constitution* for keeping a "back-yard quail farm." Yet Sister Mary Consolata remained unimpressed. "Nothing remarkable at all about her as a student," she later observed curtly. "She was a little forward with adults."

O'Connor did more than write stories starring chickens to antagonize Sister Mary Consolata. Though braces were rare, during the Depression, because they were expensive, Mary Flannery, like Mary Flemming in her untitled early story, had a mouth "full of wire where her teeth were being straightened and there were small rubber bands that hooked onto the top and bottom and had to be changed twice a day." Lillian Dowling, one of twenty-six third-graders crowded in a class picture with O'Connor, everyone outfitted with Mickey and Minnie Mouse ears and shoes — Disney having just formed the original Mickey Mouse Club in 1929 — remembers that she sometimes "pulled the rubber bands and let them sail across the room," or caked them with peanut butter. One day, she brought snuff to school after observing black servants at home pull out their bottom lips to insert a pinch. To discourage others from sharing her lunch, she would sometimes bring castor oil sandwiches.

If Sister Mary Consolata remembered O'Connor as an "unremarkable" student, she was most likely thinking of her performance in either Arithmetic or Spelling. O'Connor did much better in English, and in her social science classes, Geography and History, which were folded into the school's classical curriculum after the second grade. But misspelling remained for O'Connor a lifelong issue; as she later put it, she was "a very innocent speller." Lillian Dowling's sister, Ann, was present when the poor speller brought home one of these report cards, preparing her mother for its mixed results in her slow nasal drawl: "Mother, I made an 82 in Geography but I woulda' made a hundred, if it hadn't been for Spellin'; I made a 85 in English, but I woulda' made a hundred if it hadn't been for Spellin'; and I made a 65 in Spellin' and I woulda' made a hundred, if it hadn't been for Spellin'."

A composite of Sister Mary Consolata and other Mercy nuns shows up in O'Connor's fiction in the guise of Sister Perpetua. In an early draft of *Wise Blood,* Sister Perpetua, a Sister of Mercy, teaches at Immaculate Conception, and is seen by one cowering pupil as able to "smash an atom between her two fingers." In "A Temple of the Holy Ghost," another Sister Perpetua, also a Sister of Mercy, advises her teenage girls to warn forward boys, "Stop sir! I am a Temple of the Holy Ghost!" When the story's protagonist, an obvious stand-in for Mary Flannery — her braces "glared like tin" — visits Sister Perpetua's school chapel, a nun reaches out for an embrace, but the girl instead "stuck out her hand and preserved a frigid frown, looking just past the sister's shoes at the wainscoting." Evidently revealing her own adolescent thoughts, O'Connor writes, "You put your foot in their door and they got you praying, the child thought as they hurried down the polished corridor."

This tough attitude toward the sisters was already set by the fifth grade, and continues to register in her adult letters. Given license by the unconditional love of her father, and by the contentious attitude of her mother toward a few of the sisters — Mrs. O'Connor, for instance, felt her daughter ought to be allowed home for lunch — she might well, as a sarcastic fifth-grader, have said, or overheard, a comment along these lines, as she wrote to her friend Ted Spivey in the late fifties: "A lot of them who are teaching are competent at most to wash dishes." Writing as a thirty-two-year-old to her spiritual adviser Father McCown, she complained of having been "taught by the sisters to measure your sins with a slide rule." Elsewhere she evoked the "hot house innocence" of the cloistered nuns in her convent school. Rebellion still rising in her voice, she bragged of herself as "a long standing avoider of May processions and such-like nun-inspired doings."

Between the third and seventh grade, these tussles with the Mercy nuns spilled over into the safe haven of an upstairs room in her home. In a state of mind somewhere between a child's daydream and one of the scriptural visions she heard preached about in church, she imagined bouts with a guardian angel she pictured as half nun, half bird. As she mock-confided to Betty Hester, twenty years later: "From 8 to 12 years it was my habit to seclude myself in a locked room every so often and with a fierce (and evil) face, whirl around in a circle with my fists knotted, socking the angel. This was the guardian angel with which the Sisters assured us we were all equipped. . . . You couldn't hurt an angel but I would have been happy to know I had dirtied his feathers — I conceived him in feathers."

She was clearly conflicted. Her authority issues with the nuns were obvious, yet she loved feathered creatures. As these boxing matches did not sum up all of her juvenile feelings about the Catholic religion, she began to draw a distinction, within herself, between the sisters and the Church. On May 8, 1932, Mary Flannery O'Connor was led with the other girls by their captain up the left aisle of the cathedral, while the boys proceeded up the right, for a First Communion she felt was "as natural to me and about as startling as brushing my teeth." Two years later, on May 20, 1934, she was just as naturally confirmed in the Church. If the little girl of "A Temple of the Holy Ghost" embodied her anti-nun sentiments, she also displayed more vulnerable girlhood devotion. As O'Connor writes of the budding of the fragile seeds of faith in the twelve-year-old, "The child knelt down between her mother and the nun and they were well into the 'Tantum Ergo' before her ugly thoughts stopped and she began to realize that she was in the presence of God. Hep me not to be so mean, she began mechanically. Hep me not to give her so much sass. Hep me not to talk like I do. Her mind began to get quiet and then empty."

Mrs. O'Connor oversaw with watchful vigilance the childhood of this special daughter, who was filled with such deeply felt stirrings, as well as some weird imaginings. Her third cousin Patricia Persse judged her "a very peculiar child." In her own entertaining, Regina liked to be sophisticated and *au courant.* One of her favorite party dresses, stylish among American ladies in the 1920s, was a lavender crepe silk kimono, hemmed in lace, with long, flowing sleeves, and an Empire fitted waist clasped with a small bouquet of silk flowers in pale pink, ecru, and coral. Yet for her daughter, the mother invited into their home only those well-behaved playmates eager to participate in games and activities involving fantasy and imagination. The rumor in the neighborhood was that Mrs. O'Connor kept a list of approved playmates, and at least once turned a child away.

One of the happier events promoted weekly by the mother was a Saturday morning gathering around the radio in the parlor to listen to *Let's Pretend,* a CBS radio series for children that began broadcasting in March 1934. Opening with a jaunty musical theme, the popular show used a cast of child actors, often eight or nine years old, to render, live, such classics as "Cinderella," "Beauty and the Beast," or "Rumpelstiltskin." The announcer would roar at the outset, "Heel-looo, Pretenders!" Having listened with his brother and sister to the same program in another part of the country, the Brooklyn-born children's author Maurice Sendak could still summon for an interviewer some of its dialogue and mood seventy years later: "'How do we get to Pretend Land?' And a little boy would say, 'Let's go on a boat!' We'd *stare* at the radio."

At the end of the thirty-minute broadcast, Mrs. O'Connor served snacks of hot chocolate with homemade gingerbread or brownies to the kids, including Lillian and Ann Dowling, Cousin Margaret Persse, and Newell Turner, the daughter of an osteopath, who lived across the street on "the tall floors" of Hamilton House, built in the 1870s in the decorative style of a Second Empire château. "Mrs. O'Connor was very friendly and sweet and nice," remembers Newell Turner Parr. "And very particular. She had very definite ideas about things. I remember Mr. O'Connor more vaguely because he was not at home, he was at work. Fathers were usually not quite as available." Taking her cue from one of the *Let's Pretend* broadcasts of 1934, "The Emperor's New Clothes," Parr has said of her friend Mary Flannery, "She was really genuine . . . to adults, she would say what she thought, which wasn't always acceptable. I am sure that if she had been around, she would have been the first to tell the emperor that he didn't have any clothes on."

Many of the same playmates were enrolled in a short-lived club Mary Flannery formed about the same time the radio program first aired. She dubbed her group the "Merriweather Girls," after a series of adventure books, and nominated herself president. Its members, fancying themselves Bet, Shirley, Joy, and Kit of Merriweather Manor, met in a gazebo-like wooden playhouse, a gift of Katie Semmes. The playhouse was fitted into a corner of the backyard, otherwise teeming with Rhode Island red, Plymouth Rock, and white leghorn chickens. During several afternoons, these girls sat about a round table, straddling quaint, triangular seats constructed by an uncle, and listened as President O'Connor read to them her latest stories. "She had pages and pages of handwritten stories," Merriweather Girl Parr has admitted, "but I wasn't quite smart enough to listen attentively." Written in pencil on lined notebook paper, with her own illustrations, the tales concerned a family of ducks traveling the world.

O'Connor sometimes led a friend or two upstairs in the family house to her secret attic, a third floor kept for guests. In a remote bathroom, she liked to sit back in a large bathtub supported on porcelain feet, disconnected from any plumbing, and have her friends read aloud from her latest works. Sister Jude Walsh, a former principal of St. Vincent's, tells of Marguerite Pinckney, a child with a flair for performance, who went along with Mary Flannery's wishes as they sat together in the dry tub: "But then Marguerite would get miffed because in the middle of a paragraph Mary Flannery would say, 'Stop right there. Would you read that over again?' I guess even then she was attuned to how something was expressed. Marguerite would be annoyed because she saw no reason to stop the flow of the story."

Within a year of founding the Merriweather Club, Mary Flannery made a minor leap from fantasy into satire. Rather than writing about a family of ducks, she wrote about the members of her own family. Relying on her talent for mocking adults, she created a little collection of vignettes titled "My Relitives," which her thrilled father helped her have typed and bound. The series of portraits were so finely drawn, and uncomfortably close to life, that the relatives given this treatment by their mischievous daughter, cousin, or niece either hesitated — or simply refused — to recognize themselves. As Regina O'Connor once told an Atlanta journalist, "No one was spared." Reaction was strong enough that O'Connor brought up the scandal to her friend Maryat Lee twenty-five years later: "I wrote a book at the age of ten, called 'My Relatives.' Seven copies were printed and distributed by me. It was in the naturalistic vein and was not well received."

AT THE START of the sixth grade, Mrs. O'Connor abruptly pulled her daughter from St. Vincent's and enrolled her in Sacred Heart School. The switch was a minor scandal on Lafayette Square. A former Marist boy has recalled, even though he and his friends knew neither mother nor daughter, "We heard stories about Mary Flannery O'Connor leaving St. Vincent's and transferring out to Sacred Heart." Though her new school was located in a modern brick building on the corner of Abercorn and 38th streets, run by the more formally educated Sisters of St. Joseph of Carondelet, who taught Regina in high school in Augusta, the move to a school in a different parish was highly unorthodox.

Mrs. O'Connor may well have been responding to her daughter's annoyance with the nuns at St. Vincent's. In her fifth and final year at the school, O'Connor's absences had mounted to twenty-four. There was talk as well that the mother was more partial to the "lace-curtain" population in the more genteel Thomas Square neighborhood of clapboard houses — some rather grand, built between the late nineteenth century and the beginning of World War I — than to the "shanty" mix in the downtown school. "We were a rough and ready bunch at St. Vincent's in the old days," Sister Consolata has readily admitted. The Dowling sisters also transferred that year to Sacred Heart, possibly swaying Mrs. O'Connor's decision. But one of them, Lillian, has remarked, a bit coyly, that their friend's move really stemmed from "the strictness of a certain nun."

Katie Semmes's shiny, black electric car was pressed into service to make the mile-long trip from Lafayette Square to 38th Street, a direct drive south on Abercorn. One of only two left in Savannah, such electric models had been popular in the teens and early twenties, especially among women, because they ran on rechargeable lead acid batteries, no hand-cranking required. Each weekday morning, Mary Flannery took her place in its open carriage, with a bench in the back, two seats in front, and a vase of artificial flowers fixed to the side. Mrs. O'Connor stood commandingly in the rear, steering with a tiller, in her veil and duster and long gloves. "It reminded me of a Toonerville Trolley that you see in cartoons," says Sister Jude Walsh, then a sixth-grader, of the eccentric vehicle. "I remember a group of us standing on a corner every day to watch Mary Flannery arrive, and then we'd be out there at two fifteen to see her depart to Charlton Street."

Unlike St. Vincent's, Sacred Heart was coeducational, evenly divided between about two hundred boys and two hundred girls, taught by nine Sisters of St. Joseph of Carondelet. "They were strict," says Margaret Persse, who attended Sacred Heart with her cousin. "They were always rapping the boys over the knuckles with a ruler." Like the rest of the girls, Mary Flannery dressed in the unofficial uniform of white blouse, skirt, and bobby socks, though instead of oxford loafers she wore heavier, brown, laced shoes. Yet something about her overall demeanor struck Sister Jude Walsh as "prissy. You definitely got the impression that she was an introvert and lived a relatively sheltered existence." Like all of the other girls, O'Connor spent hours learning, by rote, the Latin words to intricate masses, such as the "Mass of the Angels." Her academic record among this order of nuns, whom she came to think of as "genteel Victorian ladies," remained unexceptional. At Sacred Heart, she never received higher than a B in Composition.

Seven years into the Great Depression, the daily lives of the students at parochial schools such as Sacred Heart were even more touched by national politics and economics. In the fall of 1936, Franklin Delano Roosevelt won his landslide victory over Alf Landon for a second term. Roosevelt's presence had always loomed large in Savannah, and many of its citizens kept time by the plot points of his presidency. Of the Bank Holiday of March 1933, Regina O'Connor remembered, decades later, "Mary Flannery was at dancing when President Roosevelt closed the banks." That November, he toured Savannah for its bicentennial and was entertained by Mayor Thomas Gamble. As the president kept a home in Warm Springs, Georgia, where he was treated for polio in the heated waters, his itinerary was closely followed. Though resisted at first out of civic pride, his New Deal was soon grudgingly, and then eagerly, welcomed for the vital jobs created by programs such as the Works Progress Administration, Civilian Conservation Corps, and the Army Corps of Engineers.

In his second inaugural address, on January 20, 1937, President Roosevelt optimistically promised, "Our progress out of the depression is obvious." Among those receptive to its message, tuned in to by a nationwide radio audience, was forty-one-year-old Ed O'Connor, whose business losses during Roosevelt's first term had amounted to a free fall. After his Dixie Realty folded, O'Connor was listed in the *Savannah City Directory,* beginning in 1934, as operating a series of short-lived companies. In 1934, he was manager of the C. F. Fulton Real Estate Company and, in 1936, its president. In 1937, the Fulton Company disappeared, succeeded by O'Connor and Company, advertised as dealing in "real estate, loans, and general insurance." Among the failed real estate interests O'Connor was said to have "jumped around" were the Tondee Apartments at 37th and Bull streets, and the "Venetian Terrace" on Tybee Island. He wound up in the 1937 *Savannah City Directory* once again listed as a salesman for his father's wholesale grocery company, his financial failures having sent him back to square one.

As fewer business prospects presented themselves, Ed O'Connor sought personal satisfaction by becoming more active in the American Legion, where his good-natured personality helped him flourish. The failing real estate agent possessed an entire checklist of traits for a successful salesman, and in another economic climate might have done well. As a parishioner who saw him at church in Milledgeville with his wife and young daughter recalled, "He was so tall and so handsome. He always smiled." Regina O'Connor never approved of her husband's redirecting his energies to the Legionnaires, or of his new Legion friends. Yet he was not swayed. His quick ascent in the Legion began in 1935, with his election to the position of commander of Chatham Post No. 16 in Savannah. In June 1936, according to the *Savannah Morning News,* he was "swept into office by unanimous vote" to the post of state commander for all of Georgia.

A likeable politician, Ed O'Connor was not simply a glad-hander. He was far more complicated, with an almost dreamy side that could sometimes be construed as diffidence, or lassitude. To Katherine Doyle Groves, who knew him when she was a little girl, he seemed "aloof" or "snooty," a man with his head "sort of in the clouds" and his nose "a little elevated." A longtime resident of Savannah reported an impression of him around town as "a dreamer." O'Connor would later write to her friend Betty Hester, "I am never likely to romanticize him because I carry around most of his faults as well as his tastes." Fitzgerald surmised that these unnamed "faults" included "sloth," a vice Flannery O'Connor often claimed for herself, combined with the stubbornness her father showed in pursuing his Legion life against his wife's wishes. "More likely, she was told this of him," Sally Fitzgerald guessed, "or heard him being told it of himself, or overheard it implied in some conversation among adults that she was not meant to overhear."

His touch of poetic inwardness, combined with the patriotism of a boy who grew up in Savannah as a uniformed junior hussar, contributed to his great strength as a Legion commander: speechifying. "He was quite an orator," says Angela Ryan Dowling, a Sacred Heart classmate of his daughter. Her positive assessment was backed up by the *Savannah Morning News,* which regularly carried reports on the speeches he gave as he traveled around the state to preside at meetings and initiate new projects. "Head of Legion Talks to Rotary" was the headline of a half-column summary of O'Connor's 1936 pre–Armistice Day talk at the Hotel De Soto in Savannah: "How veterans have picked up the ends of a normal life, disrupted by the World War, gone about constructive pursuits, and the service the American Legion has rendered in aiding the young men to re-orient themselves was brought out in an address yesterday by E. F. O'Connor, Jr."

Reading through handwritten pages of some of these talks twenty years later, Flannery O'Connor felt reassured that writing constituted her most intimate bond with her "writer" father. On a visit to O'Connor's family farm, Andalusia, during the summer of 1956, Betty Hester revealed that her own aunt and uncle were active in the American Legion, and had known Ed O'Connor personally. Hester said that her aunt had described him "in tones not usually applied to members of the Legion." A few weeks later, O'Connor wrote back to her, "Last year I read over some of the speeches he made and I was touched to see a kind of patriotism that most people would just laugh at now, something childlike, that was a good deal too good and innocent for the Legion. But the Legion was the only thing provided by the country to absorb it."

Still pondering in her heart the few words of praise from Hester's aunt, she added two weeks later, really giving him credit for her vocation, "My father wanted to write but had not the time or money or training or any of the opportunities I have had. . . . Anyway, whatever I do in the way of writing makes me extra happy in the thought that it is a fulfillment of what he wanted to do himself." In a month-long series of exchanges — a rare expression of her tender feelings toward her father — she stressed his likeability: "I suppose what I mean about my father is that he would have written *well* if he could have. He wrote all the time, one thing or another, mostly speeches and local political stuff. Needing people badly and not getting them may turn you in a creative direction, provided you have the other requirements. He needed the people I guess and got them. Or rather wanted them and got them."

At the height of his term as state commander and public speaker, in 1937, a whitish patch appeared on Edward O'Connor's forehead. Seemingly innocuous, this skin rash turned out to be the first, visible symptom of an autoimmune disorder that causes the body to produce antibodies that attack its own healthy tissues. Initially thought to be rheumatoid arthritis, the disease was eventually diagnosed as lupus erythematosus, or "red wolf," after a facial rash associated with it. As an adult suffering from the same disease, following the development of diagnostic blood tests in the 1940s and new treatments, Flannery O'Connor tersely assessed her father's earlier treatment: "at that time there was nothing for it but the undertaker." Asked about the disease, Regina O'Connor once surmised, "Oh, I don't know. He may have had it when we got married."

The flaring of this mysterious disease, with no known cause, ten times more likely to occur in women than men, combined with a downward business spiral to create a life crisis. Due to declining health, Edward O'Connor resigned midterm from his position as state commander. Traits that had been thought of as laziness — such as coming home to take afternoon naps — were now understood as symptoms of the illness. Toward the end of a difficult year, O'Connor began a letter-writing campaign to lobby for a job in President Roosevelt's newly created Federal Housing Administration. On December 23, 1937, he wrote to Erwin Sibley, a well-connected attorney friend of the Cline family, "Tried to get in touch with you while in Milledgeville the other day, but was unable to catch you. Wanted to ask a favor of you." He hoped Sibley would plead his case with the two Georgia senators and with Congressman Carl Vinson, representative from the Sixth District of Georgia and chairman of the Naval Affairs Committee.

"WHEN I WAS twelve I made up my mind absolutely that I would not get any older," O'Connor wrote in 1956 to her friend Betty Hester, who had pointed out a childlike quality in her. "I don't remember how I meant to stop it. There was something about 'teen' attached to anything that was repulsive to me. I certainly didn't approve of what I saw of people that age. I was a very ancient twelve; my views at that age would have done credit to a Civil War veteran. I am much younger now than I was at twelve, or anyway, less burdened. The weight of centuries lies on children, I'm sure of it."

Some of that burden, "the weight of centuries," was her father's illness, and the forces set in motion by his troubles amounted to the abrupt end of her childhood. In the spring of 1937, she was still the little girl who arrived at school in "the electric," and was taken occasionally by Mrs. Semmes for swimming lessons in the pool of the De Soto, Savannah's fanciest hotel. During the summer, she wore a yellow-and-white-striped seersucker sundress with shoulder straps tied together in a simple bow, hand-sewn by her mother. She donned, as well, the unlikely green serge dress and jacket uniform of the Girl Scouts; disliking troop hikes, she rarely attended meetings, even though they were held just across Lafayette Square in the carriage house of the pink Italianate villa where Juliette Gordon Low founded the national organization as the Girl Guides in 1912.

Between the lines of this life as usual, though, the watchful girl with keen eavesdropping abilities would have sensed something amiss, as news of her father's sickness remained hushed and secret. "She never knew her father had lupus," said her childhood friend Newell Turner Parr. "She never had any idea. In those days, they didn't tell children those things. You might be told Grandmother's deaf or Mrs. So and So can't see very well, be nice to her, don't knock her down, but diseases and death and things like that, children weren't told." In her early, autobiographical story about Mary Flemming, the father is likewise only half seen, imminent, as the mother, slicing tomatoes at the sink, orders "MF," as she calls her, to the bathroom to wash her hands after "fooling with those chickens" in the backyard: "'Your father will be here any minute,' her mother said, 'and the table won't be set. Hold your stomach in.'"

During her twelfth year she began a journal that amounted to a collection of random rants. Venting injustices, her funny, outraged voice sounds off in its pages, which she bound together, writing a warning hex on the front: "I know some folks that don't mind their own bisnis." She complained that her teacher corrected her spelling, but Mary Flannery thought that skill was unimportant. She likewise brushed off the usefulness of most mathematics, such as geometry, which used letters instead of numbers, as well as multiplication tables, and even having to learn to add and subtract. She railed against her dance classes, and mandatory cleaning of her room, which she preferred to keep filled with all of her own "litter." She confides of her mother, "R. said I was clumsie."

Reading books was as dear to the little girl as writing and binding them; her approach was just as personal. During the summer of 1937, she traveled with her mother to enroll in a Vacation Reading Club offered by the Carnegie Library of Atlanta, which awarded a certificate to any child reading and reporting on ten books over the summer. According to a library bulletin from the summer before, the most popular books with the twenty-four hundred children who completed the program were Louisa May Alcott's *Little Women* and *Little Men,* and Jack London's *The Call of the Wild.* O'Connor agreed about Alcott, as she wrote on the flyleaf of her copy of *Little Men,* "First rate. Splendid." Mother and daughter stayed with relatives in Atlanta, and spent time with family friend Helen Soul. Back in Savannah, with her inscribed

Vacation Reading Certificate, O'Connor wrote a thank-you note to Soul for encouraging her to "read those books," and ended with a strangely abrupt promise that "Regina says she'll write you when she has time."

She kept up this habit of reading and "reporting" as sister activities, becoming her own book reviewer almost as soon as she was a reader. On the flyleaf of Lewis Carroll's *Alice's Adventures in Wonderland,* she wrote, "Awful. I wouldn't read this book"; on Shirley Watkins's *Georgina Finds Herself,* one of a series of "Books for Girls": "This is the worst book I ever read next to 'Pinnochio.'" She held on to these opinions into her thirties, when she wrote to Betty Hester, "Peculiar but I never could stand *Alice in Wonderland* either. It was a terrifying book; so was *Pinocchio.* I was strictly a *Peter Rabbit* man myself." A cousin once bought her a subscription to *National Geographic* because, whenever she visited her home, she headed straight to the latest issue of the shiny, colorful magazine of global exploration and science. Much of its appeal, O'Connor later admitted, "wasn't a literary or even a geographical interest. It has a distinct unforgettable transcendent apotheotic (?) and very grave odor. Like no other mere magazine."

Nothing Mary Flannery was writing, or reading, directly addressed the "ancient" or "weighted" sense she remembered from that year. Yet later on she did evoke these feelings. In a fragment of another early story, an "MF"-style girl named Caulda mourns when her dog trots up carrying in his mouth her pet chicken, Sillow. She thinks of Sillow as her "brother" and fights with her mother to allow her to keep the dead chicken in her bed. Her mother, annoyed at the carcass that "was stiff already and he smelled some," tries to scare her by telling her that the man in white she spotted walking up the road is Death coming to get her. In an eerie passage, the frightened little girl confronts the fears raised by this shadow of death. "'Will he cut my tongue?'" she asks. "'That and more,' her mother said. 'That for yer lyin.'"

Trapped in bed, Caulda feels as if she's running: "She had the feeling like a stone was creeping all over her and she was facing a wall of it and another was behind her and one was pushing in on one side and he was coming up the other."

She may well have sensed the same convergence of threatening forces in her home life at the time. In January 1938, Ed O'Connor received positive news from Erwin Sibley of Congressman Vinson's intention to help. He responded to Sibley, "Can't tell you how much I appreciate your kindness." But the good news was accompanied by a shake-up. By March, with the politicking completed, her father needed to move to Atlanta to take a position as senior zone real estate appraiser for the Federal Housing Administration, or FHA. As he went ahead to arrange a living situation for himself and his family, Mary Flannery was quickly removed from Sacred Heart School, and enrolled, for April and May, the last two months of her seventh grade, in the Peabody Elementary School in Milledgeville. This arrangement began an unsettled two-year period for mother and daughter of shuttling between Atlanta and the Cline familial home in Milledgeville.

At first, her father kept alive the hope of returning to their pleasant town house in Savannah. In the 1939 *Savannah City Directory* he was listed as "on govt. service in Atlanta." In 1940, his name was still listed at 207 East Charlton, but the notice changed to a more final "moved to Atlanta." The family never did return, and Ed O'Connor never paid off his loan to Katie Semmes, who remained its owner. When Mrs. Semmes died in 1959, she left the property to Flannery O'Connor, who reported the news, simply, to the Fitzgeralds: "Cousin Katie left me the house in Savannah I was raised in." As its new landlady, she rented out the premises, even though she once complained to a friend of two properties her mother owned, "My papa was a real-estate man and my mamma has two apartment houses and we have gone nuts with renters for years."

Flannery O'Connor rarely returned to Savannah. Her adult letters contain only a few references, when someone from there sends her mother an azalea, or mother and daughter give three-dollar donations to St. Mary's Home for girls, or she expresses relief at being unable to accept an invitation to speak to a Savannah Catholic women's group. Yet for the writer who claimed, "I think you probably collect most of your experience as a child — when you really had nothing else to do — and then transfer it to other situations when you write," her time in Savannah registered as a strong afterimage in her work. Especially in the guise of the unnamed twelve-year-old girl in "A Temple of the Holy Ghost," pacing back and forth in her upstairs bedroom "with her hands locked together behind her back and her head thrust forward and an expression fierce and dreamy both, on her face."

Chapter Two

MILLEDGEVILLE: "A BIRD SANCTUARY"

In 1934, the city council of Milledgeville voted to designate the town a "Bird Sanctuary." Writing up "the glad news" of the town's nickname, the local historian and poet Nelle Womack Hines, in her *Treasure Album of Milledgeville,* gave credit to a "bird conscious" population, especially a circle of avid bird-watching professors at Georgia State College for Women. She whimsically recorded that, after the vote, "The rumor spread that several Robin Red Breasts were building nests in various parts of town — something almost unheard of." To advertise the special event, the council and the local Audubon Society ordered road signs posted at all the main entrances to the city:

MILLEDGEVILLE, GA.

A BIRD SANCTUARY

These sturdy metal signs mounted on poles captured the attention of Mary Flannery O'Connor, as she moved to Milledgeville to complete the final two months of seventh grade. A wry version of this fascination still shows up in her adult letters. She occasionally liked to put as her return address, "Milledgeville / A Bird Sanctuary." When one of her stories, "The Life You Save May Be Your Own," was televised in 1957, she reported to a former high school teacher, "It was *well* received here in the Bird Sanctuary and everybody thinks that I have now arrived." Extending a backhanded invitation, in 1960, to her friend Maryat Lee, who was living in Manhattan, she asked, "Why don't you take yourself a real vacation in that land of happy retreat, Milledgeville, a bird sanctuary?"

For the thirteen-year-old O'Connor, her family's spring 1938 move to Milledgeville, though sudden, was not a total disruption. Her parents had been spending time in Milledgeville ever since she was a baby. The visits were regularly covered on the Social and Society page of the *Union-Recorder,* the local newspaper. When she was just fifteen months old, the paper reported, "Mrs. E. F. O'Connor and little daughter, of Savannah, are visiting the Misses Cline." In November 1937, four months before their move from Savannah, an item appeared: "Mr. and Mrs. Ed O'Connor and daughter, of Savannah, were the week-end guests of Misses Mary and Katie Cline." The motor trips of Mrs. Katie Semmes were all documented, as were trips by the Cline aunts to Savannah.

Milledgeville was *Our Town* done with a middle Georgia drawl. Described by one journalist as "a styling epicenter for the Deep South," the sleepy community at the dead center of Georgia, with barely six thousand residents, blended provincial conservatism with much local color. "We have a girls' college here," O'Connor wrote, in the early fifties, "but the lacy atmosphere is fortunately destroyed by a reformatory, an insane asylum, and a military school." Georgia State College for Women did provide the town's grace notes — a steady supply of male and female professors. The reformatory was Georgia State Training School for Boys; the military school, Georgia Military College. Yet because of State Hospital, previously named Milledgeville Lunatic Asylum, the town was mostly synonymous, in Georgia slang, with "going crazy." As one miffed character says to another in *Clock Without Hands,* by Carson McCullers, who grew up in Columbus, 130 miles away, "'A thing like this makes me think you ought to be in Milledgeville.'"

Though hardly as cosmopolitan as Savannah, this fourth capital of Georgia from 1803 until 1868 was built on a similar geometric plan. As Nelle Womack Hines pointed out in her *Treasure Album,* the capital city, named for Governor John Milledge, "probably has the distinction of being one of two cities thus molded into shape for such a purpose, the other being our National Capital, Washington, D.C." The original plan reserved four large squares for a capitol, governor's mansion, penitentiary, and cemetery, with nineteen wide streets intersecting at right angles. Dubbed "a town of columns," Milledgeville became identified with a "Milledgeville Federal" style of architecture, marked by colossal porticoes, cantilevered balconies, pediments adorned with sunbursts, and fanlit doorways. When O'Connor's professor friend Ted Spivey visited, he found this early style "idealistic," as opposed to the town's midcentury Greek Revival mansions, recalling "the fanaticism of cotton barons defending slavery and states' rights."

Peabody Elementary, where Mary Flannery completed seventh grade, was an all-white school, mostly attended by girls. White boys typically went to Georgia Military College, fittingly located in the Gothic Revival Old State House of the Confederacy, with pointed arch windows and gray battlements, the scene of the Secession Convention of 1861. ("If war comes I'll drink every drop of blood that's shed," Robert Toombs promised in one of the convention's rallying speeches.) The Milledgeville City Cemetery, where Mary Flannery's Cline and Treanor relatives were buried, was divided, with graves for whites on higher ground, and those for blacks, including slave plots, on the southern edge running steeply down to Fishing Creek. The Cline family had a decent legacy with the blacks in town, though. When Mayor Peter Cline, Jr., died, in 1916, the pastor of the Colored Presbyterian Church wrote a tribute, praising the mayor's advocating "in public the rights of our race."

The Ward-Beall-Cline Mansion at 311 West Greene Street, where mother and daughter moved that spring, while Ed O'Connor visited on weekends, was one of about forty remaining antebellum homes. A traditional Federal clapboard house, with four white, fluted, Ionic columns — built by General John B. Gordon in 1820 and used briefly as the Governor's Mansion in 1838 and 1839 — the Cline Mansion developed into a showpiece with the slow accretion of architectural details: a pitched Victorian red metal roof, a wraparound front porch, a widow's walk, a lace-brick wall, built by slaves, and an antique lamppost, imported from Savannah. Each spring, as the azaleas, dogwoods, and redbuds bloomed along the town's elm-lined streets, the Cline Mansion ranked as an attraction for garden club tours and, beginning in the spring of 1939, the annual State Garden Club "pilgrimage of old homes." O'Connor watched, as a young girl, while her neighbors "trouped through in respectful solemnity." She signed the guest book with her own name and the names of all of her chickens and listed their joint address as "Hungry."

The impresario of the Cline Mansion was Aunt Mary Cline, her mother's oldest sister, then in her midfifties. A tall, thin woman, her salt-and-pepper hair tied back, with an elegant, patrician air and regal posture, "Sister," as O'Connor called her, was the family's ersatz matriarch. O'Connor's college friend Betty Boyd assumed the nickname was a private joke on Aunt Mary's appearance: "an austere nun . . . always in white." Yet Regina O'Connor corrected this impression in a note she penned in the top margin of a memoir Boyd showed her years later: "Sister was the first girl to arrive in the family after five boys and everybody in the family called her Sister." Indeed Mary Cline was the only girl in Peter Cline's first family of seven children. When her father died, as had the two Mrs. Clines, she declined Katie Semmes's invitation to move to Savannah; she chose instead to take on the responsibility of matron for home and family.

Extending hospitality to the O'Connor family during a time of trouble was a natural response for Aunt Mary. According to O'Connor's first cousin Dr. Peter Cline, "Sister would always add another room on when somebody got sick." The other residents in the home at the time were all unmarried women. A blunt, formidable companion was her sister Katie, working as a mail order clerk in the post office. Nicknamed "Duchess" by her clever niece, Aunt Katie — often dressed in a long coat with a big fur collar — was recalled by Betty Boyd Love as bearing "a strong resemblance to the illustrator John Tenniel's Duchess in *Alice in Wonderland.* She was a woman of vigorous appearance, vigorous language, and vigorous opinion." A satiric portrait of both aunts, Mary and Katie, worthy of "My Relitives," shows up in Aunts Bessie and Mattie of "The Partridge Festival": "The two of them were on the front porch, one sitting, the other standing. . . . They were box-jawed old ladies who looked like George Washington with his wooden teeth in. They wore black suits with large ruffled jabots and had dead-white hair pulled back." On the top floor of the Cline Mansion lived a third relative, the more diminutive Great-aunt Gertie Treanor, white-haired, less than five feet tall, who devoted hours to stitching muslin covers for St. Christopher medals on her little sewing machine.

The interior of the Cline Mansion was as grand, and full of character lines, as its façade. Passing in the entrance hall under a cut-glass chandelier, guests to the home, or on a garden club tour, would walk into either a drawing room to the left, or a parlor to the right, where the Clines gathered in the evenings to recite the Rosary. Dominating the drawing room was a rosewood concert grand piano; on the Colonial mantel, silver candelabra were set on either side of a large, painted portrait of Katie Semmes as a three-year-old girl in a pretty blue dress. The parlor room, lit by a pair of crystal hurricane lamps, was a flickering vision of desks, chairs, and highly polished end tables, with a long portrait of a handsome cousin, John MacMahon. Following a visit to the virtually unchanged mansion in the midsixties, the scholar Josephine Hendin recorded her impression of many family pictures, hanging on walls and propped on tables, of "Infants, girls with sausage curls, and impressively mustachioed men."

A step down, behind the parlor, was a dark wood–paneled dining room, its mahogany banquet table set with family silver and porcelain, and lined by Jacobean chairs. Miss Mary presided here over groups of sixteen or eighteen for large midday dinners, with the children seated at two little tables under far bay windows. Everyone helped themselves to trays of biscuits, and platters of sweet potatoes and fried chicken, prepared and served by a staff of three or more black cooks and servants. "We'd have these big Sunday lunches," remembers O'Connor's first cousin Jack Tarleton. "Mary Cline would sit at the head of the table and tinkle that silver bell, and here would come this entourage of people from the kitchen serving everybody around this big table. She could play that role to the hilt." Great-aunt Julia Cline was said by her son-in-law to have been "a speaking likeness" of the grandmother in O'Connor's story "A Good Man Is Hard to Find." Of a couple of reputed "alcoholic" uncles, Peter Cline says, "There were some oddballs in that family, too, but they kept them out of sight."

When Mary Flannery, still the only child living in a houseful of adults, left the main floor and climbed the central staircase that split forward and backward — called "good morning stairs" for the greetings exchanged on the middle landing — she found herself in a familiar world. While Sister and Duchess kept bedrooms on the first floor, and Aunt Gertie stayed in "the big room" on the east side of the cavernous second floor, her parents' bedroom adjoined hers in a separate apartment on the west side. Here the teenage girl could shut the door and be alone in her long, narrow, high-ceilinged bedroom, once again overlooking a backyard — where she kept geese and her mother planted daffodils — as well as the formal boxwood gardens of the Old Governor's Mansion. She spent countless hours on her stool at a high-legged clerk's desk, drawing and writing. To further escape the bustle downstairs, she retreated to a vast attic room, full of trunks and chests (a garret much like the third floor in Savannah) and with a front gabled window that looked out over Greene Street to the cemetery beyond.

The school where she was hastily enrolled was quite unlike either St. Vincent's or Sacred Heart. First known as Peabody Model School when it was founded in 1891, Peabody Elementary was a lab school for practice teachers from the education department of Georgia State College for Women. Many of their supervising professors had studied at Teacher's College at Columbia, testing ground for the liberal pedagogy of John Dewey, so the favored methods were eclectic and experimental. Mary Flannery's classroom was on the second floor in the middle of a series of "Choo-Choo" buildings, connected by overhead walkways, on the main college campus. As of 1935, a new principal, Mildred English, an educator with a national reputation, made sure that all of her pupils were taught and graded not only in Reading, Social Studies, Science, and Arithmetic, but also in Arts, Health Activities, and Social Attitudes and Habits.

Though she had been in class for only two months when the year ended, her instructor, Martha Phifer, filed a full report card, including a special note: "Mary Flannery needs to work on her spelling this summer." Otherwise she was rated satisfactory in most areas: "Speaks distinctly with well-pitched voice"; "Contributes information to group"; "Enjoys singing with the group"; "Has good posture." Responding to a survey, Mrs. O'Connor answered with snappy honesty about her daughter. To the question "Approximate time spent on home work?" she answered, "Very little." To "Does he have any home responsibilities?" the answer was "No." To "Does he prefer being alone rather than with others?": "Occasionally enjoys others." She listed as her daughter's only physical defect "Error in vision."

Mary Flannery's only friend in Milledgeville in the seventh grade was Mary Virginia Harrison, the daughter of the postmaster Ben Harrison and her mother's friend Gussie Harrison. Their match was made by the mothers. "Her mother handpicked her few friends in Milledgeville," recalls Jack Tarleton. Mary Virginia was an unlikely choice for the newcomer. While Mary Flannery was chronically shy, on the tall side for her age, gawky, and wearing glasses akin to her character Mary Flemming's "gold-rimmed spectacles," Mary Virginia was strikingly pretty, vivacious, and didn't like being alone for a minute. Yet the girls clicked. Mary Flannery remade the Merriweather Club into a secret society for two, with its own official flower, the dandelion. She designed a pin for her friend inspired by the colors of a pet parrot, and together the girls memorized the signs for Burma Shave along the highway to Macon, where they visited their dentist.

Staying, otherwise, mostly to herself, O'Connor expressed her inner life through her birds. "I remember sitting on the swing on the front porch of Greene Street, and Flannery walking by with this little bantam on a leash, and that is really my first memory of her," says her first cousin Frances Florencourt. Naming a pet quail "Amelia Earhart," following the pilot's disappearance over the Pacific in the summer of 1937, she startled a teacher and other girls on a field trip in nearby Nesbit Woods when she shouted, of her missing bird, "Oh, I've found Amelia Earhart! I've found Amelia Earhart!" Fellow Girl Scout Regina Sullivan has recalled one of her chickens with the middle name of her uncle Herbert Aloysius Cline, in Atlanta: "She would bring Aloysius to Scout meetings and he was dressed in little gray shorts, a little white shirt, a jacket, and a red bow. He just walked around us as we had our troop meeting." As O'Connor explained in "The King of the Birds": "I could sew in a fashion and I began to make clothes for chickens."

During the summers the Cline Mansion grew livelier with the annual visits of Aunt Agnes and her four daughters — distant models for the two visiting Catholic schoolgirl (second) cousins of "A Temple of the Holy Ghost." Agnes Cline had met her husband, Frank Florencourt, a signal designer for Central of Georgia Railroad, in Savannah, where she and Regina moved after high school. In 1924, the Florencourts even lived briefly with the O'Connors in their Charlton Street town house, before the birth of their first daughter. Having moved up North, near Boston, Agnes, who spoke with a Southern accent her entire life, brought her daughters to Georgia each summer for refreshment in their heritage. Greatly amplified for weeks at a time by these four girls — Margaret, Louise, Catherine, and Frances — the large Cline household sometimes included, as well, Cousins Betty and Peter Cline, from Atlanta, and Frank Cline, from Louisiana.

"They played better," remembers Peabody classmate Charlotte Conn Ferris, of the Florencourt girls. "Being in a family of four they knew better how to interact with other children." Elizabeth Shreve Ryan recalls, "I was always interested in listening to them because we didn't hear many Northern people speak. It was like listening to a foreign language." Mary Flannery mostly sat on the porch with the two oldest sisters, while the littler ones played in the yard. "I think the times I saw her talk the most was when the cousins were visiting," said Kitty Smith Kellam. "You didn't hear her laugh very often except when they were there. They would sit on that porch and rock *all* day long and I used to think how horrible that would be — just watching the world go by and rocking." Peter Cline says, "We had a running Monopoly game set up on the landing, and Mary Flannery was very much a part of it. She was a very sweet girl, very funny, with a keen wit."

While Edward O'Connor remained "the invisible man" to many children and young people in the neighborhood who never met him, he did visit during the summer. He would not have stayed away long from the daughter who was the single great joy and consolation in his life. "I remember sitting on the front porch at Greene Street in the middle of the day," says Frances Florencourt. "They had a big dinner at noonday, and afterwards they would sit in these big white chairs on the front porch and slap mosquitoes and fan themselves. I was sitting in Edward O'Connor's lap. He was playing that game, 'I got your nose' with me. I'd giggle. Then I said, 'No, I've got your nose,' and I pulled hard at his nose. I think I really must have really hurt him. He didn't look at all sick at that time. Though I wonder how much a six- or seven-year-old could really perceive."

A regular summertime destination for all of these cousins was Sorrel Farm, later called Andalusia, the 550-acre working dairy farm owned by their uncle, Dr. Bernard Cline, from Atlanta, and named for the sorrel-colored horses he kept there. Off Eatonton Road, two miles outside town, the former Stovall Place plantation was their pastoral playground, complete with white farmhouse, cow barn, horse stables, milk shed, fishing ponds, and fields for riding. One of Dr. Cline's hobbies was raising prizewinning show horses, including Rocky Barrymore and Jim Dandy, a Tennessee walker. "To this day I have bowlegs and I think it was from riding horses all over that farm when I was seven," says Jack Tarleton. The girl cousins, dressed alike in brown jodhpurs, pale yellow shirts, and shiny brown boots, rode Shetland ponies they named Shirley Temple, Devonshire Duke, Lady Luck, or Brownie. A snippet of home-movie color footage exists of Mary Flannery, in jodhpurs as well, looking quite assured in the saddle.

Yet she never simply became one of the gang of girls. She often held back, or acted in an off-putting manner. She would give inexperienced riders "wild horses" and then "laugh if you fell off," complained Loretta Feuger Hoynes, a childhood friend from Savannah. Like the three little bullies in "The River," she got a kick out of luring unsuspecting victims into a pigpen. Lucia Bonn Corse remembered being a guest at a summer party given for the Florencourt cousins during which "Mary Flannery spent the evening in a corner by herself." One Milledgeville resident has recalled that her own mother once invited the visiting Florencourt cousins to enjoy a fresh harvest of black cherries. While the girls were off riding horses, Mary Flannery, an "obligatory" guest, sat unhappily on the back porch spitting out cherry pits while muttering, "I didn't want to come."

※

Edward O'Connor did eventually secure a short-term home for his family on the outskirts of Atlanta in the Peachtree Heights neighborhood of Buckhead, still a small town of ten thousand residents, with upscale housing developments interspersed among its wooded areas. The rental at 2525 Potomac Avenue, quite a change from the Cline Mansion, was a one-story brown-frame foursquare, built in 1920. Like most of the homes in the planned "garden suburb" of curved streets, lush landscaping, and mature willow trees, the square bungalow fit a type of quintessential American construction provided by mail-order companies such as Aladdin and Sears, Roebuck, including complete plans and materials, and money-back offers of a dollar for each knot found in the lumber. In choosing the modest home on hilly ground, Ed O'Connor would have been aware of an appealing feature for his daughter: its porch fronted over the duck pond of the community park.

By moving to Buckhead, the O'Connors were also moving closer to other members of the Cline and O'Connor clans. Just a mile and a half away in Peachtree Park, another suburban development from the twenties, lived Regina's brother, the real estate agent Herbert Aloysius Cline, his wife, Edward O'Connor's sister Nan, and their two children, Peter and Betty, the regular summertime visitors to Milledgeville. Also in Peachtree Park, three blocks south of the Clines, was John Tarleton, an auditor at a building supply company, married to Regina's sister Helen Cleo Cline, and their horseback-riding son, Jack. Of the divvying up of this matriarchal world, O'Connor later explained to a friend that her mother had three main sisters, "Miss Mary, Miss Cleo, and Miss Agnes. Miss Cleo's domain is Atlanta and Miss Agnes' Boston."

All three families attended the same church, and sent their children to the same public school. Although Regina and her sister Cleo had a testy relationship, Jack Tarleton recalls that "My mother and I went once or twice to the O'Connors' house on Potomac Avenue to see them, or to pick them up." He remembers a party at the time at the Tarleton home at 3061 Piedmont Road: "Flannery was there, and the Florencourt cousins. They were all dressed in hoop skirts. Sometime during the afternoon, Flannery got caught outside on the porch and couldn't get in. So she simply went through the little window, hoop skirt and all. I was a little boy, standing there watching her. She was going to get into that house one way or another. Convention didn't mean anything to her."

Christ the King Cathedral was a three-block walk from the O'Connors' home. Dedicated in January 1939 as a sister church to St. John the Baptist in Savannah, marking the cohering of a Savannah-Atlanta diocese, this Gothic Revival cathedral, built of Indiana limestone, stood on four acres on Peachtree Road that had belonged a few years earlier to the Ku Klux Klan. The shadow history of Buckhead throughout the twenties and early thirties included lots of Klan activity. The Buckhead robe factory pumped millions of dollars into the city's economy, attracting such firms as Coca-Cola and Studebaker to advertise in the Klan newspaper. Christ the King was actually built on the site of the Klan's former national headquarters, the antebellum "Imperial Palace." As Jews and Catholics had both been targets of the Klan, the foreclosure of the property by a Jewish banker, and its subsequent sale to the Catholic Church, was a bit of revenge.

During the academic year 1939–40, Mary Flannery was enrolled at North Fulton High School, a segregated public school built in 1932 to serve the white children on this expanding edge of northern Atlanta. Designed by the neoclassicist architect Philip Trammell Schutze, North Fulton was a quintessential high school, a classical Georgian Revival brick building, trimmed in white wood, with towering Ionic pillars, through which more than a thousand students and nearly fifty teachers passed daily. "Mary Flannery and I were there at the same time," recalls Dr. Peter Cline, "but not in the same classes. You could be in the same grade, and take the same courses, but have different teachers. It was a relatively large school. . . . I used to walk to North Fulton every day. People didn't have two cars back then. It was still the Depression." Also at North Fulton, unknown to her, was O'Connor's future poet friend James Dickey, then a football player.

Every bit as progressive as Peabody, North Fulton's up-to-date layout included twenty-three classrooms, two lecture halls, seven science labs, an auditorium, cafeteria, gym, armory, shooting gallery, the newly opened W. F. Dykes Stadium, named for the school's first principal, and an industrial arts building with house-drawing, electrical, and woodworking studios. Of the young girl's uneasy reaction to this cutting-edge display case of learning, her friend Caroline Gordon later reported, "She once described her early education to me as a vacillation between the convent school and what she called 'the life of Riley.' The nuns whom she had for teachers in Savannah stressed discipline, as nuns do. The 'progressive' schools which she attended in Atlanta and later in Milledgeville offered an eclecticism which the convent-bred child evidently found bewildering."

The local patriarch of the Cline family was Dr. Bernard Cline, presiding in Atlanta as Aunt Mary did in Milledgeville. At holiday dinners at the Cline Mansion, Uncle Bernard would sit across from Aunt Mary in the place of his deceased father. A single gentleman, tall and handsome, nearly sixty, with fine silver hair, light blue eyes, and a dignified bearing, he was an ear, nose, and throat specialist, a graduate of Emory Medical School, with further medical studies in New York City and Vienna. "Our uncle Bernard footed the bills for a lot of things," explains Dr. Peter Cline. Uncle Bernard's best friend was Louis Cline, his affable, low-key, younger brother. While Mary Flannery was in school in Atlanta, Uncle Louis was selling used cars, perhaps giving her a special angle on Haze Motes's purchase of his old Essex at Slade's used-car lot in *Wise Blood*. "He's never mentioned my father to me," she later wrote, of Louis, to Betty Hester. "If he did, he'd say something like, 'He was a nice fellow,' and wag his head."

Bernard and Louis lived together at Bell House, Atlanta's elite boardinghouse for confirmed bachelors and a few widowers. Housed in a Victorian mansion, with four Tiffany stained-glass windows, on the northeast corner of Peachtree and Third streets, Bell House required that residents be recommended by three members in good standing. The house rules were no drinking; coats worn downstairs and on the veranda; no smoking in the dining room. In exchange, the men were well attended by a staff of cooks, waiters, and housekeepers. As Elinor Hiller wrote in the *Atlanta Journal Magazine* in 1929, "Being an ex–Bell House boy is something like Roman citizenship, a thing to be proud of, a thing with just a touch of distinction in it." Of visits to his uncles, Jack Tarleton recalls, with less mythology, "Bell House was musty, with high ceilings, leather furniture, and big magnolia trees out front. It was a fancy men's club that had begun to age a bit."

Dr. Bernard Cline was quite the gentleman-about-town. His social portfolio included not only Bell House, but also the Piedmont Driving Club, boasting the city's first golf course, and the

Capital City Club. Both of these exclusive clubs were "restricted" to the wealthiest of Atlanta's white society — meaning, closed to Jews and blacks. Even before moving to Atlanta, Mary Flannery and her Florencourt cousins were accustomed to fetes in their honor at the Piedmont Club, or on the front lawn of Bell House, where the main event featured black men in white coats driving up in ice cream trucks full of fancy desserts. The *Atlanta Journal* covered one of Uncle Bernard's "old-fashioned" lawn parties for eighty-five guests at Bell House, under the heading "Dr. Cline Hosts Affair Feting Nieces": the girls pinned the tail on Mickey Mouse, and released colorful balloons into the air.

Yet for the fourteen-year-old Mary Flannery, Atlanta was less a lawn party than a perfect storm of yet only dimly understood troubles. Even as an adult, she held on to a juvenile animus for the place. "My idea about Atlanta," she wrote Ted Spivey, "is to get in, get it over with and get out before dark." The sources of these negative feelings were her experiences in 1939 and 1940. During that unsettled period, her father was ill, even if temporarily asymptomatic. Every weekday he would put on a jacket and tie and travel downtown to the FHA offices on the fifth floor of the Austell Building at 10 Forsyth Street, working at one of Roosevelt's many "alphabet agencies" to help ease the city's housing crisis. As adjustment to the city was proving difficult for the family, his daughter would spend these same hours, ill at ease, in the corridors of her modern high school.

Given the extra stress, tensions between Regina Cline and the O'Connor family resurfaced. "Regina and my mother did not see eye to eye at all," reports Dr. Peter Cline of relations between Regina and her sister-in-law Nan, at whose wedding she met her husband. "All the other in-laws called my Grandmother and Grandfather O'Connor, 'Mother' and 'Father.' Regina never called them anything except 'Mr. and Mrs. O'Connor.' That gives a little clue as to what she was like. . . . Edward O'Connor was a sweet, charming man. He was tall, good-looking, very warm, the total opposite of his wife. The O'Connors were warm, loving people, very loving, very outgoing." As O'Connor herself later summed up these dynamics, especially on the Cline side, "I come from a family where the only emotion respectable to show is irritation. In some this tendency produces hives, in others literature, in me both."

The Atlanta that O'Connor knew, growing up in the thirties, suffered even more than most cities from the poverty and distress caused by the Great Depression. The South had already experienced an economic turnaround brought about by the destruction of King Cotton by the boll weevil, described by stunned cotton farmers in the 1920s as "a cross between a termite and a tank." The region was the hardest hit in the nation when the stock market crashed. Even in bucolic Buckhead, in 1932 six hundred families were considered "destitute." A year later, only half the workforce of Atlanta was employed. Although by 1939, relief from the destitution was finally evident, O'Connor was familiar with streets thick with panhandlers and apple sellers, long "hunger marches" and breadlines. On either side of Bell House, where she visited her uncles, half the stores were boarded shut on Peachtree Street — a decade earlier, the city's most fashionable stretch of boutiques.

Images of hard times, and down-and-out types, are often found in O'Connor's fiction; according to Ted Spivey, her "absurdist vision of cities" was drawn from "the few months O'Connor spent in Atlanta." Certainly Taulkinham, in *Wise Blood,* with its street peddlers, vacant lots, and railroad yards is a depressed city. O'Connor told Spivey that the novel's City Forest Park Zoo was based on Atlanta's Grant Park Zoo. When her editor Catharine Carver visited in 1960, Flannery took her on a tour of the Cyclorama next to the Grant Park Zoo, one of Enoch Emery's favorite spots: "We met her in Atlanta and took her to the cyclorama in the mvsevm where Enoch got the mummy." In "The Artificial Nigger," Atlanta is compared to Dante's Hell, especially a sewer system that the ten-year-old Nelson imagines as "the entrance to hell." Both the building of new sewers, and the refurbishing of the panoramic painting of the 1864 Battle of Atlanta in the Cyclorama, had been WPA projects much in the news in Atlanta during the thirties.

Even closer to O'Connor's heart was the adolescent homesickness she put into the mouths of a trio of bad boys in "A Circle in the Fire." In the story, their ringleader, Powell, waxes nostalgic for his early boyhood on a farm that closely resembles Sorrel Farm, with its main house and white water tower rising up behind it. His itinerant father then moved "out to one of them developments" in Atlanta. Although their cluster of ten four-story concrete buildings was much more down-market than Peachtree Heights, the term "development" covered both. "So you boys live in one of those nice new developments," says Mrs. Cope, the farm's owner. Powell's sidekick W.T. sets her straight: "All the time we been knowing him he's been telling us about this here place. Said it was everything here. Said it was horses here. . . . He don't like it in Atlanta." Evoking the all-important naming of Shetland ponies at Sorrel Farm, Powell says, in a nostalgic reverie, "I remember it was one name Gene and it was one name George."

The biggest public event in Atlanta during O'Connor's stay, if not in the city's entire cultural history, was the grand premiere of *Gone With the Wind*. Yet all the hoopla over the novel and film left her merely irked. For O'Connor, as both girl and woman, there was no escaping the endlessly popular historical romance about Scarlett O'Hara, the daughter of an Irish Catholic immigrant, surviving the Civil War years in Atlanta and on Tara plantation in North Georgia. When O'Connor was eleven years old, living in Savannah, the novel first appeared and sold a record 250,000 copies in five weeks. As John and Cleo Tarleton were early friends of Margaret Mitchell and her first husband, the family rumor was that the novel's Tarleton twins owed their name to

O'Connor's aunt and uncle. Street guards for crowd control at the gala movie premiere in Atlanta were all drawn from the ROTC chapter (of which James Dickey was a member) of O'Connor's high school.

On the evening of December 15, 1939, five giant searchlights clashed like crossed swords above Loew's Grand Theatre downtown. Confederate flags whipped in the wind along Peachtree Street as the lead actors Clark Gable and Vivien Leigh and the novelist Margaret Mitchell arrived. Pathe and Movietone crews filmed more than two thousand celebrities, and the governors of five Southern states, disappearing into a lavish façade redone as a Greek Revival plantation home. Many of these Confederate-themed festivities stretched out over the entire week, enacted along a fault line of Jim Crow tension. The black actress Hattie McDaniel, who won a Best Supporting Actress Oscar for her role as Mammy, was not invited to the premiere. The sixty-voice Ebenezer Baptist Church Choir, directed by the Reverend Martin Luther King, Sr., entertained at a whites-only Junior League ball associated with the opening event; choir members, including the ten-year-old Martin Luther King, Jr., were dressed as slaves.

For O'Connor, a rare Southerner of her generation to complain "I sure am sick of the Civil War," neither the book nor movie was a draw. Her irritation at the reception only intensified when relatives later needled her for not writing a popular moneymaker like her fellow Georgian woman author. She took revenge by sending up the gaudy opening night as the high point in the life of 104-year-old Confederate veteran General Sash in "A Late Encounter with the Enemy": "'I was in that preemy they had in Atlanta,' he would tell visitors sitting on his front porch. 'Surrounded by beautiful guls. It wasn't a thing local about it. It was nothing local about it. Listen here. Every person in it had paid ten dollars to get in and had to wear this tuxseeder. I was in this uniform.'" And parroting her own mother's criticism, the mother of the fledgling writer Asbury, in "The Enduring Chill," advises, "We need another good book like *Gone with the Wind*. . . . Put the war in it. . . . That always makes a long book." In "The Partridge Festival," Aunt Bessie, a stand-in for Aunt Mary, remarks hopefully to her aspiring-writer nephew, "Maybe you'll be another Margaret Mitchell." For the twenty-five years following the premiere, *Gone With the Wind* remained a running joke in O'Connor's life and work. Dean Hood, a friend from Florida, recalled that when she and her husband, Robert, visited Milledgeville during the 1960s, a Sunday edition of the *Atlanta Journal* ran a memorial feature on Margaret Mitchell and *Gone With the Wind,* "which Flannery sputtered over all day long."

IN THE FALL of 1940, the silhouette of Death that O'Connor described, in an apprentice story, as a man in white "coming slow up the road, to take you," grew more distinct. Because their daughter was unhappy in school in Atlanta, her parents enrolled her for the tenth grade back in Peabody High School, in Milledgeville. Edward O'Connor, under the care of physicians in Atlanta, moved in alongside his two brothers-in-law in Bell House. Soon even this shaky arrangement fell apart. A worst-case scenario came true. As his health deteriorated, O'Connor could no longer hold down his government job. By the end of the year, he retreated to the Cline Mansion to spend his last months as an invalid, dependent on the kindness of his wife's family for care. His fifteen-year-old daughter watched as the father she adored — a middle-aged man, otherwise in his prime — suffered a mysterious, painful, wasting death from the fatal illness.

Edward O'Connor's death on Saturday, the first of February 1941, came exactly a month after his forty-fifth birthday. Its apparent suddenness was a shock, especially to those outside the immediate family circle. Just a year earlier, a holiday party at the Cline Mansion had been billed as both a New Year's Day celebration and a birthday party for Edward O'Connor, with decorative yellow calendulas in a large silver bowl on the dining room table, and his daughter assisting with the entertaining. His mysterious illness had been kept enough of a well-guarded secret that a brief obituary in the *Atlanta Constitution* claimed that he died "following a two-week illness." A *Union-Recorder* obituary more fully reported, "In recent months his health had not been good, but his death was unexpected. His cordial personality, his leadership and ability won for him many friends. He waged an unrelenting fight to lift some of the tax burden from real estate."

The burial service took place on Monday, February 3, a gray, wintry day, at Sacred Heart Church on Milledgeville's North Jefferson Street. This simple sanctuary, topped by a steeple and cross, had been the scene of all of the important Cline and Treanor rites of passage for nearly three-quarters of a century. Built with bricks and Gothic-arched, hand-pressed, clear-glass windows from the handsome Lafayette Hotel that once stood on the site, the church was constructed mostly with help from Flannery O'Connor's great-grandparents. Its first wedding was held on February 8, 1875, when her grandfather Peter J. Cline married Katie Treanor. Its first funeral was that of Mary Treanor, daughter of Hugh and Johannah Harty Treanor. Edward and Regina had been married there just nineteen years earlier by Father Morrow. The current church organist was Aunt Gertie Treanor.

The chapel was an intimate, confined space, like a small country church. To the left, behind the altar rail, was a baptismal font; to the right, a freestanding pulpit. The Reverend James E. King conducted a traditional requiem mass, in Latin, facing the main altar, looking up toward a hanging, nearly life-sized, loin-draped Christ on the cross. An honorary escort for the casket, resting in the center aisle, was made up of local and state officers of the American Legion. Among the pallbearers was Dr. C. B. Fulghum, the Cline family doctor. Edward O'Connor was interred in a Cline and Treanor family plot on the northern edge of City Cemetery, and a special Rosary was said for the repose of his soul in the front parlor of the Cline Mansion. "I went to the funeral as I was a Peabody class officer," recalls Elizabeth Shreve Ryan. "It was a very cold day, and it was a very sad, dreary occasion. I don't think any of the rest of us had ever lost a father." Mary Flannery consoled her mother by reminding her that he was now better off than they were.

O'Connor rarely spoke of her father again. Yet not speaking of him did not imply that she did not feel his loss deeply. She would often keep a discreet silence about subjects that mattered to her the most, beginning with her relationship with her father. Her very silence was a stolid marker of its depth. "I think she did have a wholehearted love for her father," says Louise Abbot, a close friend of O'Connor's, beginning in the midfifties. "The love was of a kind we most often think of children having for their mother." In talking about her personal feelings about God in her religious life, O'Connor, tellingly, once wrote Betty Hester, "I've never spent much time over the bride-bridegroom analogy. For me, perhaps because it began for me in the beginning, it's been more father and child." While many have noticed the dominant place of widows in her fiction, every widow, or orphan, implies a missing husband or father. O'Connor's two novels, and many of her stories, are filled with the eraser marks of all these dead fathers.

In a jumbled notebook that O'Connor kept during her first year of college, about two years after the death of her father, she did meditate briefly on her grief. A spiritually precocious seventeen-year-old, she gave a rare glimpse into the private wisdom she earned from the tragedy:

The reality of death has come upon us and a consciousness of the power of God has broken our complacency like a bullet in the side. A sense of the dramatic, of the tragic, of the infinite, has descended upon us, filling us with grief, but even above grief, wonder. Our plans were so beautifully laid out, ready to be carried to action, but with magnificent certainty God laid them aside and said, "You have forgotten — mine?"

Soon after their return to Milledgeville in the fall of 1940, Regina O'Connor got in touch with George Haslam, the adviser to the high school newspaper, the *Peabody Palladium*. She knew that her daughter was too shy to make such a move herself. Yet she also knew how much time and effort went into the drawings and writings she was always doing in her attic studio. With her husband ill and living separately in Atlanta, her mother had hoped to find some school activity to occupy her. Haslam agreed to the suggestion and asked the extremely introverted girl to contribute to the paper. "I don't know how to write," Mary Flannery answered. "But I can draw." As a result, she was made art editor in October, and, almost immediately, began to flourish in the role.

For the October issue of the *Palladium,* she painstakingly created a linoleum-block cut, her first, titled *One Result of the New Peabody Orchestra.* The cartoon shows a girl wearing a tasseled hat, sweater, pleated skirt, and saddle oxfords, blowing on a large saxophone, as "BLAH," all in caps, emerges from the horn. A background figure, in skirt and jacket, frowning, cups her hands to her ears. The cartoon accompanied the article "Students Join Concert Group." With a knack for difficult, idiosyncratic crafts, the new art editor produced 120 of these block prints over the next five years: drawing a sketch on a piece of linoleum, gouging away the white portions, applying oil-based ink to the ridges, printing a reversed paper copy on a special press. Her first few cartoons — a girl at her desk with a thought bubble of a turkey, for Thanksgiving; a dozing pupil with Z's stringing from her mouth — were rough, scratchy affairs. As one critic has described her genre, they were "single-frame satires."

Although Mary Flannery claimed not to be a writer, she was really writing nearly as much as drawing. For her, the two activities were joined from the start. Appearing in the same November 1940 issue as her Thanksgiving cartoon was her debut poem, "The First Book." Profiled a few years later in the local newspaper by Nelle Womack Hines as "a female Ogden Nash," O'Connor aspired in her first effort to the terse, doggerel style of the popular *New Yorker* poet:

> *His mind began to wander,*
> *And his bean began to rage.*

Her light verse winds up as a paean to books, the source of her earliest enthusiastic collaborations with her father:

> *Thus the ancestor of books was born,*
> *On slides of stone and clay.*

While her father had been homebound, she was working on a send-up of Marcel Proust, though she had certainly not read much, if any, of *Remembrance of Things Past*. In a letter to Maryat Lee, in 1956, she admitted that she had read only *Swann's Way,* the first of the seven volumes of the French novel. But at fifteen, she knew enough of Proust's central conceit — the sensation of biting into a madeleine cookie to release a flood of childhood memories — to write a four-paragraph burlesque. In writing, as in cartooning, satire was her signature adolescent style. In "Recollections on My Future Childhood," she makes fun of Proust, as Ogden Nash was making fun in the 1930s of literary greats such as James Joyce, in his "Portrait of the Artist as a Prematurely Old Man." "Fish oil," not a French pastry, is her narrator's mnemonic trigger: "It was my first sardine . . . bruised & blue from the crowding." She winds up concluding, "Proust wanted past time. I'll take any old time."

Her own reading was far from orderly or comprehensive. She spent many hours during her childhood visits to the Cline Mansion reading about Greek and Roman myths, and lots of other topics, in an 1898 set of the children's encyclopedia *The Book of Knowledge* that had once belonged to her grandmother. As fascinated by the graphics as by the text, she later wrote a friend that she particularly remembered "the illustrations about a young man of about six in a sailor suit and round hat. He stood on a wharf and watched a ship come in. In each illustration the ship was bigger. He therefore came to the conclusion that the world was round. He did this without assistance. I was mighty impressed and will never forget the Book of Knowledge. I reckon it's deteriorated though." She complained that "the rest of what I read was Slop with a capital S."

After "the Slop period," she became absorbed, "for years," with a ten-volume "commemorative" edition of Poe's work she found on the family bookshelf. She enjoyed *The Narrative of Arthur Gordon Pym,* a short lyric novel about a stowaway on a whaling ship whose survivors resorted to cannibalism. But her favorite was volume eight, the *Humorous Tales,* including "The Spectacles," "The Man That Was Used Up," and "The System of Doctor Tarr and Professor Fether." She later recalled, "These were mighty humerous — one about a young man who was too vain to wear his glasses and consequently married his grandmother by accident; another about a fine figure of a man who in his room removed wooden arms, wooden legs, hair piece, artificial teeth, voice box, etc. etc.; another about the inmates of a lunatic asylum who take over the establishment and run it to suit themselves." She added, "I'm sure he wrote them all while drunk too."

According to Elizabeth Hardwick, who met O'Connor at Yaddo, the Poe collection was a staple in many educated homes of the period. "We didn't have a lot of books in my house but we did have the complete Poe," said Hardwick, of her childhood in Kentucky. "I bet they had the same edition. I remember sitting on the front porch in Lexington and reading 'Murders in the Rue Morgue.' I've often looked back and thought, 'How did that happen?' You have nothing to read when you're twelve and you're reading Poe." For O'Connor, Poe continued to haunt: showing up in the coffins and "walling up cats" of *Wise Blood,* and as an inspiration for the Misfit's spectacles for sizing up the grandmother in "A Good Man Is Hard to Find," and for Hulga's unscrewed wooden leg in "Good Country People." Most immediately, though, the tales were grist for "Recollections of My Future Childhood," in which Aunt Bertha locked her fiancé in her left bureau drawer and "never opened it."

During the spring of 1941, Mary Flannery completed writing and illustrating three books of her own, all about geese — "Elmo," "Gertrude," and "Mistaken Identity." "She wrote these books about her animals when she was growing up," says fellow Peabodite Deedie Sibley (known in high school as Frances Binion). "I remember them being pink cardboard. They had spiral binding and you just flipped them open. There was a picture of a duck, and then some little sentence or something she wanted to say about the duck." Impressed by the mechanics of publishing by her father, she was quite professional about these handmade books. "M.F. has finished three books on her geese, and put each in a box," Aunt Gertie informed Aunt Agnes in March 1941. "Nearly all who have seen them think they are good. She is thinking about having them copyrighted if she just finds the right way of going about it. Louis seems to think he knows a party in Atlanta who could put her on the right track."

She paid the most attention to "Mistaken Identity," her seventeen-page poem, with colored illustrations, about a case of gender confusion among geese. The poem was occasional, based on the true incident of her pet gander Herman laying an egg and hatching a brood of eight goslings, leading to the conclusion that "Herman's HENRIETTA." In December 1941, the *Peabody Palladium* picked up the story of her foiled attempts to find a publisher for the three books in a piece titled "Peabodite Reveals Strange Hobby." The interviewer asked, "Mary Flannery, what's your hobby?" She replied, "Collecting rejection slips." "What?" the confused reporter responded. "Publisher's rejection slips," she explained. The piece ends with the upbeat news: "As for Mary Flannery's ambition, she wants to keep right on writing, particularly satires." When she eventually self-published *Mistaken Identity* as a bound booklet, she added a preface: "The following is a drama especially prepared for highly intelligent adults and precocious children."

Seemingly custom-made for the young writer, Peabody High School had purposely been designed as just such a meeting place for intelligent adults and precocious children. Her school's idealistic motto was "The Good, The True, The Beautiful." Elizabeth Shreve Ryan recalls, "We were always told, 'Leave the world a better place than you found it.'" There were no "classes," only "activities." In Home Economics, students planned and executed a formal dinner at one of their homes. A semester of Chemistry began with the instructor asking her pupils what they wished to study, and then helping them fulfill a desire to learn about photography or cosmetics. "The teacher did run in a little bit about the elements and the periodic table," one student remembered. Literature appreciation was favored over diagramming sentences. History began with reading and reporting on the front page of a daily newspaper. The choir, of which Mary Virginia Harrison was a member, was a cappella, involving mostly reciting poetry in unison.

Yet the newspaper's contrary art editor had nothing but scorn for such experimental teaching. She got her wish to be liberated from the nuns only to be equally disdainful of their polar opposites, the freethinkers. "I went to a progressive highschool where one did not read if one did not wish to," she complained to Betty

Hester in 1955. "I did not wish to (except the Humerous Tales etc.)." In an early draft of *Wise Blood,* the Peabody principal Mildred English becomes "Mr. English the principal who had graduated from Teacher's College, Columbia," and the school becomes Tilford High School.

While putting down the principles of original thought and free expression, and teachers playing to their audience at the next meeting of the PTA, she was actually a beneficiary of the system. Cutting a highly original profile, Mary Flannery was generally accepted as the "creative" girl dressed in a plaid skirt, rolled sleeves, and a pair of brown Girl Scout shoes, her school notebook painted in oils and covered with cellophane. She often waved "hello" with a salute as she strode the halls with her head thrust forward. "I can see her plodding along," says Charlotte Conn Ferris. "That's how she walked, with her hands behind her back, just clumping along, thinking about something, who knows what." For life drawing in Art, she brought her goose of a gander, Herman, as a portrait model. She played clarinet, and bull fiddle, because, she said, "I am the only one who can hold it up." As an adult, she told an interviewer that all she remembered of high school was "the way the halls smelled and bringing my accordion sometimes to play for the 'devotional.'"

Her greatest bit of meticulously planned showmanship took place in Margaret Abercrombie's Home Economics section. The "activity" for the semester was sewing, and all the other girls busily sewed aprons, or underwear, for weeks on end, while O'Connor sat idly off to the side, not participating. "Now next Wednesday is the examination day for this course," Miss Abercrombie finally announced, a bit exasperated. "All members who expect to receive a grade are to bring and display the various garments made during the quarter. I hardly see how you are going to get a whole outfit finished and ready, Mary Flannery, by that time." As a fellow student has reported, "On the appointed day Flannery arrived with her pet duckling, and a whole outfit of underwear and clothes, beautifully sewn to fit the duck! The class in great glee all gathered round and helped dress the duck. Flannery successfully passed the course."

By now she had a full menagerie of birds to choose from for her models. On the eve of America's entrance into World War II, Mary Flannery was particularly drawn to names for her pets lifted from the daily newspapers she was required to read for History class. With an instinct for shock value, the author who would later warn, "The topical is poison," went straight for the headlines. She named her black crow, rescued when the bird was shot by a neighbor for stealing pecans, Winston, after Winston Churchill. Her pet rooster, another of her models in Art class, was Haile Selassie, for the emperor of Ethiopia, reinstated in 1941 after being routed by the armies of Benito Mussolini. Most controversial was her second rooster, Adolph, the pen mate of Haile, as Adolf Hitler, the führer of Germany, had just declared war on the United States in December 1941. She changed its name only after neighbors were disturbed by calls of "Here, Adolph!" issuing from the Cline backyard.

Cartoons turned out to be a happy medium for this quiet, yet extremely critical girl. Through her monthly cartoons, she could bare her teeth in the guise of a smile. As a more mature O'Connor wrote, in 1959, to Ted Spivey: "From 15 to 18 is an age at which one is very sensitive to the sins of others, as I know from recollections of myself. At that age you don't look for what is hidden." Among the sins that she exposed was the pretense of senior plays: in "Senior, Senior, Wherefore Art Thou, Senior," she conjured two girls in a histrionic balcony scene to accompany the article "Seniors Present Annual Plays." Like any good cartoonist, she was alert to the mood of her audience. A week following the bombing of Pearl Harbor, in a December 1941 cartoon, she modulated her tone with "In Hopes That a Jimmie Soon Will Be There": a girl sits next to a fireplace, with a soldier's jacket hung from the mantel as a Christmas stocking. (Jimmie was a nickname for a cadet at Georgia Military College, many of whom enlisted in the war effort.)

Most unsuitable for the physically awkward girl was gym class. "She just thought playing sports was the biggest bore," says Elizabeth Shreve Ryan. "We had to put on our blue bloomers and go out to a grassy area behind the school on the main campus and play volleyball. I can just remember her standing in her gym uniform making no effort to give the ball a hoist. She'd kind of nudge her shoulder as if that was all she was willing to do. She did that very cheerfully, but it was just not her bag." Likewise "not her bag" were dance invitations to battalion balls at Georgia Military College, and the chance to dress up in the retro gowns of Southern belles to match the gray uniforms of the boys. She was much happier adding to her collection of 150 replicas of birds, and other animals, in china and glass, or designing another of the original lapel pins she sold out of a local drugstore.

O'Connor was most in her element in English class, especially a six-week segment devoted to creative writing. Her Composition teacher, Frances Lott Ratliff, has remarked on how surprised she was that a fifteen-year-old could show such talent. "How she looked didn't seem to matter," she added. Elizabeth Shreve Ryan recalls the sensation caused by O'Connor's writing: "Being in a creative writing class with Mary Flannery in high school was sheer torture. I remember she wrote a very strange story with weird characters. I don't know whether it was a ghost story, but it was gripping. As World War II was just beginning, I wrote some drivel about a soldier and his girlfriend. Her stories were written with panache, and a wry sense of humor. But they were just weird."

She did agree to go on one double date. The special event was arranged by Flannery's friend Mary Virginia Harrison, who has been described by Elizabeth Shreve Ryan as "the belle of the ball. She had beautiful clothes, and never lacked a date, or an invitation to a dance." Mary Virginia's date was Reynolds Allen, one of the few male students at Peabody. He had recently won a Baldwin County essay contest, in May 1942, by writing about U.S. Representative Carl Vinson. Allen's first-place essay, awarded a full college scholarship, won over Mary Flannery's second-place effort, awarded ten dollars, on the college president Dr. Melvin Parks. Her "blind date" that evening was Reynolds's cousin Dick Allen, a slight, bookish boy. The quartet went to the country club and drank Coca-Colas. At some point in the evening, Mary Flannery blurted out, "My dad-gum foot's gone to sleep."

While she complained about having attended a high school where you could "integrate English literature with geography, biology, home economics, basketball, or fire prevention," she graduated with a solid list of credits in a standard array of academic subjects. She even received a credit in Latin. "At that time they said the same things they usually say about Latin," says fellow Peabodite Dr. Floride Gardner. "That it gives you such a good basis for English, particularly verbs." But O'Connor's Latin teacher, Lila Blitch, later claimed to be "terribly disappointed" by the negative Southern character portrayed through Haze Motes, in *Wise Blood,* by her former pupil. O'Connor also received two credits in French, taught by Miss Adams.

The culmination of her time at what she dismissed ever after as "the progressive high school" was a graduation ceremony at eight thirty on the evening of May 28, 1942, at Russell Auditorium. Her graduation day cartoon in the *Palladium* the year before was titled "At Long Last . . ." and pictured a girl in cap and gown rushing with arms outstretched and head bent toward a door marked "EXIT" in big, block letters. Actually, all the girls wore evening dresses rather than caps and gowns. The program opened with the singing of the class song, to the tune of "The Sweetheart of Sigma Chi": "When our schooldays are gone, / As they're bound to go, / We'll be broken hearted but true." Class President Mary Virginia

Harrison addressed "our mothers, our fathers," and spoke of the occasion as "the most significant one we have ever known."

Afterward, Mrs. O'Connor and Mrs. Harrison threw a party at the Cline Mansion for their daughters, the graduating class of forty-six seniors, and Peabody faculty. Frances Binion helped ladle punch at a dining room table decorated with garden flowers and lighted tapers. Lila Blitch volunteered as one of the hostesses. "I recollect Mrs. O'Connor serving us little pink cakes, and little sandwiches, and punch at our graduation party," says Elizabeth Shreve Ryan. "She was a genteel Southern lady, full of graciousness. But her daughter was on the couch looking as if she'd been *crammed* into her evening dress. She made it plain to everyone that she was not about to be a gracious hostess." In contrast to her "very pretty" mother, Mary Flannery sat out the entire affair alone, her face fixed in a look of utter boredom.

Chapter Three

"MFOC"

❋

Georgia State College for Women in Milledgeville proved to be a good fit for seventeen-year-old Mary Flannery O'Connor. The "girls' college" did remain a lifelong target for her satire, sent up as Lucy Gains College, the "local college," in a draft of "The Partridge Festival," and as Willowpool Seminary, "the most progressive Female Seminary in the state," in a draft of a graduate thesis story, "The Crop." In her Iowa "Biography," she leveled her alma mater for its emphasis on high school teaching, her early career path, by default, describing the training as qualifying her only for a job in Podunk, Georgia, earning $87.50 a month. Yet to her friend Janet McKane, in 1963, she admitted the bottom line of her feelings about high school and college: "I enjoyed college and despised the progressive high school but only remember people and things from both."

With classes starting almost immediately in the summer of 1942, the laboratory school and the college were at first nearly indistinguishable. Like all of her Peabody classmates — except one, who went away to college in Alabama — O'Connor simply "moved over" to Georgia State College for Women, or GSCW, but continued to live at home. Registering for a special wartime three-year program that required summer sessions as well as the fall, winter, and spring semesters, she was already enrolled by June 9, a mere ten days after her Peabody graduation. In classrooms exactly like those in high school, she took four courses in Biology, Composition, Math, and Humanities that she later remembered as survey courses she had merely endured.

Of a lifelong friendship that began almost at once during that ten-week summer session, while most of the college buildings were shut against the Georgia heat, and most of the faculty away on vacation, Betty Boyd Love has written, "I first met Flannery O'Connor in the summer of 1942. We were both freshmen entering a new accelerated college program at Georgia State College for Women. There weren't many of us in the program. Most of the summer students at GSCW were public school teachers returning to renew or upgrade a credential, so the small group of us who were 'regular' students got to know each other quite soon." O'Connor met Betty Boyd while she was enduring Math 110, or Functional Math, in which she received a 75, her lowest academic grade.

A poet and mathematician from Rome, Georgia, with wavy hair, round eyeglasses, and a bright smile, Boyd was the first friend Mary Flannery truly chose on her own, without her mother's oversight. The two young women discovered that they shared unfocused literary ambitions and, in the first flush of their friendship, both were writing poems. Two of Boyd's were published in the fall 1942 issue of the college literary magazine, the *Corinthian* — "Fairies" and "Reflection," a sensitive meditation on roses "twining over the wall . . . built around my soul." O'Connor tended to stilted odes, like "Pffft," published two years later. Its first line was "Some new, unheard-of thought I would put down!" Both later cringed at these "pretty terrible poems," said Love. Hearing a rumor, in 1949, of a sighting of a published poem, O'Connor wrote her in a panic:

"have not written anything but prose since I got out of stir. But several awful ghosts come to mind. Do you remember the poems we sent to an anthology and had accepted — called *America Sings,* printed by offset somewhere in California?"

Yet the thrill of being literary coconspirators was an important bond. Appealing, too, for the extremely guarded Mary Flannery, was Betty Boyd's quiet earnestness. She later portrayed herself as a "horribly serious" college student, her studiousness counterbalanced by O'Connor's "same dry whimsical humor." The *Corinthian* editor Jane Sparks Willingham concurs that "Betty Boyd was a deep-thinking person, not somebody who sat around and cracked jokes about what you did the night before on your date." Boyd's sensitivity was evident in an essay published in the fall 1942 *Corinthian,* tremulously recording her summer arrival at GSCW. She wrote of bidding good-bye to her parents, "the two people I love more than all others"; having "walked up the steps to the library to register"; and looking forward to "companionship with a fine group of smiling, quiet, friendly girls."

If not handpicked, Betty Boyd was approved by Mrs. O'Connor, and often invited to the Cline Mansion, where she spent "a great many hours" enjoying the "large and high-ceilinged and cool" rooms: "I soon became a regular visitor there and enjoyed many a Sunday dinner at the wonderful long walnut table with its silver napkin rings and the little pot of demitasse coffee served to pour over the ice cream at dessert. They had trouble keeping a cook because of the demands of Miss Katie. . . . In retrospect, this seems to me a somewhat unusual household, but at the time it appeared perfectly unexceptional, and I'm sure they all looked on it as such." Although Aunt Gertie died just four months after Edward O'Connor, Aunt Mary kept the mansion as a haven for single women by inviting two college teachers as occasional boarders, Miss Bancroft and Miss Kirby.

The most unusual aspect of the house might have escaped the

notice of the young Betty Boyd: the group of women was self-sufficient. "Miss Mary was a businessman from the word 'go,'" reported one Milledgeville resident. The GSCW History professor Dr. Helen Greene has remarked that "Miss Mary . . . inherited many rental properties and often a person in need of a place to live would come to the house to speak with her. The family employed a number of black people for the maintenance of their house and yard, and some of these employees were truly devoted." The younger sisters contributed as well. Following Edward O'Connor's death, Dr. Bernard Cline brought Regina to Atlanta to train as a bookkeeper for Sorrel Farm; in the spring of 1941, they received a sweet-milk contract from State Hospital. Aunt Katie worked her entire life at the postal job she secured in the 1920s when elder brother Hugh T. Cline was the Republican-appointee postmaster.

Not only did O'Connor discover, over the course of this summer, her capacity for close friendship, but even the introductory courses she later brushed aside provided intellectual awakening, and at least one challenge. Most important for her was Survey of Humanities, with Dr. Paul Boeson, of the Classical Language Department. Because Dr. Boeson was a Roman Catholic, and a Latin scholar, she trusted him as her first guide to the world of philosophical ideas. On the cover of the winter 1943 *Corinthian* was a photograph, reprinted from his personal collection, of a nun, in stark wimple and habit, reading a book illuminated by light streaming through a window. "She and Dr. Boeson would talk every day before the class would start," recalls a fellow student, Lou Ann Hardigne. The following year O'Connor took the second half of his survey, buying the editions of Plato, Aristotle, and the *Selected Essays* of Montaigne that she would keep her entire life.

More trying was her first college writing class, English 101, General College Composition, with Miss Katherine Kirkwood Scott. Nearly twenty years later, in January 1960, Flannery O'Connor was invited back to the college, as a local literary celebrity, to speak at Chapel in Russell Auditorium. Her topic was "Some Aspects of the Grotesque in Southern Fiction," but she added personal comments that she left out when giving the same talk some months later at Wesleyan College, in Macon, Georgia. These thoughts, tailored to her GSCW audience, suggested insecurities that had haunted her ever since college. She confided that morning: "When I sit down to write, a monstrous reader looms up who sits down beside me and continually mutters, 'I don't get it, I don't see it, I don't want it.' Some writers can ignore this presence, but I have never learned how."

An early reader, who may well have said, "I don't get it, I don't see it," in not so many words, was Miss Katherine Scott. Although she gave O'Connor a grade of 92, Miss Scott was the steel magnolia version of Sister Mary Consolata at Sacred Heart. A writer herself, Scott later published a nostalgic memoir about Milledgeville titled *The Land of Lost Content.* While O'Connor was in college, Scott delivered a talk billed as "poetic and romantic" on "Greece: A Pioneer in Democracy," to the local chapter of the Daughters of the American Revolution. She liked to hold at least one class session at her 1838 Victorian family home that she claimed was haunted; she brought along to school her three prized Boston bulldogs.

"They would not have been a happy combination," says Mary Barbara Tate, later an English teacher at GSCW, and a friend of Katherine Scott's. "She thought Flannery had great talent, but she wanted her to write like Jane Austen. She was the kind of teacher who expected to be a mentor, and to be the one who gives out of this box of knowledge." As Scott was a family friend, and had been in a small fourth-grade class with Regina Cline, both teacher and pupil were perfectly civil. Fran Richardson, a student in the class, has reported, "They would start talking and forget the rest of us were there. I told Mary Flannery once that I wished I could borrow some of her creativity, and she replied, 'I'd exchange it for your ability to attract men.'" Yet when a journalist asked Scott, decades later, about her famous pupil, she revealed a lifelong ambivalence. "Even then, it was obvious she was a genius," she replied, "warped, but a genius all the same."

❉

ON SEPTEMBER 28, the fall semester officially began with the arrival of the entire student body of 948 students, mostly from middle-income families in rural areas and small towns in Georgia, paying a yearly tuition of $67.50. The scale of O'Connor's campus had suddenly expanded from the three "Choo-Choo" buildings, a few steps in from a side street, to include nearly twenty neoclassical brick buildings, trimmed in limestone, and striped with white Corinthian columns. Set in the middle of Milledgeville, this twenty-three-acre quadrangle of firs and plumed elms, courtyards laced with flowering shrubs, and wide promenades and stone fountains constituted a humble postcard version of a Southern women's college. "I found my ideal," wrote Betty Boyd of its "old stately buildings" in her *Corinthian* piece on "My First Impression of GSCW."

Much of the charged atmosphere of the time made these years at GSCW indelible in the memories of alumnae from the early forties. Influencing all of their moods was the sensation of a nation now fully mobilized for war on two fronts. Students returning that fall remembered well the evening of December 7, 1941, when they had filed into Russell Auditorium for the annual choral singing of Handel's *Messiah,* having just heard news of the bombing attack on Pearl Harbor, resulting the next day in a declaration of war against Japan. "Girls were crying, although we didn't fully realize why we were crying," says Louise Simmons Allen of the class of '44. "The next day I listened carefully to President Roosevelt's 'day of infamy' speech on the radio. Our boyfriends were in the service and writing back about new experiences. The war was always with us."

From the start of the fall semester of 1942, the women at GSCW gathered regularly in a large room set aside in Porter Hall to roll surgical dressings for the Red Cross, and pack khaki gift kits for soldiers. Many consumer goods popular with students were rationed, including radios, phonograph records, even rolled cigarettes. Bicycles were in vogue, as few of their male dates, or even family members, could spare rationed gasoline for pleasure driving. "Sugar was scarce, but they had Ribbon Cane syrup, and fig preserves, on the table every meal," recalls one dormitory resident, Virginia Wood Alexander, of "meatless" and "breadless" suppers in Atkinson Dining Hall. Reacting to the shock of a number of unexpected American defeats early in the conflict, one student confessed in the college paper, the *Colonnade:* "This war is making us think."

The young women were also beginning the academic year at a college that had its academic accreditation suddenly pulled the previous December by an irate Governor Eugene Talmadge, not to be restored, retroactively, until January 1943. GSCW was that most unusual of institutions for middle Georgia in 1942: a progressive college, with a faculty of about sixty men and women, including a number of bright lights with PhDs from the University of Chicago and Columbia, some even transplanted Northerners. Embodying its contradictions was its longtime president, Dr. Guy H. Wells. A gruff, cigar-chomping, stout, and jowly gentleman who mangled his grammar and lacked polish, he was also a liberal on race. As early as a talk in Chapel in 1932, he was "calling attention to the prejudice against the negro." Governor Talmadge was punishing Wells with de-accreditation for his "foreign ideas" in forming a campus "Race Committee."

With all these challenges, the women who blithely nicknamed themselves "Jessies," eliding the GSC initials, operated on a cusp between the "Woman Power" called for in the homeland during the Second World War, and the more traditional giddiness of co-eds away at college. Especially for women from farm communities, the four-block strip of downtown Milledgeville had its draws: Culver Kidd Drug Store, with its lunch counter specializing in hot dogs and ham-and-cheese sandwiches, a favorite spot to meet cadets from Georgia Military College; Benson's Bakery; E. Bell's Beauty Shop, which O'Connor turned into "Palace Beauty Salon" for a college composition exercise; the Darling and Peggie Hale dress shops; and two movie theaters, the Campus and the Co-ed, charging fifteen cents for students, with separate entrances for blacks to segregated balconies.

Known as "Georgia State College for Wallflowers," because of the reduced number of available cadets and town boys, college house rules still chafed: signing out to go to the movies; ten o'clock curfew; a limit of two dates per week, one in a public parlor, with a chaperone. If Dr. Wells was liberal on race, he was a stickler on female propriety. "I grew up in Madison, Georgia, where we felt safe and as free as butterflies," complains one alumna, Gladys Baldwin Wallace. "Upon entering GSCW I felt as though I had been clapped into irons. Shortly before, two girls had been suspended for smuggling two Cokes into the dorm. One girl stood outside the window with the Cokes, the other dropped a cord out the upstairs window and hoisted them upwards." Wallace also remembers sightings of Regina O'Connor, "a hide-bound Southern lady, always wore hat and gloves in public."

Some of the more serious young women became involved in the YWCA, a center among campus clubs for race politics and social feminism. "People find it odd when I tell them that I was radicalized at this women's college in Georgia in the forties," says the 1946 yearbook editor Helen Matthews Lewis. She credits support for such leanings from a cadre of "older spinster-suffragette teachers: strong, independent women who were among the first generation of women to vote." The director of the YWCA, Emily Cottingham, once boldly drove a car full of GSCW students to Atlanta University to live in the dorm, and eat in the cafeteria, with black women students. When the Milledgeville paper printed an editorial critical of an AFL-CIO speaker, brought to campus by the YWCA, Betty Boyd and Helen Matthews composed a ringing "Letter to the Editor": "Ours are girls with a vivid realization that the pattern set for the coming world will deeply affect their future well-being and happiness and those of their children."

Living in an "imposing" terraced home, like the aunts in "The Partridge Festival," about "five blocks from the business section," O'Connor, as a freshman, was insulated, either by her design or her family's, from many of these burning issues among her peers. As she was a "town girl," she didn't fully reside in "Jessieville." "Most of the time Mary Flannery walked home alone when she had a break from classes, but sometimes she stayed in the Town Girls Room," remembers Zell Barnes Grant, who lived on a farm a mile outside town. "She always had her nose stuck in a book." Tellingly, the only club O'Connor joined her first year was the Newman Club, which met weekly in the Sacred Heart rectory and included about ten girls, the total number of Roman Catholic students at the college; they all woke up at dawn to attend monthly First Friday masses together.

She kept her friendship with Betty Boyd during all their years at school. "They were so close," remembers their mutual friend Jane Sparks Willingham. "They had a kindred spirit. Yet Betty was not awkward like Flannery. She was a very polished person, and much more into things on campus." Within the first few weeks of the fall semester, Boyd had already grown beyond the circumference of summertime at the Cline Mansion. She was living in Terrell, the freshman dormitory, with a roommate coincidentally named Mary Boyd, an English major from Calhoun, Georgia, who worked on the literary magazine. And she became active in student government. The tall, shy, reticent young woman showed such a knack for engaging in policy issues at meetings that she was elected freshman class secretary.

As Betty Boyd's roommate, Mary Boyd was also invited many times to Sunday dinner at the Cline Mansion. "She was very fond of her mother in Flannery's way of liking people," Mary Boyd Gallop has recalled. "Being the only child, the mother seemed just as fond of her girl as were two maiden aunts living there." Yet there was tension between Betty's two friends. Mary Flannery once told Betty Boyd that she found her roommate "just a bit too pedantic." More to the point, Mary Boyd made constant comments along the lines of her observation, years later, that "O'Connor never seemed interested in the opposite sex. She was happy just being herself." Mary Flannery did avoid dating. Yet she was uncomfortable at having such a private topic openly discussed.

Her defense was to cast Mary Boyd as a husband hunter, or simply boy crazy. O'Connor's letters to Betty Boyd in the years following graduation are peppered with jokes about Mary Boyd and marriage, obviously continuing a college routine. In 1949, O'Connor received a letter from Mary Boyd asking point-blank if she planned to get married. "Now let me see," O'Connor pretended to muse. "Do I or do I not want to get married?" When Betty Boyd announced her own impending wedding later that year, O'Connor's humorous response was: "This should reassure Mary Boyd." Pushing the matter to its extreme, O'Connor wrote Betty Boyd Love, in 1951, that she expected a letter from Mary "shortly, probably asking me if I like men, or some such."

If Mary Flannery stood on the sidelines of the mating rituals of many of her fellow Jessies, she was just as removed from their liberal campus politics. "We kept trying to get her to come to these things," says Helen Matthews Lewis, of the YWCA events. "But she was apolitical or nonpolitical." She saw leading campus characters as figures of fun, rather than as serious role models. The "country bumpkin" side of President Wells impressed her more than his being "ahead of his time" on race issues. Six years after graduation, she wrote to Betty Boyd, in her collegiate tone, "I read in the local paper where Guy H. Wells was going somewhere to give a talk entitled, 'Humor of Many Lands.' Now, I said, ain't that a laugh?" Bringing up the "spinster-suffragette" professors to Betty Hester in 1955, she skipped over their social feminism for a funny remark that turned on a novel by the Atlanta author Frances Newman: "she did write a novel called The Hard Boiled Virgin I find, which now I must read. I am going to see if they have it in the GSCW Library — the title may keep it out of there, a natural inconsistency, since half the teachers at that place are surely such."

The first official gathering of the entering freshman class, in September 1942, was a formal tea at the Old Executive Mansion, the residence of President Wells. Once home to Confederate Governor Joseph E. Brown, as well as to General Sherman during his March to the Sea, the Palladian high Greek Revival governor's mansion, with its soaring fifty-foot rotunda and gilded dome, was located on the same block as the Cline Mansion. Mary Flannery could spy its massive rose-colored masonry walls from her bedroom window, just beyond the backyard where, according to Betty Boyd Love, she still "kept ducks." Yet her family had to force her to walk around the block to the social event. "Flannery did not want to go but was pressured into it," remembers their classmate Harriet Thorp Hendricks. "She donned the required long dress — but wore her tennis shoes." When asked why she was sitting alone in a corner, she replied, "Well, I'm anti-social."

A tradition that elicited nothing but scorn from her was Rat Day, which began as Freshman Initiation Day in the thirties. A mass hazing of the freshman class, Rat Day commenced at four thirty in the morning. By evening, freshmen who had not shown enough servility were put on trial before a screaming jury of juniors in a Rat Court in Peabody Auditorium. Among the punishments meted out, in a 1943 Rat Court reported in the *Colonnade:* "Connie Howell was sentenced to wash her mouth out with soap. Sarah Pittard was seen sitting on a Coke bottle and washing clothes." Earlier that day, Mary Flannery had been tested by just such a group of hazing sophomore girls, ordering her to wear an onion around her neck. When she flatly refused, they commanded her to kneel and beg their pardon. "I will not," she responded with disdain, and walked off.

Even more trying for her than Miss Scott's creative writing class was English 102, the sequential General College Composition, taught that fall by Dr. William T. Wynn. Known to his students as "Willie T," the Southern-lit buff did not give the young writer even the benefit of the doubt of a high grade; she earned an 83, keeping her off the first-quarter dean's list. "Dr. Wynn was a gentleman of the old school who was soon to retire," reported a class member, Kathryn Donan Kuck. "He did not enjoy her style of writing and he tried hard to change it. He wanted her to be ladylike and graceful." When the time came to declare a major, she chose Social Science to avoid taking two requirements for the English major taught only by Dr. Wynn, a grammar course, using a little textbook he had written, and Shakespeare. "He was a laughingstock," says Mary Barbara Tate. "She just did not want to have him again. That's how she evaded him."

A sample of her writing style that would have stoked Dr. Wynn's ire was "Going to the Dogs," the first of a number of satires she published in the *Corinthian.* The parody appeared in the fall 1942 issue, with its black-and-white cover photograph of a thoughtful Jessie penning a "Dear Soldier" letter while lying on the campus lawn. "A few days later I was further startled by seeing another group of students chase a cat up a tree on the front campus," complains her narrator, reminiscent of the myopic groom of Poe's "The Spectacles," as she mistakes roving dogs for college students. She signed this effort "M. F. O'Connor," a half step to "Flannery O'Connor." Tenderly echoed in the neutral signature, too, were the initials used by her father, "E. F. O'Connor."

By the middle of the fall semester, Mary Flannery clicked into a congenial role for herself in the GSCW community: campus cartoonist. As she simply "moved over" from Peabody High to Georgia State, she likewise "moved over" as a cartoonist. The faculty adviser to the *Colonnade* was the same journalism instructor, George Haslam, who had invited her to contribute to the *Palladium*. Together they agreed that she would raise her rate of production to a cartoon every week and take over as art editor, beginning in November, in the newspaper offices in the basement of Parks Hall. She quickly adopted the campus as the setting for her cartoons, signified by a Greek column or a stone pediment. But instead of aligning herself with the idealistic view of Betty Boyd's first-impressions piece, O'Connor fixed her gaze on its eyesores: packs of stray dogs; boards patching holes in the muddy lawn; glaring nighttime spotlights.

As with her first published college story, O'Connor marked her new artistic venue with a new signature, a monogram. Such monograms, formed by turning initials, or the letters of a name, into heraldic pictures, representing a person or a job, and used on stationery, handkerchiefs, and business cards, were a wartime fad; they were even highlighted in the popular Paramount Pictures "Unusual Occupations" series of ten-minute color newsreels, in a 1944 segment titled "'What's in a Name' Monogram Art." For her own identifying emblem, she mined her dearest obsession, scrambling her initials to make a design suggesting a bird: "M" for a beak; "F," a tail; "O," a face; "C," the curve of a body. "It may look like a bird," Betty Boyd Love wrote of the witty final result, "but I'm sure she would have said it was a chicken."

O'Connor's debut cartoon appeared on October 6, with her chicken logo fixed in the lower-left corner. Titled "The Immediate Results of Physical Fitness Day," its subject was a spent girl in baggy sweater, skirt, and saddle oxfords, stiffly supporting herself with a cane, her tongue hanging out. The illustration accompanied a feature story: "Keeping Fit: Physical Fitness Program to Be Daily Feature at GSCW." Over the next months, she concocted an unfolding frieze of such challenged types — some, like a harried, limp-haired girl, staggering under a load of books, an obvious self-portrait. "I thought of her then as a cartoonist who also tried her hand at writing," says Gertrude Ehrlich, an Austrian "refugee student." "She was a genius at depicting us 'Jessies' running around campus, with scarves hanging out of pockets, or messily draped on our heads."

By the time O'Connor completed her eight cartoons of the first fall quarter, she had developed her favorite situation — a short, fat girl and her tall, thin sidekick, bouncing caustic remarks off each other. In an October 24 spoof of a faculty-student softball game, one of the pair of girls, loaded down with books, grouses to her friend, "Aw, nuts! I thought we'd at least have one day off after the faculty played softball!" The accompanying article: "Faculty Score 13 Over Seniors' 12." The steady outfitting of her odd couple with raincoats, galoshes, and umbrellas was a wink to a knowing audience. "It seemed to rain a lot in Milledgeville and we wore khaki-colored cotton gabardine raincoats most of the time," explains Virginia Wood Alexander. "This is the way I remember Flannery. She would come 'slouching' along like the rest of us."

A rare campus event that O'Connor truly enjoyed was the Golden Slipper, an annual drama contest between the freshmen and sophomore classes, with a small golden slipper as the award. "I remember her being behind some of the brilliant backdrops and scenery in this competition," says her classmate Frances Lane Poole. The production that November was especially important to her, as the freshman entry, "Blossoms on Bataan," was directed by Betty Boyd. It was set in a foxhole during the Battle of the Philippines, an American defeat in April 1942. The equally topical sophomore production "The Bell of Tarchova" took place in a village church during the 1939 Nazi annexation of Czechoslovakia. When the sophomore class won, O'Connor's November 14 cartoon featured her trademark girls, defeated, in highly elongated saddle shoes, with the caption "Doggone the Golden Slipper Contest. Now we have to wear saddle oxfords."

Enough excitement was generated by these cartoons that at the end of her first school year the *Macon Telegraph and News* ran a profile, written by Nelle Womack Hines, alongside a freshman photo of a grinning O'Connor wearing round glasses, her hair done in the typical pin-curled style of the 1940s. The piece was headlined "Mary O'Connor Shows Talent as Cartoonist." Hines found herself with an easily quotable subject in the girl she characterized as "fast making a name for herself as an up-and-coming cartoonist": "When asked how she went about her work, Miss O'Connor replied that first — she caught her 'rabbit.' In this case, she explained, the 'rabbit' was a good idea, which must tie up with some current event or a recent happening on the campus." Hines rightly observed, with coaching from the cartoonist, "Usually Mary presents two students in her cartoons — a tall, lanky 'dumb-bunny' and a short and stocky 'smart-aleck' — female, of course." The interviewer's conclusion was politic: "A keen sense of humor enables her to see the funny side of situations which she portrays minus the sting."

※

IN JANUARY 1943, World War II came marching onto the campus of Georgia State College for Women. By that winter, the global conflict had intensified. GSCW students and faculty heard daily news reports of battles from Guadalcanal to Tripoli and Stalingrad, as they worked in the Civilian Morale Service's Key Center, operating out of Russell Library. But the war came home in a more startling way when Waves began drills on campus, and moved into their dorms and classrooms. Women Accepted for Volunteer Emergency Services were among eighty-six thousand female soldiers pressed into navy service on the home front. With lobbying from the powerful Milledgeville Congressman Carl Vinson, House chairman of the Naval Affairs Committee (who helped Ed O'Connor win his FHA appointment), GSCW was chosen as one of four campuses for on-site training (Smith was the only other women's college).

The first of four hundred initial "Ripples" (a nickname that never caught on) "weighed anchor" on campus on January 15, taking over the prime dorms of Ennis, Sanford, Mayfair, Beeson, and the top floor of the Mansion, their numbers eventually adding up to a startling fifteen thousand between 1943 and 1945. As regulations required the women to speak navy language, Ennis became the "U.S.S. Ennis," and its floors, "decks"; its stairs, "ladders"; its windows, "ports." As part of their training to replace navy men at shore stations, the Waves woke to reveille, marched sixteen miles daily, attended six lectures in Arts Hall, typed two hours, exercised one hour, and went to bed to taps at ten p.m. Their uniforms were navy blue suits, blue hats, black gloves, and low-heeled black shoes. "They'd get out every morning at six marching between the dining hall and the library," remembers Jane Sparks Willingham. "It wasn't a happy mix, but it was necessary."

Many of the Jessies, now crowded three or four to a room, had mixed feelings about this reverse invasion, as the Waves transformed their women's college into a battleship in dry dock. But they usually cut their resentment with a grudging patriotism. "We had very little contact with them," Dr. Elizabeth Knowles Adams has recalled. "Some of us were probably a little jealous because they seemed so glamorous in their uniforms." For the proponents of the social equality of women, the presence of independent female soldiers on campus could be seen as a bonus. "Woman Power" became essential in the national emergency, and the radical-sounding slogan was adopted for regular use by the United States government, as well as by the Board of Regents of Georgia. Yet even the social feminist Helen Matthews Lewis found their unavoidable presence invasive: "They were always in the way, keeping us from getting to class."

Mary Flannery skipped the patriotism and went straight for the comedy; in the Waves, she found her most reliable cartoon topic. Not since the nuns she liked to mimic at Sacred Heart had she seen so many single women together in uniform. The first of her series of Waves cuts appeared on January 23, a day after fifteen staff officers were introduced to the students during morning Chapel. The setting is a campus corner, where two girls espy a couple of Waves walking toward them. "Officer or no officer," says one in a plaid skirt, "I'm going to ask her to let me try on that hat." There followed two years of girls butting their umbrellas along the backs of marching Waves' legs; girls clinging to tree trunks, like cats, to escape a drilling platoon; girls sneaking to check if Waves carried gunpowder in their handbags; or using Waves for archery practice.

Not only women, but male soldiers also bivouacked more and more in Milledgeville. Few showed up in O'Connor's cartoon world, yet they were a force in the town and on campus. Although the only local "base" belonged to the navy women at GSCW, there were many military bases nearby: Camp Gordon, Augusta; Fort Benning, Columbus; Camp Wheeler, Cochran Field, and Warner Robins Field, Macon; as well as a naval hospital in Dublin. On weekends, throngs of servicemen with leave passes crowded into Milledgeville. As there were not enough hotels to house them, or families to take them in, they often slept on porch swings, or in sleeping bags, on campus. "When convoys passed, the soldiers threw down notes for the GSCW students to pick up," recalls Charmet Garrett, who lived in Ennis Hall across Hancock Street. The military presence in town was dense enough for Bob Hope to broadcast his NBC radio show live from Russell Auditorium, for an audience of Waves and Jessies, on May 18, 1943.

Male soldiers became known to Mary Flannery mostly through Sacred Heart Church, and the USO, or United Service Organizations. A number of Roman Catholic soldiers would show up at her church on Sunday, and the Clines often invited them home for a family dinner. As early as 1941, Aunt Gertie reported to Agnes Florencourt that "two of the soldiers came over from Macon — Louis met one and asked him over, so Mary told Louis to ask him to dinner. . . . they were both at church." The Clines were just as involved with the USO — Aunt Katie was appointed chairman after the opening of its social club, in December 1943, in a storefront at the corner of Hancock and Wilkinson streets. On Sunday mornings, soldiers who crashed on the campus of GSCW sauntered across the street to the USO to clean up and enjoy free coffee and doughnuts.

While short, solid, gray-haired Katie Cline was a regular presence at the post office, she had known other more engaging moments in her life. As a young woman, she was a member of the Georgia Military College Players Club, acting in light comedies with Bardy, brother of Oliver Hardy, later of the Laurel and Hardy comedy team, then a rotund, teenage, silent-movie projectionist at the Palace Theatre in town. The second most memorable chapter of her life, locally, was her generous hospitality to soldiers during the war. "Miss Katie used to sit out on the porch on a Sunday morning and talk to all the passers-by," Betty Boyd Love has recalled. "If a lone service man happened by, he might be invited to dinner." One wounded soldier later wrote to her from Camp Wheeler, "I can still remember vividly the first time I had dinner in your home. It was just grand, Miss Cline." Another wrote her from Fort Benning, "About this time of day I'd be sitting on your veranda, begging for a Coca-Cola and cake — if I were in Milledgeville."

One Sunday, Aunt Katie invited home from church John Sullivan, recently assigned as a sentry to the naval training station at the college. As Sally Fitzgerald, who met Sullivan once, in Cincinnati during the 1980s, told the story, he had been "a handsome Marine Sergeant, resplendent in his dress blues." Following the service, he was handed a note, written by Miss Katie, inviting him to be the guest of "the Cline sisters" for a midday dinner at their home on Greene Street. He accepted, and met their cherished niece, in her freshman year at GSCW. The two quickly developed a rapport based partly on a similar family background: an Ohio boy, Sullivan came from a large Roman Catholic family. They were able to trade funny stories, and share suppressed giggles, as he became a regular visitor, a "fixture" welcomed by all the aunts and uncles.

Of course, he and Mary Flannery were quite different. He was blithe, outgoing, confident, and at ease with his good looks. She was painfully shy, given to awkward gestures, and, as Mary Boyd was fond of pointing out, not used to the company of boys. Yet because Sergeant Sullivan appreciated her offbeat wit, and wry inside tips about Southern mores, they went on what amounted to "dates" — long walks, an occasional movie. He even escorted her to one college dance, though he quickly discovered that she was truly a bad dancer — she later claimed to have a "tin leg." The foiled attempt may have contributed to her April 1943 cartoon on the opening of the college gym for dances, portraying a "wall-flower" of a girl in a long striped skirt, with glasses, sitting alone, watching other couples dance. The caption: "Oh, well, I can always be a Ph.D."

When Fitzgerald interviewed Sullivan, forty years later, he claimed that theirs had been "a close comradeship," not a romance. Yet the two played at romance enough to tease a hopeful mother. Once, as they sat together on the couch in the parlor, Regina called liltingly over the stairwell, "Mary Flannery, wouldn't you and John like to polish the silver?" After an exchange of amused glances, her daughter wickedly answered with a flat "No." Following Sullivan's transfer to a training camp for the Pacific war zone, O'Connor did show signs of a modest "crush." She wrote many drafts of her own "Dear Soldier" letters, stashing them between the pages of her college notebook. In a journal entry, she made fun of herself for "casually" dropping to her family that she had just heard from John. This exchange of letters lasted until he entered St. Gregory's Seminary, just after the war, briefly studying for the priesthood.

Her "crush" was enough of a blip — or a carefully concealed secret — that no relatives or classmates in Milledgeville remember the marine sergeant. What remained for O'Connor, though, was the PhD thought balloon that she floated during their time together. For at eighteen, she was hatching a plan for a life away from Milledgeville — studying journalism, or working as a newspaper cartoonist. No one in her family took these plans seriously. John Sullivan did, and he offered "admiration and encouragement." She must have felt in him some of her missing father: the handsome man, occasionally in uniform, who was both confidant and supporter. Like one of the suitors in her later stories — the less likeable Mr. Shiftlet, for instance, who comes walking up the road in "The Life You Save May Be Your Own" — his surprise visit had subtly enlivened things.

DURING THE TIME she was getting to know John Sullivan, coincidentally enough, Mary Flannery took a class with an English teacher who finally responded with understanding and enthusiasm to her writing. The professor who "got" her work was Miss Hallie Smith, a large and nurturing woman, one of those in the cadre of GSCW professors who belonged to the Audubon Society, and qualified in all respects as a "suffragette-spinster." In the spring 1943 quarter, while O'Connor was in her class, Smith gave her own talk to the DAR on "Woman, a Strength in Freedom's Cause," trumpeting the importance of "womanpower in this war and other wars."

The elective course O'Connor took with Miss Smith that spring quarter was English 324, Advanced Composition. As the capstone of the composition sequence, the class included only a dozen young women. "Miss Hallie required us to write something for each class — then, to my chagrin, she expected us to read it aloud," recalls Marion Peterman Page. "It wasn't long before I realized that the only writer in the class was Mary Flannery. The efforts of the rest of us were so juvenile compared to her. She seemed to be very shy and very modest. She was a mousy looking young lady, but one forgot that when she read what she had written." Another member of the class, Karen Owens Smith, who usually sat in the front row with Mary Flannery, a few feet from the teacher, remembers "a twang to her voice that I can still hear."

On March 24, O'Connor handed in her first assignment, two descriptions of a street scene, one photographic, the second poetic. Naming her street Raphael Street, after Katie Semmes's husband, she evoked Charlton Street in Savannah with a lineup of "six, tall grey buildings." Yet she had obviously been reading James Joyce's short story "Araby," too, and precociously tried to copy the style of the Irish Catholic writer. On Dublin's North Richmond Street, in Joyce's story, "The other houses of the street . . . gazed at one another with brown imperturbable faces." On O'Connor's Raphael Street, "gaunt houses all of somber, grey stone, gaze austerely at each other." Miss Hallie was thrilled with the effort. On the single typed page, signed "M. F. O'Connor," she wrote in red pencil, "A+."

Five days later, O'Connor handed in a typed, one-page character study. "Nine out of Every Ten" was signed with a pseudonym that could have popped out of a Merriweather Girls novel, "Jane Shorebanks." The sketch details a vapid young lady walking along chewing gum to the beat of the "Missouri Waltz." In red pencil, Miss

Hallie wrote an exclamatory "A!" and added, "Won't you submit something to the Corinthian?" Miss Hallie sensed in O'Connor's depiction of a face "sagging and contracting" as a girl chews a "slippery mass" of chewing gum a different tenor of writing talent. O'Connor had previously published, in the winter 1943 *Corinthian,* a mock review of a children's book about Ferdinand the bull, deeming the book "highly recommendable literature for the college student," and a satire on replacing cars with horses, "Why Worry the Horse?"

Over the next ten weeks, O'Connor wrote a series of short, descriptive exercises: lemon gelatin ("translucent mush"); celery (tastes like "sucking warm water out of a dish rag"); a kitchen; a velvet collar; and a mahogany table, much like the one in the dining room in the Cline Mansion. A description of a general store proprietor, for which she received an "A, An excellent use of the details at your disposal!" included "loud-labeled tin cans," close in wording to the "tin cans whose labels his stomach read" in the general store in Faulkner's "Barn Burning." She created vignettes of a black laundress talking to a white woman, a third-grade teacher on a bad day, and a Mrs. Watson reading movie magazines under a hair dryer. A single-scene character study of an imperious Mrs. Peterson being ushered to her seat at the theater was titled "The Cynosure," signed with another silly, feminine pseudonym, "Gertrude Beachlock," and marked "Excellent. Let me have a copy. A."

The one full-blown story she wrote for class was her most startling work of the semester, revealing a grasp of materials that her classmates never suspected from the "plain looking girl, unassuming." Says Marion Peterman Page, "At the time it seemed too deep for me to understand." The graphic tale, titled "A Place of Action," transpires on Saturday night in a black neighborhood, complete with a "zuit-suited" character who is stabbed by a woman he is hassling. While the story is melodramatic, and turns entirely on a stereotyped cast of characters, its use of violence as its climax, and its downbeat setting — "a dingy corner" — signal a writer finding her voice. Miss Hallie wrote "good" next to the description of the knife: "A thick, red coating hid its glimmer." Her final comment: "You might call your theme Saturday Night. Would you like to submit this to the *Corinthian*?"

O'Connor took Miss Hallie's advice. She began to publish stories as well as satires, though nothing as edgy as "A Place of Action," as its racy treatment of urban blacks was a definite taboo for a young Southern lady of the time. Her first published story, printed that spring, was "Elegance Is Its Own Reward," a weird tale, in the style of the "humorous" Poe, about a husband murdering both his wives, one with a hunting knife, the second by way of strangulation. Another written about the same time, and published in the fall 1943 *Corinthian*, "Home of the Brave," was set in wartime Milledgeville, turning on two snobbish matrons rolling bandages at a ladies' aid society while engaging in a lot of gossip, as "belligerent," she wrote, as "the Battle of Stalingrad," including their criticizing of Eleanor Roosevelt for not staying home enough.

She followed the writing course with two summer literature courses, The Short Story, taught by Miss Hallie Smith, and a Survey of English Literature. O'Connor later developed a selective memory about what she had read and when. "When I went to Iowa I had never heard of Faulkner, Kafka, Joyce, much less read them," she later claimed to a friend. Yet her early stories bear traces of the fingerprints of both Faulkner and Joyce. And *The Story Survey*, her textbook for her English 311 course, with her name, "M. F. O'Connor," and address, "305 W. Green Street, Milledgeville" carefully inscribed on the front page, has a checkmark in the table of contents next to Faulkner's "That Evening Sun," a star next to Joyce's "A Little Cloud," and lots of underlining of the explanation of "gothic" in the write-up on Poe's "Cask of Amontillado."

She was obviously mining authors for ideas for her own experi-

ments in writing, and for kindred sensibilities. So her take on literature courses could be likewise highly personal, creative, often
"smart-aleck." Unimpressed by Emily Dickinson, O'Connor compared the New Englander's poetry to the froth on a glass of Alka-
Seltzer. When a friend once asked if she had read Robert Browning's
The Ring and the Book, she reported back, "I had a course in college
entitled 'Tennyson, Browning,' and it looks like they would have
made us read it. I don't remember anything about it though. All I
remember from the whole course is 'Come into the garden, Maud,
for the black bat, night, has flown.' I thought that was hilarious."
She loved telling of the freshman in Miss Hallie's class who piped
up that the moral of Hawthorne's *Scarlet Letter* was "Think twice
before you commit adultery."

During her junior year of 1943–44, she paid the price for
her spiteful Social Science major by needing to take a series of
sociology courses, beginning with Sociology 301: Introduction to
Sociology. "In college I read works of social-science, so called," she
complained in a letter years later. "The only thing that kept me
from being a social-scientist was the grace of God and the fact that
I couldn't remember the stuff but a few days after reading it." The
other second-year requirement that she put on an equal plane of
disdain, though earning her much lower grades — C's rather than
A's — was Physical Education. "She was considered dangerous
with a golf club in her hand," one Phys Ed classmate of hers has
recalled. "She was apt not to look around or yell 'Fore.' She wasn't
particularly athletic, but she was a good sport and laughed at
herself."

Mary Flannery could be particularly irate and funny about
Social Science 200, Contemporary Georgia Problems. As Ana
Pinkston Phillips, a student in her class during the winter of 1944,
recalls, "My introduction to her was when she slammed her book
shut and said, as she left the room, 'I don't need to know how many
pigs were born in Georgia in 1932!'" (A couple of her later fic-

tional young women with Southern, feminine double names were book slammers, as well — Mary Elizabeth in "The Partridge Festival" and Mary Grace in "Revelation.") Her reaction to the course was already set when she laid eyes on the syllabus the quarter before; a November 1943 cartoon of hers depicts a lumpy student, hair in disarray, soliciting a snappily uniformed Wave: "Could I interest you in buying a Contemporary Georgia syllabus?"

With one eye on "Podunk," she dutifully fulfilled, during the same academic year, requirements toward a minor in Education. As she accurately reported to her friend Janet McKane, in 1964, "I had 3 education courses in college. Pure Wasted Time." Of one of those classes, with only four students enrolled, the fellow pupil Jane Strozier Smith, says, "I remember Flannery as outstanding, not only for her brilliance, but because she never flaunted it at all." She produced the equivalent of her "Contemporary Georgia" cartoon in three satiric essays for the *Corinthian* — "Doctors of Delinquency," in fall 1943, about Hayden Struthers III, getting a "Master of Rotating Tops Degree" at Columbia Kindergarten; "Biologic Endeavor," in spring 1944, on the modern miracle drugs Tums and Ex-Lax; and "Education's Only Hope," in spring 1945, with its loopy parting shot:

> *. . . until students quit school in the grammar grades,*
> *higher education will not attain that ultimate goal*
> *which the poet, Ridinghearse, expressed so beautifully*
> *when he wrote:*
>
> "*Gee,*
> *It's chilly*
> *Up here!*"

A reprieve from "progressive education" was provided by two single women professors, Miss Mary Thomas Maxwell and Miss

Helen Greene. Many of O'Connor's college friendships wound up being drawn not so much from other students as from a circle of professors closer in age to her aunts, perhaps explaining what one student called her "old fashion wardrobe — long dark skirts, long sleeves." Joan DeWitt Yoe, a staff member at the *Corinthian,* was put off by her: "I was an art major and my job was to illustrate Mary's short stories. I regret now that my drawings weren't abstract to be in the same mood as her stories. She would hand me a copy of her story without a word or looking me in the eye. It was a strange situation that I still don't understand. She wouldn't let me in her space. . . . I do know that all of the teachers adored her and were constantly around her."

Miss Mary Thomas Maxwell, the first of these teacher-friends, was nicknamed Tommy. "She was one of the most inspiring, exciting, and beautiful teachers," remembers Helen Lewis of the sparkling woman in her thirties. "She introduced us all to Walt Whitman. Her exam would be imagining a dinner party with Mark Twain sitting next to another author, and you would have to develop a conversation between them." O'Connor respected Tommy Maxwell enough to take her English 308 course in Spoken English during the summer of 1944, even though she cringed at public speaking. When Miss Maxwell queried her, she replied, "Well I know it won't do any good, but I have to show Regina and Sister." At the end of the summer, she received a B, not because her delivery had noticeably improved, but to acknowledge the "splendid" content of her talks.

Confiding to Betty Boyd that she felt Dr. Helen Greene, with her PhD from the University of Chicago, was "the smartest woman at that college," she took her course in European History. As a member of an honor society, the International Relations Club, she attended evening meetings in Dr. Greene's faculty apartment in Beeson Hall on Montgomery Street; afterward, another student would walk the "very carefully brought up" girl home. "My survey of European History was of special interest to her, I thought," Dr. Greene has reminisced, "because the author of our textbook, one of those widely used, was a noted professor at Columbia University who, while working on his studies of Martin Luther in Germany, had changed his membership to the Roman Catholic Church."

SPRINGTIME WAS TREATED as a happy cliché at GSCW. Each year, the *Spectrum* yearbook published a few pages of black-and-white shots with a caption, much like that in the 1945 edition: "Springtime brings with it Dogwood blossoms and flowering Iris." One entry, a few years earlier, had filled in the scene with more local color: "Elms form a stately avenue for academic processions, dogwoods flaunt their beauty in Terrell Court. The formal garden accentuates the classic architecture of the buildings." M. F. O'Connor added to the spring theme, while purposely getting it backward, in "Effervescence," an ode printed in the spring 1943 *Corinthian,* in which the sun rises on dogs sleeping beneath dogwoods. Its opening line, "Oh, what is so effervescent as a day in the spring," was a parody of "And what is so rare as a day in June?" in "The Vision of Sir Launfal" by the American Romantic poet James Russell Lowell, a granduncle of Robert Lowell.

The spring of 1945, as O'Connor began her final quarter at GSCW, felt, even more than usual, to the young women and their guests, the Waves, as if the world was making a historic turn on its axis. During the previous summer, the D-day invasion had taken place with 155,000 Allied troops landing on the beaches of Normandy, opening a wedge in the Nazi domination of continental Europe. On February 23, 1945, Joe Rosenthal snapped his iconic photo of a group of marines and a navy corpsman raising a huge American flag over the Japanese island of Iwo Jima. By March 1945,

Hitler was confined to his bunker in Berlin while American bombers attacked the city, and American troops liberated the first Nazi concentration camp, Buchenwald. Within two months, on May 8, 1945, VE-day was declared, marking the official end of the war in Europe.

In the midst of so many positive historic events, the sad news came on April 12 that Franklin Roosevelt, recently inaugurated to an unprecedented fourth term, had died in Warm Springs, Georgia. "My roommate and I went to an afternoon movie, returning to campus around five, and someone told us 'The president has died,'" remembers Betty Anderson Bogle, a student from Atlanta. "We assumed she meant Guy Wells. When we realized she meant Roosevelt, we were stunned beyond belief." A performer at one of the GSCW Monday musical events had been Navy Chief Petty Officer Graham Jackson, a black accordion player. When *Life* magazine appeared, many of the women recognized him in a photograph, playing "Going Home" on his accordion, tears rolling down his face, as the president's hearse rolled past the steps of the Warm Springs polio hospital.

As she prepared to graduate, at twenty years old, O'Connor was far more active on campus than might have been expected. She had made enough of a name for one classmate to remember her as a "B.W.O.C." ("Big Woman on Campus"). The girl whose only campus activity her first year had been the Newman Club was now editor in chief of the *Corinthian* literary magazine, feature editor of the *Spectrum* yearbook, and art editor of the *Colonnade* newspaper, as well as having been elected to all the honor societies — the Phoenix, Who's Who in American Colleges and Universities, and the International Relations Club. The tone of her first Editor's Letter in the fall 1944 *Corinthian,* titled "Excuse Us While We Don't Apologize," was unmistakable: "Although the majority of you like the 'my love has gone now I shall moan' type of work, we will give you none of it. Although the minority of you prefer consistent punctuation and a smack of literary pretension, we aren't going to worry about giving it to you."

She had grown particularly ambitious for her cartoons. With the *New Yorker* cartoonist James Thurber a household name in America during the forties — his *My World and Welcome to It* was published in 1942, *The Thurber Carnival* in 1945 — she submitted cartoons to *The New Yorker,* only to receive what she later described as "a lot of encouragin' rejection slips." Says the *Colonnade*'s feature editor Bee McCormack, echoing a common sentiment among the students, "I thought then she might become the new James Thurber." As O'Connor later reported to Janet McKane: "I like cartoons. I used to try to do them myself, sent a batch every week to the New Yorker, all rejected of course. I just couldn't draw very well. I like the ones that are drawn well better than the situations." A sheaf of her cartoons from the time includes a classic of her sensibility: one fish saying to another, "You can go jump out of the lake!" While taking a two-semester course on "The United States" with a new history professor, James Bonner, she focused on the textbook *A Century of Political Cartoons,* imagining for herself a future in the profession.

Impressed by the splash her cartoons made in the student newspaper, Margaret Meaders, a journalism instructor and editor of the *Alumnae Journal,* asked the senior to contribute some work for the upcoming issue. Meaders later recalled looking out her office window in Parks Hall one afternoon and catching sight of Mary Flannery sauntering across Hancock Street, entering the campus, and making her way up the broad front walk beneath the overarching elms. She was on her way to their meeting, toting a pile of her "wonderful, merry cartoons." Meaders wrote, "We Southerners would say that she 'moseyed.' I never remember seeing her hurry." She summed up O'Connor's understated presence at the college as "slow-spoken, quiet-mannered," rather than that of "a campus big shot, a professional bright-girl-sure-to-heap-glory-on-all-of-us."

The climax of O'Connor's stint as campus cartoonist was the 1945 *Spectrum*. The endpapers of the yearbook were panoramic views of the campus, a reprise of her greatest hits: chins-up, eyes-forward Waves marching in columns; girls balancing books and umbrellas; hounds curling their long tails. She also designed an entire "Pilgrimage through JESSIEVILLE" of ink drawings, re-doing her tall-short pair with a sketch, from the rear, recognizable as the tall dean of women, Ethel Adams, and the short, stout dean of studies, Hoy Taylor. Her friend Robert Fitzgerald later judged these illustrations less successful. "In the linoleum cuts the line was always strong and decisive with an energy and angularity that re-call the pen drawings of George Price, drawings that in fact she admired," he wrote, noting the influence of a lesser-known, but brilliant *New Yorker* cartoonist. "For the yearbook . . . she tried a rounder kind of comic drawing, not so good."

Because all of the student publication offices were located in Parks Hall, Editor O'Connor spent many hours in its basement. In her spare time, she took on herself the project of painting murals on the walls of its student lounge. "Mary Flannery decorated the walls with some of these Thurberesque types," Dr. Helen Greene has written. She also completed a painting, *Winter,* included in a traveling exhibition through Georgia. A posed yearbook photo shows her sitting at a desk, in a cramped office, dressed in classic coed style — sweater, bobby socks, scuffed saddle shoes, with coiffed dark hair — surrounded by her staff of ten young women. In an-other shot, she leans against a pillar, one leg coyly tucked up, exam-ining a copy of the magazine with her business manager, Peggy George. "We were laughing," recalls Peggy George Sammons. "That is the only picture I have ever seen of her where she even had a smile on her face."

On April 11, the evening before the death of President Roosevelt, the Pulitzer Prize–winning New England poet Robert Tristram Coffin spoke at Peabody Auditorium and was given a reception at the Cline Mansion. When Janet McKane happened to quote some of the poet's lines in a 1963 letter to O'Connor, she triggered O'Connor's memory of the event and of her own college poems, which she compared to a work of thudding end-rhymes by Edwin Arlington Robinson: "Your quoting of a poem of R.P.T. Coffin took me back. He visited our college when I was about 18, read some poems of mine and came to our house for some kind of program. That was the only time in my life when I attempted to write poetry. All my poems sounded like 'Miniver Cheevy.'"

Described by O'Connor as a "striking-looking old man," Coffin had been subjected at the party to an earnest Q-and-A session by many of the young women present. According to Margaret Meaders, one of them asked Coffin — "a bit breathlessly but, oh, so charmingly in the manner of one poetic soul to another" — to unlock for them the symbolism of a fox in one of his poems. The poet sputtered, in an unguarded moment, "My God, just a fox, just an ordinary, everyday fox!" Looking over at Mary Flannery, Meaders caught her "busy disciplining the mirth that twinkled in her eyes."

The most important class O'Connor took at GSCW turned out to be one of her last, Social Science 412: Introduction to Modern Philosophy. Its professor, George Beiswanger, had been hired, along with his wife, Barbara, in the fall of 1944. They quickly were nicknamed "Dr. He-B" and "Dr. She-B." The son of a Baptist minister, with a PhD from the University of Iowa, Beiswanger had just moved from Manhattan, with his wife, a dancer who had studied with Martha Graham. Over the past five years he had worked as associate editor of *Theatre Arts Monthly,* written dance criticism for *Dance Observer,* and taken part in an arts symposium at the

Mary Flannery O'Connor, age two or three. (Courtesy of the Flannery O'Connor Collection, Georgia College and State University Library, Milledgeville, Georgia.)

Edward Francis O'Connor, about 1930. (Courtesy of the Flannery O'Connor Collection, Georgia College and State University Library, Milledgeville, Georgia.)

Regina Cline O'Connor posing for a formal portrait with her daughter. (Courtesy of the Flannery O'Connor Collection, Georgia College and State University Library, Milledgeville, Georgia.)

Mary Flannery O'Connor, age three. (Courtesy of the Flannery O'Connor Collection, Georgia College and State University Library, Milledgeville, Georgia.)

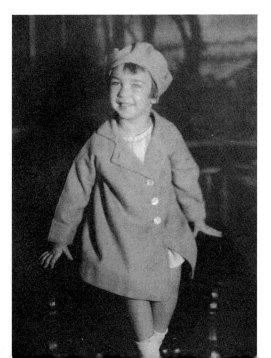

Aerial shot of the Cathedral of St. John the Baptist on Lafayette Square. (Courtesy of the Catholic Diocese of Savannah: Archives.)

St. Joseph's Hospital, now demolished, where Mary Flannery O'Connor was born on March 25, 1925. (Courtesy of the Catholic Diocese of Savannah: Archives.)

The O'Connor home at 207 East Charlton Street, Savannah, present day, next door to Katie Semmes's former home. (Courtesy of Flannery O'Connor Childhood Home Foundation. Photograph by Bill Dawers.)

Mary Flannery O'Connor, First Communion Day, May 1932. (Courtesy of the Flannery O'Connor Collection, Georgia College and State University Library, Milledgeville, Georgia.)

The Ward-Beall-Cline Mansion, 311 West Greene Street, Milledgeville. (Courtesy of the Catholic Diocese of Savannah: Archives.)

Mary Flannery O'Connor, "a very ancient twelve." (Courtesy of the Flannery O'Connor Collection, Georgia College and State University Library, Milledgeville, Georgia.)

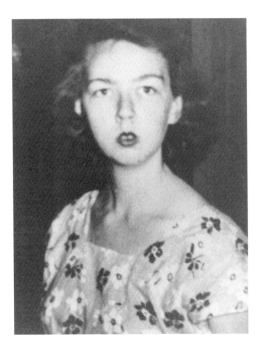

Mary Flannery O'Connor, as a teenager. (Courtesy of the Flannery O'Connor Collection, Georgia College and State University Library, Milledgeville, Georgia.)

Mary Flannery O'Connor, at Georgia State College for Women. (Courtesy of the Flannery O'Connor Collection, Georgia College and State University Library, Milledgeville, Georgia.)

Mary Flannery O'Connor, editor of the college literary magazine, with the college yearbook editor, 1945. (Courtesy of the Flannery O'Connor Collection, Georgia College and State University Library, Milledgeville, Georgia.)

Surrounded by the staff of the *Corinthian,* 1945. (Courtesy of the Flannery O'Connor Collection, Georgia College and State University Library, Milledgeville, Georgia.)

Flannery O'Connor at the side door of Currier House, Iowa City, 1946–47. (Courtesy of Barbara Tunnicliff Hamilton.)

In her fifteen-pound muskrat coat, February 1948, Iowa City. (Courtesy of Barbara Tunnicliff Hamilton.)

O'Connor in the Tower Room of the main Mansion, Yaddo, 1948. (Courtesy of The Corporation of Yaddo.)

O'Connor, third from left, in conga line with fellow artists at Yaddo, 1948. (Courtesy of The Corporation of Yaddo.)

Robert Lowell, in his office as poetry consultant to the Library of Congress, Washington, DC, 1948. (Courtesy of AP Images.)

avant-garde Black Mountain College, in North Carolina. Hired as chairman of the departments of Art, Philosophy, and Religion, the dapper gentleman, always dressed in a suit, and his wife, hired to teach modern dance techniques, brought with them a gust of cosmopolitanism.

Mary Flannery had already taken note of "Dr. He-B" the previous quarter. His debut address to the student body had been on the dull topic "Good Manners and Campus Courtesies." As assigned by the Student Government Association, the subject was far afield from his ten-page spread in *Theatre Arts Monthly* on his high hopes for modern dance as "humanizing the machine." As a jumping-off point, the rookie professor used a quotation from Ralph Waldo Emerson: "Manners are the happy way of doing things." In the next, February 7, issue of the *Colonnade,* O'Connor printed her riposte — a drawing of a girl entering a classroom in a strapless evening gown, long white gloves, pumps, a fluffy boa draped over one arm, and a load of books clutched in the other, while a second annoyed student, dressed in one of the exaggeratedly long knit sweaters popular in the period, whispers to her friend, "I understand she says it's the happy way of doing things."

Dr. Beiswanger's class was a survey of modern philosophers, the assigned textbook, *The Making of the Modern Mind,* by John Herman Randall, Jr. As Beiswanger has recalled, the book was "an academic best-seller whose viewpoint (and mine) was secular humanist (grounded in Pragmatism) and took for granted that the Renaissance and the Age of Enlightenment set the Western mind free from the benightedness of Medieval thought (from Thomas Aquinas, etc.)." The hero of the course was the seventeenth-century French philosopher Descartes, for relying in his *Discourse on Method* (1637) on mathematics and science to unlock the secrets of a purely material world. Yet a few weeks into the course, the professor became aware of a persistent, subtle scowl: "Flannery sat in class, listened intently, took notes, and without her saying a word, it became clear that she didn't believe a word of what I was saying."

Although Beiswanger saw Mary Flannery as confident, behind her poker face she was actually rattled enough to have to think twice about what the instructor was saying. "What kept me a sceptic in college was precisely my Christian faith," she later confided to the young poet Alfred Corn, going through his own period of doubt as a student at Emory University in 1962. "It always said: wait, don't bite on this, get a wider picture, continue to read." By the end of the quarter, though, she had emerged from her shell enough to give the professor a hard time. As she relived one exchange with him, in a letter to the Fitzgeralds, in 1952: "[He] is the one that one day in a class says, 'The Medieval Church was politheistic.' I rise and say, 'The Medieval Church was not politheistic.' [He] fixes me very coldly, 'I am speaking,' says he, 'as an anthropologist.'"

Helen Matthews Lewis, a student in the class, remembers a few other charged exchanges between professor and pupil. Once O'Connor went up to the blackboard to diagram, in detail, what she saw as the contrast between Aquinas and modernism. "Philosophy class was early in the morning, and most of us would be pretty sleepy and would have missed breakfast," says Lewis. "We would run across campus, sometimes trying to hide our pajamas under our raincoats, to get to class. Flannery was always there, bright and ready to go, ready to argue with the professor." As Beiswanger summed up O'Connor's position: "It was philosophical *modernism* that had blinded the Western mind."

What registered most strongly was the certainty that he had before him no ordinary girl: "She knew Aquinas in detail, was amazingly well read in earlier philosophy, and developed into a first rate '*intellectual*' along with her other accomplishments. . . . It soon became clear to me that she was a 'born' writer and that she was going that way." A classic example of a teacher making a difference, Beiswanger encouraged his A student to apply for graduate school at his alma mater, the University of Iowa. She sent in applications to both Duke University and to the journalism program at Iowa, mulling a possible career in newspaper political cartooning. The professor lobbied his contacts at the school to secure her a scholarship. When offered a journalism scholarship from Iowa, providing full tuition and sixty-five dollars a term, she quickly accepted.

At eleven o'clock on Monday morning, June 11, 1945, the fifty-fourth annual commencement of Georgia State College for Women opened with a procession of graduating seniors, O'Connor among them, accompanied by the well-worn organ strains of the "Grand March" from *Aïda*. Taking place on a hot Georgia summer's day, with temperatures expected to rise to the midnineties by afternoon, the procession might well have "plodded stolidly along" to Russell Auditorium, like that of Sally Poker Sash and her graduating class in "A Late Encounter with the Enemy":

> *The black procession wound its way up the two blocks and started on the main walk leading to the auditorium. The visitors stood on the grass, picking out their graduates. Men were pushing back their hats and wiping their foreheads and women were lifting their dresses slightly from the shoulders to keep them from sticking to their backs. The graduates in their heavy robes looked as if the last beads of ignorance were being sweated out of them.*

Like the commencement speaker in "Late Encounter" who "was through with that war and had gone on to the next one," Georgia Governor Ellis Arnall assured the 165 GSCW graduates that "the hope for lasting peace lies not in Washington nor on the battlefronts of the world, but in the hands of the 1945 graduates." All were then "hooded" by Miss Katherine Scott. In the flurried ritual of yearbook autographing, Mary Flannery wrote as her standard entry, simply, "The usual bunk — M. F. O'Connor."

In its coverage of the graduation, the *Colonnade* reported that "the realm of further study" had claimed five graduates, including Student Government Association President Betty Boyd at Chapel Hill, and "Mary Flannery O'Connor at Iowa State." Yet this salutary, now definite news was not being entirely celebrated at the Cline Mansion. The notion that Mary Flannery was going off, by herself, to a school in the Midwest was nearly unthinkable. Up until graduation, O'Connor's classmates were still walking her home at night, the two blocks from college meetings at Beeson Hall. Yet fragile appearances to the contrary, their sheltered niece obviously had a mind of her own, and her father's quiet, stubborn will to back up her decisions. With Savannah in her past, having met John Sullivan of Ohio, and reading far and wide, she knew well the limits of Milledgeville.

As O'Connor later summed up her personal longitude and latitude at this juncture, in her "Biography," written at Iowa, she felt that her big opportunity came in the form of the fellowship to graduate school. She hoped that the experience would either verify her suitability for little else but the job of teaching ninth-graders in Podunk, Georgia — the horizon line for most women majoring in English at GSCW — or that she would discover a happier means of making a living. Writing in her journal during the summer of 1945, Mary Flannery's response to the wishful, dire predictions of a number of her relatives that she would be home in three weeks came down to one word — "Humph!"

Chapter Four

Iowa

❋

Sitting in his office early in the fall of 1945, Paul Engle, the director of the Iowa Writers' Workshop, heard a gentle knock at the door. After he shouted an invitation to enter, a shy, young woman appeared and walked over to his desk without, at first, saying a word. He could not even tell, as she stood before him, whether she was looking in his direction, or out the window at the curling Iowa River below. A tall, hulking poet, in his thirties, with wavy dark hair, alert blue eyes, and expressive eyebrows, Engle quickly took the lead. He introduced himself and offered her a seat, as she tightly held on to what he later claimed was "one of the most beat-up handbags I've ever seen."

When she finally spoke, her Georgia dialect sounded so thick to his Midwestern ear that he asked her to repeat her question. Embarrassed by an inability a second time, to understand, Engle handed her a pad to write what she had said. So in schoolgirl script, she put down three short lines: "My name is Flannery O'Connor. I am not a journalist. Can I come to the Writers' Workshop?" Engle suggested that she drop off writing samples, and they would consider her, late as it was. The next day a few stories arrived, and to his near disbelief, he found them to be "imaginative, tough, alive." She was instantly accepted to the Workshop, both the name of Engle's writing class and of his MFA graduate writing program, the first in the nation, to which she would switch her affiliation from the Graduate School of Journalism by the second semester.

For all of her outward timidity, she had quickly found her way to Engle, and her vocation. Just a few weeks earlier, the third week in September, she and her mother had departed Milledgeville together. In Atlanta, they boarded a train to Chicago, where they transferred at La Salle Street Station. They then made the four-hour trip west to Iowa City on the Rock Island Railroad, through a countryside of cornfields, apple orchards, and colts grazing on grassy hillocks. Anticipating subzero winters, O'Connor arrived carrying a fifteen-pound muskrat coat. Mrs. O'Connor stayed long enough to make sure that her only child was comfortably settled in Currier House, at 32 East Bloomington Street, a two-story, old-brick, corner building, housing fifteen or twenty graduate women in double rooms.

Iowa City was a nearly rural university town of about eighteen thousand year-round residents. Downtown consisted of four or five banks, a couple of hotels, as well as drugstores, bookshops, tea rooms, and beer halls rigged for student trade. Like Milledgeville, this Johnson County seat had once been the state capital, until the government moved to Des Moines, in 1855. Left behind was the gold-domed Old Capitol, revamped as the State University of Iowa main administration building, set high on a hill in the center of town, near a Masonic Temple. Quiet residential backstreets were lined with dull clapboard houses, interspersed with some Victorian follies. O'Connor later told Robert Lowell that she quickly responded to the "naturally blank" tenor of the place: "I always liked it in spite of those sooty tubercular-looking houses."

In September 1945, more than 11,600 students enrolled for the fall term, expanding the town's population by more than half, and helping to bolster its extravagant nickname, "The Athens of the Midwest." With the highest percentage of full-time, resident PhDs in the country, town-gown friction was not a problem. The 425-acre campus was viewed more as an extension of the city, like a municipal park sloping down from the Old Capitol to sturdy footbridges spanning the muddy Iowa River. Its nine colleges, housed in fifty-odd gray stone buildings, on both the east and west banks of the bisecting river, introduced into the life of the city each fall aspiring doctors, dentists, lawyers, engineers, businessmen, actors, musicians, writers, and artists. The Iowa Hawkeyes, a Big Ten college football team, generated alarming civic frenzy at home games in the monumental Iowa Stadium.

This influx was greatly exaggerated in 1945 by a spike in enrollment from returning veterans, increasing through the spring and peaking in the fall of 1946. In the wake of the formal surrender of the Japanese to General Douglas MacArthur, on September 2, marking the end of World War II, millions of demobilized soldiers started streaming back from Europe and the Pacific. A large number took advantage of the GI Bill of Rights, or Servicemen's Readjustment Act of 1944, providing a free college education and one year of unemployment compensation. "Iowa City was a bustling place," recalls one graduate, "because it was flooded with GI Bill students, as well as droves of foreign exchange students."

To returning vets, with more worldly experience, the county seat, its feeder roads crowded with trucks full of pigs, could look ominously "hick." Many had been in the position of Haze Motes, in O'Connor's novel *Wise Blood,* which she began in the Workshop the next year: "The army sent him halfway around the world and forgot him." Yet as John Sullivan was moved by wartime experiences to study for the priesthood, others resolved to lead creative lives: they wanted to write the great American novel, play jazz, or paint. To their relief, they soon discovered a homegrown artistic tradition of "regionalism," as exemplified in *American Gothic,* the iconic portrait of a stately farmer, with pitchfork, and his spinster daughter, painted in the thirties by the faculty member Grant Wood. Arriving to sign up for the Workshop in midsemester the next spring, still in his "Eisenhower jacket" and parachute jump boots, James B. Hall wrote of "a new Bohemia, albeit in cornfields."

Yet no amount of prairie-flower bohemianism, or postwar euphoria, could assuage O'Connor's first reaction to her new surroundings: homesickness. Far from her extended family, and speaking a dialect routinely treated as a foreign language, she experienced an acute ache. As she later wrote to her friend Maryat Lee, of "The Geranium," her first published Iowa story, "I did know what it meant to be homesick." At Currier House, she roomed with a couple of rumba-loving suitemates who cranked up the volume on the record player. While remaining friendly toward them, she soon relished their weekend departures. Every day, she wrote a letter to her mother, who wrote back daily replies, as well as forwarding the weekly Milledgeville newspaper.

Her home away from home did not turn out to be Currier House — and certainly not the Airliner, a long, narrow tavern, just across from campus, with white tile floors and a jukebox, popular with other students. Instead she found the antidote for her homesickness two blocks away at St. Mary's Catholic Church, on East Jefferson Street. A modest, brick structure with a clock-tower steeple, built in 1869, St. Mary's provided a worship experience enriched by seventeen church bells. Its high altar was crowded with Victorian paintings and pastel statues of St. Patrick and St. Boniface, reflecting the mixed demographic of Irish and Germans in the parish. In the fall of 1945, the church pastor, Monsignor Carl Bernstein, offered daily morning masses at six thirty and seven thirty. As O'Connor told Roslyn Barnes, a young woman enrolled in the Workshop, in 1960, "I went to St. Mary's as it was right around the corner and I could get there practically every morning. I went there three years and never knew a soul in that congregation or any of the priests, but it was not necessary. As soon as I went in the door I was at home."

With the same deliberation that she applied to coming up with her "MFOC" monogram signature for her first college cartoon, and a revised name, "M. F. O'Connor," for her first published college story, she decided nearly from day one at Iowa to introduce herself, and to sign her papers, as "Flannery O'Connor." Everyone who met her in Iowa City knew her simply as "Flannery." Yet unlike her character Joy, who spitefully changed her name to Hulga when she went away to college in the story "Good Country People," O'Connor asked her mother's permission in advance. Partly she wanted to lose the lilting double name that exaggerated her oddity as a Southern lady in Iowa City, but she also looked forward to her byline when she fulfilled a wish to write what Engle said she described to him as "shom storrowies." As she later joked to the writer Richard Gilman of calling herself Mary O'Connor: "Who was likely to buy the stories of an Irish washerwoman?"

Enrolled for the fall semester in the Graduate School of Journalism, Flannery had a course load that was tilted, at first, in the direction of magazine work. She took Magazine Writing, with William Porter, a mustached pulp-fiction writer, given to wearing rumpled checked shirts, who had sold a couple of crime stories to the movies. He geared his course to "selling stories to magazines." O'Connor wrote for Porter her short, somewhat flat-footed "Biography." In Principles of Advertising, with Mr. Gordon, she studied commercial art. Her single political-science course, American Political Ideas, was a survey of "representative American thinkers," from Roger Williams to James Madison, including a discussion of political cartooning. She received a grade of B in all three courses.

Still holding out for a possible career as a cartoonist, Flannery submitted cartoons and drawings to the Art Department to be admitted to the two-semester course Advanced Drawing, and to Individual Instruction. Hoping for some extra income, she submitted her cartoons to trade journals, expecting the competition would not be as steep as at *The New Yorker,* but with no success. As the Art Building was located on the west campus, she would walk to her life-drawing classes over a bridge, just below the Iowa Memorial Union and along gravel paths crowded with familiar enough companions — flocks of mud-caked geese. The department was lively during that era: the artist Philip Guston, an associate professor, won first prize in a Carnegie Institute "Painting in the United States, 1945" show; Mauricio Lasansky was setting up a world-class print studio.

Yet by knocking at the door of Paul Engle that fall afternoon, O'Connor had begun to shift her direction away from art toward what was called "imaginative writing" at Iowa. He immediately enrolled her in two of his classes, Understanding Fiction and Writers' Workshop (the double-listed Workshop was credited as "Journalism" in her fall semester, and as "English" afterward). Engle was the one-man band of the Workshop. During the war years, it had been simply an informal class with eight or ten students. Earning one of the first creative graduate degrees in America, at Iowa, in 1932, for his collection of poems, *Worn Earth,* published in the prestigious Yale Series of Younger Poets, Engle became a tireless champion of the MFA concept. As he liked to brag of his program, "You can get an M.A. degree without counting the commas in Shakespeare."

The title of his lit course was actually the title of its textbook, an anthology of stories that O'Connor later said Engle "was able to breathe some life into" — *Understanding Fiction.* Published in 1943, it had been edited by Cleanth Brooks, Jr., and Robert Penn Warren, with interspersed explanations. An academic marker for the fashionable school of New Criticism, its editors emphasized "close reading," paying attention to the art and craft of stories, rather than to historical or cultural concerns, or to mining fiction for a series of psychological clues to a writer's life. Many of the selections were eye-openers for Flannery: Caroline Gordon's "Old Red"; Guy de Maupassant's "The Necklace"; Nathaniel Hawthorne's "The Birthmark"; William Faulkner's "A Rose for Emily." In an exam essay, in November, she argued that Thomas Thompson's "A Shore for the Sinking" was about "a man's realization that he has been 'left out.'" Engle wrote on her blue book, "A+. Admirable."

All of the creative writers at Iowa, and many painters and musicians, too, passed through Engle's Workshop. Still in its nascent wartime stage in the fall of 1945, the writing seminar was taught in the English Department faculty offices, or in a small classroom in the University Building, next to the Old Capitol on the Pentacrest of five buildings. "It was a plain little room in an old building on campus that nobody was competing for," recalls one student. A dozen chairs would simply be drawn into an informal semicircle around a reading desk set on a platform a wooden step up from the floor. As Paul Engle described the class routine, in the *Des Moines Register,* "Each meeting consists of the reading of manuscripts by, customarily, two students. . . . The students are quite merciless in criticizing each other's work, as well as in challenging the faculty before them."

One of a small minority of women in the 1945 Workshop, Mary Mudge Wiatt, from Sioux City, was present the first time Flannery read a story. "Her voice was quiet, with a nice, rich Southern accent," remembers Wiatt. "I thought she seemed not really at ease. She colored easily, flushed. I remember one scene where a white woman answers the door. A black man had some business with her. They spoke back and forth." The story, a draft of "The Coat," was Flannery's attempt to mimic a selection she admired in her *Understanding Fiction* anthology, "The Necklace," by Maupassant.

In the original French moral tale, a string of paste jewels, mistaken for diamonds, destroys the heroine's life. In her Southern rewrite, Rosa, a black washerwoman, invites tragedy on her husband, Abram, by wrongly imagining that he killed a white man for "dat coat."

O'Connor wrote about this shaky period in Iowa, trying to find her way as a writer, for the *Alumnae Journal* at Georgia State College for Women, when the magazine was running a series on choices in career paths. In a piece titled "The Writer and the Graduate School," which appeared in the summer of 1948, she confessed her initial doubts: "What first stuns the young writer emerging from college is that there is no clear-cut road for him to travel on. He must chop a path in the wilderness of his own soul; a disheartening process, lifelong and lonesome. Therefore, of what use graduate work?" She answered her own question, with some of her arch high school humor, by claiming that a creative writing program at least saved a few authentic writers from becoming one of the scholarly "dead birds" in "the literary woods": "Some of these were laid away with Ph.D.'s and doubtless all with an excellent knowledge of Beowulf." The MFA program was an alternative, she concluded, to "the poor house" and "the mad house."

An early boost came with a classroom visit from the poet John Crowe Ransom, the founder and editor of the *Kenyon Review,* the house organ of the New Critics. Visits from such writers deemed, by Engle, "of the right sort," were an important component of the Workshop. When Ransom chose one of O'Connor's stories to read to the class, she was encouraged to be singled out, and by such a prominent Southern writer. Yet the work was in the mode of her high school story "A Place of Action," or "The Coat." She was trying to render the dialogue of poor whites and blacks in the South. When Ransom came across the word "nigger," he refused to read it aloud, substituting the word "Negro." "It did spoil the story,"

Flannery complained to Robie Macauley, after he arrived as a Workshop instructor in 1947. "The people I was writing about would never use any other word."

For one of her next stories, she turned again to *Understanding Fiction,* and Caroline Gordon's "Old Red," for a model. By now, winter had dramatically fallen on Iowa City. Flannery had been home to Georgia for the Christmas holidays and discovered that she had grown more than an inch her first semester, up to about five five. By the time she returned for the February 3 resumption of classes, the cornfields were a silent blur of thick, fallen snow. Fellow Workshop member Norma Hodges recalls walking out after one evening Workshop meeting into the bracing Iowa air: "Flannery was so cold, she was shivering all over. I said something about, 'Not quite your Southern weather.'" Always tense around the "little pale girl with big glasses," Hodges felt her silly pleasantry returned with "one of those dirty, dirty looks. I didn't mess with her much."

Yet on the day Flannery read her "Old Red"–inspired story, Hodges was "flabbergasted. I was real excited about Flannery when I heard her. But then the men gave her a hard time, which seemed funny." The story she read was a draft of "The Geranium." In Gordon's "Old Red," an old Southern gentleman finds a symbol for his life in a wily red fox. In O'Connor's story, a Southerner, Old Dudley, living in a tenement in New York City, finds a symbol for his homesickness in a potted red geranium. As she later wrote to Maryat Lee of this story, expressing the underlying emotion of her first winter in Iowa City, "I couldn't though have written a story about *my* being homesick." Instead she embodied the experience in "an old man who went to live in a New York slum — no experience of mine as far as old men and slums went."

The early mimeographed draft Flannery read in a contentious Workshop session had a more extreme ending that was later cut.

Upon finding that the pot had fallen off a windowsill, the old man, rather than merely feeling crushed, as in the final version, according to Hodges, "pitched himself out of the window. I think his daughter asked, 'Where are you going?' and Old Dudley said, 'After that damned geranium!'" But feelings among the men in the class were already stacked against O'Connor as she began reading the story with what Hodges called a "broad Southern drawl": "After a few lines, groans arose from the oval of chairs and the story was given to a man with more recognizable diction." When the old man leapt to his death — a finale Hodges found "mythical" — "They all went, 'No . . . couldn't happen . . . it's too much,' and so on."

"The only day I felt she fell flat on her face was when she tried to write about a boy-and-girl situation," Hodges added, of O'Connor's talent for these "mythical" stories. "It wasn't her thing. And one about an educated black became labored." Engle likewise noted her awkwardness in writing about sex or romance. In the corridor, following one Workshop session, he tried to make a few suggestions. "'This scene of the attempted seduction just is not correct, I want to explain,'" he said. "'Oh no, don't, not here!'" Flannery quickly replied, looking nervously about. "So we went outside, across the street to the parking lot and into my car. There, I explained to her that sexual seduction didn't take place quite the way she had written it — I suspect from a lovely lack of knowledge."

If Engle felt that her sex scenes were not graphic enough, Flannery was still worried about their mere existence in the work of a young Catholic writer. As she later wrote of this crisis of literary conscience, "I was right young and very ignorant and I thought what I was doing was mighty powerful (it wasn't even intelligible at that point) and liable to corrupt anybody that read it and me too." Her solution was to visit one of the local Iowa City priests and carefully explain the problem. The priest drew out from his stash "one of those ten cent pamphlets that they are never without" and told her that she didn't need to write for fifteen-year-old girls. While this permission to write for a wider adult audience was helpful, his pamphlet failed to impress when she discovered that its Jesuit author deemed *A Tree Grows in Brooklyn* "about as good as you could get."

O'Connor later told an interviewer, concerning the Workshop, "When I went there I didn't know a short story from an ad in the newspaper." In spite of her insecurities, Engle encouraged her to keep submitting work for publication. Her first submission to the *Sewanee Review* was rejected over Christmas break. But in February, she mailed off two more stories, "The Geranium" and "The Crop," to *Accent* magazine. A broad satire in the style of some of her juvenile fiction, "The Crop" concerned a spinster schoolmarm with pretensions of becoming a writer of "social problem" stories. Like the young Miss O'Connor, trying on different author's story lines, the assiduous Miss Willerton, sitting in front of her typewriter, "discarded subject after subject and it usually took her a week or two to decide finally on something."

In March, close to her twenty-first birthday, O'Connor received word that "The Geranium" had been accepted for publication in the summer issue of *Accent.* Flannery was now "published," a crucial distinction in the Workshop. A "little magazine" from the University of Illinois, credited with printing the first stories of J. F. Powers and William Gass, *Accent* was on a short list of publications considered "of the right sort" among the Workshop members. Flannery admitted to a fellow student that she had not begun to think of herself as a fiction writer until the respected literary magazine had taken her first story, adding, "Although I reckon I got a long way to get yet before I'm what you call good at it." As she simply parsed her achievement at Iowa to the TV interviewer Harvey Breit, in 1955, "Then I began to write short stories, publicly."

Mixed feelings about having been picked out, but mildly cen-
sored, by John Crowe Ransom, were transformed into pure pleasure when Robert Penn Warren selected a story of hers from a pile
of student work during a visit to the university in April 1946. Warren had delivered a talk in the Senate Chamber of Old Capitol
on his story "Blackberry Winter"; his new novel that year, *All
the King's Men,* was awarded the 1947 Pulitzer Prize. Another
Southerner, and an editor of her *Understanding Fiction* anthology,
"Red" Warren was one of the more influential writers and critics
of the moment. As James B. Hall has recalled, "When R. P. Warren cocked one eye and said, 'By god, I like this paragraph right
heahr!' — well, something happened. You were stronger, more
daring, more resolved the next time out."

Just as important to Flannery's maturing as a writer was advice
she received before the end of the spring semester from Paul Horgan, her instructor in Imaginative Writing, a backup course to the
Workshop. Hired in February, "Lt. Col. Paul Horgan," as the student newspaper identified the recently discharged officer, was a
novelist and 1946 Guggenheim Fellow. O'Connor later told Betty
Hester that "Horgan never even knew I was in the room, I am
sure — though once he noted about forty things wrong with a
story of mine and I thought him a fine teacher." His advice to the
girl he did indeed later remember as "a sort of waif of the art of
writing" was to set aside a number of hours daily for writing —
same time, same place. That habit became her lifelong regimen,
the very soul of her artistic credo. She later shared her discipline
with a young writer, in 1957: "I write only about two hours every
day because that's all the energy I have, but I don't let anything interfere with those two hours, at the same time and the same
place. . . . Something goes on that makes it easier when it does
come well. And the fact is if you don't sit there every day, the day
it would come well, you won't be sitting there."

Having flown home for summer break in May because of a national railroad shutdown, in spite of President Truman's call for "strike curbs," O'Connor continued to submit her stories to literary magazines, though with less luck, from Milledgeville. She received two rejection notes over the summer, both from Allen Maxwell, the editor of *Southwest Review,* and both addressed to *Mr.* Flannery O'Connor. Either purposely, or inadvertently, her pen name — especially when stories lacked any stereotypical female romantic touches or domestic details but were full of guns and violence — often caused her to be mistaken for a male writer. In June, Maxwell rejected "Wildcat," a story about an old black man's fear of a prowling beast that was highly imitative of Faulkner's "That Evening Sun." In July, he rejected "The Coat" for moving along "in a rather uncertain manner."

ON HER RETURN to Currier House in September 1946, for the second year of the two-year program, Flannery was better adjusted to her surroundings and roommates than she had been when she first arrived in Iowa. Now living in a quieter back bedroom on the east side of the ground floor, she was able to experience the plus side of the Iowa Workshop that she later described as "an easier, freer childhood." Her roommate the first semester was Sarah Dawson, a former Wac (Women's Army Corps) from Des Moines, and, the second semester, Martha Bell, a former Wave from Mount Pleasant. In the adjoining double bedroom — four women shared a single bathroom — lived Jean Newland, of Belle Plaine, and Barbara Tunnicliff, a business major from Emmetsburg.

Barbara felt that she and Flannery had found in each other "kindred spirits," as they often took walks together around Iowa City, steering clear of any dating or frenzied weekend parties. "They would have house parties once in a while and invite men, but I just didn't feel comfortable with those people," says Barbara

Tunnicliff Hamilton. "I don't think either of us went to such things." Together they concocted a pipe dream in which Barbara, the "business woman," would become the "patron" who would contribute to the financial support of the "artist" Flannery. "We both had a sense of humor, almost a sense of the ridiculous," said Barbara Hamilton. "We were both a little offbeat." They exchanged bulky sweatshirts: Flannery's bore a University of Iowa insignia; in return, she gave Barbara one emblazoned with "Georgia" in big, red capital letters.

Yet mostly Barbara just heard, or sensed, Flannery on the other side of the closed door, working. "I didn't bother her when she was doing that," says Barbara Hamilton. The young writer liked to keep things plain: no curtains on the windows; a bare bulb hanging by a long cord from the center of the ceiling. When she was alone, she would pull down the shades and sit at her typewriter with a pile of yellow paper, writing and rewriting. If she wasn't writing, she was reading. As there was no food service in "Grad House," she usually took her breakfast and lunch in the room, often snacking on tins of sardines, or perishables that she kept cool on the windowsill. When Barbara asked Flannery why she worked so obsessively at her writing, she replied that she "had to."

"She was very serious about her mission in life, and had a sort of sense of destiny," says Barbara Hamilton. "She knew she was a great writer. She told me so many times. If I would have heard that from other people, I would have laughed up my sleeve, but not with her. We both agreed that she might never be recognized, but that wasn't the point. The point was to do what she thought she was meant to do." Another graduate woman in the Workshop, Ruth Sullivan, already looked up to Flannery as a writer, and treated her as an authority. "With the door open between our rooms, I often heard bits of their conversations," says Hamilton, of Sullivan soliciting Flannery's opinions. "I remember Ruth once saying she thought maybe she'd better give up trying to write, get married, and have a 'a pack of kids.' Flannery seemed always glad to try to help with advice."

In the fall of 1946, the Workshop moved into a sheet-metal Quonset hut on the banks of the Iowa River north of the Iowa Memorial Union; its next move, soon afterward, was to four corrugated-iron barracks. Quickly assembled to accommodate the influx of GI Bill students, in a style dubbed "World War II Ghastly" by knowing vets, these rows of official metal buildings constituted a fitting stage set for much of the fiction being written. "When more than half the class are returned servicemen, and when a good proportion of the fiction being written concerns war experiences, one would naturally expect veterans to disagree on the psychological reactions of story heroes," the *Cedar Rapids Gazette* reported of the Workshop, now numbering thirty-five students. "Men who have served in the navy question the motives of the air corps story heroes; infantry men do the same about the navy."

While not writing about the war, Flannery did try her hand at a topical subject for a next story, "The Barber." In November, a married couple had opened University Barber Shop on East Market Street to accommodate black students unable to get haircuts at "Jim Crow barbers" in town or on the campus. The State University of Iowa president, Virgil M. Hancher, refused to take a position on this divisive issue. For weeks, the Workshop had been abuzz with the topic as its only black member, Herb Nipson, who later became an editor of *Ebony* magazine, needed to travel twenty-one miles to Cedar Rapids to get a haircut. At about this time, Nipson was present at Flannery's reading of a story of hers involving relations between blacks and whites. Afterward a student complimented her dignified, respectful portrayal of a black servant. Nipson has recalled that "Flannery's answer went something like this, 'No. That's just the way he was.'"

In "The Barber," she reset the racial tension to Joe's Barber Shop in Dilton, a fictional college town in the rural South. The story turns on three visits made by Rayber, a liberal college professor, when he argues with its patrons, all supporters of Hawkson, a populist and racist conservative candidate. With little personal knowledge of men's barbershops, she pulled off a convincing evocation of hot lather, tinted windows, and good old boys spitting tobacco. But from its opening line, "It is trying on liberals in Dilton," Rayber was more a brunt of jokes than heroic, lending credence to a suspicion among some in the Workshop that she displayed too much of the "Southern attitude." James B. Hall reports, "She once said to my wife, also a Southerner, 'Momma and me got a nigger that drives us around.' My wife was privately critical of that order of talk."

Yet Flannery's personal attitudes about race were actually quite progressive during her years in Iowa. "I see I should ride the bus more often," she wrote to Betty Hester, in 1957. "I used to when I went to school in Iowa, as I rode the train from Atl. and the bus from M'ville, but no more. Once I heard the driver say to the rear occupants, 'All right, all you stove pipe blonds, git on back there.' At which moment I became an integrationist." Having become friendly for a while with a black woman graduate student, she bucked warnings from her mother that interracial friendships were dangerous, refusing to be swayed by such issues. She joked of "Verge" Hancher, complicit in Southern-style segregation on campus, as being president of the "Iowa Barber School."

Another story she wrote that year was equally a departure. While she had created a morning discipline of daily mass, followed by hours of writing, she had yet to put the two activities together. She had not treated the religious faith that was sustaining her in a story, even a darkly comic one. Her first attempt was "The Turkey," which used as its central symbol the bird she had once drawn in a preschool cartoon. In the story, a little boy, Ruller, "captured" a wild turkey, already shot dead in a ditch, interpreting the prize as a sign of favor from God. The juvenile preacher in training fancies himself, in one draft, "like Billy Grahme." Imagining himself into the 1938 film *Boys Town,* "He thought of Bing Crosby and Spencer Tracy. He might found a place for boys to stay who were going bad." But when his bird is swiped by just such bad boys, his faith becomes mixed with terror: "He was certain that Something Awful was tearing behind him."

As important to the young writer as assiduously imitating the masters were her reading courses. She took Seminar in Literary Criticism, taught by Austin Warren, another rising star among the New Critics, at work at the time with Iowa Professor René Wellek on their landmark *Theory of Literature.* For her supplementary texts in the class of this cultivated, Jamesian gentleman, with a national reputation as an organist, she chose Joyce's *Dubliners* and Brooks and Warren's *Understanding Fiction.* During the class segment on Joyce, Warren treated her as the resident expert in Roman Catholicism, asking, "Now, Miss O'Connor, what are we talking about here?" She took, as well, a two-semester course, Philosophy in Literature; Aesthetics in the Philosophy Department; and Select Contemporary Authors, concentrating on modern European novelists.

By far her most significant literature class was a two-semester independent study, Reading for Final Exam, directed by Engle. "I didn't really start to read until I went to Graduate School and then I began to read and write at the same time," she rattled off her regimen to a friend:

> Then I began to read everything at once, so much so that I didn't
> have time I suppose to be influenced by any one writer. I read all
> the Catholic novelists, Mauriac, Bernanos, Bloy, Green, Waugh;
> I read all the nuts like Djuna Barnes and Dorothy Richardson
> and Va. Woolfe (unfair to the dear lady of course). I read the
> best Southern writers like Faulkner and the Tates, K. A. Porter,

Eudora Welty and Peter Taylor; read the Russians, not Tolstoy
so much but Dostoevsky, Turgenev, Chekhov and Gogol. I became
a great admirer of Conrad and have read almost all his fiction.

Around Christmas 1946, Flannery started work on a new story, "The Train." She began with the conscious intent to build a novel from its tale of Hazel Wickers, a nineteen-year-old, homesick, country rube returning South after the war. In choosing a first name as unisexual as her own, she relied on a custom she happily noticed among rural families who occasionally gave their sons feminine names — June, for instance. Her readings in Joyce and Faulkner were echoed in neologisms like "greyflying" to describe the train whizzing by. Yet what truly caught her imagination was a train ride home for the holidays. As she later explained the genesis of the story, "It started when I was on a train coming from Chicago. There was a Tennessee boy on it in uniform who was much taken up worrying the porter about how the berths were made up; the porter was so regal he just barely tolerated the boy."

On the first leg of that holiday trip, Flannery made her way across downtown Chicago from La Salle Street Station to Dearborn Station, "a journey that never impressed me as beautiful." She then caught the Dixie Limited, to travel from Illinois through Tennessee to Georgia. A discarded draft gives a glimpse, through Hazel's eyes, of "the dilapidated [Dearborn] station, where the southern trains came in. There was a strange feeling in it for him, of awayness and homeness mixed. . . . It was a sooted red brick with turrets and inside it was grey and smoked and there were spittoons parked at the end of every third bench." O'Connor later delighted in telling a friend of one of her own encounters at the terminus, "I sat down next to a colored woman in the waiting room at the Dearborn Street station in Chicago once. She was eating grapes and asked me to have some but I declined. She was very talkative and kept talking and eating grapes. Finally she asked me where I was from and I said, 'Georgia,' and she spit a mouthful of grape seeds out on the floor and said, 'My God,' and got up and left."

Flickering through various drafts of "The Train," marked "Workshop," is the presence of a more military Haze, recently demobilized, among army buddies en route, like Flannery, from Chicago to Chattanooga. In one version, he is the life of the party, buying them all beers in the club car and passing out cigarettes. While keeping quiet in class, Flannery had evidently been listening closely to the war stories of classmates, like Jim Eriicson, at work on a novel about a veteran in a hospital, suffering, he told the *Cedar Rapids Gazette,* from "the Oedipus complex." She borrowed from these war-torn heroes for her own more comic antihero. And although Iowa City never left many traces in her fiction, the minute she hit Dearborn Station, where Hazel felt "a thump of recognition" at hearing "flat and twangish" country voices, her imagination clicked on.

When she returned to Iowa City, in January 1947, Flannery set to work finishing "The Train," the last of the six stories in her thesis collection, the writing requirement for an MFA degree. She also began adapting the story as the first chapter of her novel in progress. The novel was inspired not simply by themes of "awayness" and "homeness," but also by Paul Engle's announcement in November of an award from Rinehart Publishers of a $750 advance for a novel, to be awarded to a Workshop student in May, with an option, upon acceptance, of another $750. Engle had already sent two of her stories to his friend John Selby, the Rinehart editor in charge of the prize. Flush from the success of their recent bestselling novels, *The Lost Weekend,* by Charles R. Jackson, and *The Hucksters,* by Frederic Wakeman, the publishers hoped to sign up hot new talent.

For help with writing the required outline and four chapters, or twelve thousand words, she turned to Andrew Lytle, brought in by Engle as a visiting lecturer and instructor in February and put up in Quonset hut no. 244. In his midforties, Lytle was a wiry, card-carrying Southerner and gentleman farmer. As an undergraduate at Vanderbilt University, in Nashville, he had been one of the original members of the Agrarians, a literary movement nostalgic for Old South rural, aristocratic values. Before leaving college to go off to Yale Drama School and a stint as a Broadway actor, he was friendly with the founding Fugitive poets, including Allen Tate, Donald Davidson, and Robert Penn Warren. In "The Hind Tit," the essay he contributed to the 1930 Agrarian manifesto, *I'll Take My Stand,* he wrote of Tennessee yeomen farmers, much like Hazel, displaced from the land by the "pizen snake" of industrialism.

Lytle first encountered Flannery while sitting in on a Workshop class, where he was asked to read her student story aloud: "I was told later that it was understood that I would know how to pronounce in good country idiom the word chitling which appeared in the story. At once it was obvious that the author of the story was herself not only Southern but exceptionally gifted." Flannery responded to Lytle as a protective big brother and consummate prose stylist, known to "make a federal case out of a comma." It fell to Lytle to help her through a scene involving Hazel and a prostitute that wound up in the novel's second chapter: "She would put a man in bed with a woman, and I would say, 'Now, Flannery, it's not done quite that way,' and we talked a little bit about it, but she couldn't face up to it, so she put a hat on his head and made a comic figure of him." He advised her to "sink the theme" and "clobber" her reader more subtly.

Their master-apprentice relationship irritated those students baffled by the growing recognition of the young lady meanly described by one as having "a bale of cotton in her mouth." Aware of the rumblings, Lytle said, "She was a lovely girl, but scared the boys to death with her irony." Lytle did not help matters by talking widely of her talent. "Why, she can just walk by a poolroom and know exactly what's happening by the smell," he told James B. Hall, the "second-best" writer in class. As the Brooklyn native Eugene Brown explains, "People who were favored in the Writers' Workshop at that time were Southern writers." This suspicion of Southern loyalty was only confirmed with the campus visit during the week of April 21 of the Fugitive poet and *Sewanee Review* editor Allen Tate. In his class "critique," Tate likewise paid special attention to Lytle's protégée.

Flannery was busily filling out applications and gathering together her finished manuscripts by early May 1947. First she applied for several college teaching positions, just in case. "It comes to us all," she moaned of the dreaded profession. She then enlisted Barbara Tunnicliff to type her thesis project, *The Geranium: A Collection of Short Stories.* "She paid me for doing it and watched over me as I did," recalled her former suitemate. O'Connor dedicated the work, for his extraordinary support, "To Paul Engle, whose interest and criticism have made these stories better than they would otherwise have been." Norma Hodges remembers helping Flannery and a mutual friend, Carol Nutter, carry stacks of its pages from the print shop. According to Hodges, continuously feeling shunned by her, when they arrived at the door of Nutter's second-floor apartment, Flannery coldly discouraged her from entering, wishing to be alone with her friend Carol: "Her magnified eyes swam up punctuating an unspoken, 'Don't you dare come in!' "

In the synopsis required for her Rinehart application, O'Connor hinted that a starting point, if not blueprint, for Haze's quest might be found in T. S. Eliot's shattered epic of modern life, *The Waste Land,* a poem revered by her New Critic writer-instructors: "His search for a physical home mirrors his search for a spiritual one, and although he finds neither, it is the latter search which saves him from becoming a member of the Wasteland and makes him worth 75,000 words."

Partly the reference was parody, a use of a buzzword. But unlike her joke on Proust in high school, she was reading Eliot's poems and essays very closely and sympathetically. As a poet at once modern and devout, having converted to Anglo-Catholicism a decade after writing his poem of "fragments I have shored against my ruins," Eliot was a figure of fascination to O'Connor. Traces of this deep interest dot her Iowa pages: a "dead geranium" is a central image of his poem "Rhapsody on a Windy Night"; the fortune-teller Madame Sosostris of *The Waste Land* shows up in a draft of her novel as Madame Sosistra; her mummy's colloquial museum label, "once as tall as you or me," is lifted from Eliot's line about Phlebas the Phoenician, "once as handsome and tall as you."

All of this hard work finally paid off during the fourth week in May, when she received official word that she was the winner of the Rinehart-Iowa Award, and that Engle had pulled strings to secure her a teaching assistantship for the following year. In an interview accompanying her photograph and front-page story in the *Daily Iowan,* she insisted that her novel about a man searching for a spiritual home was not a "typed" novel: "Any author who follows a hard and fast outline allows himself to become a slave to the typewriter." To celebrate, on May 29 she traveled by car to Cedar Rapids with her roommate, Martha Bell, and housemother, Sarah Dawson. "We had dinner there," Bell recorded in her diary, "did some window-shopping and then went to see *The Egg and I.*" The plot of the light romantic comedy they chose concerned a society girl (Claudette Colbert) who is persuaded by her new husband (Fred MacMurray) to start a chicken farm.

Also celebrating the end of the semester, Paul Engle and his wife, Mary, threw a picnic at Stone City, their Victorian summer house, previously belonging to Grant Wood, next to a limestone quarry. Charles Embree, a Missouri writer whose first Workshop story, "Concerning the Mop," about jazz, had just been published in *Esquire,* drove Flannery to the party in his 1936 Ford coupe. Because of his Southern accent, Flannery often asked him to read her stories in class. "She was a loner," says Embree. "Yet everybody re-spected her talent. It was apparent." In one photograph of a dozen guests taken that day at the quarry, Flannery stands off to the side, in a heavy dark skirt and checked jacket. In a crowded group por-trait in the living room, she is hidden behind the woman next to her, with only her knee showing. "It was wholly typical of Flan-nery that the part of her visible is the right knee," wrote Engle. "There is a spirit about that knee."

Springtime parties, no matter what the excuse, were the norm in Iowa City because of the demands of the extreme winters; the guests at Stone City that afternoon were mostly in high spirits sim-ply from the mild break in the weather. "In spring, it was as though we had come through," wrote James B. Hall. "The Iowa country-side was one long, low lyric of fields growing." For the trip back, Andrew Lytle offered rides to both James Hall and Flannery, who tucked herself silently into the back seat, her extreme quietness making her more a potent presence. Hall recalls that "Andrew was talking about Flannery's recent distinction, her Rinehart Award. He was driving, but looked closely at me, also in the front seat. I thought he was rubbing it in, and also seeing how I was taking the news."

In the days immediately following, Flannery returned to Milledgeville for the summer, where she joined the Cline family, still mourning the sudden death of Uncle Bernard at the end of January. Her relatives were trying to deal with the practicalities of his will, including his bequest of Sorrel Farm to Regina and Louis. On a bus trip to Atlanta in the fall of 1946, Flannery had chanced to sit next to a descendant of the Hawkins family, the original own-ers, who informed her that the farm, in the nineteenth century, had been called Andalusia, after a province of southern Spain. She wrote her mother, pushing for reinstating its fanciful name, and her uncle Bernard had been willing. So Andalusia it now was. "I was in Milledgeville in the summer of 1947 with my mother," says

Frances Florencourt. "I remember Flannery was very happy, up-beat, smiling." The hopeful twenty-two-year-old was in a good humor that season.

❊

A POSTGRADUATE STUDENT on a fellowship, Flannery made inde-pendent living arrangements when she returned to Iowa City in September for her final year. As a teaching assistant, she was given an office in the Old Dental Building, next to University Hall, re-served for junior members of the English faculty. After looking at a number of boardinghouses, she settled on renting a single room in a big, gray, wood-frame house at 115 East Bloomington Street, owned by a Mrs. Guzeman. Like the boardinghouse of Haze Motes in *Wise Blood,* her new address was "clapboard . . . in a block of them, all alike." And like Haze's Mrs. Flood, her own "Mrs." land-lady, whom she surmised "was most a hundred then," could be pe-nurious. As she later groused, "Mrs. Guzeman was not very fond of me because I stayed at home and required heat to be on — at least ON. It was never UP that I remember. When it was on you could smell it and I got to where I warmed up a little every time I smelled it."

On the opening day of the Workshop, she made friends with Jean Williams, a new student-writer from Indianapolis, who sat down in the seat beside her. "Flannery was sitting alone in the front row, over against the wall," wrote Jean Williams Wylder. "She was wearing what I was soon to think of as her 'uniform' for the year: plain gray skirt and neatly-ironed silkish blouse, nylon stockings and penny brown loafers. Her only makeup was a trace of lip-stick . . . there was something of the convent about Flannery that day — a certain intentness in the slight girlish figure which set her apart from the rest of us. She seemed out of place in that room composed mostly of veterans returned from World War II. Flannery was only 22 years old then, but . . . could easily have passed for 17 or 18."

Jean Williams saw her only a few times that fall, outside of the Monday afternoon Workshop sessions. As Mrs. Guzeman didn't serve Sunday dinner, Flannery occasionally took her noon meal at the Mad Hatter Tea Room, over Bremer's Clothing Store, on Washington Street, where Williams worked as a "salad girl." They once bumped into each other as she was exiting Woolworth's Five-and-Ten-Cent Store with a single cake of Palmolive soap. "I doubt if Flannery ever bought two of anything at one time," she recalled. When Williams visited O'Connor's room at Mrs. Guzeman's, she was struck by the "monastic simplicity" of its "neatly-made bed, the typewriter waiting on a desk. There was nothing extraneous in that room except a box of vanilla wafers beside the typewriter. She nibbled on cookies while she wrote, she said, because she didn't smoke."

A more involved friendship began at the same time with Robie Macauley. On leave for the year, Engle put Andrew Lytle in charge of the Workshop and brought in Macauley as both a student and instructor, teaching a course in Russian literature. "He was a brilliant young professor," says Bernie Halperin, a Workshop writer who took his course. "He was a thin, nice-looking fellow, with a tremendous knowledge of those massive Russian novels." At the age of twenty-eight, the Michigan native had earned a BA at Kenyon College, where he studied under John Crowe Ransom; served during the war in the Army Counterintelligence Corps; taught at Bard College; and worked as an editor at Henry Holt and Company. Upon first hearing O'Connor read from her novel in progress, he was immediately impressed by the work as "entirely original, strange."

"I used to date Flannery and I remember sitting with her long hours on the porch swing of her boardinghouse . . . discussing a number of deep matters or reading the new chapters of *Wise Blood*, which she was writing at the time," Macauley later recounted. "As for the deep matters, I remember that Flanders Dunbar had become intellectually fashionable that year and we'd both read her, and so we spent a lot of time discussing psychosomatic medicine." The Dunbar book was *Mind and Body,* its author also a medievalist with an interest in Dante, a favorite of the two new friends. Macauley also occasionally escorted Flannery, with Workshop instructor Paul Griffith and his girlfriend, to Sunday lunch in Amana, the historic German Pietist community, twenty miles from Iowa City: "We ate in a big barnlike dining hall with everybody at long tables. Flannery liked that."

During the fall, Macauley introduced Flannery to his friends Walter Sullivan, a Workshop writer from Tennessee, and his wife, Jane. "Robie took care of Flannery . . . he had a gift of making her relax," Sullivan has observed of their easygoing relationship. When Macauley first brought her by a small party at their home, promising, "There's a little Georgia girl here you've got to meet," she found an audience highly receptive to spun tales of her childhood, especially her centerpiece story of the Pathe News arriving to film her backward-walking chicken. "Flannery would get strung out and start telling stories about the South," said Jane Sullivan of her many visits. "Funny stories, and it was hysterical, but this required a small group for conversation; it wasn't party stuff."

Regarding his friendship with Flannery, Macauley used the term "date" a couple of times with interviewers. Yet whatever dating occurred was of the lightest sort. As he explained when pressed, "Flannery and I had no 'romantic' relationship. I was engaged to Anne Draper (who was in New York) and Flannery was well aware of it. . . . We did spend a lot of time talking and reading manuscripts." Her bond with the tall, soft-spoken intellectual, not a "party man," was more as a "soul mate." Like the soldier John Sullivan, he was a good-looking, somewhat unavailable, slightly older guy who protected and encouraged her. And she brought a similar excitement to their friendship. Once Jean Williams saw Flannery on her way to the library to check out Gogol's *Dead Souls,* which Macauley told her was a must-read for every writer. "So I reckon I better do it," Flannery said.

The first week in October a dorm mate of Macauley's from Kenyon, Robert Lowell, arrived to give a poetry reading in the Old Capitol and to critique Workshop poems. A Boston-born disciple of the Fugitives, Lowell had camped out during the summer of 1937 in the backyard of Allen Tate and his wife, Caroline Gordon, in Tennessee, to learn at the feet of the Vanderbilt masters; he then broke with family tradition by leaving Harvard to study, like Macauley, as one of "Ransom's boys," at Kenyon. Later describing Iowa City as "tame and friendly," the thirty-year-old poet, in 1947, was treated as a wild celebrity. Chain-smoking, curly-haired, and unruly, he cut a poetic figure. "He was so sensitive, he trembled as he read to us," recalls James B. Hall. Flannery was quite impressed by Lowell, at the reading and at a dinner, where he held forth one night during his four-day visit.

A visitor altogether different from Robert Lowell arrived later in the month for a weekend stay — Mary Virginia Harrison, her attractive "best friend" from high school. Mary Virginia stayed at a hotel, and one night the girlfriends shared a double bed at Mrs. Guzeman's. Flannery had written that she could meet her train at any hour, as her own life was "simple, austere." As for clothing, she advised, "The well dressed Iowa Citian is usually seen in a sweat shirt, trousers or skirt (as the sex may dictate), heavy coat and limp cigaret." A Jessie classmate they both knew was Faye Hancock, married to the Workshop writer Hank Messick, and living in Victory Park, a student trailer park for veterans. Messick later recalled that on her visits Flannery preferred bottled Blue Ridge springwater. "When it was gone," he wrote, "she returned to mixed drinks, claiming a lot of Scotch was necessary to make the water drinkable."

For her third holiday trip home to Milledgeville that December, Flannery was accompanied as far as La Salle Street Station in Chicago by Jean Williams. The train ride in high-backed swivel chairs in the parlor car was their longest time spent together. Flannery convinced the porter it would be "right nice" if he would "allow" her friend into the first-class section, too. She was putting the final touches that month on "The Train," which would be published in April in the *Sewanee Review,* the prestigious quarterly from Tennessee's University of the South, edited by both Lytle and Tate. "They know exactly what they're doing all the time," she said, eyeing the porter. "No dilly-dallying atall." She then took out a snapshot of the Cline Mansion from her purse to show. "Flannery was glad to be going home that Christmas," wrote Jean Williams Wylder. "She looked very pretty, more like a college girl . . . almost tall in a blue plaid suit and tan polo jacket."

When they both returned to Iowa City, Jean accompanied Flannery on a walk that doubled as a fact-finding mission. At work on a chapter about Haze's lone friend, Enoch Emery, at City Forest Park Zoo, Flannery suggested they visit the local City Park Zoo, a half-mile walk along the Iowa River. Here she got her inspiration for Enoch's fixation on a cage of "two black bears . . . sitting and facing each other like two matrons having tea," which she worked into her story "The Heart of the Park." According to her friend, on this bleak Sunday afternoon in February, a "completely absorbed and interested" Flannery stared at "the two sad and mangy bears, the raccoons, and the special foreign chickens they had." O'Connor later remembered "two indifferent bears . . . and a sign over them that said: 'These lions donated by the Iowa City Elks Club.'"

If her "barbarous Georgia accent," as she joked of it, had been a liability two years earlier, during the spring of 1948 readings by Flannery were much sought after. One circle where she felt comfortable sharing her work gathered on Sunday evenings at Austin Warren's elegant home. The in-group included Robie Macauley;

Andrew Lytle; Warren Miller, reading from a Kafkaesque novel in progress; and Clyde McLeod, one of only three women in the Workshop that year, who sang a ballad with a "Hootie, Hootie" refrain. "Flannery's novel is sure going to be very beautiful," Paul Griffith reported in mid-February to Engle, still on leave; "her chapter at AW's was polished and colored to perfection." Hansford Martin, an instructor in the Workshop, annoyed by her endless revisions, complained to Engle that "Flannery, in spite of all that Paul and I say, is still rewriting her first chapter."

Another such informal Midwestern salon took place in the rented rooms of the writer John Gruen and the painter Jane Wilson, then both MFA students at Iowa. "We would invite her to our house because we had little gatherings, and ask her to read," says Gruen. "She would sit quietly at first until she was asked to read. 'Okay, Flannery, did you bring your story?' 'Yeeees.' 'Are you going to read it?' 'Yeeees.' I believe that she read the first chapters of her novel in an accent that was even fiercer than the way she regularly spoke. She took on all the characters. She would read in this kind of very heavy singsong but not really singing. It was a performance. It became totally hypnotic. So that all of us sitting there, young people in their teens and twenties, were totally struck."

In early drafts of her novel, Hazel had a sister, Ruby Hill, a "modern" type who lives in a boardinghouse and, upon discovering she is pregnant, wishes to have an abortion. The bit Jane Wilson recalls Flannery reading was a version of this subplot, later spun off by the "demon rewriter," as Robie Macauley dubbed his friend, into "Woman on the Stairs," published the next summer in *Tomorrow,* a small literary magazine, and eventually revised and published as "A Stroke of Good Fortune." "She read the story in this rhythm of a woman climbing a stair," remembers Wilson. "It was so persuasive. It was a monologue of silly miseries and dismay. 'Oh this waistband is so uncomfortable on me. Oh, God!' Then in the end when she gets to the top of the stairs her worst fears have burst through.

It's not weight gain. She's pregnant. . . . The writing was scary. But she emanated warmth while she was reading it . . . affection, in a way."

Over the course of the spring, Flannery was given guidance in planning her future. As Norma Hodges suggests, "She had this air of dependence about her, as if she needed someone to take care of her." Engle arranged a teaching fellowship for the following year. Griffith suggested applying for a summer residency at the Yaddo artists' colony in Saratoga Springs, New York. He then helped her gather a strong list of recommendations. Austin Warren endorsed her as "a personally shy but kind and charming young Southern writer." Andrew Lytle wrote that she had "as much promise as anyone I have seen of her generation." Engle praised her as "one of the best young writers in the country." Her application was successful, and Hansford Martin reported to Engle in April, "Flannery seems happiest of all, blossoming like a rose, packing for Yaddo."

She was happy enough even to overcome her reluctance to read aloud in the Workshop. In the class run that spring by Lytle, Flannery had rarely spoken up. Once, when her mentor asked her to comment on a student's story, she paused a beat, then in a deadpan voice, she replied laconically, "I'd say the description of that crocodile in there was real good." For her memorable late-April performance, she chose to read the vignette of the woman on the stairs, which she introduced as the second chapter of her novel. Her "flat, nasal drawl" reminded the Workshop writer Gene Brzenk of the comic screen actress Zasu Pitts, known for her switchboard-operator voice. "She never looked up," he recalled, "and acknowledged her audience only when the laughter drowned out her voice. When she finished reading, we all applauded and the meeting broke up in high good humor."

At the close of the afternoon, Flannery quickly disappeared through the door to return to her room, while the other students regrouped for beers at the Brown Derby, a hangout on Dubuque Street. But Jean Williams turned to Clyde McLeod, unsatisfied. "For once there was not going to be any critical dissecting," Jean Williams Wylder has written. "That we had said nothing about Flannery's story was a tribute to her genius. But, the other girl writer and I wanted there to be something more — some more tangible token of our admiration. We went around Iowa City on that late spring afternoon, walking into people's yards as if they were public domain, to gather arms full of flowering branches — taking only the most beautiful — and we carried them up to Flannery."

Chapter Five

Up North

❋

Arriving on the first of June for her stay at Yaddo, located on the outskirts of Saratoga Springs, near the Adirondack region of upstate New York, Flannery found herself among a crush of summer invitees on overlapping two-week to two-month residencies. Many had taken the morning train from New York City, reaching the local station at around four in the afternoon. Courtesy Cab Company then offered a special fifty-cent rate for the short ride past ornate hotels, once catering to visitors "taking the waters" in the nineteenth-century spa town; a string of Edwardian and Victorian mansions on Union Avenue; and the Saratoga Race Course for thoroughbreds, with its low fences and practice tracks, bordering the estate of Jock Hay Whitney as well as the grounds of the artists' colony.

"It did not take Georgia for me to appreciate Yaddo," Flannery joked that summer of the four-hundred-acre estate, arrived at by passing between stone pillars and driving down a long, curving road lined by tall evergreens and occasional ponds. Better preparation for appreciating the rarefied style of Yaddo might have been her early favorite, Edgar Allan Poe, rumored to have written "The Raven" on a lower lake during a visit to the property in the 1840s. For looming on a piney mountain ridge, surrounded by dark woods, formal rose gardens, fountains, and rockeries, was a fifty-five-room, turreted, late-Victorian, stone mansion, as Gothic as anything Poe imagined. Built by the stockbroker Spencer Trask and his wife, Katrina, in 1893, along with sixteen outlying buildings, the puzzling name of the estate was first lisped by one of their four children to rhyme with "shadow."

By the time Flannery arrived in the summer of 1948, Yaddo had been open for creative business since 1926, bequeathed by Katrina Trask, who outlived her husband and all her children, as a center for "creating, creating, creating." Earning his keep as a summer assistant during the early thirties, the novelist John Cheever later credibly claimed, for the acreage, "more distinguished activity in the arts than any other piece of ground in the English-speaking community, or perhaps in the entire world." Guests walking across the sloped lawn in just its first two decades included the poets Louise Bogan, Langston Hughes, and Delmore Schwartz; the critics Philip Rahv and Lionel Trilling; the philosophers Hannah Arendt and Sidney Hook; the photographer Henri Cartier-Bresson; the novelists Paul Bowles, James T. Farrell, and Jean Stafford; and the composers Virgil Thomson and Aaron Copland, who wrote his "Piano Variations" in the Stone Tower on Lake Spencer.

Like the Iowa Writers' Workshop, Yaddo had recently been hosting a Southern renaissance. Katherine Anne Porter shared a chicken dinner with her fellow guest Eudora Welty — and had the dubious pleasure of finding Carson McCullers stretched across her doorway in the main mansion, professing undying love, as she simply stepped over her admirer on the way to dinner. Porter was so taken with the place that she soon bought South Hill Farm nearby. During the summer of 1946, Truman Capote was ensconced in Katrina Trask's uppermost Tower Room, with its ornate Gothic tracery windows, writing his first novel, *Other Voices, Other Rooms*. Following Capote's suggestion to apply for a Yaddo fellowship, the Texas-born Patricia Highsmith had arrived in mid-May, coinciding with O'Connor's stay for six weeks, to work on her own first novel, *Strangers on a Train*.

Flannery was put up for her two-month summer residency on an upper floor of the mansion, along with most of the other twenty-three guests, including two composers, six painters, and fifteen writers. The coveted, rose-motif Tower Room that season went to Clifford Wright, an exuberant young Scandinavian American painter from Seattle, by way of Mott Street in lower Manhattan, who became friendly with her, noting in his June diary entry cataloging the arriving guests: ". . . and Flannery O'Connor who is a youngster working on her first novel." Highsmith pegged her as "very quiet, stayed alone . . . while others of us were shockingly gregarious and unwriterlike." A decade later, O'Connor was still passing along her favorable first impressions of Yaddo to Cecil Dawkins: "I really think you ought to look into the Yaddo business. The food is very good. The quarters are elegant. The servants are very nice. The scenery is magnificent."

In a polished atmosphere of grandeur past, not unlike the Cline Mansion, though more ostentatious, Flannery descended the red-carpeted staircase each evening for dinner. With the other guests, she lingered in the Great Hall, an eccentric repository of Persian carpets, pink velvet sofas, a Tiffany chandelier and glass mosaic of a phoenix rising above the fireplace, oversized oil portraits of the Trasks, and a pair of painted sleighs, gifts of Queen Marie of the Netherlands. At six thirty, a silver bell rang and everyone passed across oiled hardwood floors and through velvet drapes, to be seated around a carved Tudor table with high-backed, dark oak chairs, the Trasks' silverware glinting from sideboards. The dress code was jacket-and-tie for men and evening wear for women.

Presiding at the head of the table was Elizabeth Ames, the director of Yaddo since its first season, when she was appointed by Mrs. Trask's second husband, George Peabody. A widowed schoolteacher from Minnesota, Mrs. Ames affected an imperious, affable air. "She is like a well-meaning early Hanoverian king — but she's a liberal and doesn't approve of kings," commented Robert Lowell, a guest during the summer of 1947. She was also half-deaf, and recycled stories. The novelist Frederick Morton, in residence with O'Connor, recalls someone telling a story that summer about the Hollywood actor Monty Woolley. Mrs. Ames caught his name, and retold exactly the same gossip. "There was the same laughter, mostly staged," says Morton. "Everybody was very scared of her, because she had a decisive voice in who would be invited."

Equal parts Mother Superior and monarch, Mrs. Ames ran Yaddo with many of the strict rules of a convent, except for chastity — though spouses *were* discouraged from visiting. This regimen was made to order for Flannery, who suddenly found herself in a world where at least some others, like her, worked "ALL the time." Following breakfast, the guests were handed a black tin workman's lunchbox and thermos, and sent off to their studios. Those favored by the kitchen staff sometimes found an extra raw carrot. "I would have been happier writing in my room," O'Connor said, "but they seem to think it proper you go to a studio." A great silence, straight out of the Rule of St. Benedict, was imposed from nine until four in the afternoon, with no visiting or talking among guests allowed, and invitees were restricted to the hours of four to ten at night.

Flannery made her way each morning down a dirt road, through the pinewood, most likely to Hillside Studio, built in 1927 as a piggery but never used for that purpose. Instead its hearth and chimney, constructed for smoking hams and curing sides of bacon for Yaddo meals, qualified the outdoor wooden studio as one of the more desirable, along with Meadow Studio to its east, with views all the way across the Hudson Valley to the Green Mountains of Vermont. O'Connor remembered her cottage for June and July simply as "a long single room with a fireplace and chaise longue and a couple of tables and straight chairs." When not writing, she took "nice walks . . . around the lakes and back towards the race tracks." Her constant companions were a "studio squirrel," as well as some "chipmonks and a large important-looking woodchuck."

Animals turned out to be fitting company that summer, as her own imaginary companion was Enoch Emery, the zoo guard who winds up near her novel's end donning an ape suit. While many of the characters she was inventing were fated for the cutting-room floor, or spun off into other stories, "grinning" Enoch, in his "yellowish white" suit, "pinkish white" shirt, and "greenpeaish" tie, somehow stuck. First noticed by Haze, in a seventy-five-hundred-word draft, marked "Yaddo," looking "like a friendly hound dog with light mange," he became his faithful, if abused, sidekick. "In my whole time of writing the only parts that have come easy for me were Enoch Emery and Hulga," O'Connor later admitted. During her Yaddo summer, she was sending out, getting back, and rewriting the two stories that brought Enoch to life, "The Peeler" and "The Heart of the Park."

The downside of Yaddo for Flannery was its artiness, or the "arty" pose she felt that many of her fellow guests adopted. "At the breakfast table they talked about seconol and barbiturates and now maybe it's marujana," she warned Dawkins. "You survive in this atmosphere by minding your own business and by having plenty of your own business to mind, and by not being afraid to be different from the rest of them." The summer was marked by many of the legendary Yaddo parties, of which O'Connor claimed, "I went to one or two of these but always left before they began to break things." The more extreme action usually took place on weekends at Jimmy's Bar, on Congress Street, in the black section of town.

But at one official Yaddo event, a woman writer, ginned up, felt inspired to perform a combination cancan and cooch dance.

"Miss Highsmith and Mr. Wright had a taxi driver follow them around from bar to bar and then didn't have any money to pay him so were taken to jail in a highly uncooperative mood, but managed to talk themselves out before morning," Clifford Wright recorded of his high jinks with Highsmith, who characterized herself, at Yaddo, as falling "between those two stools" of writing and partying. All of the alcohol consumption — "in any collection of so-called artists you will find a good percentage alcoholic in one degree or another," sniped O'Connor — combined with late hours, led, of course, to sexual escapades. "In such a place you have to expect them all to sleep around"; she went on, observing satirically, "This is not sin but Experience, and if you do not sleep with the opposite sex, it is assumed that you sleep with your own."

Having defensively decided that "the help was morally superior to the guests," Flannery's initial response was to shrink back from the others, and to make friends, instead, with Jim and Nellie Shannon, the Irish caretaker and head cook, who lived with their three kids in East House, one of three smaller buildings on the property. "Dad had been a ragpicker on the docks until he got in a brawl and someone put a bale hook in his skull, so he moved upstate," says his son Jim. Although Flannery couldn't reproduce her daily Iowa City ritual, each Sunday morning she drove with the Shannons in their 1930s Ford station wagon to mass at St. Clement's Church on Lake Avenue in Saratoga Springs. She kept a close watch, too, on the staff of mostly Irish maids, a type she was familiar with — "all well over forty, large grim and granit-jawed or shriveled and shrunk."

Flannery did, soon enough, form a close friendship with one other woman writer, Elizabeth Fenwick. A Texas-born author of both thrillers and lyric novels, Fenwick was living on the Upper

West Side of Manhattan, working for a Columbia professor. "I remember she was a kind of sexy creature, very attractive physically," says Frederick Morton. The coincidence that brought Flannery together with the easygoing "Miss Fenwick," as she liked to call the more facile writer, was that they were both working on novels for John Selby at Rinehart. As O'Connor later told Betty Hester of Elizabeth Fenwick Way, who remained a lifelong friend: "She lives by a kind of rhythm, has nothing to say but is full of lovely feelings, giggles, is a big soft blond girl and real nice to be around except that she bats her eyelashes. . . . She *is* a kind of complement to me, and we get on famously."

As in Iowa City, she took up as well with a few protective men who helped her along. One was Paul Moor, who wrote about music, described by Mrs. Ames in her notes as "an accomplished pianist and a socially graceful person." Moor had an unfortunate summer: he collapsed from heat exhaustion on a visit to Manhattan and had to be flown back to Yaddo; at the end of July, his studio accidentally burned to the ground. Yet he made a most important difference in O'Connor's professional life by recommending her to Elizabeth McKee, his literary agent. "Elizabeth McKee was a wonderful woman," recalled Robert Giroux, who eventually became O'Connor's publisher. "For New York, she was really genteel and didn't act like most literary agents I knew. She was very loyal to Flannery, was a damn good agent for her, and really helped her."

In her introductory letter to McKee, on June 19, Flannery apologized for writing to her "in my vague and slack season," and warned, "I am a very slow worker. . . . I have never had an agent so I have no idea what your disposition might be toward my type of writer." Evidently charmed by the candor and self-deprecation, McKee responded within a few days: "Your work sounds very interesting. . . . Please don't let it worry you that you are not a prolific writer." As they began to discuss the details of the contract for her novel with Rinehart, Flannery, who reported that she was working on the twelfth chapter, further defined her "type of writer" as decidedly not formulaic: "I don't have my novel outlined and I have to write to discover what I am doing. Like the old lady, I don't know so well what I think until I see what I say; then I have to say it over again."

McKee showed commitment to her new writer by asking George Davis, a fiction editor at *Mademoiselle,* for a chance, as her agent, to look over the galleys of "The Turkey," set to be published as "The Capture" in the magazine's November issue.

The gentleman most taken with the taciturn young lady from the South was Edward Maisel, a musicologist, author, and Harvard graduate in his early thirties, who had published a successful biography of the American composer Charles T. Griffes five years earlier. A confidant of Mrs. Ames, he lived with an overflow of guests out at North Farm, on the far side of Union Avenue, where he could sing at the top of his lungs while writing. He was fond of picking up Flannery after working hours to take long strolls in the woods, and he even led her on a boating expedition on a nearby lake. The two occasionally walked into downtown Saratoga Springs, where he introduced her to some of the townspeople he found amusing. She obviously responded, as she later wrote: "after a few weeks at Yaddo, you long to talk to an insurance salesman, dog-catcher, bricklayer — anybody who isn't talking about Form or sleeping pills."

Maisel was caricatured by Robert Lowell, in a letter to Elizabeth Bishop, as "a real Yaddo ringer who knows everything and everybody — is in on everybody — and is sort of a pain." He was fond of telling guests' fortunes with a deck of tarot cards. Yet his very nature as a learned and amusing busybody stood Flannery in good stead when he took it upon himself to become her advocate. As silence was the rule at Yaddo, much communication took place by note passing; Mrs. Ames's favorite medium was a blue slip on which she often warned guests of infractions. In one typed missive,

Maisel diplomatically urged her to notice Flannery's distinction: "By the way have you got to know Flannery O'Connor at all? Probably not, because she's so very silent and withdrawn, and needs bringing out; but I have been on several evening walks with her, and find her immensely serious, with a sharp sense of humor; a very devout Catholic (thirteenth century, she describes herself). I think you would enjoy her, Elizabeth."

Flannery's describing herself as "thirteenth century" on their walks shows the weightiness of some of these crepuscular conversations; she wasn't much for small talk. The phrase was also a passkey to her more private thoughts. "She was completely intellectual, and cerebral," assured Giroux. "She was a thinker. And in those days encountering a philosophical woman thinker was rarer." The most "thirteenth-century" book she was reading, and avidly underlining, at the time was *Art and Scholasticism,* by Jacques Maritain, a French Thomist, who was teaching at Princeton and helping to make the thought of Thomas Aquinas relevant in forties America. Its eighth chapter, "Christian Art," was a thunderclap to O'Connor; she drew line markings next to the passage "Do not make the absurd attempt to sever in yourself the artist and the Christian."

Maisel's crusade worked, and on July 26, a mere three days before Flannery's departure, Mrs. Ames sent a note inviting her to return: "Then you may count on staying, definitely, to the end of the year: and I shall do my best for you to remain well after that date." In a note of thanks, Flannery claimed, "I have worked with much peace here." Her invitation was a coup, treated as a loud secret, in keeping with the intrigue around most of Ames's decisions. "Dear Flannery is leaving tomorrow, but is coming back in September to stay all winter (this is a secret from the rest of the guests)," Clifford Wright confided in his diary. Soon after her return to Milledgeville, Flannery wrote "Dear Elizabeth," that "were it not for my mother, I could easily resolve not to see Georgia again."

Her news of an open-ended stay at the artists' colony, though, was greeted with far less enthusiasm by Regina, irritated that her daughter would give up a practical Iowa teaching fellowship.

Still, Flannery pushed ahead, writing Paul Engle a postcard suggesting he transfer her grant to Clyde McLeod, while including an inside joke about Haze's casketlike upper berth in "The Train": "I sleep in my coffin beginning every evening at 7:30." The biggest excitement on her visit home was an August 12 rally of 350 Klan members on the steps of the Milledgeville Court House, which she reported, dryly, to Ames: "It's too hot to burn a fiery cross, so they bring a portable one made with red electric light bulbs." Likewise regaling Clifford Wright with tales of visiting her "ancient wealthy" cousin Katie, who told her to mind her manners more, she confided her tactic of not telling tales of Yaddo for fear of upsetting her relatives, who "think the height of Bohemianism is wearing slacks out of the house."

When Flannery returned to Yaddo on the early afternoon of September 16, she joined a reduced group of fifteen guests. Among them, until the end of the month, was Elizabeth Hardwick, a Kentucky-born *Partisan Review* writer in her early thirties, already a lively presence on the literary scene in Manhattan. "She was a brilliant creature, a wonderful conversationalist, who fainted once that summer on the tennis court," says Morton. When Mrs. Ames invited Hardwick back for January, she signed her note, with unusual warmth, "My love to you." Staying until mid-October was Malcolm Cowley, assistant editor of the *New Republic* from 1929 until 1944 and one of the Yaddo board members who approved O'Connor's application, with the comment "She seems to have talent." (The only naysayer on the board, the Smith College professor Newton Arvin, found her submitted stories "hard to like . . . unrelieved, gray, uncolored.")

As the main mansion was shut for the winter months, Flannery was put up, for "the small season," in a modest bedroom, and separate work studio, on the first floor of West House, where Mrs. Trask had spent her final years, until her death in 1922. A miniature version of the mansion, with an attached stone tower, the whimsical wooden farmhouse had its own Victorian parlor with chandeliers, marble mantelpiece, shelves lined with cracked library sets, and a grand piano. Flannery loved the quieter mood, as fall transformed Yaddo into what the critic Alfred Kazin, author of the highly successful *On Native Grounds* and among a half-dozen visitors that winter, called "a thorny mysterious return to another century on the rim of the Adirondacks, a mixture of primeval woods and the genteel tradition." O'Connor assured Cecil Dawkins, "It is beautiful in the fall and winter, and most of the creepy characters take off at the end of summer."

Flannery felt herself on deadline at West House to finish a draft of her novel, to send to John Selby at Rinehart in hopes of an advance to cover a year of rewriting. Yet she was already bracing herself — and Elizabeth McKee — for rejection: "I cannot really believe they will want the finished thing." Laid out on the table before her were chapters in varying states of completion: the opener, "The Train"; a third chapter, "The Peeler," where Haze (now Motes) meets Enoch, as well as the fake blind man who begins to tap his way through her novel like the truly blind prophet Tiresias of *The Waste Land;* "Woman on the Stairs," then chapter four; and "The Heart of the Park," chapter nine. Though unsure about Selby, she was encouraged to learn that Philip Rahv, editor of *Partisan Review,* had decided to publish "The Heart of the Park" in the February issue.

Into Flannery's seclusion and her pile of plans, six days after her own arrival, walked Robert Lowell, assigned a West House bedroom and studio for the fall and winter, too. Crackling with the sudden literary fame that she had seen him manifesting in Iowa City, Lowell had a knack for stirring up controversy. He arrived fresh from the post of poetry consultant to the Library of Congress — and from a fight, eventually successful, with supporting votes from Eliot, Auden, and Tate, to award Ezra Pound the 1948 Bollingen Prize for his *Pisan Cantos*. Protests had come from leftist poets over Pound's wartime radio broadcasts for Mussolini. Indeed, one of Lowell's first letters from Yaddo was to Pound, under sanatorium arrest for treason at St. Elizabeths Hospital in Washington, DC, informing him that "Yaddo is a sort of St. Elizabeths without bars — regular hours, communal meals, grounds, big old buildings etc."

Except for Elizabeth Hardwick, whom he found charming and convinced to return in midwinter, Lowell could be sharp about the skeleton crew remaining. Clifford Wright was "pleasant," but with "a rather withering old-maidish torpor." The English professor J. Saunders Redding and the painter Charles Sebree were pegged as "an introverted and extroverted colored man," the painter James Harrison as "a boy of 23 who experiments with dope." He judged Malcolm Cowley likeable but boring. For his part, Cowley was stressed by the endless table talk about politics, both literary and national. Off-season dinners took place on the second floor of the Garage, and the charged topic, in the fall of 1948, was the Progressive Party candidacy of Henry Wallace for president, described by one guest as "the friend of Moscow." Asked whom he was voting for, Cowley, a radical Marxist during the thirties, cautiously replied, "There's not one of them I want to see elected." Then "Someone gave a nervous laugh," he recalled, "and conversation resumed."

Lowell's favorite was Flannery, who treated him at dinner to the surefire story of her backward-walking chicken that had delighted their mutual friend Robie Macauley. Lowell found her "acute and silent," and quickly became her champion, writing Caroline Gordon, who was teaching Creative Writing in the General Studies program at Columbia: "There's a girl here named

Flannery O'Connor, an admirer of yours, a Catholic and probably a good writer, who is looking for a teaching job. Is there anything at Columbia?" Gordon later told Sally Fitzgerald, of O'Connor's feelings for her new, larger-than-life friend, "She fell for him; she admitted it to me." Arriving back in January, Edward Maisel opined theatrically, "I lost her to Robert Lowell." Whether or not her ardor was romantic remained a well-kept secret. Giroux surmised, "She wasn't in love with him; she was *impressed* by him." Yet she did write Betty Hester eight years later, "I feel almost too much about him to be able to get to the heart of it. . . . He is one of the people I love."

Lowell's feelings for Flannery were not romantic, but they were full of excitement for her Roman Catholicism and her rare brand of Southern literary talent: "I think one of the best to be when she is a little older," he promised the poet Elizabeth Bishop. "Very moral (in your sense) and witty." Of strong-jawed New England Puritan stock, Lowell had converted to Catholicism during his marriage to his first wife, Jean Stafford, partly from reading Jacques Maritain; when he left the marriage, he left the Church. As O'Connor later put it, "I watched him that winter come back into the Church. I had nothing to do with it but of course it was a great joy to me." Writing by day of a "Christ-haunted" character, she confronted one at dinner each night. He, in turn, liked the glamour of canonizing a new saint. As late as 1953, Caroline Gordon wrote to friends, "Cal Lowell says she is a saint, but then he is given to extravagance."

Lowell was extremely tender, and full of elegy and exactitude, when he later wrote Elizabeth Bishop, on hearing of Flannery's death. Their Yaddo autumn had been a sort of parenthesis in both their lives, as she worked on her novel, and he on his long narrative poem *The Mills of the Kavanaughs:*

> *It seems such a short time ago that I met her at Yaddo, 23 or 24,*
> *always in a blue jean suit, working on the last chapters of* Wise

Blood, *suffering from undiagnosed pains, a face formless at times, then, very strong and young and right. She had already really mastered and found her themes and style, knew she wouldn't marry, would be Southern, shocking and disciplined. In a blunt, disdainful yet somehow very unpretentious and modest way, I think she knew how good she was.*

At the time, of course, his tone about her was far more gossipy, and bemused, as he shared news, usually with Robie Macauley, as if she were a little sister passed from the care of one brother to another: "She's run through the local library, put out crumbs for birds, bought a sternostove — I think she's planning a sort of half-hibernation to never leave a small dark cheerless room where she'll subsist on vitamin B soup capsules, and Dr. E. Flanders Dunbars psycho-somatic summa. But we've learned her ping-pong."

The library Flannery read her way through was an ugly brick building at Skidmore, the small liberal arts college housed mostly in antiquated Edwardian and Victorian buildings in downtown Saratoga Springs. Especially absorbing to her was the dark fiction of the eminent French Catholic novelist François Mauriac, which addressed the irreconcilability of sexual passion with the world of pure spirit. Wright complained that he heard so much about Mauriac at dinner that he finally gave in and made a painting titled *The Desert of Love,* after Mauriac's novel about the romantic triangle of a father, his son, and a fatally attractive woman. Of Mauriac's books, at least fifteen of which she came to own, Flannery was especially drawn to the novel *Destines,* published in English under the title *Lines of Life,* about a middle-aged widow infatuated with a troubled, dissolute young man. As she later wrote of the novel, to Betty Hester, "I read it about ten years ago in the Skidmore College Library and remember nothing about it but the last sentence, which in that translation was: 'And (she) was again one of those corpses floating down the stream of life.'"

Flannery received from the lost, often amoral characters of this living Catholic novelist the same thrilling permission she received theologically from the Thomist definition of art, in Maritain's *Art and Scholasticism,* as a "habit of the practical intellect," rather than a speculative or moral activity — the territory of theologians and saints. As Maritain concluded, "The pure artist considered in the abstract as such, is something completely unmoral." The job of the Christian writer, understood in this "thirteenth century" way, was pure devotion to craft, to telling strong stories, even if they involved atheists, hoodlums, or prostitutes — the same craft lifted up by O'Connor's New Critic teachers. As she would later spell out this enabling notion in folksier language to Betty Hester, "you don't have to be good to write well. Much to be thankful for."

As being at Yaddo and having a Guggenheim fellowship (of about twenty-five hundred dollars) were nearly synonymous in the late 1940s, Flannery decided that fall to apply. Clifford Wright, himself applying, described Lowell, when he arrived, as "Guggenheiming it." Hardwick, likewise "enGuggenheimed," had received hers in June. Flannery did find herself in the fortunate spot, shared by Lowell but few others, of having crossed a Mason-Dixon Line of literary politics — published by the *Sewanee* and *Kenyon Reviews,* associated with conservative, even reactionary Southern writers, as well as by *Partisan Review,* the provenance of left-leaning, often Jewish, New York intellectuals. Her own recommenders were George Davis; Philip Rahv; Paul Engle; Robert Penn Warren; Theodore Amussen, a Rinehart editor, who had moved to Harcourt Brace; and Robert Lowell, providing the inside information that she wrote "sentence by sentence, at snail's pace."

In December, pleading economic worries, Flannery made the bold decision to spend Christmas away from home. Instead, she hunkered down with the two remaining Yaddo guests, Lowell and Wright. By then, their social rhythm was comfortable. After Thanksgiving, Ezra Pound's son, Omar Shakespeare Pound, visited, and Lowell reported, in a letter to T. S. Eliot, "I introduced him to our Yaddo child, Miss Flannery O'Connor. Weird scenes of Omar trying to help her into her muskrat coat — a new experience for both." When Lowell recalled her tripping up stairs with a bottle of gin, she corrected him: "It was not gin but rum (unopened) and the steps were slick." Wright appreciated Flannery's "high moral tone," and found "ingeniously funny and ominous" the zoo chapter from her novel, which she told him was titled *The Great Spotted Bird*. He found the title "perfect," summing up the "grotesque" book as "short . . . the main character is a boy."

The Christmas holidays were a bit milder than Lowell might have liked. "My suggestion that we have bottled egg-nog for Christmas breakfast fell rather flat," he complained of his housemates, who were "not celebrating types." But he consoled himself on Christmas Eve by reading *Pride and Prejudice* "aloud to the two Yaddonians," and listening to the "Gloria" from three masses — Bach's B Minor, a Palestrina, and a Gregorian. Remembering her last holiday on the train from Iowa City with Jean Williams, Flannery wrote her friend:

> It would be nice to meet you again this year on the train. However, I am glad I won't be fooling around with any trains this Christmas. I am not budging from this place. The Yuletide Poorhouse fare is very decent. The cook will be off and we three will be sent to the New Worden Hotel for dinner. We have a Christmas tree but will not hang up any stockings. We three are myself, Robert Lowell, and a stray painter.

Indeed the next day, after a week of light snowfall, the three were driven into town for a holiday dinner at the only year-round hotel, courtesy of the Yaddo Corporation.

Soon after the New Year, Flannery mailed her agent a freshly typed manuscript of the first nine chapters of her novel, adding up to 108 pages, with a note: "please show John Selby and let us be on with financial thoughts." But her steady misgivings came true when the editor in chief responded with his impression that the work needed revision, allowing that its author was "a pretty straight shooter." McKee forwarded Selby's letter, which Flannery promptly showed to Lowell. She eventually passed on the poet's comments to Paul Engle, now caught in the middle: "He too thought that the faults Rinehart mentioned were not the faults of the novel (some of which he had previously pointed out to me)." Engle pleaded, "Send me, please, like a good girl (and whether that designation fits or not) some sense of what the rest of the novel will be about."

Hardly resistant to rewriting — indeed Selby wondered about "some aspects of the book that have been obscured by your habit of rewriting over and over again" — Flannery was more annoyed by his tone. She asked McKee, "Please tell me what is under this Sears Roebuck Straight Shooter approach," and she resented the jauntiness of a reply "addressed to a slightly dim-witted Camp-fire Girl." Emboldened by having Lowell on her side, she wrote back to Selby of her choice to take the high road of art, responding to his sense of a limiting "kind of aloneness in the book, as if you were writing out of the small world of your own experience": "I am not writing a conventional novel, and I think that the quality of the novel I write will derive precisely from the peculiarity or aloneness, if you will, of the experience I write from." Because Selby was disturbed by what he termed "the hardening of the arteries of her coopera-tive sense . . . most unbecoming to a writer so young," a decision was made that she come down from Yaddo for a late-February meeting, to clear the air, or part ways.

In the meantime, Yaddo was going through one of its seasonal reshufflings, the deck held entirely in the hands of Mrs. Ames, who informed Flannery that she was free to stay until the end of March, and perhaps beyond — as long as she swept the hallway carpet, each Sunday. Added to the mix, in January, were James Ross, brother-in-law of the Southern novelist Peter Taylor; Edward Maisel, *redux;* and Alfred Kazin, staying with Mrs. Ames at Pine Garde, her English Tudor cottage on the grounds. Kazin's first impression was that Flannery "seemed to be attending Robert Lowell with rapture." But he quickly became more interested in her writing, as he read pages from her novel, tipping off Giroux at Harcourt Brace, for whom he was working as a scout. "No fiction writer after the war seemed to me so *deep,* so severely perfect as Flannery," wrote Kazin. "She would be our classic: I had known that from the day I discovered her stories."

The arriving guest having the most catalytic social effect was "dimpled agreeable" Elizabeth Hardwick, returning on January 5, as she excited Lowell's already teeming passions. If their quickly escalating romance bothered Flannery, she did not let on. Indeed for the young lady who wished to remain on the prepubescent side of twelve, and with Lowell who saw her as "our Yaddo child," the development may have been tolerable, even comfortable. "Lizzie Hardwick and Cal Lowell have become about as close as two people can get," Wright reported. "I have not infra-red photo phlashes to prove it. Flannery is playing it cool." As Kazin, who engaged in heated nightly political debates with Lowell, crankily recalled, "Lowell and Elizabeth Hardwick were a brilliant couple, but Lowell was just a little too dazzling at the moment."

Hardwick, too, tended to view Flannery as even younger than her twenty-three years, about seven years younger than she and Lowell: "Most of all she was like some quiet, puritanical convent girl from the harsh provinces of Canada." Remembered Hardwick, "She was a plain sort of young, unmarried girl, a little bit sickly. And she had a very small-town Southern accent . . . whiney. She whined. She was amusing. She was so gifted, immensely gifted. But the first thing I saw of hers after we met her at Yaddo, I'm sort of ashamed to admit, maybe I saw pages of *Wise Blood,* and I thought, 'What on earth is this?' It was just so plain, so reduced, after reading really startling things like *Ulysses*. Of course now I think it's wonderful, I later did. But at first it didn't hit me. . . . I think she and Cal were quite friendly. He was very interested in her."

By early February, political controversies overtook aesthetic distinctions, or became intensely enfolded in them. Engagé Marxists of the thirties, many of whom found a home at Yaddo, had mostly, by 1949, evolved into non-Stalinist leftists, disillusioned by the Trotsky trials and the Nazi-Soviet Non-Aggression Pact of 1939 — just as *Partisan Review* outgrew its original thirties stance as official magazine of the Communist-dominated John Reed Club. Yet more conservative Southern Agrarians, and modernists such as Eliot and Lowell — with sympathies for religion, and a visceral response to Communist atheism — still distrusted these reformed "fellow travelers." Such complex partisan issues were being played out in a nation just a year away from Senator Joseph McCarthy's speech denouncing Communist infiltration in the State Department and already engaged in "red-baiting," and a Cold War with the Soviet Union.

During the fall, Lowell's foil for dinnertime political rows had been Charles Wagner, who was writing a "pious" history of Harvard. "I wouldn't give the life of one American soldier he betrayed for Pound's," Wagner snarled one evening. To which Lowell shot back, "But no one lost his life because of Pound." Wagner's adversarial role was taken up by Kazin, who complained in his memoir *New York Jew:* "It was a gloomy time for me; listening to Lowell at his most blissfully high orating against Communist influences at Yaddo and boasting of the veneration in which he was held by those illiberal great men Ezra Pound and George Santayana, made me feel worse." Wright reported Lowell's intent to turn Yaddo by the next summer into a haven for "the agrarian–little magazine entente." Pleading writer's block, and marital problems, Kazin fled back to Manhattan.

The spark finally set to all this Yaddo tinder was a front-page story in the *New York Times* on February 11, 1949: "Tokyo War Secrets Stolen by Soviet Spy Ring in 1941." Including an accusation by General Douglas MacArthur, the article reported evidence from the army that Agnes Smedley had run a Soviet spy ring out of Shanghai. A friend of Mrs. Ames, with the special dispensation of being a Yaddo guest from 1943 until March 1948, Smedley was in the midst of writing a biography of Marshal Zhu De, founder of the Chinese Red Army. "She idolized Mao Tse-tung," remembers Jim Shannon. "She walked around the place like a man, like a soldier marching through the paddy fields." Eight days later, the army disowned its report. Opposite a February 20 notice of Smedley thanking the army for clearing her name ran the announcement: "Pound, In Mental Clinic, Wins Prize for Poetry Penned in Treason Cell."

Yet by the date of the retraction, paranoia had been heightened by the appearance, on February 14, of two FBI agents, questioning Hardwick and Maisel about Communist sympathies at Yaddo, tipped off by Mrs. Ames's secretary. The first casualty of this "Red Scare" was Clifford Wright — sent packing as Mrs. Ames had the "fantastic idea" that he was the FBI informant. At Saturday dinner, with Flannery and Elizabeth Hardwick, Mrs. Ames defended Smedley as "an old-fashioned Jeffersonian Democrat." Lowell, incensed by Ames's control of guests' stays and by the liberal left in general, pushed for a meeting with the board of directors to demand her ouster. Shortly before the meeting, James Ross took off. "I had refused to join with the other guests in bringing charges against you," he wrote Ames, "and had expressed my opinions rather violently one night at dinner."

A bizarre inquisition, orchestrated by Lowell, and attended by eight of the directors of Yaddo, as well as the four remaining guests, took place in the Garage on Saturday morning, February 26. "I shall compare the institution to a body and the present director to a diseased organ," Lowell began, with an extended simile, "chronically poisoning the whole system." Hardwick spoke of a summer party where "Molotov cocktails" were served, and jokes made, "Is it too pink for you?" In an *Et tu, Brute?* moment, Mrs. Ames confronted her accusers: "They frequently came to my house for music or cocktails, a harmonious life, with now and then little affectionate notes . . . then all of this changed with the morning of Tuesday." The director Everett Stonequist, a Skidmore sociologist, mused aloud that the FBI investigation released "some of the excitement, hysteria, perhaps, which seems to be part of the post-war period in American history."

Its least likely participant was Flannery O'Connor, ever silent, and keeping a canny distance. Yet the combination of Lowell's mesmerizing personality, some annoyance with Mrs. Ames's autocratic style, and a simple view of Communism as evil, all led her to take part. Her cross-examination by Lowell was the least expansive of the testimonies, just a single page of a sixty-page transcript. Describing her relations with Mrs. Ames over the summer as "very pleasant. I saw little of her," she said matters had devolved to being "precariously cordial": "I felt more like Mrs. Ames' personal guest than a guest of the Corporation." To Lowell's leading question, "Has Mrs. Ames said anything contrary to her official position?" she replied sharply, "Mrs. Ames said that Agnes Smedley had been living in fear for a long time . . . that seemed different to me. It did not seem to fit in with an impression of her as an old-fashioned Jeffersonian democrat."

In her testimony on Ames's arbitrary rule, Flannery told prosecuting Lowell, "I asked to stay through July, largely through economic pressure, which has not improved, but I am leaving next Tuesday." The last four guests did hastily depart Yaddo within a day or two. Of the "little mix-up," Hardwick claimed, "It wasn't as much as it seems now. Flannery wasn't so much in that." All was forgiven enough for Elizabeth Ames to invite O'Connor to return, in 1958; she declined, writing back of her peacocks, "When I look at my birds I often think of Yaddo and how well a few of them would go with the place." Yet at the time much *was* being made, and aftershocks followed the group to New York City, where a board meeting was scheduled the next month to decide the issue. Having been present at the feverish Garage meeting, Malcolm Cowley reported back to a friend: "The guests departed, vowing to blacken the name of Yaddo in all literary circles and call a mass meeting of protest. . . . I left too, feeling as if I had been at a meeting of the Russian Writers' Union during a big purge. Elizabeth went to a nursing home. Her secretary resigned. Yaddo was left like a stricken battlefield."

※

THE SELF-IMPOSED EXILE of the group from Yaddo threw Flannery into confusion, vexing for a young woman whose writing depended so much on cloistered regularity. "We have been very upset at Yaddo lately and all the guests are leaving in a group Tuesday — the revolution," she reported to Elizabeth McKee on February 24. "All this is very disrupting to the book and has changed my plans entirely." Arriving in Manhattan during a winter storm that covered everything in snow and ice, with gusting winds, she was nearly as disturbed as she had been during her abrupt girlhood removal to Atlanta. As Enoch cries to Haze, of Taulkinham, in "The Peeler," published nine months later in *Partisan Review,* "There's too many people on the street . . . all they want to do is knock you down. I ain't never been to such a unfriendly place before."

Flannery was oblivious to most of the changes that were making

New York City the "first city" of the postwar world: its population, during the administration of Mayor William O'Dwyer, approaching the 1950 census figure of 7,891,957; construction beginning along the East River of the United Nations Secretariat, the world's first glass-walled skyscraper; African American sharecroppers migrating from Southern cotton farms to Harlem; Puerto Ricans arriving on daily flights from San Juan. Yet she was painfully aware of the numbers on the streets, the crowds captured in the canonic images of the *Life* photographer Andreas Feininger, using a telephoto lens, to compress lunch-hour workers on Fifth Avenue into even more of a cliché of a "rat race" in a "skyscraper jungle." As she told Betty Boyd of the anomie she was witnessing daily, "There is one advantage in it because although you see several people you wish you didn't know, you see thousands you're glad you don't know."

Her first stop was Elizabeth Hardwick's apartment in Devonshire House, a 1920s building in the "Hispano-Mooresque" style at 28 East 10th Street, where she stayed briefly, while Lowell checked into the Hotel Earle, off Washington Square. Always retaining fond feelings for Hardwick, she later wrote of the "very nice girl" to Betty Hester, "I think Elizabeth is a lot better writer than she gets credit for being. She is a long tall girl, one of eleven children, from Kentucky. . . . I used to go up to Elizabeth's apartment to see her when I lived in New York and the elevator man always thought I was her sister. There was a slight resemblance." Hardwick felt the mistake had to do with their accents, adding, "But mine was upper South, hers was very deep, small-town Southern."

She moved next into a two-dollar-a-day room that smelled like "an unopened Bible," in Tatum House, a "horrible" YWCA residence, at 138 East 38th Street, on Lexington Avenue. The building provided breakfast, and she took most of her other meals at a nearby "very good co-op cafeteria," on 41st Street between Madison and Park: "The only place in New York that I could afford to

eat downtown where I didn't feel I was going home with pyoria."
She was hardly alone her first week in the city, though, as Lowell
introduced her around. Including her in visits to friends, he rallied
support for his Yaddo crusade, while announcing his "reconver-
sion" to Catholicism, having attended mass, with Flannery, for the
first time in over a year, before leaving Saratoga Springs. Both issues meshed in his psyche into an apocalyptic struggle of good versus evil.

Yet Lowell was quite intuitive in his introductions, helping
Flannery make contacts crucial for her life and career. He brought
her to meet Robert and Sally Fitzgerald, living with their two
young children in a small, two-room apartment on York Avenue. A
poet (*A Wreath of the Sea*), critic, and translator of Euripides and
Sophocles, Robert Fitzgerald, nearly forty, had been brought up
Irish Catholic in Springfield, Illinois, left the Church — O'Connor
liked to say, "to become an intellectual" — and then returned to the
fold, resulting in an annulled first marriage. Sally, thirty-two, the
daughter of a Texas judge, was an aspiring painter who studied at
the Art Students League in New York, served as an officer in naval
intelligence during the war, and had become an intense convert
to Catholicism, briefly considering entering a convent before her
marriage.

Responding to their doorbell on the gray, wintry afternoon, the
Fitzgeralds discovered, standing in the hallway, their disheveled
poet friend, "shooting sparks in every direction," accompanied by
Flannery, slender, sandy-haired, with a straightforward blue-eyed
gaze and shy half smile, dressed in corduroy slacks and a navy pea
jacket. She bore out Lowell's account of Yaddo as she sat facing the
windows reflecting light off the East River. "She did this with some
difficulty, frowning and struggling softly in her drawl to put whatever it was exactly the way it was," remembered Robert Fitzgerald. "We saw a shy Georgia girl, her face heart-shaped and pale
and glum, with fine eyes that could stop frowning and open bril-

liantly upon everything. We had not then read her first stories, but we knew that Mr. Ransom had said of them that they were *written.*"

She made a strong impression on Sally, too, who grew curious to discover "how this affable, smiling girl from Georgia who didn't have much to say, wrote, how she went about it." Finding a copy of "The Train," she quickly became riveted by its intense tale of Hazel Wickers, "shapes black-spinning past him," hurtling toward Taulkinham: "I was unprepared for it, for the force, the sheer power of the writing. When I finished the story my hair was standing on end." By the time Flannery left that afternoon, a sort of familial triangle was already forming, with Robert as the paterfamilias, a font of literary knowledge, and Sally, an older-sister figure. "Mrs. Fitzgerald is 5 feet 2 inches tall and weighs at most 92 pounds except when she is pregnant which is most of the time," Flannery nailed her in one of her caricatures. "Her face is extremely angular; in fact, horse-like, though attractive, and she does have the pulled-back hair and the bun."

Equally profound was Lowell's next introduction, Robert Giroux at Harcourt Brace. Still a junior editor, with an alert, open face, Giroux had already published the early novels of Jean Stafford; the poetry of Lowell and T. S. Eliot; Hannah Arendt's first book, *The Origins of Totalitarianism.* When Lowell brought Flannery by the firm's modern offices, at Madison Avenue and 46th Street, Giroux was instantly convinced of his "unusual" visitor's literary future. "She was very quiet," said Giroux. "She was very chary of words. Lowell of course was vocal and full of interesting phrases, a great talker. But she had electric eyes, very penetrating. She could see right through you, so to speak. I was a young publisher, interested in acquiring writers. I thought, 'This woman is so committed, as a writer, she'll do whatever she's made up her mind to do.'" But he knew that she was signed to Rinehart and felt sure she would not go back on an agreement.

"At first, her speech was difficult to understand because she had a deep Georgia accent," remembered Giroux. "I had to concentrate. I was amazed when Paul Engle told me he couldn't understand a word she said. I could hear the words. It was the rhythm and accent that required attention. It occurs to me that Robert Lowell had a Southern accent, too. He was born in Boston. But he went to Kenyon, and Ransom had a definite, very nice, genteel Southern accent, and he sort of picked up on that." Flannery's only request was for a copy of Giroux's surprise bestseller that season, *The Seven Storey Mountain,* a memoir, by his Columbia classmate Thomas Merton, of abandoning the literary life of Manhattan to become a Trappist monk in Kentucky. When she left his office that day, book in hand, she felt the same sympathetic tug of interest in the young editor, educated in a Jesuit high school, whom she would later call "my good editor," that he felt for her.

As the first week in March, and Lent, progressed, so did Lowell's religious fervor, and Flannery's special role in his vivid imaginings. His was to be a poet's conversion more dramatic than even Merton's. On March 4, he phoned Robert Fitzgerald to inform him that on Ash Wednesday, March 2, his thirty-second birthday, he had "received the shock of the eternal word." He went on, "Today is the day of Flannery O'Connor, whose patron saint is St. Therese of Lisieux." At Lowell's direction, Fitzgerald got out a pad and pencil and took notes, writing, "He filled his bathtub with cold water and went in first on his hands and knees, then arching on his back, and prayed thus to Therese of Lisieux in gasps. . . . He went to the Guild Bookshop to get Flannery a book on St. Therese of Lisieux but instead before he knew it bought a book on a Canadian girl who was many times stigmatized." Lowell then left town on a weeklong meditative retreat for absolution and counsel at his own chosen Trappist monastery in Rhode Island.

Word of these visions, and of Lowell's insistence on canonizing Flannery, began to circulate at Manhattan cocktail parties. When

Betty Hester heard such tales, independently, during the sixties, and asked her friend about them, she obviously hit a tender topic. "Let me right now correct, stash & obliterate this revolting story about Lowell introducing me as a saint," O'Connor fired back, about the part played by her and Robert Fitzgerald. "At the time it was happening, poor Cal was about three steps from the asylum. He had the delusion that he had been called on some kind of mission of purification and he was canonizing everybody that had anything do with his situation then. I was very close to him and so was Robert. I was too inexperienced to know he was mad, I just thought that was the way poets acted. Even Robert didn't know it, or at least didn't know how near collapse he was. In a couple of weeks he was safely locked up."

When Lowell returned to New York on March 16, he appeared much calmer, as he awaited the Yaddo board meeting scheduled for March 26, following the inconclusive Garage meeting a month earlier. During that week, he and Hardwick brought Flannery along to dinner at the midtown apartment of the novelist Mary McCarthy and her husband, Bowden Broadwater. In O'Connor's words, McCarthy, a lapsed Catholic, prominent in the *Paris Review* circle, was "a Big Intellectual." Arriving at the apartment at eight, the group engaged in fast-moving dinner conversation, with Flannery never adding a word — it was "like having a dog present," Flannery said, "who had been trained to say a few words but overcome with inadequacy had forgotten them." At a defining moment toward one o'clock in the morning, she did finally speak. As O'Connor told the story, "Mrs. Broadwater said when she was a child and received the host, she thought of it as the Holy Ghost, he being the 'most potable' person of the Trinity; now she thought of it as a symbol and implied that it was a pretty good one. I then said, in a very shaky voice, 'Well, if it's a symbol, to hell with it.'" Of what became a well-known response, Hardwick, McCarthy's close friend, said defensively, "It did become famous, in Flannery's favor, so to speak. But I don't consider it a proper answer. . . . Considering how intelligent she was, she was more pious than any other Catholic I've ever known."

Flannery was not present for the denouement of Lowell's *mise-en-scène,* his temporary downfall. For to his great disillusionment, a counterpetition in support of Mrs. Ames was signed by fifty-one writers, including Kazin, Porter, McCullers, Delmore Schwartz, and Cheever, accusing him of "a frame of mind that represents a grave danger both to civil liberties and to the freedom necessary for the arts." At their March 26 meeting, the Yaddo board dismissed Lowell's charges. Stung by the rebuke, and following an appearance at a Cultural and Scientific Conference for World Peace at the Waldorf-Astoria, where he introduced himself as "a poet and a Roman Catholic," Lowell flew off to Chicago to visit Allen Tate and Caroline Gordon. There his behavior grew extreme enough for him to finally be hospitalized at Baldpate, in Massachusetts. Of what he felt was their enabling of Lowell's delusions, Tate chidingly wrote to Hardwick, "But you are a woman and Miss O'Connor is a woman, and neither of you had the experience or knowledge to evaluate the situation in public terms."

A few days before the Yaddo board meeting, Flannery was already on the train home, where she celebrated her twenty-fourth birthday and stayed through Easter. When Giroux had handed her a copy of *The Seven Storey Mountain,* he did so for her "to take with her to her mother's house in Milledgeville." She read there of the importance to Merton of Maritain's *Art and Scholasticism* in reconciling his identities as novelist and contemplative, and of a religious conversion played out in apartments and Catholic sanctuaries in Manhattan. In Georgia, arguments were stacked against her living in Manhattan. Mrs. O'Connor worried about her daughter alone in the most notorious of northern cities. Money was tight; as Flannery wrote Paul Engle, "I didn't get any Guggenheim." Yet her Yaddo friend Elizabeth Fenwick had helped her secure a rented room in the uptown apartment of an acquaintance, and Flannery had every intention of returning.

During her month down South, she continued to bristle from the Yaddo incident. Even Lowell would later joke of the time they "blew our lids there" and "tried to blow the roof off." Her upset at the time, though, was nearly as charged as his. Her GSCW history professor Helen Greene remembers Flannery agitatedly stopping by her office in Parks Hall during this spring visit, asking reproachfully, "Why didn't you teach me about Communism?": "I told her that her major in social studies had included a great deal on the subject and that she had probably made an A on it, or surely a B+. She was really shocked to find that many of those gifted fellows appointed to do creative work at Yaddo were unwilling or unable to believe in God. Their main reason, perhaps, was the appeal of Communism — whatever it meant to them. She had no patience with such attitudes."

In a letter to Betty Boyd that summer, Flannery was every bit as shrill, and apocalyptic, in her damning of Communism, as Lowell, the Catholic Church, or even Billy Graham, who preached, in a career-making, eight-week mission in Los Angeles in 1949, "On one side we see communism . . . against God, against Christ, against the Bible."

She vehemently reported on the Yaddo incident to her college friend, "Our action gained a good deal of publicity — not through us — and we have been assailed as people who want to destroy civil liberties etc etc. . . . As to the devil, I not only believe he is but believe he has a family . . . Yaddo has confirmed this in me."

When she did return to Manhattan, Flannery survived a muggy summer, marked by heat waves "much worse than Georgia." She lived for four months in a furnished room on the twelfth floor of the Manchester, a pre–World War I brick apartment building, at 255 West 108th Street and Broadway, in Morningside Heights, a neighborhood teeming with Columbia students, Jewish families, and Puerto Rican immigrants. Replicating her Iowa City routine, she began each morning by walking around the block to pray at the white marble Church of the Ascension, a mostly Irish parish, near Amsterdam Avenue. "I liked riding the subways and busses and all," she reminisced, "and there was a church on 107th and I got to Mass every day and was very much alone and liked it." She told Betty Boyd, "All the women over sixty-five in New York are wearing sun back dresses."

But she spent most of her time in her room, writing; any progress achieved by training her attention on what she called, near the end of *Wise Blood,* "the pin point of light but so far away that she could not hold it steady in her mind." Claiming that her own knowledge of the complicated layout of the city was limited to "uptown" and "downtown," she later admitted to a friend, "I didn't see much of the city when I stayed in New York. . . . I didn't go to a single play or even to the Frick Museum. I went to the natural history museum but didn't do anything the least cultural. The public library was much too much for me. I did well to get out and get a meal or two a day. I finally ended up eating at the Columbia University student cafeteria. I looked enough like a student to get by with it, and it was one of the few places I suspected the food of being clean."

A rare visitor to her small, comfortably arranged apartment was Lyman Fulton, a Tennessee native, who had begun a residency at New York Hospital–Cornell Medical Center on July 1. A friend of Mary Virginia Harrison, Fulton visited three or four times in the company of Flannery's first cousin Louise Florencourt, and he found her "not overly talkative. I decided she was reclusive, probably a bookworm. . . . I had the impression she spent most of her time at the apartment." A running joke between them was the meal she served her guests of "goat's milk cheese and faucet water." The longest conversation between the two Southerners concerned Truman Capote's *Other Voices, Other Rooms,* published with much controversy the year before. Added into the scandal, still being discussed at Yaddo, was Capote's summer affair with Newton Arvin. "I do remember that she had a definitely negative opinion of Truman Capote," said Fulton.

Her greatest consolation, outside the featureless room where she wrote, was two trips to the medieval collection of the Metropolitan Museum of Art at the Cloisters, the assemblage of monastic chapter house and chapels, imported from France and Spain, and reconstructed stone by stone just a decade before, on a dramatic crest overlooking the Hudson River, at Fort Tryon Park. The Cloisters was a must-see destination for postwar visitors, its energetic curator, James J. Rorimer, excelling at public relations. Shortly after, as Flannery returned from Georgia, the *New York Times* ran a double-column photograph of a thirteenth-century sculpture of the Virgin from a choir screen of the Cathedral of Strasbourg as "An Easter Attraction at the Cloisters"; in a *New Yorker* "Talk of the Town" piece, James Rorimer, "a pipe smoker, in the best detective and curatorial tradition," escorted a reporter through the popular Nine Heroes Tapestries exhibition.

But Flannery's favorite was not the striking statue of the Strasbourg Virgin, celebrated in the daily press. In the soft light of the Early Gothic Hall, illuminated by three thirteenth-century windows carved by stonecutters in Normandy, she was drawn instead to a smaller, four-foot-high statue of Virgin and Child, with both parties "laughing; not smiling, laughing." She imagined that "the Child had a face very much like the face of a friend of mine, Robert Fitzgerald." What chiefly pixilated her in the sculpture was its artistic sensibility. As she wrote to a friend, "Back then their religious sense was not cut off from their artistic sense." Embodying a profound spirituality that could accommodate humor, even outright laughter — a recipe she was working toward in her own novel — the statue, which "wasn't colored," was living proof of Maritain's writings on the breadth of expression possible in religious art.

Another entertainment that fascinated her, in August, was of a different sort altogether, satisfying her countervailing taste for the more ludicrous products of popular culture. She either saw or closely followed reports of the premiere of *Mighty Joe Young,* a film that opened to wide success at the Criterion Theatre in Times Square. Its publicity campaign of a man in an ape suit greeting customers in front of the theater made the August 8 edition of *Newsweek,* with a photograph of the ape-man dangling from a line stretched across Broadway. Flannery lifted features of its simian hero, and its publicity gimmick, for her novel; when Enoch, the embodiment of all things goofy, slips into a cinema to watch a film "about a baboon named Lonnie who rescued attractive children from a burning orphanage," he was actually engrossed in the finale of *Mighty Joe Young.*

Lyman Fulton rightly enough concluded, "I don't think New York City was Flannery's cup of tea." At her most excoriating, she complained to Betty Boyd of its thick "culture fog" and even its "fornication." More immediately, she was bothered by its hay fever season, accompanied by a high pollen count that "comes in there August 15 and don't leave for three weeks." So she quickly accepted an offer from the Fitzgeralds to move, as a "paying guest," to a large country house they had bought, in July, in the woods of Connecticut. The plan had been put forth by Robert Lowell — now out of Baldpate and married to Elizabeth Hardwick, as of July 28. Anticipating more children, the Fitzgeralds were feeling constricted by New York apartment life; the agreement was that O'Connor would pay sixty-five dollars a month, and babysit one hour each afternoon.

※

"Me and Enoch are living in the woods in Connecticut with the Robert Fitzgeralds," Flannery proudly reported her change of address to Robie Macauley. Her new rural retreat, "miles from anything you could name," was actually a stone and timber house on a wooded hilltop in Redding, Connecticut, a two-hour drive from the city. Located on Seventy Acre Road — a dirt road at the time — and set back in a wilderness of laurel and second-growth oak, the rambling structure included an attached garage with an upstairs bedroom and bath. In this modest garret, with a gable roof and three casement windows overlooking a boulder-strewn field, Flannery set up her typewriter. To make the room more welcoming, the Fitzgeralds rolled a coat or two of paint on the beaverboard walls, and painted the Sears, Roebuck dresser a bright sky blue. When the nights turned frosty, their clever boarder pushed pins into the walls, to "hurt their feet," she said of the field mice pattering between the timbering.

Each morning, Flannery and one of the Fitzgeralds drove to low mass at Sacred Heart Church, in Georgetown, four miles away, while the other parent stayed behind. Upon returning, Flannery boiled herself a breakfast egg and lingered at the kitchen table, with highchairs pushed up to it, until Robert left for his commute to Sarah Lawrence College in Westchester. Flannery then disappeared up the interior back stairs, to put in four hours of writing — "which I find is the maximum," she wrote Betty Boyd. At noon, dressed in a sweater, blue jeans, and loafers, "looking slender and almost tall," she reappeared with a daily letter to her mother, posted by walking a half mile to the mailbox at the bottom of the hill. At least one hour every afternoon was spent in her room babysitting for Ughetta, the eldest girl. As Sally Fitzgerald recalled her style of child-rearing, "Flannery would lie on the bed and watch the child as she would play around the room. I remember once she told me that she listened to her howling . . . and finally, when she paused for breath, Flannery said, 'Your mom can't hear you over here.' The child waited, then walked over to the door and started howling out, which Flannery reported to us."

When Fitzgerald returned from teaching, and the children were tucked into bed, the three adults re-created some of the mood of Yaddo by mixing a pitcher of martinis, sharing a meal, gossiping — Mary McCarthy and Randall Jarrell taught at Sarah Lawrence, and were vital sources — and discussing books. The Fitzgeralds outdid even Flannery in the piety of their lengthy Benedictine grace, recited in Latin, as she ruefully recalled, "while the dinner got cold." They circulated among themselves volumes by Catholic writers — Lord Acton, John Henry Newman, a history of the Reformation by Father Philip Hughes. Flannery recommended Nathanael West's defiantly original novel *Miss Lonelyhearts,* as well as Faulkner's *As I Lay Dying,* its central image of a mother's coffin a fixation in the novel she was writing. "They were our movies, our concerts, and our theatre," wrote Robert Fitzgerald of these talks that often went on until midnight.

Yet not all of the conversation was so high-minded. Flannery learned that she could always get a rise by telling droll tales of Georgia and her family. Daily letters from her mother, who also mailed hand-sewn baby clothes, fruitcakes, and arcane recipes, provided a rich inventory. Flannery told, too, of affable Uncle Louis, who sent "gewgaws" from the King Hardware Company in Atlanta, where he was now working as a salesman. Because of the prevailing familial tone — O'Connor dubbed the Fitzgeralds "my adopted kin" — Robert was one of the only people she ever spoke with about her father's death; his father, too, had died when he was fifteen, and the loss had been equally devastating. "Perhaps this *ménage a trois* plus provided her with an easier and freer family life," Sally Fitzgerald surmised. Dinners wound up at the kitchen sink as Sally and Flannery chatted while sudsing and drying, and the "master of the house" busied himself elsewhere.

Meanwhile, upstairs, the pile of yellow second sheets on which Flannery was composing her novel was mounting. She was making progress, thinning out and pacing the opening. "Well I can't sustain that," she told Sally when her friend praised "The Train." "I have to tone it down." Haze Motes, in his "glaring blue" suit and "hat that an elderly country preacher would wear," was coming into focus as a slightly demented saint in the making, a shift in direction that Sally thought perhaps "due to criticism by Lowell." Yet Flannery proudly wrote Elizabeth McKee, "The novel is going well, almost fast." The biggest problem remained Rinehart. In October 1949, Giroux sent a provisional Harcourt contract. But Selby was refusing to let her off so easily, accusing her of being "unethical," the worst word he could have chosen. To right the "malicious statement," Flannery agreed to show Rinehart more pages, in March, she hoped for the last time.

Flannery was moving closer to achieving her goal of being "a writer on my own," residing, like so many young American authors at the time, in New York City, or one of the many small towns within a hundred-mile radius. If she was unaware of the solitude of her chosen path, news that fall of the wedding plans of two girlfriends reminded her. From each event, she kept a stiff distance. When Mary Virginia Harrison invited her to be a bridesmaid at her wedding, she invoked canon law forbidding Catholics to participate in "outside" religious services, even though the reception was being held at Andalusia. She sent Betty Boyd a congratulatory note on her engagement to James Love, with a tiny line drawing of three disheveled violets, and the telling admission, "Marriages are always a shock to me." According to Sally Fitzgerald, "She *did* husband her energies. She knew she had much work to do. And she knew that she had to do it alone."

In December, Flannery returned to Milledgeville for what was expected to be a routine holiday visit. Lowell and Hardwick kept her company as she awaited her train in New York City. "We spent an hour and a half in the station with Flannery," Lowell informed Robert Fitzgerald, "more or less on tip-toe because her train was

'reported' an hour late, which meant it might leave any minute."
Yet, once in Milledgeville, she fell seriously ill, and was told that
she would need to be hospitalized for an operation for a floating
kidney — upsetting news that she relayed lightly to friends. "I
won't see you again," she wrote Lowell, of a planned rendezvous,
"as I have to go to the hospital Friday and have a kidney hung
on a rib." In early January, she was admitted, for a month, to the
Baldwin Memorial Hospital — a two-story redbrick building on
Greene Street, formerly the Richard Binion Clinic, consisting of
four doctors' offices on the first floor and a small patient facility on
the second — just a few blocks east of the Cline Mansion.

As Lyman Fulton was in training as a physician, she went beyond her usual vague, comic report that she was "having a kidney
tacked up" when telling him of her situation. "She wrote to me
about having had a so-called Dietl's crisis," said Fulton. "This is a
condition, often very painful, in which a kidney slips out of place so
as to cause a kinking and obstruction of the ureter. Surgery is often
necessary. I wrote expressing my condolences." When he learned
later of her lupus, he understandably wondered if "the Dietl's crisis,
if that's what it really was, may actually have been the opening salvo
in her battle with that cruel disease." Spending the month of February recuperating at the Cline Mansion, Flannery indicated the serious toll of the "radical cure" on her energies only to her agent: "I'm
anxious to be on with the book but don't have any strength yet."

When she did finally return to Connecticut, near the end of
March, the seasons were already turning, as Robert Fitzgerald has
poetically recalled: "We worked on at our jobs through thaws and
buds, through the May flies, and into summer, when we could take
our evening ease in deckchairs on the grass." In May, the Fitzgeralds' newly born third child, Maria Juliana, was ready for baptism,
and Flannery held her as godmother, standing with her fellow
godparent Robert Giroux. "I noted what good spirits Flannery was

in," said Giroux, "as we gravely performed our roles as godparents, renouncing the devil and all his works and pomps." For Flannery, as for the Fitzgeralds, the sacrament confirmed not only Maria's, but Flannery's, place among them. "She was now one of the family," Robert Fitzgerald wrote, "and no doubt the coolest and funniest one."

The warmer months in Redding were highly productive for the novelist. During the spring, she invented central episodes involving the radio preacher Hoover Shoates, a shyster's name much celebrated by the Fitzgeralds. In the summer, when she reached an impasse with the character of Haze, she found a startling solution by reading the copy Robert Fitzgerald had inscribed for her of his translation of Sophocles' *Oedipus Rex*. Meditating on Oedipus blinding himself in recognition of his sins, she dared to have Haze sear his own pecan-colored eyes with quicklime. Having closely read, as well, over the past year, three women saints — Catherine of Siena, Catherine of Genoa, and Teresa of Avila — she added some dark, medieval touches, including Haze lining his shoes with broken glass and wearing a shirt of barbed wire. Now reflecting physical pain, and compunction, her novel was growing doubly deep, and far more ambitious.

She humorously complained to the Fitzgeralds, in December, of heaviness in her "typing arms." She had retyped her entire novel to set up Haze's self-blinding, and blamed the ache on her labors, because she could no longer raise her arms to the typewriter. Flannery insisted, in later years, that hers had not been a particularly sickly childhood. "I am wondering where you got the idea that my childhood was full of 'endless illnesses,'" she corrected Betty Hester. "Besides the usual measles, chickenpox and mumps, I was never sick." Yet even before the Dietl's crisis, she noticed problems while living at Yaddo, and in Manhattan, as she "ran from one end of it to the other looking for an honest doctor." When the condition in her arms worsened, she began to fear having a contagious disease that the children might catch. So, at Flannery's request, Sally drove her to Wilton for an appointment with Dr. Leonard Maidman, the Fitzgerald family physician.

Dr. Maidman offered a provisional diagnosis of the joint pains as rheumatoid arthritis; he said the symptoms checked out, but not perfectly. Since she was soon traveling to Milledgeville, he recommended a complete physical examination at her local hospital. "She had disguised her symptoms," explained Sally Fitzgerald, "and had not told us how severe they were." When Sally saw her off for the Christmas holidays, she noticed some stiffness in gait as Flannery walked away from her along the boarding platform. But otherwise she seemed fine, "smiling perhaps a little wanly but wearing her beret at a jaunty angle," promising to be back in January. On the overnight train trip south, though, she became desperately ill, and by the time of her arrival, Uncle Louis, who had not seen her in nine months, said his niece resembled "a shriveled old woman." The Fitzgeralds were in "a state of complete shock" when Mrs. O'Connor telephoned, a few nights later, to break the startling news that Flannery, at twenty-five, was dying of lupus.

Part Two

Chapter Six

THE LIFE YOU SAVE

❋

Her pivotal train ride from New York City back to Georgia, at Christmastime 1950, was a strong enough plot point in O'Connor's life to show up nearly intact in her fiction. She once insisted that "any story I reveal myself in completely will be a bad story." Yet when she wrote "The Enduring Chill," seven years after the event, her depiction of a homecoming was barely camouflaged. The playwright Asbury Fox, returning, ill, from New York City, is a young man, but he is also twenty-five, and the detail of putting three thicknesses of the *New York Times* between his blankets to stay warm in his apartment, during winter, reminded Robert Fitzgerald of conditions in Connecticut: "I know for a fact that she had to stuff newspaper in the window cracks; we did, too."

Although Asbury's train, in the fictional rendering, is met by his widowed mother, the shock described is familiar from the recounting by Uncle Louis of Flannery's disembarking. As soon as Mrs. Fox catches a first glimpse of her son, bracing himself behind the conductor, with a bloodshot left eye, "puffy and pale," she gasps: "The smile vanished so suddenly, the shocked look that replaced it was so complete, that he realized for the first time that he must look as ill as he was." Through the medium of this snotty young artist, O'Connor allows a glimpse of some of her own fears while experiencing her reversal of fortune: "The train glided silently away behind him, leaving a view of the twin blocks of dilapidated stores. He gazed after the aluminum speck disappearing into the woods. It seemed to him that his last connection with a larger world were disappearing forever." The difference is that Asbury's dread disease turns out to be undulant fever, heightened by self-dramatizing and hypochondria. Flannery would be a longer time coming to understand the true nature of her illness and its more serious significance.

"Borne home on a stretcher, all out helpless," as she put it, she was immediately admitted to Baldwin Memorial Hospital, where she had spent the previous yuletide season. This Christmas she found the place "full of old rain crows & tree frogs only — & accident victims — & me." On December 23, she informed Betty Boyd Love, "I am languishing on my bed of semi affliction, this time with AWRTHRITUS or, to give it all it has, *the* acute rheumatoid arthritis, what leaves you always willing to sit down, lie down, lie flatter, etc. . . . I will be in Milledgeville Ga. a birdsanctuary for a few months, waiting to see how much of an invalid I am going to get to be . . . but I don't believe in time no more so its all one to me."

Lying in her "horsepital" bed, she thought back on Dunbar's *Mind and Body,* which had so fascinated her in Iowa City. "These days you caint even have you a good psychosomatic ailment," she wrote Betty. And she read T. S. Eliot's *Murder in the Cathedral,* earning her a reputation among the nurses as a "mystery fan."

Not unlike bald, round-faced Dr. Block, a stethoscope hung about his neck, in "The Enduring Chill" — so "irresistible to children" that "they vomited and went into fevers to have a visit from him" — Flannery's attending physician, Dr. Charles Fulghum, was a beloved general practitioner in Milledgeville. "He was a little fella, sort of makes me think of Old Doc on *Gunsmoke*," says town resident Margaret Uhler. "He was delightful and everybody loved him." He was an internist, when, according to his partner Dr. Zeb Burrell, "Internal medicine was the Cadillac of specialties, not in income but intellect. Internists were thought of as *the* diagnosticians of the time. Physicals consisted of an hour-long conversation with the patient, followed by an hour-long checkup." Dr. Fulghum had for many years been one of the Cline family's regular doctors, and had served as a pallbearer at the funerals of both Flannery's father and her aunt Gertie.

Dr. Fulghum initially concurred with Dr. Maidman's diagnosis of rheumatoid arthritis, treating his patient with cortisone, a hormone produced by the adrenal gland, with powerful anti-inflammatory properties. As Flannery informed her agent, "Am in the hospital, taking Cortisone, a new drug for that, & am improving." While correct about the recent discovery of the treatment — earning a 1950 Nobel Prize in Medicine and Physiology, for Drs. Kendall, Hench, and Reichstein — her expected improvement turned out to be wishful. The cortisone kept her alive, but her alarming fevers continued rising. Given the crisis, Dr. Fulghum contacted Dr. Arthur J. Merrill, an internist and Georgia's first kidney specialist, at Emory University in Atlanta. Over the telephone, Dr. Merrill suggested a likely diagnosis of disseminated lupus erythematosus. He also spoke quite honestly and directly with Mrs. O'Connor about her daughter's chances.

In February, on the recommendation of Dr. Merrill, Flannery was transferred to Emory University Hospital. Located on the main campus, in the residential Druid Hills neighborhood of Atlanta, the Italianate-style hospital, built in 1922 as Wesley Memorial, was a 320-bed facility, treating more than 11,500 patients a year. Under the care of the forty-two-year-old physician she came to refer to as "Scientist Merrill," or, simply, "the Scientist," she underwent a battery of tests. As she told Betty Boyd Love, "I stayed there a month, giving generous samples of my blood to this, that and the other technician, all hours of the day and night." The LE cell test — the first lupus test, developed in 1948 — confirmed Dr. Merrill's diagnosis. Yet her mother, fearing the shock of her discovering that she had the same disease that killed her father, chose to conceal the news. "She was already weak and it would have been too awful," concurred Sally Fitzgerald.

A disorder in which the immune system forms antibodies that attack its own connective tissue, causing chronic inflammation and often affecting multiple organs, systemic lupus erythematosus (SLE), with no certain viral or genetic trigger, remained nearly as elusive to her doctors as it had in her father's day, due to a confusing array of possible symptoms. While syphilis, treatable with penicillin, had earned the title "the great imitator" in the nineteenth century, lupus, frequently misdiagnosed as rheumatoid arthritis on first examination, inherited this same distinction by the early fifties, because no two patients exhibited exactly the same symptoms. Like a more virulent undulant fever ("It'll keep coming back," Dr. Block warns in "The Enduring Chill"), the disease complicated matters by oscillating between "flares" and "remissions." As Flannery later wrote to Robert Lowell, "It comes and goes, when it comes I retire and when it goes, I venture forth."

Since the disease could compromise joints, blood vessels, lungs, kidneys, heart, or brain, its diagnosis involved identifying at least two to four items on a checklist of nearly a dozen symptoms, including rashes, high fevers, photosensitivity, oral ulcers, hematologic disorders, and arthritis. Suffering from a severe case, Flannery manifested a number of these markers during her great "flare" of 1951. Of the disease that often announced itself with a wolfish rash across the bridge of the nose, she reported, in 1957, to a friend, "I have not had the rash in several years." And she wrote to Maryat Lee, "When I was nearly dead with lupus I had these sweats. They are a sign of serious chemical imbalance." Indicating a low white blood cell count, she recalled, "In '51 I had about 10 transfusions." Most obvious, in her case, were the painful, inflamed joints of arthritis.

The lifesaving treatment Dr. Merrill prescribed was a high dosage of ACTH, or adrenocorticotropic hormone, derived from the pituitary glands of pigs. She would eventually sing the praises of this natural hormone, discovered by the same group of scientists who had developed cortisone for treatment: "I owe my existence and cheerful countenance to the pituitary glands of thousands of pigs butchered daily in Chicago Illinois at the Armour packing plant. If pigs wore garments I wouldn't be worthy to kiss the hems of them."

As a corticosteroid — one of the hormone groups generally produced by the outer part, or cortex, of the adrenal glands on top of the kidneys — ACTH stimulated the body's secretion of cortisone. Yet all such new cortisone-related treatments, especially at high doses, had potent side effects. "I was an intern at Columbia Presbyterian Medical School, in the fifties, when cortisone came into widespread use in hospitals," says the psychiatrist and O'Connor scholar Robert Coles. "One gets stirred by cortisone. I don't want to turn this into a federal case, or an interpretation of her writing. But the drug that was saving her life was also, to some extent, stirring her body and mind."

Flannery certainly felt this stirring, lying ravaged in an Atlanta hospital bed, her hair having fallen out during high fevers, her face bloated and "moon-like" from the cortisone. As she later described the mental over-stimulation to Betty Hester, "I was five years writing that book and up to the last I was sure it was a failure and didn't work. When it was almost finished I came down with my energy-depriving ailment and began to take cortesone in large doses and cortesone makes you think night and day until I suppose the mind dies of exhaustion if you are not rescued."

She imagined a connection between the disease and the novel

that she had worked on so strenuously. By a sort of magical thinking, propelled by the treatment — "the large doses of ACTH send you off in a rocket and are scarcely less disagreeable than the disease" — she wondered if she had perhaps predicted, even shaped, this illness through her writing: "during this time I was more or less living my life and H. Mote's too and as my disease affected the joints, I conceived the notion that I would eventually become paralyzed and was going blind and that in the book I had spelled out my own course, or that in the illness I had spelled out the book."

Though her imaginings may have been delirious, she did hit on a critical truth. For while she "never had a moment's thought over Enoch . . . everything Enoch said and did was as plain as my hand," Haze did not truly cohere as a character until the stretch of time between her two hospital visits. In sickness and near death, the author bonded with her "morbid" character. Only in the last few months, and last dozen pages, had Haze moved beyond his snarling sermons atop his "high rat-colored" Essex for the Church Without Christ — preaching that would strike a *Newsweek* reviewer as "a subtle parody of Communist soapboxing" — to a glimmer of humility and self-awareness. As she would tell one interested reader, "I just unfortunately have Haze's vision and Enoch's disposition."

Following a month's stay, Flannery emerged from Emory, and the harrowing debut of her illness, with a novel that finally felt balanced, after she continued to make changes in the hospital. Recuperating in Milledgeville, she was put by Dr. Merrill on a strict salt-free, milk-free diet, and she learned to give herself four daily shots of ACTH. But, mostly, she focused on preparing for submission the pages that had been typed for her in Atlanta. With Rinehart officially declining to publish the novel, she was now free to mail her manuscript to Robert Giroux, which she did on March 10. Having long ago discarded "The Great Spotted Bird," and whittled down "Wise Blood and Simple," the author, who had just been through four months of blood tests and blood transfusions, was set on a title, as well. "I have finished my opus nauseous and expect it to be out one of these days," she wrote Betty Boyd Love, on April 24. "The name will be *Wise Blood.*"

※

IN THE SPRING of 1951, shortly after her twenty-sixth birthday, Flannery and her mother moved to Andalusia, a practical change motivated by her difficulty navigating all the steps at the Cline Mansion, and allowing more privacy for recovery and writing. Regina O'Connor had already been spending more time at the dairy farm, as she became that most daunting of figures in a small Southern town, a tough businesswoman. After a summer marked by several returns to the Atlanta hospital, Flannery filled in the Fitzgeralds on her situation: "Me & maw are still at the farm and are like to be, I perceive, through the winter. She is nuts about it out here, surrounded by the lowing herd and other details, and considers it beneficial to my health. The same has improved."

The austere farmhouse where Regina and Flannery took up residence, expecting to stay through the summer, was the two-story, white-frame Plantation Plain–style house, with a steeply pitched red metal roof, built in the 1850s, where the writer had spent so many summer days and evenings with her cousins as a child. From any of the rockers always set in a row on its columned, screened front porch, mother and daughter could look out over a sloping front lawn, full of oak trees, and onto a 550-acre estate of rolling hills, ponds, pastureland, and pine forests, with Tobler Creek, a spring-fed waterway, meandering through hayfields and wetlands at the rear of the property. Sunsets, as O'Connor often paints them in her stories, might be a "purple streak," or "flame-colored," or "like a red clay road." "Does it every evening," the mother, Lucynell Crater, reminds shiftless Tom T. Shiftlet as he admires one in "The Life You Save May Be Your Own."

When they arrived that spring, the property was at its most inviting. The four-mile ride northwest from town on the main paved road toward Eatonton cut through dense woods. Just before Andalusia was a half-mile stretch of fields filled with kudzu vines, and the fragrant purple buds and flowers of tree-climbing wisteria. "You could, literally, with your windows down in the car, smell it coming," remembers the O'Connor scholar Robert Strozier of passing the spot in the early fifties. Regina, driving her black Chevrolet, would turn left off the public road onto a driveway that cut through a red clay bank and curved gently uphill for a quarter mile, until she swerved around the back of the house to an open carport, paved with flagstones. Rarely using the half-dozen, wide, brick front steps, mother and daughter generally entered by way of the low-ceilinged rear kitchen porch, Regina often fussing with packages, and Flannery moving along more slowly behind.

Due to her convalescence, they chose to set up quarters on the main floor, leaving for guests two upstairs bedrooms, reached by a steep, railed, central staircase, its landing brightly lit by a long window. Flannery claimed, as her bedroom-study, the front corner room on the west side of the south-facing house. She soon had in place a narrow bed with a high Victorian headboard pushed against one tall front window; a few steps away she positioned a writing desk smack onto the back of an armoire, turned away from two corner windows, her attention focused inward rather than on any pastoral views. Her mother's bedroom was directly behind hers, connected by a doorway. Across the entrance hall was a plain, high-ceilinged, gray-walled combination parlor and dining room; to the rear, the kitchen, where they met for morning coffee — always efficiently prepared by Regina the night before and poured into a thermos — and listened to news on the radio.

Not having lived at home since college, Flannery now found herself faced with coping, as an adult, with her mother, in close quarters. Regina was both a godsend and a challenge for the daughter she persisted in calling "Mary Flannery." Having matured from a comely Southern belle into a feisty, formidable widow, with a straight back, sharp nose, small chin, and enormous blue eyes, she countered Flannery's near silence with endless garrulousness, and a zest for moneymaking. As overseer of the farm, she was a natural. According to one friend, "Regina was very petite, in charge. She was a very capable manager." She was also an ideal nurse and caretaker, but, at times, as trying a companion for Flannery as she had been for Edward. "With me, Flannery tended to be a bit joking and sarcastic about her mother," remembered Robie Macauley. "But the idea that Regina was a tyrant — though a beloved one — also came through."

While their former plantation house on a rise of land was the main attraction of the twenty-one-acre central farm complex, its working plant had grown more productive since Uncle Bernard willed the operation to Louis and Regina. Outbuildings now included a low horse barn; a vast, two-story cow barn with hayloft; brick milk-processing shed; well house; pump house; and a white wooden water tower on tall spindly legs. The tenants' house was an early-nineteenth-century, two-story plantation cottage, with an open porch, just two hundred feet from the main house. Three other workers' shacks were located in low-lying fields farther out on the property. By the time the *Union-Recorder* ran a feature on Andalusia, in 1958, the dairy farm boasted eighty-five Holstein, Guernsey, and Jersey cows, grazing on fescue grass and crimson and white clover, and supplying milk to the Putnam County Cooperative: "the cows are fat and sleek and giving plenty of milk."

As Regina busied herself with driving about the property in her stick-shift automobile, inspecting fencing, or planning a livestock pond at the bottom of the hill, her daughter stayed in her room, shades drawn, having reinstated an inviolable regimen of writing for several hours in the morning. Yet during her first season at Andalusia, most of this writing consisted of rewriting. Although she felt that her novel was essentially finished, the publication process was full of starts and stops, beginning with a long silent spell that made the first-time author nervous. In April, she tugged at her agent: "Would you check on my manuscript at Harcourt, Brace? . . . I am anxious to get it off my mind." She was not aware that Robert Giroux had run into some blank, uncertain reactions from the editorial board and sales department. "I thought, Wow, this is really taking a chance, but it's the right chance to take," said Giroux. "It was all against the grain."

In June, word finally came of the acceptance of *Wise Blood,* and Flannery was "mighty pleased." Following the good news, Giroux sent a list of suggested additions and corrections. She had also mailed the manuscript to the Fitzgeralds, her steady correspondents throughout her convalescence. With her permission, Robert Fitzgerald passed the manuscript on to Caroline Gordon. Like her husband, Allen Tate — just asked by the Fitzgeralds to stand as godfather for their fourth child, Michael — Caroline Gordon was a recent convert in search of a Catholic literary "renascence." In *Wise Blood,* and in the manuscript of another first novel, *The Charterhouse,* sent to her almost simultaneously by Walker Percy from Louisiana, though never finally published, she saw some of her wish realized. As she reported the coincidence to Brainard Cheney, a friend in Nashville: "It is no accident, I'm sure, that in the last two months the two best first novels I've ever read have been by Catholic writers. The other novel is by Flannery O'Connor. Harcourt, Brace say it is the most shocking book they have ever read but have finally agreed to publish it." And to Fitzgerald, she wrote back excitedly, "This girl is a real novelist. She is already a rare phenomenon: a Catholic novelist with a real dramatic sense, one who relies more on her technique than her piety."

True to character, Gordon did find herself "wanting to make a few suggestions" on improving two "muffed" scenes, and was "presumptuous" enough to send them along. Yet for countless young writers, as Gordon knew, her opinion was most welcome; the literary pedigree of this fifty-five-year-old Kentucky-born author of a half-dozen Southern novels and of such classic stories as "The Captive" and "Old Red" was impeccable. As she liked to point out, she had been Ford Madox Ford's secretary in Greenwich Village in the 1920s, and he had once been Henry James's secretary; Lowell thought of her as "almost my mother." Her fiction workshops at Columbia, where she had taught since 1946, were coveted. One of her students recalls, "She presented herself in class as a correct Southern lady, wearing a frilly dress, polished black shoes, and a hat. But she told fascinating tales of friendships with Hemingway, in Paris, and Hart Crane, and was incredibly generous with her time, and her pages of typed comments."

Flannery was quite grateful for the "touch here and touch there," indicated by Gordon, whose criticism obviously struck her as more apt than Selby's earlier "vague" comments that she suspected were designed to "train it into a conventional novel." She made her corrections, in ink, while "a lady around here types the first part of it." But rereading the revised draft in mid-September felt to the novice author like "spending the day eating a horse blanket." So she asked "Mrs. Tate" if she would mind taking yet another look. Emboldened by the request, Gordon typed back a staccato, nine-page, single-spaced list of suggested edits. Jammed into these tight lines was a crash course in the basics of her fictional creed: Henry James advising a "stout stake" around which the action would swirl; the practice of Flaubert to never "repeat the same word on one page"; Yeats's recommendation to offset every tense line with "a numb line."

Beginning with this "St. Didacus' Day" letter, November 13, 1951, Flannery entered into an informal, and lifelong, correspondence course that Sally Fitzgerald dubbed a "master class." *Wise*

Blood was six years in the making partly because Flannery was learning on the job, teaching herself to write as she went along. Although she would eventually wean herself from Gordon's absolute authority, in the fall of 1951 she was an eager, nearly obedient student. Gordon was quite strict. For instance, she insisted that the omniscient narrator should speak in "Johnsonian English." Under her guidance, Emory's necktie was changed from "greenpeaish" to "the color of green peas." Gordon deemed many scenes "so stripped, so bare." At her prodding, Flannery added an expansive night sky above Taulkinham that turned into one of the more lifting passages in the book:

> *His second night in Taulkinham, Hazel Motes walked along down town close to the store fronts but not looking in them. The black sky was underpinned with long silver streaks that looked like scaffolding and depth on depth behind it were thousands of stars that all seemed to be moving very slowly as if they were about some vast construction work that involved the whole order of the universe and would take all time to complete.*

As Caroline Gordon was now a literary confidante, Flannery felt that she might express to her some vulnerable feelings on the frustrations of exile in middle Georgia. Under the delusion that her ailment was acute rheumatoid arthritis, she was still viewing recuperation at the dairy farm as an inconvenient detour on the way back north to Connecticut, and to her "adopted kin," the Fitzgeralds. "All these comments on writing and my writing have helped along my education considerably and I am certainly obliged to you," she thanked Gordon in a draft of a letter. "There is no one around here who knows anything at all about fiction (every story is 'your article,' or 'your cute piece') or much about any kind of writing for that matter. Sidney Lanier and Daniel Whitehead Hickey are the Poets and Margaret Mitchell is the Writer. Amen."

Yet during these same weeks that she was deriding her fate, she was simultaneously settling, nearly imperceptibly, into the new life that was awaiting her. If she had foretold her own debilitating illness through Haze Motes in *Wise Blood* — a book that she once described as "autobiographical" — she also sensed her new direction while thinking about her work. In a telling comment to Robert Fitzgerald (he passed it on to Caroline Gordon), Flannery claimed that while her first novel was about "freaks," her next book would be about "folks." This prediction began to come true as she adjusted to the land and folks at Andalusia. During this period, she took up oil painting, using scenes of farm life as subjects, and was delighted to be back among those dear companions of her youth, farmyard birds. "I have twenty-one brown ducks with blue wing bars," she informed the Fitzgeralds. "They walk everywhere they go in single file."

The "folks" looming largest in the immediate ken of this young author, discovering the subject matter of her own mature style, were the Stevens family — her mother's dairyman, his wife, and two daughters — living just beyond the farmyard gate, in the unpainted, gray, wooden plantation cottage, with two front entrances and a long porch. "He was sort of like the foreman," remembers a friend of Mr. Stevens. "He was a country fellow . . . real easy to get along with." Flannery enjoyed spying on this tenant family (the house was visible out her bedroom window), picking up dialogue, and mailing off snippets for the amusement of her friends up north. She first introduced Mr. Stevens, much like a character in a story, to the Fitzgeralds in a mid-September letter: "I have just discovered that my mother's dairyman calls all the cows *he:* he ain't give but two gallons, he ain't come in yet. — also he changes the name endings: if its Maxine, he calls it Maxima. I reckon he doesn't like to feel surrounded by females or something."

Even more fascinating to Flannery was the talkative Mrs. Stevens, a homemaker, who did not participate in the working farm, except for the occasional feeding of some yard chickens. Yet she quickly insinuated herself in the lives of the O'Connors, appearing daily at their back door. "She always tells us every morning what the weather is in different parts of the country, giving exact time and location"; or, feigning surprise at having intruded into a roomful of guests, "with some unnecessary message — so as to get a look at them." Flannery was particularly bemused by Mrs. Stevens's enthusiastic brand of Protestantism. On Saturday afternoons, Mrs. Stevens regularly had her church ladies over to the house and was charged with preparing an uplifting moral lesson: "She says she ain't studied it very good yet but she is going to work it up by the time the ladies meet. They have a book with all these lessons in it and I suppose have a lesson each meeting."

What she could not discover by direct observation, she picked up by reading, closely, the weekly *Union-Recorder,* along with Georgia's agricultural tabloid, the *Farmer's Market Bulletin;* she later told a friend that she "gleaned many a character" from its pages. The previous September, the newspaper ran an article, "Want to Win Movie Pass? Shake Hands with Live Gorilla," on the appearance at the Campus Theatre of Congo, the star of *Mark of the Gorilla,* in time for her to swipe its handshaking stunt, and the phrase "first ten brave enough," for *Wise Blood.* In August 1951, the paper featured the 106-year-old Confederate veteran General William J. Bush, photographed in a "dashing" full-dress uniform and military hat, attending the graduation of his 62-year-old wife from GSCW. O'Connor lifted and doctored the item when she returned to story writing the following summer, in "A Late Encounter with the Enemy."

Flannery gained full exposure each noonday, as well, to the social class of ladies, usually in their hats and white gloves, who filed in with the O'Connors for lunch, the main meal of the day, at Sanford House. Opening that fall — just as Flannery was reemerging into daily life — the new tearoom was located in an 1825 Federal-style white-pillared home on Wilkinson Street, directly across from the college. Dubbed by Flannery "the local High Dining Establishment," the restaurant was the creation of Miss Fannie White, the senior partner, and Miss Mary Thompson, dieticians from Wesleyan, a women's college in Macon. The two ladies stayed true to the building's antebellum spirit: in the entrance hall they hung a copy of the Secession Ordinance, printed on silk; over an Adams mantel in the dining room was a large etching of General Robert E. Lee.

"It seems like the O'Connors were coming from the beginning," remembers Mary Jo Thompson. Likewise, Frances Florencourt recalls, "If it opened at twelve, they were right there at quarter to twelve on the front porch, sitting, waiting for people to gather." They would always request the same corner table, Regina facing the bustling dining room, her daughter staring out a front window toward the Second French Empire clock tower of the brick courthouse, where the Klan had rallied three years earlier. "Flannery mostly ate in silence," recalls Dorrie Neligan, a town resident, "while Regina visited with everybody she knew." The menu was typed twice daily, with dishes billed as "unusual": grits soufflé, rolled flank steak, hand-churned cranberry sherbet. Flannery's favorites were fried shrimp, on Fridays, and peppermint chiffon pie for dessert.

WISE BLOOD WAS finally published on May 15, 1952, in a modest run of three thousand copies, selling for three dollars apiece. Its abstract, cream-colored cover did not give buyers many clues for prejudging the book, evoking a stylish *noir* thriller, or an Agatha Christie suspense novel. The words "Wise" and "Blood" were isolated in pools of red and olive, surrounded by jagged, pencil-like ripples emanating outward. The entire back of the book was taken up by a black-and-white portrait of O'Connor, her thinned hair fixed in a standard pageboy. She was still puffy from cortisone and was dressed in a blouse and dark blazer. She resisted having the photograph taken, sending the print a month later than Giroux requested, and was horrified, when first shown a "very pretty" copy by a local bookseller, to find herself "blown up on the back of it, looking like a refugee from deep thought."

A lone "imprimatur" from Caroline Gordon was printed on the inside flap, comparing her work favorably with the absurdist fables of Franz Kafka, very much in vogue in smart circles in America (Anatole Broyard would title his memoir of postwar Greenwich Village *Kafka Was the Rage*). Gordon's blurb claimed, "Her picture of the modern world is literally terrifying. Kafka is almost the only one of our contemporaries who has achieved such effects."

Yet this praise could backfire for Flannery, who had never made it through Kafka's novels *The Castle* and *The Trial*. As she reported reaction on the home front to the Fitzgeralds: "Regina is getting very literary. 'Who is this Kafka?' she says. 'People ask me.' A German Jew, I says, I think. He wrote a book about a man that turns into a roach. 'Well, I can't tell people *that*,' she says." When speaking with students from Dr. Helen Greene's history class at the college, O'Connor was "distressed" to find them thinking that she shared in the European intellectual pessimism associated with Kafka that was "just getting to the young people of this country" — a harbinger of misunderstandings to come.

Not simply the neutral package, but the 223-page, unconventional novel itself invited high-contrast reactions. Written in a poker-faced style, its tale of lanky Hazel Motes — truculently arriving in the fictional town of Taulkinham, preaching in his "sharp, high, nasal, Tennessee voice," conjuring a church where "the blind don't see and the lame don't walk" — was evidently satiric, but the object of the satire could be a question mark. Playing Sancho Panza to Haze's Don Quixote, Enoch has the "wise blood" of the title, but he winds up exiting the scene in a foolish monkey suit. Haze is pursued by the hormonal fifteen-year-old Sabbath Lily Hawks, the fake-blind Asa Hawks's daughter, but no sex or romance occurs. In its final chapters, the episodic novel changes tone, revealing itself to be a morality play, as Haze — his pulpit of a junk car pushed over a cliff by a redneck cop — removes the "mote" in his own eye by self-blinding, and eventual death in a ditch.

Since this singular story of a pilgrim's backward progress was expressed in poetic shorthand, indicating a high order of talent, the slim novel could not be ignored. Yet by crossing two literary wires — a Southern gothic tale with a medieval saint's life — O'Connor opened herself up for criticism, somewhat unwittingly, as she was a newcomer to publication. "One reason I like to publish short stories is that nobody pays any attention to them," she would tell an interviewer several years later. "In ten years or so they begin to be known but the process has not been obnoxious. When you publish a novel, the racket is like a fox in the hen house." By the time she knew enough to dread the review process, though, she also understood why Haze Motes may have missed his mark with some early readers, a lesson learned: "he was a mystic. . . . The failure of the novel seems to be that he is not believable enough as a human being."

Critical reaction was mixed. Especially during the postwar decades, most of the attention of reviewers was taken up with books in competition for the laurel of the Great American Novel — that year Ernest Hemingway published *The Old Man and the Sea;* John Steinbeck, *East of Eden;* and Ralph Ellison's *Invisible Man* won the National Book Award. Yet some quieter Catholic literature was succeeding, too: Dorothy Day released her memoir, *The Long Loneliness;* and François Mauriac, once said by O'Connor to be her single greatest influence, won the 1952 Nobel Prize in Literature. Another adolescent, male antihero was cutting a wide swath across the popular imagination — Holden Caulfield, in J. D. Salinger's

Catcher in the Rye, published the year before; Flannery thought "that man owes a lot to Ring Lardner. Anyway he is very good."

Yet Haze Motes's spiritual agon was not as legible to the first line of critics, the guardians of public taste, as Holden Caulfield's more general teenage angst. "I can tell you that from a publishing point of view *Wise Blood* was a flop," said Robert Giroux. "It got three or four bad reviews right off. Then a good one came that began to see something. But I was shocked at the stupidity of these, the lack of perception, or even the lack of having an open mind. The review in the *New York Times Book Review* was by a Southern writer. He was embarrassed later, too late. Another reviewer said that it's a work of insanity, the writer is insane." Giroux succinctly wrote, "I was disappointed by the reviews more than she was; they all recognized her power but missed her point."

A prepublication notice, in *Library Journal,* labeled *Wise Blood* "odd," and set the sharp tone of the more negative reviews: "Written by another of that galaxy of rising young writers who deal with the South, this one was penned at deep-freeze temperatures." The all-important Sunday *Times* review, "Unending Vengeance," by William Goyen, introduced O'Connor as "a writer of power," but slighted her style as "tight to choking" and her novel as "an indefensible blow delivered in the dark." An anonymous review in *Time* accused her of being "arty," using Gordon's blurb as ammo: "All too often it reads as if Kafka had been set to writing continuity for L'il Abner." The unnamed *New Yorker* critic wondered "if the struggle to get from one sentence to the next is worth while." After reading Oliver LaFarge in *The Saturday Review* — "sheer monotony" — Flannery wrote to Giroux, "I am steeling myself for even more dreadful reviews."

Yet the novel eventually found some critical acceptance as more thoughtful notices began to appear. The first break in all the tough talk was a review by Sylvia Stallings, "Young Writer with a Bizarre Tale to Tell," in the *New York Herald Tribune Book Review:*

"Flannery O'Connor, in her first novel, has taken on the difficult subject of religious mania, and succeeds in telling a tale at once delicate and grotesque." *Newsweek* gave her celebrity treatment by running a profile, including a photograph of her "ancestral mansion": "Flannery O'Connor is perhaps the most naturally gifted of the youngest generation of American novelists, and her first book, 'Wise Blood,' has an imaginative intensity rare in any fiction these days." John W. Simons, in *Commonweal,* touted *Wise Blood* as "a remarkably accomplished, remarkably precocious beginning."

Like many a young author, Flannery soon discovered that no critic could cause as much anxiety, or be as incisive, as relatives and friends. Before a single review had appeared, she knew that she had a scandal on her hands in Savannah and Milledgeville. Her mother's reactions had always been muted, perhaps from sheer incomprehension. When the second draft was completed, she told the Fitzgeralds, "My mother said she wanted to read it again so she went off with it and I found her a half hour later on page 9 and sound asleep." Cousin Katie Semmes was far more alert to the prospect of her precocious niece in print. She ordered advance copies to be mailed to her inner circle, the priests of Savannah, including Monsignor James T. McNamara, who joked around town that he genuflected whenever passing Mrs. Semmes's home, as she was a major donor.

Trepidation about Cousin Katie's reaction was palpable for weeks at Andalusia. If Regina missed some of the subtlety of the work, or its Kafkaesque technique, she knew well that men's room graffiti and a teenage nymphomaniac in black stockings — a *Chicago Sun* critic would later praise O'Connor for having anticipated *Lolita*, in Sabbath Lily, five or six years before Nabokov — were far more incendiary than the material in Mary Flannery's previous scandal, "My Relitives." "My current literary assignment (from Regina) is to write an introduction for Cousin Katie 'so she won't be shocked,' to be *pasted* on the inside of her book," she explained to the Fitzgeralds, when the first hardback copies arrived. "This piece has to be in the tone of the Sacred Heart Messenger and carry the burden of contemporary critical thought. I keep putting it off."

The pasted disclaimer did not convince her overly high-minded cousin. Savannahians still gossip that "Mrs. Semmes went to bed for a week after that incident," while penning notes of apology to all the priests who received copies. "Wherever did she learn such words?" Cousin Katie cried. In Milledgeville, Aunt Mary Cline was equally horrified, and theatrical. "I can see her right now, after that book came out," recalls a neighbor, Charlotte Conn Ferris, "drawing herself up, raising her head, crossing her arms, and saying, 'I don't know where Mary Flannery met those people she wrote about, but it was certainly not in *my* house.'" One relative remarked, "I wish you could have found some other way to portray your talents." Yet Flannery weathered the family drama. As she encouraged John Lynch, a writer and teacher at Notre Dame, four years later: "I also had an 83-year-old cousin who was fond of me and I was convinced that my novel was going to give her a stroke and that I was going to be pursued through life by the Furies. After she read it, I waited for a letter announcing her decline but all I got was a curt note saying, 'I do not like your book.' She is now 88."

Reaction among the ladies who lunch in Milledgeville was just as disapproving. Upon reading the description of Mrs. Watts, lounging in her place of business — "the friendliest bed in town" — Flannery's first college writing instructor, Katherine Scott, threw the novel across the room. In an interview with a journalist, decades later, Miss Scott said, "When I read her first novel I thought to myself that character who dies in the last chapter could have done the world a great favor by dying in the first chapter instead." Some townspeople later claimed that they circulated *Wise Blood* among themselves in brown paper bags, and one upright citizen boasted that she burned her copy in the backyard. "I read *Wise*

Blood when I was ten," says Mary More Jones, a Sanford House waitress during her college years. "I was attracted because it was hidden in Mother's and Daddy's closet."

Even a few of the men of Milledgeville held opinions. A doctor working at Milledgeville State Hospital read the novel, and remarked, "I enjoyed it, but I know one thing. She don't know a damn thing about a whore house." Flannery later admitted to a priest friend that she indeed leaned on conjecture in the brothel episode. And Reynolds Allen, who had once defeated her in the high school essay contest, was attempting to write mystery stories and found that Flannery (they had resumed their friendship when she returned to town) was adept at "spotting inconsistencies in character very quickly." But she disapproved of some of the British writers he appreciated — Somerset Maugham, Aldous Huxley — and urged him to read Faulkner. When *Wise Blood* appeared, he recalled, "I was pleasantly surprised. It was wittier than I would have guessed."

All of these social tensions were politely ignored when the time came for a public response to the appearance of Mary Flannery's novel. The headline in the college newspaper was "Flannery O'Connor Wows Critics with New Book"; in the *Union-Recorder,* "Top Literary Critics in Nation Are High in Praise of 'Wise Blood.'" Brought up with the rubric "pretty is as pretty does," many of the same women who expressed distaste were the most active in arranging lovely teas and luncheons for the book's celebration. Flannery soon found herself preferring the bad reviews to this round of local book parties, which she forbade on all subsequent publications. As she complained to Robie Macauley, whose first novel, *The Disguises of Love,* would soon be published, "I hope you won't have as much trouble about keeping people from having parties for you as I am having. Around here if you publish the number of whiskers on the local pigs, everybody has to give you a tea."

On Thursday morning, May 15, from ten o'clock until noon, a

kickoff "Autograph Party" was held for "Miss O'Connor" at the Beeson Reading Room at the college library. The room was decorated with bouquets of cut flowers, and several of Flannery's recent oil paintings hung on the walls. Nearly three hundred guests, including Katie Semmes, driving up from Savannah, and Flannery's college nemesis Mary Boyd, were received by Regina O'Connor and Mary Cline. Visibly mended from her bout of illness, the prettily made-up author wore a sleeveless silk dress, pinned with a large corsage. She signed copies, seated in a striped chair at a wooden table. "Cocktails were not served but I lived through it anyway and remember signing a book for you sometime during it," she wrote Betty Boyd. In a thank-you note, she praised the library staff for having been "most brave."

"I have rarely enjoyed a situation more," remembered *Alumnae Journal* editor Margaret Meaders.

> For situation it was, first of all, and function only — and barely — second. Having read her book, I understood perfectly the quandary that had befallen so many of the dressed-up visitors. . . . What to do? Everybody liked the child. Everybody was glad that she'd got something published, but one did wish that it had been something ladylike. What to say to her? What to do with your book once you bought it and she had signed it. If you read it, did you say so? If you owned it, did you put it out to be seen — or slip it behind Mama's copy of The Poems of Father Ryan? . . . From time to time that morning I saw what I'm sure was the quick light of laughter in Flannery's eyes.

A companion event, a week later, was a luncheon in honor of the book's publication, held on May 22 at Sanford House, and hosted by Mrs. Nelle Womack Hines — unkindly characterized by Flannery to the Fitzgeralds as "an old dame that I abide with gritted teeth." Seated around a white-covered table, decorated with sprays of pine and two silver candelabra with green tapers, members of the Milledgeville Book Club were asked to tell what childhood book had impressed them most. "I have been told that everyone tried hard to come up with an impressive choice," wrote one Milledgeville resident, Mary Barbara Tate, "and the statements were, as Huck said of those in *Pilgrim's Progress,* 'interesting but tough.'" When her turn came, Flannery punctured the pretension by drawling flatly, "The Sears-Roebuck Catalog." Departing guests were then presented with autographed copies of Hines's *Treasure Album of Milledgeville.*

Among her more sophisticated, now epistolary, friends, reactions were just as conflicted. Robert Lowell remained one of the most ardent and committed supporters of the novel. Not yet having seen the final, published version, as he was living in Amsterdam, he did read the "Enoch and the Gorilla" excerpt, sold as second serial rights by Harcourt, in *New World Writing,* and he dashed off an enthusiastic response in early June: "When I was through reading I could have hugged the gorilla. The whole incident is rather epically dismal." He suggested for her next book the story of Lizzie Borden, accused of murdering her father and stepmother in 1892. Lowell later informed Flannery, from Manhattan, that the *Partisan Review* editor Philip Rahv "now goes about enraging New York literati by telling them they should write a *Wise Blood.*"

Andrew Lytle was not as pleased, though he did not relay his disapproval directly to his former student. Having encouraged her during an early, fecund stage of the novel, Lytle did not appreciate the severe religious turn the novel had taken at Yaddo and in Connecticut; he rightly suspected theology in the retooling of the main character into what O'Connor herself later called "a Protestant saint, written from the point of view of a Catholic." When the *Shenandoah* editor Thomas Carter asked Lytle to review *Wise Blood,* he declined, explaining, "I think she left out too much circumstance of sardonic humor. . . . There is a move towards the

Old Church on the part of some of my friends, and I'm afraid an extraneous zeal is confusing their artistry." Mary McCarthy's husband, Bowden Broadwater, remained unmoved, saying, "I still can't read Flannel Mouth."

To try to get out a more sympathetic message about the book, Giroux began to solicit comments that might be useful in ads. He wrote especially to the English Catholic novelist Evelyn Waugh, whose satiric *Loved One* had been cited in the *Wise Blood* flap copy. Waugh wrote back,

> *Thank you for sending me WISE BLOOD, which I read with interest. You want a favorable opinion to quote. The best I can say is: "If this is really the unaided work of a young lady, it is a remarkable product." End quote. It isn't the kind of book I like much, but it is good of its kind. It is lively and more imaginative than most modern books. Why are so many characters in recent American fiction sub-human? Kindest regards, E.W.*

When Giroux forwarded the pulled quote, Regina was "vastly insulted." Putting the emphasis on *if* and *lady,* she asked, of the author she called "Evalin Wow": "Does he suppose you're not a lady? . . . WHO is he?"

Open season on *Wise Blood* ended by early summer, culminating with a mostly negative review in the *New Republic* from Isaac Rosenfeld. His extreme interpretation was that O'Connor "writes of an insane world peopled by monsters and submen, Motes the first among them. . . . Motes is plain crazy. . . . How then can one take his predicament seriously?" He found the characters revealed "in a pallid light reflected mainly, I should say, from Faulkner and Carson McCullers." As O'Connor reported on the review with humor, seemingly able to rise to any challenge, "He found it completely bogus, at length." Yet even Rosenfeld allowed that the author exhibited "a variety of sensibility out of which the kind of fiction that matters can be made." As her friend and champion Robert Fitzgerald put the best face on three months of critical dissonance: "But Rosenfeld and everyone else knew that a strong new writer was at large."

IN EARLY JUNE, Flannery finally realized her wish to return to the Fitzgeralds' Connecticut home, a year and a half later than anticipated. Almost immediately upon her arrival, Robert Fitzgerald needed to depart for six weeks of teaching at the Indiana School of Letters. They now had four children all under four years of age, and he was frantically working wherever he could to support his rapidly multiplying family. But he was present when Flannery arrived, "looking ravaged but pretty, with short soft new curls" and having smuggled three baby ducks on the plane from Georgia, to delight the children. And he remembered joining in the first few meals of cress and herbs that Sally prepared, as their guest was still on a restricted, salt-free diet.

Except for a day trip to New York for lunch with Caroline Gordon, Flannery tried her best to settle back into her former existence in her garret studio over the garage. But life did not cooperate, and the summer proved much more difficult than the bucolic season, two years earlier, when their greatest nuisance had been swarms of flies. The stone house on the remote, wooded ridge was fuller, with the children growing in size and in their ability to cause trouble. A leader in this trend, three-year-old Benedict, as Flannery reported to Gordon, "climbed in the car, drove it twelve feet over a chair and into a pile of rocks, climbed out the window, looking exactly like Charles Lindburg, and received a whipping from me (Sally was in bed sick) as if it were a great honor." Flannery remained a proponent of such old-fashioned "cutting a switch" in child rearing.

Two other additions to the household added to an atmosphere of unruliness, emphasized by the absence of the patriarch subtly depended on by both Flannery and Sally. To help in the care of their clan of small children, the Fitzgeralds had brought over from Yugoslavia Maria Ivancic, an old shepherdess. The Roman Catholic Church was active at the time in putting such "displaced persons," or "DPs," whose lives had been disrupted by World War II, in American homes as immigrant workers; Mrs. O'Connor had been trying to secure just such a mutually beneficial arrangement for Andalusia. Yet, as Robert Fitzgerald explained, the old woman from Gorizia, on the border of northern Italy, "after being helpful for a year, had learned from Croatian acquaintances of the comparative delights of life in Jersey City, and had begun to turn nasty."

A second unlikely guest, to whom Flannery claimed Maria was "allergic . . . on first sight," was Mary Loretta Washington, a twelve-year-old African American "slum child" from New York City, charitably invited by Sally Fitzgerald for a country holiday through the Fresh Air Fund. Her two-week stay coincided with the second half of the visit of Flannery, who snitched in a letter to Robert Fitzgerald that Loretta "had to stay in the room with Sally and she was full of wise sass and argument. . . . Loretta would perhaps have been controllable if there had been a Federal Marshall in the house, though I have my doubts." Such unsympathetic remarks caught Sally up short, and she dismissed them to her husband as "pure Georgia rhetoric," claiming that Loretta had been "too shy during her visit to do anything but stand around caressing the blond heads of our young."

While their time together was chaotic, Sally did use the occasion to share an important truth with Flannery, after uneasily holding back. A few weeks into the visit, they drove to Ridgefield to do household errands. On the way back, on a lovely summer's afternoon, she glanced over at her passenger, wondering how she could disturb such peace; but she had made up her mind, following much inner struggle, that Flannery should finally know the true nature of her illness. At that instant, Flannery happened to mention her arthritis. "Flannery, you don't have arthritis," Sally said quickly. "You have lupus." Reacting to the sudden revelation, Flannery slowly moved her arm from the car door down into her lap, her hand visibly trembling. Sally felt her own knee shaking against the clutch, too, as she continued driving along Seventy Acre Road.

"Well, that's not good news," Flannery said, after a few silent, charged moments. "But I can't thank you enough for telling me. . . . I thought I had lupus, and I thought I was going crazy. I'd a lot rather be sick than crazy." Reassured that her friend was not going to fall to pieces, Sally pulled off the hilly road, and up the long driveway. They then walked into the kitchen, where Flannery dutifully drank one of her twelve daily glasses of water, on doctor's orders, as the sounds of the voices of the children playing in the yard, watched by Maria Ivancic, bounced through the open windows. "There's not much to say about it," she went on. "But don't ever tell Regina you told me, because if you do she will never tell you anything else. I might want to know something else sometime."

Sally was only too happy to agree, relieved that she would not need to confess to Mrs. O'Connor. Their intimate conversation was broken, though, as a baby began to wail. "I have to go," Sally apologized tentatively, unsure about leaving her alone. "Well, I think I'll go take a little rest," Flannery responded. Before walking out the kitchen door to the inner staircase, she turned back once; using the polite Southern expression, she added, "I'm obliged to you."

"This was devastating knowledge," Sally Fitzgerald later recalled. "That she was going to have to live with uncertainty, that

she would not be autonomous and independent. I didn't minimize
what she would have to go through up in her room over the garage
when she left that afternoon after I had told her. But I never really
regretted it. I knew it was what Flannery wanted. The atmosphere
was cleared."

Flannery had initially been planning an open-ended stay with
the Fitzgeralds, over Regina's objection, "You always overdo!" But
even her six-week visit to Connecticut was cut short a week by a
string of unforeseen problems. Having never before encountered a
black person, the Slavic nanny, increasingly upset by the presence
of Loretta, began scowling and muttering foul phrases in Slove-
nian. After a protracted spell of such irrational tantrums, Sally,
pregnant with a fifth child, became ill and took to her bedroom,
threatened with a miscarriage. And Flannery contracted a virus.
But rather than panic at her own momentous news, or the mounting illnesses in the house — Benedict soon came down with chicken
pox, too — she went about efficiently arranging for Sally's care
while scheduling her own return to Georgia.

Flannery cleverly recruited a neighbor, Elsie Hill, described by
Sally as a "strong-minded Lucy Stoner," because of her early feminist leanings and strong leadership style, to watch over the situation until Robert Fitzgerald returned. She then brought Loretta
along with her on the train to New York City, plying her with
candy and a dollar bribe for remaining quiet, until handing her
over at the gate to her mother. As she reported on the exchange to
Sally Fitzgerald, "She was a very nice-looking pleasant woman
and said that she had been very worried that Loretta might have
misbehaved. I assured her this wasn't the case. A noble lie, I
thought." Though her reunion with the Fitzgeralds had been the
epitome of a cherished plan run amok, she was sincere when she
added her thanks to Robert: "It was a great boon to me to be able
to spend a month in Connecticut."

From New York City, Flannery flew to Atlanta, where Regina

had arranged an immediate appointment with Dr. Merrill, whose offices were located in an old home downtown at 35 Fourth Street, with a lab and X-ray machine on the second floor. The doctor concluded that the lupus had been reactivated by the viral infection, accompanied by an onset of high fevers; he ordered two blood transfusions, and raised her ACTH dosage from 0.25 cc to 1 cc a day. Yet she was able to find good news in the cost of the medicine, not covered by insurance, which she described as "a kind of Guggenheim. The ACTH has been reduced from 19.50 to 7.50." She felt palpable relief, too, at having the nature of the disease finally out in the open. As she wrote Robert Fitzgerald, in Indiana, "I know now that it is lupus and am very glad to so know." She even broached the matter with Regina, without implicating Sally as her informant — her mother taking personal pride in informing her that Dr. Merrill had diagnosed lupus before even seeing her, "over the phone."

Again forced back home by disease — an unmistakable echo of her return eighteen months earlier — Flannery clearly appraised the meaning of her difficult situation. She did not know whether she would be allotted the same three years of borrowed time as her father, following his diagnosis, or if indeed "the Scientist" possessed a miracle cure. She had her doubts. As Mr. Shiftlet speechifies in "The Life You Save May Be Your Own": "There's one of these doctors in Atlanta that's taken a knife and cut the human heart . . . and held it in his hand . . . and studied it like it was a day-old chicken, and lady . . . he don't know more about it than you or me." Yet she was certain that Connecticut was no longer to be her home, and so asked Sally Fitzgerald to please mail back her things: two suitcases, coat, camera, a copy of *Art and Scholasticism*, and her Bible.

If her old life could fit into a couple of trunks, shipped, as old man Tanner's body would be transported in a rickety casket from up north in her story "Judgment Day," Flannery was simultaneously looking forward to another crate arriving by rail from the opposite direction: Eustis, Florida. This crate was charged with a contrary significance, as a beginning rather than a closure. After spending six weeks in bed, following her "flare," but avoiding Emory Hospital — "a gret place to avoid" — Flannery had been reading through the Florida *Market Bulletin,* when she came across a listing for three-year-old "peafowl," at sixty-five dollars a pair. Never having seen or heard a peacock, she unhesitatingly circled the ad, seized, as if by instinct, and passed it to her mother. "I'm going to order me those," she said. "Don't those things eat flowers?" Regina asked. "They'll eat Startena like the rest of them," Flannery answered with fake certitude.

On a mild day in October, the shipment finally arrived via Railway Express. Driving up to the station, Regina and Flannery saw that the wooden crate had already been unloaded onto the platform. As O'Connor later remembered, "From one end of it protruded a long royal-blue neck and crested head. A white line above and below each eye gave the investigating head an expression of alert composure." Flannery jumped out of the car and bounded forward as the bird quickly withdrew its head at her approach. Transporting the box back to Andalusia, mother and daughter, with help, undid the lid, unpacking a peacock, a hen, and four seven-week-old "peabiddies." Knowing the bird so far only by its literary reputation, as the pet of Hera, the wife of Zeus, Flannery would have to wait for the display of its full complement of tail feathers — "a map of the universe" — shed in late summer, and not fully regained until Christmas.

"As soon as the birds were out of the crate, I sat down and began to look at them," O'Connor remembered nine years later, in her essay "The King of the Birds."

I have been looking at them ever since, from one station or
another, and always with the same awe as on that first occasion;

though I have always, I feel, been able to keep a balanced view and an impartial attitude. The peacock I had bought had nothing whatsoever in the way of a tail, but he carried himself as if he not only had a train behind him but a retinue to attend it. On that first occasion, my problem was so greatly what to look at first that my gaze moved constantly from the cock to the hen to the four young peachickens, while they, except that they gave me as wide a berth as possible, did nothing to indicate they knew I was in the pen. . . . When I first uncrated these birds, in my frenzy I said, "I want so many of them that every time I go out the door, I'll run into one."

By the time of the arrival of these first peacocks — a sure sign of her intention to settle at home, in earnest — Flannery was already finding new inspiration for her fiction, as well, in the vagaries of small-town life. She had made a first sketchy attempt at rendering down-home material in her savage satire "A Late Encounter with the Enemy," based on the Milledgeville *Union-Recorder* article about a Confederate general's appearance at the graduation of his much younger wife. In O'Connor's tall tale, General Tennessee Flintrock Sash, his name a send-up of Stonewall Jackson, dies of a stroke, following his granddaughter's graduation. His corpse is then wheeled to a Coca-Cola machine by a clueless Boy Scout — the local paper having likewise been running ads for the Georgia-based soft drink featuring the Scouts. While the conceit of a corpse treated as if it were still alive owed its weirdness to Faulkner's "A Rose for Emily," O'Connor sidestepped the master's tone and language, in what she disparagingly called "my one-cylinder syntax."

This same vernacular prose and comic clarity helped her agent to place "A Late Encounter with the Enemy" in August, with Alice Morris, the fiction editor at *Harper's Bazaar,* a glossy women's magazine, which indicated the popular appeal that Flannery's high art potentially possessed. When the news reached Lowell, he wrote her, "Someone said you had something in *Harper's Bazaar,* but I can't believe it." She wrote back, of the story not published until the next September, "I did have one in *Harper's Bazaar* about a Confederate General who was a hundred and four years old, but nobody sees things in those magazines except the ladies that go to the beauty parlors." Actually, under Editor in Chief Carmel Snow, whose motto was "well-dressed women with well-dressed minds," the magazine was including much important fiction by Capote, McCullers, Cheever, Christopher Isherwood, and Katherine Anne Porter, among all its illustrations of haute couture.

The story that truly showed O'Connor finding her most reso-nant subject matter, though, was the aptly named "The Life You Save May Be Your Own" — its title suggested by Robert Fitzger-ald, based on road signs he had seen while driving through the South, in place of her first two choices: "Personal Interest" and "The World Is Almost Rotten." For this trickster's tale, which she sent to her agent in October, Flannery used names that could be found in the local phone book — H. T. Shiftlet lived on Route 1; Lucynell Smith had attended her *Wise Blood* book party. But as she began to describe the widow Lucynell Crater, and her nearly thirty-year-old mute daughter, also Lucynell Crater, visited by the one-armed handyman, Tom T. Shiftlet, she found herself writing, too, about the grounds of Andalusia, as reflected in the purposely distorting mirror of her imagination: "The old woman and her daughter were sitting on their porch when Mr. Shiftlet came up their road for the first time. The old woman slid to the edge of her chair and leaned forward, shading her eyes from the piercing sun-set with her hand. The daughter could not see far in front of her and continued to play with her fingers."

Flannery received much praise for the subtle recalibration in her style. Described by Robert Fitzgerald as "a triumph over Er-skine Caldwell," this breakout story, marking her first treatment of a mother-daughter relationship, and introducing a "gentleman caller," used *Tobacco Road*–type poor-white characters without being clichéd, and to fierce moral ends. By December, Flannery learned that she was the recipient of a two-thousand-dollar *Kenyon Review* fiction fellowship, having been invited to apply by its editor, John Crowe Ransom. Her award was followed by publication, in the spring 1953 issue, of "The Life You Save May Be Your Own," which went on to win the second prize in the 1954 O. Henry Award. But Flannery had conveyed that something significant was stirring as soon as she wrote the opening description of the daughter, resembling, as only she knew, her recently delivered bird: "She had long pink-gold hair and eyes as blue as a peacock's neck."

Chapter Seven

THE "BIBLE" SALESMAN

※

Like all good farm folk, we get up in the morning as soon as the first chicken cackles," Flannery wrote to her friends Louise and Tom Gossett in 1961. But she could just as easily have written that report during her first few months on the farm, or any time since. Certainly by early 1953 Flannery had settled into a schedule and rhythm that remained unvaried for the rest of her life. The woman who came to believe that "routine is a condition of survival" guarded her daily regimen, with the help of her mother and a self-protective instinct, but also with contentment and joy. As she implied to the Gossetts, each day followed a pattern, beginning with her mother, up first, waiting with a thermos of coffee for the two of them to drink at the kitchen table while listening to the local weather report on the radio.

This cycle of hours and days had a religious significance for Flannery, too. As Thomas Merton, a self-described "14th century man," abandoned New York City for the life of prayer and farming of a contemplative monk in Kentucky, so Flannery, dubbing herself a "thirteenth century" Catholic at Yaddo and, at Andalusia, a "hermit novelist," framed her new life in religion. Immediately on waking, she read the prayers for Prime, prescribed for six in the morning, from her 1949 edition of *A Short Breviary*. Following coffee, she and her mother then drove into town to attend mass at Sacred Heart, celebrated most weekday mornings at seven; the priest, for a decade, was the charming, bridge-playing Father John Toomey from Augusta. "Flannery sat in the *fifth* pew on the *right* side," recalled one parishioner. On Sundays, Flannery pulled on her black wool tam-o'-shanter to get to the earliest seven-fifteen mass. As she wrote a friend, in 1953, "I like to go to early mass so I won't have to dress up — combining the 7th Deadly Sin with the Sunday obligation."

Not merely a personal peculiarity, regularity was a civic virtue, too. Flannery was surrounded by family, and friends, who arranged their lives like clockwork. Regina was a stickler, and Flannery could chafe at her rules and regulations, but as long as her own writing time and space were kept sacred (of her writing desk, she said to a friend, "Nobody lays a hand on that, boy") she could accept other impositions. "She didn't want to come back to Georgia, she had left it," observed her cousin Margaret, the oldest of the Florencourt sisters. "But she and Regina had formed some kind of agreement that Regina would not interfere with Flannery's work. I credit them with that détente, if you will, under which they would live. I think that it obviously worked out because each of them was strong, and they knew how it was going to be, and accepted it."

Appearing most Friday afternoons on his way to the Cline Mansion — following work at King Hardware Company in Atlanta, then driving back to Bell House at the same hour each Sunday evening after supper — was Uncle Louis, basically a third member of the household. "My round uncle," as Flannery described the co-owner of Andalusia, paid special attention to planting fig trees all over the property, as he had an appetite for the sweet fruit. One of his favorites, planted near the back door, was evoked in "The Life You Save May Be Your Own": "A fat yellow moon appeared in the branches of the fig tree as if it were going to roost there with the chickens." Like Regina, who disliked Flannery's peacocks for eating her Lady Bankshire and Herbert Hoover roses, Louis balked when he discovered their taste for figs. "Get that scoundrel out of that fig bush!" he would roar, rising out of his chair at the sound of a breaking limb.

Just as regular participants in the life of Andalusia, in the category of "adopted" kin, were Misses White and Thompson. By 1953, the two women were fixed in their schedule of closing Sanford House on Wednesdays and driving out to Andalusia on Tuesday night, taking one of the upstairs bedrooms and spending the next day. "That was our weekend," says Mary Jo Thompson. They would join the O'Connors for meals and afternoon car rides. "Flannery was the only person I know who liked sharp cheese on her oatmeal," recalls Mary Jo. While Mary Jo never had literary talks with Flannery, they would chat while washing the dishes (Flannery found the warm water helpful for her aching joints). One of Flannery's favorite topics was Mrs. Weber, a boarder at the Cline Mansion, who likewise helped to clean up after dinner. "Flannery said Mrs. Weber carried on a two-way conversation the entire time with her deceased husband," remembers Thompson.

The models for many of O'Connor's observations of the lives of the black tenant farmers — as surely as the Stevens family inspired early vignettes of white sharecroppers — were a few longtime African American workers at Andalusia, living in outlying shacks, and eventually in the nearby, darkly weathered clapboard cottage. Jack, "the colored milker," as Flannery called him, worked with Mr. Stevens in the dairy; Louise, his wife, was a domestic, who cooked and cleaned, "blundering around," as she said; Willie "Shot" Manson, the youngest, performed hard farm labor, such as plowing fields. Living by himself in a shanty was Henry, "around here . . . a kind of institution," as Flannery described the yardman, in his eighties, who once fertilized her mother's flower bulbs with the calves' worm medicine. "Wormless they did not come up," she gleefully reported.

Yet Flannery was adept at shutting herself away during her "set time," between nine and noon, when she applied herself to her writing. Averaging three pages a day, she told a reporter from the Atlanta newspaper, "But I may tear it all to pieces the next day." While modest, her desk began to take on the character of a folk sculpture constructed of random parts, utilitarian to her eyes alone. "I have a large ugly brown desk, one of those that the typewriter sits in a depression in the middle of and on either side are drawers," she wrote, producing a mental snapshot of the assemblage for a friend. "In front I have a mahogany orange crate with the bottom knocked out and a cartridge shell box that I have sat up there to lend height and hold papers and whatnot and all my paraphernalia is around this vital center and a little rooting produces it. Besides which, I always seize on busy-work."

During the fall of 1952, and through the spring of 1953, in this "rat's nest of old papers, clippings, torn manuscripts, ancient quarterlies," O'Connor began work on a second novel, as well as several short stories that established her control of the genre and were told in an inimitable voice, sliding in and out of the colloquial heads of her characters. Each of these stories concerned death, the powerful theme that had been dealt her, especially since the revelation of her summer visit with the Fitzgeralds. Having described herself as a girl as "a *Peter Rabbit* man," menace was always her great effect. But in "You Can't Be Any Poorer Than Dead," begun as the first chapter of her new novel, the macabre slapstick of the teenage Francis Marion Tarwater (his last name swiped from Tom T. Shiftlet's hometown) — tempted to shirk burying his great-uncle, but haunted by the old man's corpse still propped at the breakfast table — had the depth of what Henry James called "felt life." This quality was missing from the ghoulish tales of stabbings and strangling in O'Connor's juvenilia.

In "The River," finished in November 1952 and full of images of "speckled" skeletons, the preschooler Harry undergoes a drowning-baptism. The next day he tragically finds his way back to the river in the Georgia clay country, red-orange after a rain, where he was baptized by the Reverend Bevel Summers while on an outing with his sitter, Mrs. Connin. As the little boy gives himself over to the undertow of death, and possibly salvation, his parents are nursing hangovers in their city apartment — a satiric cartoon of bohemianism, cluttered with overflowing ashtrays and abstract paintings. To write Mrs. Connin's adoring attitude toward their hymn-singing minister — "He's no ordinary preacher" — O'Connor borrowed freely from Mrs. Stevens, who had recently told her of a dramatic sermon by her own preacher, also a fine singer: "Evy eye is on him. . . . Not a breath stirs."

Conceiving "A Good Man Is Hard to Find," she connected the dots of a few articles that had mesmerized, or tickled, her: the *Atlanta Constitution* reported on a petty bank robber with the alias "The Misfit"; she clipped a photograph of a tartly made-up little girl, in a tutu, incongruously mimicking Bessie Smith's rendition of "A Good Man Is Hard to Find" at a talent contest. Yet the laughter in her light tale of a fifties' suburban Atlanta family waylaid on a road trip is silenced by the gunshots of her own "Misfit," a prophet of existentialist nihilism, far more harrowing than Haze Motes. The scene of the family's murder is a dark wood, as foreboding as Hawthorne's in "Young Goodman Brown," which is faintly echoed in the title as well. "It was no coincidence that Flannery wrote that story within months of, metaphorically, having a gun aimed at her," said Sally Fitzgerald, of her reaction when Flannery mailed her a draft in the spring of 1953.

Flannery sent the stories, as well, to her agent and her publisher. Hired away from *Partisan Review* by Harcourt Brace's Robert Giroux, his copy editor and first reader Catharine Carver was excited about O'Connor's writing. "Catie would read them first and say, 'Bob, wait till you see this one, a new story has come in,'" Giroux recalled. "This happened, every time, over a series of months. . . . I remember one day Catharine brought me one. I didn't read it in the office. I had a batch of stuff, and I took it home that night and read 'A Good Man Is Hard to Find.' I thought, This is one of the greatest short stories ever written in the United States. It's equal to Hemingway, or Melville's 'Bartleby the Scrivener.' And it absolutely put her on the map." In his Christmas card of 1953, Lowell included praise of her recent works: "Both the baptizing and the homicidal lunatic are fearfully good."

Writing with such intensity, with "a fresh mind" during the mornings, she might well have been entirely spent by afternoon. This normal diastole and systole was accentuated in her case by the disease, generally resulting in fatigue after two or three useful hours a day. Afternoons, for Flannery, were a much slower time, marked by flu-like symptoms and overcast by some mental fog. She passed them while "receiving on the front porch": "I work in the mornings but I am at home every afternoon after 3:30," was a typical invitation. "One of the few signs of Flannery's lupus was that you could see her tiring by late afternoon," remembers Louise Abbot, a friend from nearby Louisville. "But when her eyes were sparkling, those dark blue and quite extraordinarily beautiful eyes, and she was trying to repress her laughter, I knew a story was coming."

During these waning hours, Flannery also pursued her hobbies of painting and raising birds, looking and listening. She was taking classes in town from Frank Stanley Herring, the post office muralist, and she hung on the walls of the farmhouse her simple studies of zinnias in bowls, angular cows under bare trees, a worker's shack in winter, and a rooster's angry head. "None of my paint-

228 · FLANNERY ·

ings go over very big in this house although mamma puts them up and is loth to take them down again," she wrote the Fitzgeralds. She collected an entire bestiary of "show birds": pens of pheasants and quail, a flock of turkeys, Canada geese, Muscovy ducks, Japanese silky bantams, and Polish crested bantams. Keeping her ears cocked for responses to her prized peacock, she got much mileage from a repairman who remarked, after the bird unfurled its magnificent tail, "Never saw such long ugly legs. . . . I bet that rascal could outrun a bus."

Sundown and bedtime were nearly synonymous for Flannery. "I go to bed at nine and am always glad to get there," she told a friend. Occasionally she recited Compline, the last office of the day, from her *Breviary,* set between a Sunday missal and her Bible on a low bedside table. More reliably, her habitual nighttime reading was the lofty, lucent prose of Thomas Aquinas. For just as significant as ordering peacocks as a signal of her intention to settle, was her obtaining her own copy of the seven-hundred-page Modern Library selection *Introduction to Saint Thomas Aquinas,* which she signed and dated "1953": "I read it for about twenty minutes every night before I go to bed. If my mother were to come in during this process and say, 'Turn off that light. It's late,' I with lifted finger and broad bland beatific expression, would reply, 'On the contrary, I answer that the light, being external and limitless, cannot be turned off. Shut your eyes,' or some such thing." Even resting in bed, Flannery was replenishing her writing. "I read a lot of theology because it makes my writing bolder," she once explained to a friend.

Spending hours alone in her large front room, among the phantasms of drowning boys, garrulous Southern grandmas, and mean killer-prophets, all created within a span of six months, Flannery struggled to make sense of her life. When her father died, she had compared God's grace to a bullet in the side. Faced with that same daunting grace, she developed a narrative to explain her situation. For this dedicated writer there was no surer sign of grace than writing a good story, and she had just written several. So when she broke the news of her lupus to Robert Lowell, in March 1953, she swore that "I can with one eye squinted take it all as a blessing." Spinning her own life as a parable of a prodigal daughter, forced home against her wishes and finding a consoling gift, she later encouraged the young Southern novelist Cecil Dawkins: "I stayed away from the time I was 20 until I was 25 with the notion that the life of my writing depended on my staying away. I would certainly have persisted in that delusion had I not got very ill and had to come home. The best of my writing has been done here."

※

ONE SPRING AFTERNOON in late April 1953, a striking-looking young man appeared at the front door. Tall and blond, described by Caroline Gordon as "a Dane with eyes like blue marbles," Erik Langkjaer was a twenty-six-year-old college textbook salesman for Harcourt Brace, Flannery's publisher. As his recently assigned territory was the entire South east of the Mississippi, he had been visiting with professors at Georgia State College for Women. Among them was Helen Greene, whose English history textbook was published by Harcourt. "After checking out his current offerings in that field, I asked him if he would like to meet one of his company's published authors," Greene has written. As she was his last appointment of the day, the history professor was pleased to take him "out to Andalusia to meet Mary Flannery and Miss Regina."

While Helen Greene remembered Erik's response as an enthusiastic "Of course!" he felt, in truth, puzzled. "She was sure that Flannery would be interested in meeting me," says Langkjaer, "and I must say I couldn't imagine why, because I hadn't read the novel, and I hadn't even been told that she was living in Milledgeville, and why would anyone want to meet a perfect stranger on such a flimsy pretext. But the professor said that she doesn't see too many people, living as she does with her mother. I went along with that idea. Some time in the afternoon, we rang the doorbell of Andalusia." Helen Greene judged the introduction a success: "He and Mary Flannery liked each other a great deal, and, as I recall, she guided him on a tour of Baldwin County in his car. . . . He was happily surprised to find such interesting and attractive people in the area."

Sophisticated, funny, and widely read, Erik possessed a cosmopolitan background rarely encountered in east-central Georgia. The son of a Danish diplomat and lawyer and a Russian émigré mother, he had been born in Shanghai, where his father served as consul-general. After a difficult childhood in Copenhagen, marked by bitter divorce proceedings between his parents, he eventually moved to New York City with his mother. When he graduated, on scholarship, from Princeton in 1948, he was then guided by his grandmother's cousin, Helene Iswolsky, a Catholic intellectual and activist, to study and teach at Fordham. As a religious skeptic with a Lutheran background, though, Erik did not see much of a future in a Catholic college. One of his Jesuit professors, William Lynch, a favorite theologian of Flannery's, advised him to seek his fortune elsewhere. Feeling at loose ends, he turned to the publishing industry.

Flannery thought enough of his visit to spill lots of its details into a letter to the Fitzgeralds, jumping off from a conversation she and Erik had on this first meeting about Dorothy Day, the founder of the Catholic Worker movement, a social justice ministry to the poor, forsaken, hungry, and homeless, begun as a hospitality house on the Lower East Side of Manhattan:

I never heard of Conversations at Newburgh *(sp?), but there was a man by here the other day who was a textbook salesman from Harcourt, Brace who told me that was one of D Day's farms. That man was from Denmark, not a Catholic but had some Russian aunt who was a Catholic and somebody or other with a magazine called* Nightwatch *or* Watchguard *or somesuch. Anyway he had studied philosophy at Fordham and taught German there and knew Fr. Lynch and was much interested in Dorothy Day.*

Flannery was challenged by her facsimile of a "gentleman caller," who had a strong Danish-British accent that marked him as a definite outsider. Although they talked theology, he wasn't Catholic. He was also highly opinionated, and far from shy in voicing his opinions; of Dorothy Day, "He couldn't see he said why she fed endless lines of endless bums for whom there was no hope, she'd never see any results from that, said he. The only conclusion we came to about this was that Charity was not understandable." Flannery camouflaged her interest in the young man to the Fitzgeralds with the throwaway remark "Strange people turn up." Yet she soon ordered a subscription to the *Catholic Worker,* and back issues of the *Third Hour,* the journal edited by Langkjaer's Russian relative Helene Iswolsky, a regular contributor to Dorothy Day's newspaper.

They discussed more on this first visit than Day's social activism, or the ecumenical mission of his "aunt" in reuniting the Russian Orthodox Church with Rome. Erik was quite open about his life situation, "that I had come to the U.S., that I was now traveling somewhat rootlessly in the South, and that I had all these religious concerns and problems." Flannery was tickled by a traveling salesman carrying "The Bible," a joke term in publishing for his standard loose-leaf binder of promotional materials and tables. "It amused her very much that something that was not a bible should have been called a bible," says Langkjaer. And she responded with tenderness to his rootless search. Writing to Erik two years later, Flannery recalled a first rush of empathy with his homelessness: "You wonder how anybody can be happy in his home as long as there is one person without one. I never thought of this so much until I began to know you and your situation and I will never quite have a home again on acct. of it."

Because Erik shared some troubling personal information fairly quickly — childhood in occupied Denmark during the war years, his father's subsequent death — Flannery was unusually forthcoming, too. She spoke of her lupus, and of her own father's death, two of her most private topics. The need to discuss her disease, though, was fairly obvious; she was, as she told the Fitzgeralds, in January, "practically bald-headed on top," with "a watermelon face." Langkjaer remembered his first impression of her as "a little bloated" from the steroid medicine, with slack muscle tone. "Flannery told me quite openly about her illness," recalls Langkjaer. "I was told about her father's death and the unexpected fact of the disease being hereditary, as she had not expected from what the doctors had told them. But she seemed quite composed about this."

That first afternoon, Mrs. O'Connor served Erik and Flannery tea and then withdrew to take care of various business matters. Erik immediately picked up on the wide gap in sensibility between Flannery and her mother. Not "the saint everyone thinks she was, she was rather rebellious," says Langkjaer of the young woman who struck him as still far from reconciled to her fate. "I did sense that Flannery had a tense relationship with her mother. I got the impression that she was quite dependent on her mother now that she had come down with this disease, but that she was not an easy person for Flannery to talk to. I mean they were really not of one mind, to put it mildly. It wasn't that I experienced any altercations between them, but this was something that Flannery told me."

Erik had not read a word by the writer with whom he established such sudden intimacy, but she soon gave him *Wise Blood,* with the inscription "For Erik who has wise blood too," and "A Good Man Is Hard to Find," which she was completing when they met. Holding on to his impression of Mrs. O'Connor as "pleasant," yet "rather restrictive, very much focused on the practical aspects of running the farm," he continued later in life to interpret the grandmother of the story — wearing her white cotton gloves and blue navy straw hat so that "anyone seeing her dead on the highway would know at once that she was a lady" — as a version of Regina, or others of Flannery's female relatives. "This woman represented perhaps the essence of members of Flannery's own family that she distilled into this one character," says Langkjaer. "Here was a very, very limited person. . . . The grandmother is a completely banal, superficial woman."

Erik was stimulated enough by the remarkable new friendship to schedule regular visits to Milledgeville on weekends, often needing to rearrange his itinerary and travel a hundred miles or more out of his way. As Regina made clear to Flannery that she considered his staying overnight improper, he rented a room in a local motel, and then made his "calls" to Andalusia. Textbook orders were placed seasonally, clustered over the next fall and spring, so there were ten or twelve such visits. Erik and Flannery would take long walks, go for rides, or have lunch at Sanford House, talking all the while. "Was he ever handsome," recalls Mary Jo Thompson. "Flannery reserved the table on the porch to have lunch with Erik. It was perfect for a couple." Flannery was invested enough that when Betty Hester mentioned Helene Iswolsky a few years later, she confided, with unusual candor and spunk, "I used to go with her nephew."

During the same few weeks that Erik made his surprising first appearance at Andalusia, on the cusp of April and May 1953, Milledgeville also put itself briefly, and sensationally, on the map of current events with an incident O'Connor later described as "the most melodramatic event in the history of the bird sanctuary." In honor of its sesquicentennial, the town mounted a weeklong celebration, catering exclusively to the white population, full of nostalgia for its antebellum glory days: a pageant climaxing with the Secession Convention; the printing of a half-million dollars' worth of Confederate twenty-dollar bills; a tour of antebellum homes, including the Cline Mansion; men forced to grow whiskers and sideburn chops, and women to wear hoop skirts. Yet civic pride suffered a blow on Saturday, May 2, when the grocer and money-lender Marion Stembridge, briefly put in stocks for refusing to grow the requisite beard, shot two of the town's most prominent lawyers — one had prosecuted him for the murder of a black woman, though he avoided serving a prison sentence. Stembridge then turned the gun on himself.

This double homicide and suicide made a lasting impression on Pete Dexter, then a pupil at Peabody Elementary, where he was a student of O'Connor's high school classmate Deedie Sibley. He had once even been taken on a class trip to Andalusia. "I remember there were cowbells on the front door because I broke those," says Dexter. "In the barn, I put a girl's head where you put the cow's head for milking, so she couldn't get loose." As his Boy Scout leader was one of the lawyers killed, and his stepfather, a science teacher at Georgia Military College, had also opted out of growing a beard, the shots reverberated with the young boy. Although his family left Milledgeville later that same year, Dexter was faithful to the facts of the original case when he went on to write his own account in the novel *Paris Trout,* winner of a 1988 National Book Award.

The crime evidently resonated with Flannery, too. Pete Dexter had not read her story "The Partridge Festival," turning on the same event, before he wrote *Paris Trout,* but neither had many of O'Connor's readers. Her farcical tale of Singleton slaying five members of the Partridge City Council, then being incarcerated in Quincy Asylum, was printed in March 1961 in *Critic,* a low-circulation Catholic journal specializing in book reviews. Although she portrayed her mother as oblivious to her fiction, Regina's objections when she read an early draft, begun six years after the event, obviously registered: "my mother still didn't want me to publish it where it would be read around here," she wrote Cecil Dawkins. Yet she did proudly inform the novelist John Hawkes, "Quincy State Hospital is actually two miles out of Milledgeville, the same only bigger." Of its apparent model, Milledgeville State Hospital, an institution for the insane, Langkjaer recalls, "She liked to point it out as being in the neighborhood, with a smile on her face."

She certainly did not indicate to the Fitzgeralds at the time that "the most melodramatic event" had made much of an impact on her imagination. Her letter of May 7, written five days after the killing, and following the town funerals of the two victims and the cancellation of the Sesquicentennial Grand Ball, was filled mostly with news of Erik. The only other development she shared was an exchange of letters with Brainard and Frances Cheney, Nashville friends of the Fitzgeralds and the Tates: "The Cheneys said that when they went to St. Simons they would stop by to see me so I am hoping they will." After Andrew Lytle declined, Brainard Cheney had contributed a perceptive review of the "theologically weighted symbolism" of *Wise Blood* in Washington and Lee University's literary quarterly, *Shenandoah,* and Flannery invited a friendship by writing to thank him. If mail was "eventful," so, evidently, were people who "turn up."

The first weekend in June, the Cheneys, whose appearance in Flannery's life was to be as immediately welcomed as Erik's, indeed visited Andalusia on their way to their vacation property off the southeast coast of Georgia. Nicknamed "Lon," after the Lon Chaney silent movies popular when he was a student at Vanderbilt in the twenties, Brainard Cheney was a newspaper reporter and playwright and the novelist of *Lightwood* (1939) and *River Rogue* (1942). His wife, "Fannie," had been Allen Tate's assistant when he held the Poetry chair at the Library of Congress, and, after 1945, was an instructor at the library school of the George Peabody College for Teachers, in Nashville, where she became legendary in the field. "Mrs. C. is a liberry science teacher at Peabody but she is very nice inspite of that," Flannery told the Fitzgeralds. "In fact you would never know it." With them was a Japanese Fulbright student "whose gold teeth fascinated Regina."

Within two months, her creative burst matched by a reflex to reach out to new acquaintants, Flannery boarded a plane for the first of her many visits to Cold Chimneys, the Cheneys' home in Smyrna, Tennessee, twenty miles southeast of Nashville. A large brick house in the Greek Revival manner, with a broad entrance hall, vegetable garden, and an outdoor swimming pool used daily by Fannie, Cold Chimneys — renamed Idler's Retreat after central heating was installed in 1957 — was a refuge for many of the leading figures in the "Southern Renaissance," dating from Brainard Cheney's Fugitive days at Vanderbilt. Among "the petit cercle" of visitors, as Caroline Gordon called them, were Robert Penn Warren, Randall Jarrell, Cleanth Brooks, Andrew Lytle, Eudora Welty, Allen Tate, Katherine Anne Porter, Jean Stafford, Peter Taylor, Eleanor Ross, Malcolm Cowley, Russell Kirk, Robert Lowell, and Walker Percy.

"Cleanth Brooks and others have suggested that there are some similarities between the literary renaissance in Ireland and that in the Southern United States," wrote Ashley Brown, a houseguest of the Cheneys the weekend Flannery first visited in the summer of 1953. "In retrospect it seems to me that Cold Chimneys was something like Coole Park in County Galway, Lady Gregory's house where for thirty years William Butler Yeats and his friends gathered." A natural guest at almost any time at Cold Chimneys, where he had spent long stretches while a graduate student at Vanderbilt,

Brown was a particularly apt invitee at the house party that weekend. He was a young instructor at Virginia's Washington and Lee University, and had already been in touch with O'Connor, convincing her to allow the publication of "A Stroke of Good Fortune," the revised version of "Woman on the Stairs," in the spring 1953 issue of *Shenandoah.*

Of a type in academic and literary circles pegged as knowing and cultivating *"everyone,"* Brown, who was to become a good friend of Flannery's, and a frequent weekend visitor to Andalusia, had first become alert to her byline when the episodic chapters of *Wise Blood* appeared in the *Sewanee Review* and *Partisan Review.* "At that stage, let us say 1948 or 1949, I wasn't quite sure whether Flannery was male or female," he says. Quickening his interest was Caroline Gordon's blurb on the novel's dust jacket, inspiring him to write an enthusiastic letter, to which Flannery responded, "I'm no Georgia Kafka," setting what he described as the "flippant" tone of their friendship. "She was intelligent, caustic, with a tremendous sense of humor," remembers Brown, of meeting her at the Cheneys'. But she stopped him short while he was telling her of an imminent trip to Ireland. "Whatever do you want to go *there* for?" asked Flannery.

Cold Chimneys soon became a retreat for Flannery, and the Cheneys a nearby replacement for the Fitzgeralds, whom she visited in Connecticut for the last time in August 1953, before they left for Italy on a Guggenheim grant, and where they remained for the next eleven years. The bond with the Cheneys was strengthened by their conversion to Catholicism in March, following the lead of the Tates and making them part of a small minority in the South. "I consider Caroline my literary godmother," Brainard told Flannery, "and now she is my godmother in The Church." As at the Fitzgeralds' home, Flannery felt comfortable practicing her religion. "We just hit it off," said Frances Cheney. "Flannery had a kind of Gothic humor. She used to come see us right often. Her mother always made her buy a new dress. . . . We put her in the junk room and I'd go in there — she spent a good deal of time there — and she would be saying her prayers."

The high point of the trip for the Cheneys' friends, and for Flannery, in finding a group that appreciated her sensibility, was her reading aloud of a couple of stories over the weekend in the library, the most impressive spot in the house. As the sun slanted through the blinds of the great study, with its floor-to-ceiling books and old-fashioned sliding shelf ladder, she regaled them with "The River," just published in the *Sewanee Review*. Prominently on display, the summer 1953 issue also contained essays by Warren and Lytle, and Caroline Gordon's "Some Readings and Misreadings," taking Mauriac to task for his denial of the *"natural."* "She seems a very solid sort and salty," Brainard reported to "Red" Warren on her reading. "She appeared almost simultaneously with her story, THE RIVER, in the Sewanee Review, and she read it for us in her good Georgia drawl: the exact tone of voice for the story, which I believe is her finest, perhaps."

Ashley Brown vividly remembered her reading aloud "A Good Man Is Hard to Find," just published as well in *The Avon Book of Modern Writing,* which had been compiled by the *Partisan Review* editors, William Phillips and Philip Rahv. It included stories by "today's leading writers": Colette, Diana Trilling, Eleanor Clark, and Isaac Rosenfeld. With "The Life You Save" in the spring 1953 *Kenyon Review,* "A Late Encounter" forthcoming in *Harper's Bazaar,* and Brown having in hand the current *Shenandoah* with "Woman on the Stairs," the Cheneys' friends were experiencing O'Connor's works as they appeared from several directions at once. "This seems to me her great creative moment," Brown wrote of the stories being widely published between 1952 and 1955. Of her reading of "A Good Man," he recalled that "by the time that the grandmother found herself alone with The Misfit we were stunned into silence. It was a masterful performance."

"I heard a lot of Tennessee politics and more literary talk, most of it over my head, than since I left Iowa," she summed up the sociable weekend for Robie Macauley. In spite of her barbed remark, she actually found the visit to the Cheneys "most agreeable," sharing some of Fannie's sense that "we liked to read the same things and we laughed at the same things." A photograph taken that weekend with her hosts on the rotting steps of an abandoned smokehouse, wild vines gradually taking over, shows her looking relaxed, if unsmiling, in a ladylike dark blue dress with white trim, and a rare pair of earrings, perhaps suggested by her mother. "I asked the steward on the airplane what he did with the dirty dishes," she reported about her trip home. "When we get to Chicago, he says, we push them down a slot. I would like to work out some such arrangement."

WITHIN WEEKS OF this return from Tennessee, Flannery was inspired by a newly settled family of tenant farmers at Andalusia to begin work on the story that she would read aloud in the Cold Chimneys library on her next visit, in December. The Matysiaks, a Polish "displaced family," consisting of Jan, the father; Zofia, the mother; twelve-year-old Alfred; and his younger sister, Hedwig, arrived in the fall of 1953. These Roman Catholic outsiders, speaking in accents more impenetrable than, but reminiscent of, Erik Langkjaer's, drew from O'Connor a response both moral and comic. In newsy letters to the Cheneys, echoing her story, she persisted in referring to Mr. Matysiak, like an allegorical character, by the flat moniker "the D.P.," for "displaced person."

Having arrived in Georgia from West Germany, the Matysiak family had just spent six years as refugees, following the father's incarceration during World War II in a German labor farm as a prisoner of war. "They had what were called 'camps' for people living in Germany who were not natives," recalls Al Matysiak. "We moved from camp to camp." A "jack-of-all-trades," the father's application to immigrate to the United States was finally accepted in 1951, and they wound up in Gray, Georgia. They traveled twenty miles each Sunday morning to the nearest Catholic church, Sacred Heart, where they met Mrs. O'Connor. By the fall of 1953, alert to reasonably priced labor, Regina had them resettled at Andalusia, and Alfred enrolled in Sacred Heart School, his presence at a school service noted in the *Union-Recorder:* "The boys in white marched in procession. Alfred Matysiak was the leader of the boys."

The Matysiaks were hardly an unusual case. *Life* magazine reported in July 1945, "In the American and British zones of liberated Europe there had been discovered about 6,700,000 Displaced Persons. . . . More Poles, Balts and Yugoslavs elect not to go home, fearing the Communist domination of their fatherlands. In one group of 3,500 Poles, it was reported, only 19 chose to go back to Poland now." The Displaced Persons Act of 1948, signed by President Truman, allowed entry of 400,000 of these DPs over a four-year period, against the opposition of many conservative Southern congressmen, including Texas Representative Ed Gossett, who viewed them as "subversives, revolutionists, and crackpots of all colors and hues." Because half were Roman Catholics, Bishop William Mulloy testified at a 1948 congressional hearing, "It is our Christian duty and moral obligation to remove the displaced persons from their present plight."

Milledgeville already had its share of such displaced families, with the active involvement of Father John Toomey, working through the Catholic Resettlement Commission. The first of these immigrants, the Jeryczuks, with two children, had arrived in July 1949, rating a feature story and picture in the *Union-Recorder:* "Displaced Family Arrives on Farm from Poland." After briefly stopping at the parish house of Father Toomey, they had been escorted to a three-room shack on the Thornton dairy farm. Preparing in December 1951 for another displaced family that never finally moved to Andalusia, Regina and Mrs. Stevens sewed curtains for their windows from flowered chicken-feed sacks. Flannery reported to the Fitzgeralds that when Regina complained that the green curtains did not match the pink, Mrs. Stevens, "(who has no teeth on one side of her mouth) says in a very superior voice, 'Do you think they'll know what colors even is?'"

The Matysiaks were put up in a four-room shack beyond the lower pond, with no running water and a wood-burning stove. As Jan's English was broken, and Zofia spoke only Polish, Al, having picked up English at school, served as the family translator. His father, a short man who wore plastic-frame glasses, possessed lots of technical skills. After an old John Deere tractor broke down, he astonished Regina by taking the motor apart. "Miss O'Connor could not believe it," remembers Al Matysiak. "She said to him, 'That thing will never work again.' But Daddy got her to order new parts, put it back together, and it worked just like new. Daddy could fix most anything." As an official 1951 governmental study of such displaced laborers in the South noted, "They need much less supervision than native Negro workers; they take better care of machine and farm implements — in fact, one employer complained jokingly, 'They are such darn perfectionists.'"

Al Matysiak does not remember much direct contact with Flannery, who struck him as a distant presence. "If I talked with her it was very, very little," he recalls. "I'd see her occasionally at a distance. She was really, I don't want to say *fanatic,* but she loved different types of fowl, and feeding them in the pens. I couldn't believe her peacocks when I first saw them. It was amazing, especially when they spread their feathers out. The male was beautiful. They had feathers all over the ground. Being a nosy kid, I would sometimes pick up those feathers. That was the first time I'd seen a peacock when I came, and the first time I'd seen a guinea hen, the first time I'd ever seen a pheasant, too. I'd seen chickens, ducks, and geese, but not the exotic type animals that she had."

His favorite of the O'Connors was Regina, who filled the role of a surrogate American parent: "She was like my second Mama basically. I would walk from our house to hers and tell her, 'I don't feel good,' and she would take my temperature and give me an aspirin. She loved to ride her car around the farm, two or three times a week, and she'd come get me." If crossed, though, Regina could "make you feel knee-high to a duck; she could use words to make you feel way, way down." Erik Langkjaer was present enough for Al to have a few flickering memories of the visitor: "One Sunday afternoon, a car pulled up to the house, and a tall, lanky, nice-looking young fella, dressed nicely, came out. Flannery got in the car, and they came back later that evening. I asked Mrs. Stevens, 'Who was that man?' and she said, 'That's her boyfriend. They just went on a date.'"

When she began catching glimmers of her new story, though, Flannery wasn't thinking entirely of the Matysiaks. The situation they dramatized for her was also Erik's, as his sales trips were a kind of displacement, too. And his homelessness, she felt — like her own homesickness in Iowa City — had a single antidote, a spiritual one. Sitting on the screened porch, drinking her favorite concoction of Coca-Colas laced with black coffee, they often discussed religion. "We did speak about faith, Flannery and I, an awful lot," says Langkjaer. "I think she found it extremely difficult to understand how anyone could live without faith. When I told her, soon after we met, that I was somewhere between being a watered down Lutheran and an agnostic, she saw this maybe as a challenge to her faith." Displacement became their inside joke. "Flannery told me she was working on the story," says Langkjaer, "and couldn't help thinking of me also as a 'displaced person.'"

Yet while Erik remained "displaced" in Flannery's private associations, she started her story, with bold simplicity, almost as an eyewitness account of daily life on Andalusia, even more baldly rendered than "The Life You Save May Be Your Own." Mrs. Shortley, the fictional dairyman's wife, swipes some of her dialogue directly from Mrs. Stevens. Over the complaints of the farm owner and widow Mrs. McIntyre, about a mix of red and green curtains, she replies, "You reckon they'll know what colors even is?" The priest sponsoring the Polish family is as "long-legged" a "black figure" as Father John Toomey. The Guizacs, like their counterparts, the Matysiaks, are a family of four: a father wearing glasses "perfectly round and too small"; a "short and broad" mother who can say only "Ja, Ja"; a twelve-year-old translating son, Rudolph, "pausing at odd places in the sentence"; and a younger sister, not Hedwig, but Sledgewig.

O'Connor also introduced two black characters, the old man, Astor, and "the young Negro," Sulk, who were basically life drawings of Henry and Shot. "The two colored people in 'The Displaced Person' are on this place now," she admitted to a friend. "The old man is 84 but vertical or more or less so." Having learned from the failures of her high school and college stories with black central characters, she added, "I can only see them from the outside." Such sketching could result in routines uncomfortably close to those of Stepin Fetchit, the servile, wily character created by the comic movie actor Lincoln Perry in the thirties: "Never mind," Astor tells Sulk, "your place too low for anybody to dispute with you for it." Yet the African American novelist Alice Walker — in 1953, a nine-year-old girl living in a sharecropper shack eighteen miles away in Eatonton — felt the portrayals accurate when she read O'Connor's stories "endlessly" in college, "scarcely conscious of the difference between her racial and economic background and my own."

"Her mother was probably traditional in her view of blacks, and Flannery more liberal," says Langkjaer of the attitudes toward race relations behind these scenes. "She made it very clear to me that she was opposed to the way the 'Negroes,' as they were called then, were treated, and I had a strong feeling that she looked forward to the day when things would be different." Virulent racism was certainly rampant in Milledgeville; in the fall of 1952 the Klan burned a cross on an outlying field of the O'Connor farm while initiating three new members. Alice Walker briefly attended a segregated elementary school in Milledgeville, housed in a former state penitentiary, its execution chamber barely disguised. Yet unlike her mother, an Eisenhower supporter, Flannery voted, in 1952, for Adlai Stevenson, the liberal Democrat, identified with integration. "I remember standing in the playground," says Pete Dexter's sister, "and a friend saying, 'Well, if Stevenson gets elected, we'll have to go to school with nigrahs.'"

As an ambitious tale of manners and race, "The Displaced Person" soon led O'Connor into political material with global implications, which required her to widen her scope beyond the perimeters of the wire fencing and wooden pasture gates of Andalusia. To establish a historical time line, without being ponderous, she relied on outdated *March of Time* twenty-minute documentary newsreels, popular in movie theaters in the thirties and forties. Obviously having seen one of these news features, such as "What to Do with Germany" (October 1944), "18 Million Orphans" (November 1945), or "Justice Comes to Germany" (November 1945), the fictional Mrs. Shortley "recalled a newsreel she had once seen of a small room piled high with bodies of dead naked people all in a heap. . . . Before you could realize that it was real and take it into your head, the picture changed and a hollow-sounding voice was saying, 'Time marches on!'" Stubbornly misusing the concentration-camp footage as evidence to further "suspicion" regarding the family she insisted on calling "the Gobblehooks," Mrs. Shortley concludes of the displaced family, "If they had come from where this kind of thing was done to them, who was to say they were not the kind that would also do it to others?"

That December, Flannery received in the mail a prayer card that helped her to feel her way to the end of a first draft — a process of divination she once described as "following my nose more or less." Included, as a Christmas gift, with her *Catholic Worker* subscription, which had arrived regularly since her first conversations with Erik, was "A Prayer to Saint Raphael," beginning, "O Raphael, lead us toward those we are waiting for, those who are waiting for us: Raphael, Angel of happy meeting, lead us by the hand toward those we are looking for." Touched by this nineteenth-century prayer, written by the French Catholic Ernest Hello, for the archangel Raphael — popularly considered a patron saint of friendship and marriage — Flannery would recite its invocation daily for the rest of her life. As she explained to a friend about Raphael, who guides Tobias to his wife Sarah in an apocryphal book of the Old Testament, "He leads you to the people you are supposed to meet."

"The prayer had some imagery in it that I took over and put in 'The Displaced Person,'" Flannery wrote of its concluding vision of a heavenly home, "the business about Mrs. Shortley looking on the frontiers of her true country." For at the climax of the story, the Shortleys — like the Stevens family, consisting of a father, mother, and two daughters — drive off in a jalopy, displaced by the Poles, as Mrs. Shortley, spouting Holy Roller prophecies, suffers a stroke, and finds herself, in death, finally *placed*. Borrowing from the prayer for its concluding line, O'Connor, pulling out all the stops, writes of the daughters, "frightened by the grey slick road before them, they kept repeating in higher and higher voices, 'Where we goin, Ma? Where we goin?' while their mother, her huge body rolled back still against the seat, seemed to contemplate for the first time the tremendous frontiers of her true country."

"The Displaced Person," performed by Flannery on her return to Cold Chimneys, was only part one of the final version, but she considered the story complete at the time. Missing was the trans-figuring peacock (a later version was briefly titled "The King of the Birds"), a climactic crucifixion scene leaving Mr. Guizac crushed under a tractor, and Mrs. McIntyre, herself paralyzed by a stroke, taught to make out the contours of her "true country" — purgatory — by the faithful priest. These elements would appear when she turned the story into a three-part, sixty-page "novella" the following year. Yet even part one was a hit, read aloud to a group that included the houseguest Monroe Spears, editor of the *Sewanee Review.* When "The Atlantic kept it 4 months & decided it wasn't their dish," Flannery forwarded the story to Spears, who published this version in his fall 1954 issue.

※

DURING ONE OF Erik's several afternoon visits to Andalusia, Flan-nery proudly brought out a new painting to show him. Ever one of her favorites, her "self-portrait with a pheasant cock that is really a cutter," created in the spring of 1953, could be counted on to draw mixed responses from viewers, with its full-on portrayal of her-self, oval-eyed, wearing a fiery yellow halo of a sunhat, her arm wrapped about a fearsome dark bird. "He has horns and a face like the Devil," she wrote her friend Janet McKane, of the pheas-ant. "The-self portrait was made ten years ago, after a very acute siege of lupus . . . so I looked pretty much like the portrait." Her friend Louise Abbot felt that Flannery looked "stunned" in the painting. "I praised it," recalls Erik, "but I said that she was better-looking than the portrait. Flannery responded by saying that, well, this was the way she saw herself."

Neither Erik nor Flannery based their friendship on the come-liness of her looks. On the contrary, she enjoyed flouting expecta-tions of ladylike beauty, as in this unconventional self-portrait, done in bright Van Gogh reds, oranges, and greens, with vibrant expressionist brushstrokes, which she soon hung between the two long front windows of the dining room, like a parody of the more formal portraits of aunts and cousins on display in the Cline Mansion. And Erik played right along. Of a photograph of Helene Iswolsky in a Catholic magazine, Flannery wrote to Betty Hester that "her kinsman used to tell me that she was the ugliest woman in the world and that I reminded him of her which was why he liked me." Langkjaer recalls, too, that "She loved to talk about the peacocks because they were so beautiful, and I had a feeling, or maybe she even told me so, that she thought they were so obviously much more beautiful than she was."

Whatever quality struck Elizabeth Hardwick, at Yaddo, as "plain," was magnified by O'Connor's disease and accelerating disability. At Cold Chimneys toward the end of 1953, Ashley Brown noted that Flannery was "rather careful in her movements, going down the two or three steps at the backdoor." She was beginning to limp from persistent hip pain, attributed to incipient rheumatism. By the spring of 1954, Erik recalls the appearance of a cane: "She was using a stick at the time already. But she could walk about the place, and we did take some walks." Every bit as unsparing, and funny, in describing herself as the many maimed characters in her stories, such as the "one-arm jackleg" Tom T. Shiflet in "The Life You Save May Be Your Own," she wrote Caroline Gordon in November: "I am doing very well these days except for a limp, which I am informed is rheumatism. Colored people call it 'the misery.' Anyway I walk like I have one foot in the gutter but it's not an inconvenience and I get out of doing a great many things I don't want to do."

The handicap had no impact on her brisk rate of production, which remained steady throughout the spring of 1954, Erik's last as a textbook salesman in the Southeast territory. In that season's

Kenyon Review, John Crowe Ransom published O'Connor's latest story, "A Circle in the Fire," the setting again a doctored photograph of Andalusia. Like a pair of opposite body types out of one of her college cartoons, in this savage tale of vandalism the widowed owner, Mrs. Cope, is "very small and trim," the foreman's wife, Mrs. Pritchard, "large . . . her arms folded on a shelf of stomach." Two indistinguishable black workers shuffle in and out of the action, commenting as they go. Once more relying for material on bits found in the newspaper, O'Connor has Mrs. Pritchard patter about a woman giving birth to a baby in an "iron lung," based on a front-page article in the *Atlanta Journal* headlined, "Baby Born in Grady Lung!"

The innovation in "A Circle in the Fire" is its portrait of the artist as a twelve-year-old girl, Sally Virginia, with "a large mouth full of silver bands," peering down onto the action mostly from a second-floor windowsill; and three delinquent teenage boys who wreak havoc, letting loose a black bull and eventually setting an entire farm ablaze. Crackling along with their arson is a subtext of adolescent sexuality, inseparable from violence and danger. Like Walt Whitman's woman bather peering at nude boys at a swimming hole in *Song of Myself,* Sally Virginia hides behind a pine trunk, "prickle-skinned," staring out at the naked boys as they splash in a nearby cow trough. In a moment fraught with threat, the three culprits, back in trousers, on the way to commit their crime, pass by "not ten feet from where she was standing, slightly away from the tree now, with the imprint of the bark embossed red and white on the side of her face."

When Ben C. Griffith, an English professor from Mercer University, visited Flannery and asked about a possible connection between the story's sexual hint and the ensuing violence, she was surprisingly receptive. "He remarked that in these stories there is usually a strong kind of sex potential that was always turned aside and that this gave the stories some of their tension," she wrote Betty

Hester, "as for instance in A Circle in the Fire where there is a strong possibility that the child in the woods with the boys may be attacked — but the attack takes another form. I really hadn't thought of it until he pointed it out but I believe it is a very perceptive comment." Yet she made clear to Hester that any such attack would not be a crime of "passion," but of "revenge" on Mrs. Cope.

The incipient violence of the story, though, isn't entirely an indication of sexual repression. Fires were indeed an ever-present danger much remarked on by Mrs. O'Connor at Andalusia, with all its flammable pine. An article in the *Union-Recorder* warned, "Baldwin Faces Forest Fire Season with Great Caution," and advised "the greatest care with matches and cigarets." Delinquents from the nearby Boys Training School were perceived of as a threat by mother and daughter alike. "The reformatory is about a mile away and the lads escape about this time of year," she told a friend. "Last week we had six one day, one the next, and two the next. They track them down through the woods with other reformatory boys. We would much prefer they use dogs." In 1951, Georgia was ranked highest in the nation in the rate of lynching and other murders, often a solution to farm conflicts — 18.23 per 100,000 people, against a national average of 4.88.

Written at almost the same time as "A Circle in the Fire," and serving as its companion piece, was "A Temple of the Holy Ghost." Its protagonist is again a twelve-year-old girl challenged by adolescent sexuality — this time in the guise of two visiting fourteen-year-old Catholic schoolgirl cousins. As the younger girl sharply observes, "All their sentences began, 'You know this boy I know, well one time he . . .'" The girl's fascination mounts as Joanne and Susan date two Church of God boys and whisper of a hermaphrodite exposing private parts at a traveling fair. Though O'Connor claimed to "dislike intensely the work of Carson McCullars," her story blatantly contains elements of *The Member of the Wedding,* McCullers's novel of a twelve-year-old haunted by the House of

Freaks and provoked by her brother's wedding to accept her adult female identity. When McCullers read some of O'Connor's stories she cattily remarked, "I did read enough, though, to know what 'school' she attended, and I believe she'd learned her lesson well."

Introducing "A Temple of the Holy Ghost" in *Harper's Bazaar* in May 1954, an editor's urbane note promised "a memorable addition to her gallery of hard-boiled, out-of-the-way but engaging Southerners — this time with a precocious twelve-year-old brat whose curiosity leads her into dark alleys." The author contributed a plangent, cute personal statement: "I've had poor luck with my peafowl and have only one cock and ten hens left, the rest having died of broken hearts or whatever peafowl die of." But tucked into the conclusion of "A Temple of the Holy Ghost" was a profound response to McCullers's novel. O'Connor's twelve-year-old discovers *her* identity in the body of Christ, held up at a Benediction service in a convent chapel, as the girl's face is mashed, this time, "into a crucifix hitched" on the belt of a nun who hugs her. "Sex potential" deflected can lead to violence; an alternative is evidently sexuality sublimated in religious expression.

Stimulating a response to such romantic issues and "broken hearts" outside the world of her fiction, was Erik Langkjaer, as their close relationship reached a decisive phase. On May 20, Flannery abruptly canceled a trip to visit the Cheneys in Nashville, remaining at Andalusia to entertain Erik. Not telling the full story, she apologized to her hosts: "The weekend I planned to come to Nashville, a friend of mine who was on his way to Denmark to live elected to pay me a visit and there was no way to stop him — otherwise I would have." Obviously Erik could have been stopped, especially because Flannery, claiming to be "certainly distressed" at forgoing the trip to Cold Chimneys because of her friend's choice, pointed out that "I already had the ticket." Rescheduling her visit for later in the year — now one of two or three annual trips to

Nashville — she wrote the Cheneys that "barring mortal accidents I will be along."

The "mortal accident" that kept her at Andalusia on the weekend of May 21 was Langkjaer's decision to take a six-month leave from Harcourt Brace and return to Europe for the summer. To mark this rupture in a friendship at least tinged with romance, Erik invited Flannery on a farewell car ride, their favorite pastime — for Flannery a savored chance at intimacy and a much-needed escape from farm and mother. "We drove through the countryside and I remember her saying how much she liked the red clay of Georgia," says Langkjaer, "and she would point to this red clay as we drove along. It gave her a homey feeling." On this special occasion, Erik parked the car, and decided to lean over and kiss Flannery. "I may not have been in love, but I was very much aware that she was a woman, and so I felt that I'd like to kiss her," he says. "She may have been surprised that I suggested the kiss, but she was certainly prepared to accept it."

Yet, for Erik, the kiss felt odd. Remarkably inexperienced for a woman of her age, Flannery's passivity alarmed him. "As our lips touched I had a feeling that her mouth lacked resilience, as if she had no real muscle tension in her mouth, a result being that my own lips touched her teeth rather than lips, and this gave me an unhappy feeling of a sort of *memento mori,* and so the kissing stopped. . . . I was not by any means a Don Juan, but in my late twenties I had kissed other girls, and there had been this firm response, which was totally lacking in Flannery. So I had a feeling of kissing a skeleton, and in that sense it was a shocking experience." Erik's uneasy reaction touched on unspoken feelings about Flannery being "mildly" in love with him, and of his admiring and liking, rather than truly loving her; as well as a mounting awareness of "her being gravely ill." At that moment they were interrupted by a stray couple, from a nearby parked car, poking their heads in the window and quickly withdrawing, which Flannery found "rather enjoyable."

Returning to Europe, within weeks, Langkjaer immersed himself in his new life. He registered for a six-week summer course for foreigners in Marburg, Germany, where he soon became infatuated with an attractive Finnish woman. He wrote Flannery letters about his reading of German authors, including Rilke and Mann, but much of his attention was taken up with this mild flirtation, which lasted only a short time. In the fall, he then decided to return to his native city of Copenhagen and to enroll in courses on Shakespeare, the English Romantic poets, and American writers after 1920. While at the University of Copenhagen, he met Mette Juhl, the daughter of a famous Danish stage and screen character actor. Bonded by a mutual plan of becoming high school teachers, the two began a serious love affair, which Erik did not reveal in any of his letters to Flannery.

Flannery had no such change of scenery, and her letters to Erik, at his Copenhagen address, are among her most tender. In her first letter of June 13, she writes, longingly, in a closing line, of their car rides, with an implicit memory of their last kiss, "I haven't seen any dirt roads since you left & I miss you." Erik responded with a postcard of Billy Graham autographing a Bible during a revival meeting in a public square in Copenhagen. "Thank you for the post card," she wrote back on July 18. "I put it in the Bible naturally." When Erik shared his plans to stay through the fall to study American literature, though, Flannery, on October 17, sounded concerned: "You are wonderful and wildly original and I would probably think you even more so if I still didn't hope you will come back from that awful place." She ended with a sweet tug: "Did I tell you that I call my baby peachicken Brother in public and Erik in private?"

Passing the fall anxiously anticipating word from Erik, Flannery resolutely continued her "researches into the ways of the vulgar." While correspondence from Erik was disappointingly thin, the South continued to provide fulsome inspiration. Sometime during that fall of 1954 she heard, for the first time, the dissonant word pair "artificial nigger," and instantly knew that here was a "rabbit," as she once described the trigger for her high school cartoons. Her mother had casually passed on the phrase to her daughter, when she returned from a day of cow shopping. Having asked directions to the house of a cowman, Regina recounted, she had been told, "Well you go into this town and you can't miss it 'cause it's the only house in town with a artificial nigger in front of it." "So I decided I would have to find a story to fit that," O'Connor later told an audience at Vanderbilt University. "A little lower level than starting with the theme."

Referring to the black-jockey hitching posts that Uncle Louis persisted in calling "nigger statuary," this title phrase instantly got her in trouble. Wishing to publish O'Connor's country-come-to-town misadventure of Mr. Head, a "Raphael, awakened by a blast of God's light," guiding his ten-year-old nephew, Nelson, through an Atlanta straight out of Dante's *Inferno,* John Crowe Ransom worried about its racist ring. "I hate to insult the black folks' sensibilities," he wrote her. But O'Connor viewed the story's diminutive plaster-of-Paris statue — provoking the healing of a rift between uncle and nephew — as a textbook Christ symbol, suggesting "the redemptive quality of the Negro's suffering for us all." Writing back to Ransom, who had once changed "nigger" to "Negro" when reading aloud her story in Workshop, she insisted that "the story as a whole is much more damaging to white folk's sensibilities than to black." Her jarring title stuck.

Yet even after Ransom's acceptance of the story, O'Connor remained dissatisfied and rewrote it twice over the fall. Sending the story to her trusted adviser Caroline Gordon, she confided that

"Mr. Ransom took the Artificial Nigger for the Kenyon but I think without enthusiasm. He complained that it was very flat and had no beautiful sentences in it. I rewrote it but there still ain't any beautiful sentences." Gordon agreed, and told her that she needed, in Flannery's words, "to gain some altitude and get a larger view." Working and reworking the ending, she finally achieved a nearly Miltonic description of Mr. Head's transformation as "the action of mercy covered his pride like a flame and consumed it." After the story's publication in the *Kenyon Review* in the spring of 1955, she wrote a friend with some pride, of fulfilling her mentor's wish, "In those last two paragraphs I have practically gone from the Garden of Eden to the Gates of Paradise."

Having worked on a first novel for seven years, and never feeling entirely satisfied with the result, Flannery had now written eight or nine new stories within two years, and mostly liked them all. She was especially pleased with "The Artificial Nigger," which she described as "my favorite and probably the best thing I'll ever write." Encouraged by Robert Giroux, she began putting together a collection under the title of *his* favorite story, "A Good Man Is Hard to Find," with an October delivery date and tentative spring 1955 publication. By Christmas 1954, Flannery felt assured enough to write to Sally Fitzgerald of the forthcoming volume, "Without yr kind permission I have taken the liberty of dedicating (grand verb) it to you and Robert. This is because you all are my adopted kin and if I dedicated it to any of my blood kin they would think they had to go into hiding. Nine stories about original sin, with my compliments."

But soon after the beginning of the New Year, a tenth story about original sin combusted nearly spontaneously within the author, as no story ever had before. She wrote "Good Country People" "in about four days, the shortest I have written any thing in," and with "less conscious technical control . . . than in any story I've ever written." One morning Flannery simply began writing about her familiar pair, a divorced farm owner, Mrs. Hopewell, and busybody tenant, Mrs. Freeman. To her own surprise, "Before I realized it, I had equipped one of them with a daughter with a wooden leg." Even more startling was the appearance of Manley Pointer, the Bible salesman, who tricks Mrs. Hopewell's thirty-two-year-old daughter, Joy (she prefers "Hulga") out of her prosthetic leg in a low joke of a hayloft seduction. As O'Connor later revealed at a Southern Writers' Conference, "I didn't know he was going to steal that wooden leg until ten or twelve lines before he did it, but when I found out that this was what was going to happen, I realized that it was inevitable. This is a story that produces a shock for the reader, and I think one reason is that it produced a shock for the writer."

When Flannery sent this hastily written story to Caroline Gordon, her usually critical first reader was more enthusiastic than she had ever been. Mrs. Tate had a few quibbles about "the Om. Nar." using phrases such as "kind of," or some scenes that were weakly visualized, but mostly her letter consisted of unequivocal praise: "GOOD COUNTRY PEOPLE is a master-piece. Allen and I are in complete accord on that. Can't you get it into the volume of short stories?" If Flannery wrote her shocker with unusual ease, Caroline Gordon was likewise remarkably hands-off in her editing. Allen Tate was impressed enough to telegram Robert Giroux his conviction, which he also expressed in a letter to Flannery: "It is without exception the most terrible and powerful story of Maimed Souls I have ever read." Giroux wired Tate back that the story would indeed be fit into the collection, and perhaps his praise could serve as a jacket blurb.

Yet the genesis of the story was not entirely between Flannery and her literary friends, or even her subconscious. Developments in her relationship with Erik played a part in its creation, too, even if they were only dimly understood by her. By the beginning of 1955, Flannery knew that Erik was extending his leave of absence to remain in Europe. And "Good Country People" contains many coded references to him, most obviously in Manley's job as a fake Bible salesman (his hollowed-out tome contains condoms, porn playing cards, and a flask of whiskey), his displaced origins, "not even from a place, just from near a place," and his exit "over the green speckled lake." Satirizing herself, Flannery was even sharper: limping Hulga suffers from a heart condition and is not expected to live past forty-five; a "lady Ph.D.," she reads Heidegger. For the paragraph of Hulga's philosophy book that gives her mother a chill, O'Connor copied lines from her own marked-up 1949 translation of Heidegger's *Existence and Being*. Most poignantly, Hulga has never been kissed, and her response to Manley's stolen kiss is far from indifferent: "The kiss, which had more pressure than feeling behind it, produced that extra surge of adrenaline in the girl that enables one to carry a packed trunk out of a burning house, but in her, the power went at once to the brain."

Between the few letters from Erik and her story, a red flag from the imagination, Flannery might well have controlled herself. But she persisted. In a January 9 letter, written about the time she was percolating "Good Country People," she nudged him: "Write me an unintelligible post card please so I will have an excuse to write you a letter. My mother don't think it is proper for me to send mail when I don't receive it." When Erik wrote of his summer plans to pursue charitable works with Abbé Pierre, a radical Catholic social thinker dear to the Catholic Worker houses, she wittily answered him on the back of a fund-raising letter from Dorothy Day, including her mother's response, "Do you think Erik will *like* being a ragpicker?" She then added a handwritten afterthought to the typed letter: "I feel like if you were here we could talk about a million years without stopping."

Her eager April 1 postscript crossed in the mail with a note announcing Erik's engagement to Mette, and the couple's plan to return to America, where he would resume his old job with Harcourt

Brace in the same southern territory. This was disturbing news for Flannery. If Manley's making off with Hulga's wooden leg elicited shock in the writer just ten lines before writing the fierce scene, her inklings of the finality of Erik's departure likewise did not insulate her from a shock. Years later, when Sally Fitzgerald asked Regina whether Flannery had suffered, her mother looked down, and against her customary reserve, said, "Yes, she did, it was terrible." Not only did Flannery endure the pain of unrequited affection, but also the bracing clarity that such intimacy was probably never to be hers. With great politesse, she wrote back, subtly shifting from "I" to "we": "We are glad that you plan to return South and we want you to let us help you make your wife at home in this part of the country. Consider us your people here because that is what we consider ourselves."

Not surprisingly, Flannery never shared "Good Country People" with Erik, even though she had regularly been sending stories to him in Copenhagen for comment. As late as April 1955, she thanked him for his criticism of "The Displaced Person" and promised changes in page proofs to address his confusion about Mrs. Shortley's stroke. Yet he did eventually read in print the work she called her "very hot story," and wrote of recognizing himself "in some sort of disguise." Flannery wrote back, a bit disingenuously, "Dear boy, remove this delusion from your head at once. As a matter of fact, I wrote that one not too long after your departure and wanted to send you a copy but decided that the better part of tact would be to desist. Your contribution to it was largely in the matter of properties." She did point out, accurately, "As to the main pattern of that story, it is one of deceit which is something I certainly never connect with you."

Though they never saw each other again, Flannery and Erik kept in touch. For the next three years they corresponded, through Erik's marriage in July 1955, the birth of his two children, and subsequent moves to La Porte, Indiana (he was reassigned to the

Midwest territory), and then back to Scarsdale, when he worked in Manhattan as a Scribner's editor specializing in religious books. But when he published a piece in the *Catholic Worker,* in 1958, concerning nuclear disarmament, she wrote a letter critical of his naivete and the "bezerk" house style of the magazine, and never answered his reply. In a stray reference, in 1962, she even managed to misspell his name as "Eric." Yet just as Flannery, for all her distrust of reading fiction for clues to a writer's life, could describe Hulga to the Tates as the character "I just by the grace of God escape being," so she skirted the revelation that, like Hulga, she, too, had lost "a wooden part of her soul" in the encounter with Erik, painful as it was, and that the loss may have constituted a kind of grace.

Chapter Eight

FREAKS AND FOLKS

S eated before an NBC studio camera in New York City on
May 31, 1955, Flannery was visibly ill at ease. Her host, Harvey Breit, assistant editor of the *New York Times Sunday Book Review,* had invited her to be the first guest on *Galley Proof,* his new
half-hour talk show, broadcast at one thirty on Tuesday afternoon,
on WRCA-TV. The program combined an interview with a leading author and a short dramatization from a forthcoming book —
in O'Connor's case, a scene from her story "The Life You Save
May Be Your Own." She had been nervous about the appearance
for weeks, feeling dubious about her presence on the small screen,
and mistrusting the show's awkward, midafternoon time slot. As
she had written to Robie Macauley two weeks earlier, "I will be
real glad when this television thing is over with. I keep having a
mental picture of my glacial glare being sent out over the nation
onto millions of children who are waiting impatiently for The Bat-
man to come on."

A public intellectual in his midforties, formerly married to

Alice Morris, Flannery's editor at *Harper's Bazaar,* Breit, in a sack suit — looking every inch an urban professor, with his high forehead and receding wavy hair — chain-smoked in front of a bookcase while fumbling with oversized galley pages. "*Galley Proof* is an attempt to bring forward in advance, as a kind of preview, the most exciting new books we know of," he announced. "Such a book is a collection of short stories, *A Good Man Is Hard to Find,* to be published this Friday. . . . Several years ago she wrote a novel, *Wise Blood,* which critics hailed as a brilliant book. One critic called her 'perhaps the most naturally gifted of the youngest generation of American novelists.' Here she is, Flannery O'Connor."

Caught in a close-up, Flannery stared sideways, wincing from Breit's cigarette smoke. Yet she was elegantly dressed in a skirt, a dark blouse with a wide velvet collar fastened at the neck with a clasp, a thin bracelet, and earrings. When a producer had called to warn her not to wear a white dress, she complained to a friend, "I don't know what she thought I'd come decked out in a white dress for, but anyway she didn't tell me to wear my shoes." An interviewer's nightmare, Flannery stuck, at first, to short, one-line answers. When asked about the genesis of *Wise Blood,* she replied, "Well I thought I had better get to working on a novel, so I got to work and wrote one." When Breit mentioned her life on the farm, she corrected him, as he later recalled "quietly (but with quiet fervor)": "I don't see much of it. I'm a writer, and I farm from the rocking chair."

As Flannery gradually relaxed, she grew more articulate, explaining, in response to the inevitable query about her place in Southern literature, "When you're a Southerner and in pursuit of reality, the reality you come up with is going to have a Southern accent, but that's just an accent; it's not the essence of what you're trying to do." Before enacting a staged walk with her host to a front-porch set for the dramatization of the opening scene of "The

Life You Save," performed by three actors in thrift-shop-style cos-
tumes, she displayed her characteristic grit:

> *Breit:*   *Flannery, would you like to tell our audience what*
>   *happens in that story?*
>
> *O'Connor: No, I certainly would not. I don't think you can*
>   *paraphrase a story like that. I think there's only one*
>   *way to tell it and that's the way it is told in the story.*

Although no longer showing any signs of puffiness or hair loss,
Flannery felt that she looked "very tired" when she watched herself on the kinescope. She had just arrived for the taping the afternoon before, when her Eastern Air Lines flight was met at four
twenty at Newark Airport by Catharine Carver, who then accompanied her into the city to a hotel near Grand Central Station. She
had originally been booked at the Woodstock Hotel, on the West
Side, but, traveling without her cane, wished to be situated in
shorter walking distance of the Harcourt Brace offices. Not only
was Carver her "nursemaid," on this trip, as Flannery described
her, but she had also now officially been named her editor, in a surprise shake-up as Robert Giroux left to become vice president of
Farrar, Straus, and Cudahy, and Denver Lindley took over the position of editor in chief at Harcourt.

When she had first received news of Giroux's departure, a few
weeks earlier, Flannery was dismayed. And as soon as possible,
during her visit, the two met to discuss the delicate situation. Giroux assured her that she was in good hands. Flannery told Carver
of her boss confiding that she "did all the work anyhow." He also
informed Flannery that her book was generating lots of prepublication buzz. As she relayed this news to the Fitzgeralds, "The atmosphere at Harcourt Brace, at least in regard to meself, has
changed to one of eager enthusiasm. I had tea with Giroux and he

told me all about it." They spoke of negotiations for a contract for a second novel that he shrewdly suggested to Flannery and Elizabeth McKee should include a "provisional voidance clause," allowing cancellation if Carver should unexpectedly leave the firm, too.

With its June 6 publication date still days away, Flannery already had an advance copy of her book. "I like it fine," she said. "It is nice not to have to look at myself on the back of the jacket." Giroux had not acceded to her wish to use her painted self-portrait as the author photo. "I think it will do justice to the subject for some time to come," she tried to convince him. Yet the final presentation, without any photograph at all, was just as agreeable, and projected a stylish, literary sensibility similar to their last project, *Wise Blood,* in hardcover — if not to the Signet paperback, then on the racks in a print run of 234,090, featuring a racy cover drawing of Sabbath and Haze flirting in the grass, its steamy tagline "A Searching Novel of Sin and Redemption." The jacket for *A Good Man Is Hard to Find* was again abstract, with white title words in scarlet pools against a tan background; its modest first printing, 2,500 copies — 500 less than *Wise Blood.*

Flannery remained in Manhattan until Friday, meeting with her agent and journalists, and participating in the literary life she had warily sampled during her years in the north. "I had interviews with this one and that one," she regaled the Fitzgeralds, "ate with this one and that one, drank with this one and that one, and generally managed to conduct myself as if this were all very well but I had business at home." She spent most of the time in the company of Catharine Carver, feeling comfortable with the shy, impeccable line editor, who was such a deep fan of her work. In honor of her author's visit, Carver procured two of the most coveted tickets of the season, to Tennessee Williams's *Cat on a Hot Tin Roof,* at the Morosco Theatre. Flannery found the play that went on to win a 1955 Pulitzer Prize "melodramatic": "I thought I could do that good myself," she told McKee. "However, on reflection I guess it is wise to doubt that."

Her most unusual assignation was a quick visit with Fred Darsey, a young man recently escaped from Milledgeville State Hospital, where he was committed by his parents during a troubled adolescence. Darsey first caught her interest with a blind letter, in March, from the mental institution, revealing his passion for bird-watching. She was startled when her reply was returned and the envelope marked "eloped." She sympathized, when Darsey wrote her again from New York City, "When you have a friend there you feel as if you are there yourself, so you see I feel as if I have escaped too." Carver helped arrange the date, which Flannery kept secret from Regina, in Bryant Park, at the rear of the New York Public Library, with the pen pal she had never met. "I just love to sit and look at the people in New York, or anywhere," she told him, "even in Milledgeville."

Flannery wound up her trip north spending the weekend in Connecticut with Caroline Gordon. They stayed at Robber Rocks, the farmhouse of the writer and editor Sue Jenkins, in Tory Valley, a longtime literary enclave on the Connecticut–New York border. Just down the road was a house the Tates had rented in the twenties with the poet Hart Crane. Stopping by, she noted, "There was a lot of his stuff piled up in a corner, a pair of snow shoes and some other things." In honor of this visit, Jenkins threw a party, inviting the Mark Twain biographer Van Wyck Brooks, and Flannery's Yaddo acquaintance and leader of a postwar Faulkner revival, Malcolm Cowley. When "Dear old Van Wyke" insisted that Flannery read one of her stories, she began "Good Country People" but was interrupted by Caroline Gordon, who was worried about the response to the hayloft scene, suggesting "A Good Man Is Hard to Find" as shocking enough.

"It was interesting to see the guffaws of the company die away into a kind of frozen silence as they saw which way things were heading," Gordon reported to Fannie Cheney of Flannery's reading of "A Good Man." While exiting, Brooks remarked to his hostess on the shame of someone so talented viewing life as "a horror story." He felt her characters were "alien to the American way of life." An amused Flannery added in the detail to the Fitzgeralds that "Malcolm was very polite and asked me if I had a wooden leg." The next day, Sue Jenkins drove Flannery and Caroline to mass and read the *Times* while waiting. On the way back, Flannery spoke of Guardini's *Faith and Modern Man,* and Caroline excitedly told her about Erich Neumann's *Origins and History of Consciousness,* "about the best book I ever read, next to Holy Writ," while their hostess visibly sulked. "She felt left out," Caroline wrote her husband. "How childish can grown women get?"

Upon her return to Milledgeville, by June 8, Flannery found a letter waiting from Fred Darsey, written soon after their rendezvous at the New York Public Library, addressed, "Dear Ferocious Flannery," and accompanied by a small, illustrated booklet, *The Life of Jesus.* She quickly responded that "I think I am about as ferocious as you are," adding, "I saw about a million people during the week, and I'm very glad to get back to the chickens who don't know that I write." She had indeed reached a point where her heart was decidedly in Georgia, on the farm, savoring the unsophisticated responses of her "good country" neighbors. "I am fast getting a reputation out of all proportion to my desire for one and this largely because I am now competing with The Lone Ranger," she quipped of a local newspaper announcement of her TV appearance. "Everybody here shakes my hand but nobody reads my stories."

As she recovered from her trip, on the farm that she had downplayed to Harvey Breit, this first week in June turned out to be the single most important for her public career as a writer. Beginning on Sunday, with a front-page review by Sylvia Stallings in the *Her-*

ald Tribune Book Review titled "Flannery O'Connor: A New Shining Talent among Our Storytellers," a fresh attitude toward her fiction started to take hold. On Friday, the *New York Times* ran a daily review by Orville Prescott, confirming her claim "to a high rank among our most talented young writers." Bookstores sold three hundred copies that day, and Harcourt ordered a second printing. On Sunday, a biased rave by Caroline Gordon ran in the *Times Book Review,* claiming, in its first sentence, O'Connor's fulfillment of Henry James's praise of Guy de Maupassant as exhibiting "the artful brevity of a master." Still Gordon complained to friends of being held to a five-hundred-word limit.

Of course O'Connor received her share of mean reviews. A blind notice in *The New Yorker* picked up where a 1952 "Briefly Noted" column on *Wise Blood* had left off, arguing that "there is brutality in these stories, but since the brutes are as mindless as their victims, all we have, in the end, is a series of tales about creatures who collide and drown, or survive to float passively in the isolated sea of the author's compassion, which accepts them without reflecting anything." Flannery's response, to Catharine Carver: "Did you see the nice little notice in the *New Yorker?* I can see now why those things are anonymous." And she bristled at many reviews widely considered positive, such as a piece in *Time* that "was terrible, nearly gave me apoplexy," describing her stories in punchy phrases, including "highly unladylike . . . brutal irony . . . slam bang humor . . . as balefully direct as a death sentence."

A keen observer of popular culture, Flannery had joked to Robie Macauley of her need on TV to work herself up into a heady mix of the professional wrestler Gorgeous George and Catholic Bishop Fulton J. Sheen, host of the popular ABC show *Life Is Worth Living.* She was well aware of a cultural trend toward promoting authors as celebrities in what were called "personality stories" in newspapers, and through the new genre of talk shows pioneered at NBC, such as *The Today Show* (1952) and *The Tonight*

Show (1954) with Steve Allen, and of which *Galley Proof* was a short-lived example. Uncomfortable with the "horrible pictures of me," and unwilling to reveal the medical reasons behind her life on the farm, she poked fun at this trend, hoping her private life would remain hidden behind the hard surface of her fiction.

Yet this reserve backfired in 1955, creating an aura of mystery that led only to further curiosity, and never again abated. Sylvia Stallings closed her adulatory *Herald Tribune* review by citing the "unusual reticence" of the dust jacket that "says very little about the author except that she lives in Milledgeville, Georgia, and is at work on her second novel. Even that is too much probably for the longer she keeps her whereabouts a secret, the sooner she will have finished her next book." Magazine editors did not concur. *Time* ran a photo of her looking almost boyish, à la Carson McCullers. A *Newsweek* year-end roundup of books featured O'Connor as the lead, top-left photograph. *Harper's Bazaar* blew up a soft-focus portrait of her, dressed in a work shirt, as if fresh from the typewriter, looking off winsomely, seated on the front steps of Andalusia. "The effect, though 'glamorous' as they used to say, isn't at all natural," complained Ashley Brown.

The author had to contend with another book release that month, as well. *Wise Blood* was published in England on June 26, using as its cover blurb a truncated version of Evelyn Waugh's comment: "It is a remarkable product." O'Connor wrote the Cheneys, "You should see Hazel Motes picture on the front of the British edition of my book. It came out last month, put out by somebody named Neville Spearman who is apparently always just on the edge of bankruptcy. This one will probably push him over the edge. Anyway, here is the British conception of Mr. Mote's face (black wool hat on top); also the rat-colored car is there — all this in black and white and pink and blue, the book itself being an unbelievable orange." The new edition prompted a review in the *Times Literary Supplement,* warning that the work of this lady author "from the American South" was "intense, erratic and strange."

Still Flannery could not help being pleased with the general reception of *A Good Man Is Hard to Find,* a patent departure from the flat incomprehension that had so often greeted her work. "This book is getting much more attention than Wise Blood and may even sell a few copies," the surprised author had written the Fitzgeralds. When her editor informed her that the collection was selling better than anything on their list except Thomas Merton, she cracked, "Doesn't say much for their list." In quick succession, *A Good Man* went through three printings, selling 4,000 copies over the summer, and was named a finalist for a 1956 National Book Award, losing out eventually to John O'Hara's *Ten North Frederick.* Its inevitable fate was the thirty-five-cent paperback, published by Signet the next year in a run of 173,750 copies, with a lurid cover of Hulga, in an open blouse and red skirt, her leg and foot bare, struggling in a hayloft with a dark stranger.

※

AMID ALL THESE diverging critical responses, including high praise, and book covers that could seem weird and distorted, Flannery felt something akin to a sigh of gratitude in the middle of July when she received a thoughtful letter from a young woman named Betty Hester, living in Atlanta. The stranger disagreed with *The New Yorker* review, and asked whether these stories were not truly "about God." Flannery's response, on July 20, was full of excitement: "Dear Miss Hester, I am very pleased to have your letter. Perhaps it is even more startling to me to find someone who recognizes my work for what I try to make it than it is for you to find a God-conscious writer near at hand. The distance is 87 miles but I feel the spiritual distance is shorter."

Although they would not meet in person for another year, Betty Hester and Flannery developed an instant sisterly bond. They shared many similarities, made all the more striking by their unlikely profiles as brainy, independent-minded, unmarried women in the Deep South of the 1950s. Born in Rome, Georgia, thirty-two-year-old Hester was mostly self-educated, having attended a humble local junior college, Young Harris, a two-year Methodist school in the Appalachian Mountains of rural northern Georgia. Serving as a meteorologist with the U.S. Air Force in Germany shortly after World War II, she then moved to 2795 Peachtree Road, at the corner of Rumson Road, in Buckhead, to live, again like Flannery, with a widowed female relative; in her case her aunt, Mrs. Gladstone Pitt, who went by the nickname "Clyde."

Every morning, like a character out of a Kafka novel, either doomed, or aspiring, to invisibility, Betty took a bus downtown to her job as a clerk at Credit Bureau, Inc., later acquired by Equifax. Resembling Flannery in stature, as well — she was about five three, 130 pounds, with thick horn-rimmed spectacles, a Roman nose, and ash blonde hair — Betty mostly kept to herself. According to a mutual friend, "Betty was very shy. So she and Flannery could be quiet together." Each night, the reclusive clerk returned to her aunt's apartment and took up her station on the living room couch, where she slept, as well as read and wrote, surrounded by stacks of books, ashtrays — she was a heavy smoker — and a menagerie of cats. She wrote hundreds of letters to Flannery, and was later identified as "A" in O'Connor's published correspondence, to protect her privacy.

Perhaps from reading the letters about devotional art between the Jesuit poet Gerard Manley Hopkins and his friend and close reader Robert Bridges, or simply from "apoplexy" at the incomprehension of some reviewers, Flannery, after 1955, felt a pressing need to explain her artistic intentions. Aware of the limits of her understanding of "my own work or even my own motivations," these letters gave her an opportunity to try to set the record straight, for herself as much as anyone. Already in her initial response, she vented about the *New Yorker* critic as an example of "a generation of wingless chickens" with "the moral sense . . . bred out." She set the tone for her forthcoming talks and essays when she told Hester, "I write the way I do because (not though) I am a Catholic. This is a fact and nothing covers it like the bald statement. However, I am a Catholic peculiarly possessed of the modern consciousness, that thing Jung describes as unhistorical, solitary and guilty."

As much as a sympathetic reader, of course, Flannery was in need of a dear friend. Betty's perceptive letter came just three months after the news from Erik of his engagement, and the same month as his marriage. While Flannery was in New York City, her new friend Fred Darsey had detected on her face a "disappointed look." She insisted that this expression, which she claimed others had noticed in the city, was congenital: "This is the look I have been carrying around since birth — born disenchanted." Yet she certainly had cause for disappointment, including, most recently, the loss of her confidant. Like Erik, Betty promised to be able to keep up with her intellectual breadth and curiosity, as they filled their letters that summer with lively debates on Thomas Aquinas, Etienne Gilson, Henry James, Graham Greene, Samuel Beckett, Sigmund Freud, Victor White, and Carl Jung.

Ever the fiction writer, Flannery characterized her friends quickly, and stuck to the categories she imposed. Erik was a "displaced person," the prototype of a traveling salesman. Betty, she decided early on, was Simone Weil. She saw in this homegrown intellectual — an agnostic obsessed with God — something of the tormented, brilliant French Jew, who was deeply drawn to Christianity, yet agonizing over and never taking the step to baptism. Weil had died of tuberculosis in England, in 1943, refusing food in solidarity with those living in Nazi-occupied France. In her second letter, Flannery asked if Betty had ever read Weil, and, in the next, confessed, "I have thought of Simone Weil in connection with you almost from the first." She also revealed a wish to write a novel about a character like Weil: "and what is more comic and terrible than the angular intellectual proud woman approaching God inch by inch with ground teeth?"

Their connection soon went beyond merely typing out thoughts on paper. Flannery was once moved to enclose a peacock feather, and an article on Edith Stein — a Jewish-born Carmelite nun and Catholic saint who died at Auschwitz — clipped from the *Third Hour,* the magazine edited by Erik's aunt. Betty mailed her a novel by Nelson Algren. "I have read almost 200 pages so far," Flannery answered. "I don't think he is a good writer." They soon developed a system, as they sent books back and forth by post, thriftily turning around the brown packing paper, adding Scotch tape, and addressing the stickers on the reverse side. From her own shelf, Flannery mailed off *The Lord* by Romano Guardini, a contemporary theologian in Germany. From an Atlanta public library, Betty sent back Simone Weil's *Letters to a Priest* and *Waiting for God.*

By early October 1955, Flannery was preparing to visit the Cheneys in Nashville. The challenge was steeper than usual, though, as she had to adjust to crutches. Her doctors had diagnosed a "softening" of the top of the leg bone, and believed that taking weight off the hip for a year or two might allow the bone to harden again; if not, a wheelchair or an operation to insert a steel cap would be necessary. They assured her that the condition was unrelated to lupus, though later studies established an occurrence of this condition of osteonecrosis in twenty percent of lupus patients treated with high-dose corticosteroids. She was also switched to Meticorten, a trade name for prednisone, a new pill form of the drug. "I am learning to walk on crutches," she wrote Betty, "and I feel like a large stiff anthropoid ape who has no cause to be thinking of St. Thomas or Aristotle."

She wrote a letter to Betty before leaving, hoping to strengthen their bond. If Betty instigated the relationship, Flannery tended to take responsibility for ensuring its growth. Betty had exhibited a guarded interest in the Thomism that Flannery had been spinning for her over the past three months, and she was an apprentice writer having approached a master. She showed promise as a disciple, a pupil, and a friend. "It occurs to me to ask you if I may stop calling you Miss Hester and if you will stop calling me Miss O'Connor," Flannery wrote on October 12. "It makes me give myself airs hearing myself called Miss. I have a mental picture of you as a lady 7 ft. tall, weighing 95 lbs. Miss Hester fits this image better than Betty but I think I can still make the shift without disabusing myself of the vision. You can let me know after you meditate on it."

Her time in Nashville was designed so that Flannery could meet the Cheneys' other weekend guest at Cold Chimneys, Russell Kirk, who was in town to lecture at Vanderbilt. An old-school conservative thinker in the Anglo-American tradition, popularizing the ideas of Edmund Burke, Kirk was teaching at Michigan State, and had helped found that year the journal *National Review.* Flannery admired his 1953 book, *The Conservative Mind: From Burke to Santayana,* which Brainard Cheney had reviewed in *Sewanee.* In her copy, she drew marginal lines next to a phrase that was an important seed in her thinking: "Abstract sentimentality ends in real brutality." But in person the chemistry was weak. She saw him as "Humpty Dumpty (intact) with constant cigar and (outside) porkpie hat," and their "attempts to make talk were like the efforts of two midgits to cut down a California redwood."

Kirk had never read any of O'Connor's stories. But over the weekend he grew interested, as he heard the young woman on crutches, with a bandaged leg he assumed was broken, reading her reliable "A Good Man" aloud in the library. As Frances Cheney later told a group of students, "She was no beaut, but she could tell a story." Flannery shared that evening the request of a Theater Arts major in Los Angeles to film the story because it would be cheap to produce. "Cheap and nasty," responded Kirk. On his way back to Michigan, he read O'Connor's book and was excited enough to recommend her to T. S. Eliot, his London publisher. Eliot replied that he had seen a book of her stories while in New York City and was "quite horrified by those I read. She has certainly an uncanny talent of a high order but my nerves are just not strong enough to take much of a disturbance."

O'Connor returned to a desk even messier than usual. Despite Caroline Gordon's warning that "I hope you won't let them bully you into writing a novel if you don't feel like it," she had signed the contract for a second novel. Of its working title, *You Can't Be Any Poorer than Dead,* Flannery joked to Macauley, "Which is the way I feel every time I get to work on it." She was once more embarked on a novel that would take years to finish, this time her alter ego a fierce, fourteen-year-old, backwoods boy fighting the call to be an Old Testament–style prophet in the contemporary South. To support the work, she applied for a Guggenheim, with references from Giroux, Lindley, and Andrew Lytle, but was again denied. Preparing the way for her new hero, she worked on a talk to be given the next year in Lansing, Michigan, that she was calling "The Freak in Modern Fiction."

But, in early winter, Flannery found herself once again visualizing her imaginary farm, its widow-owner visited this time by an "uncouth country suitor" in the form of a pawing black bull chewing at a bush beneath her bedroom window in the silvery moonlight. While treating novels as homework assignments to be painfully completed, stories had become for Flannery quick target practice, often resulting in her most successful productions. "I get so sick of my novel that I have to have some diversion," she told the

Cheneys of her new story. As usual, its heroine, Mrs. May, was once removed from Regina, this time in her habit of inspecting the fields. "Miss Regina always picked me up to go riding," recalls Al Matysiak. "I'd get out of the car and undo the gates and shut them back behind her." Its overhead sun "like a silver bullet" was also familiar to Flannery, who needed to wear a big hat outdoors to prevent the rash that sunlight could trigger.

Yet her new story, "Greenleaf," was as much myth as *tranche de vie,* its scrub bull, let loose from his pen by the unreliable tenant farmers, the Greenleaf boys, sporting a hedge-wreath on his horns, "like some patient god come down to woo her." Flannery had recently befriended Ben Griffith, liking his review of *A Good Man* in the *Savannah Morning News* — "Stories of Gifted Writer Acquire Stature of Myths" — for having "brought out a lot of points I wanted to see brought out." And "Greenleaf" almost seemed written to prove his theory about the mythic, folkloric elements in her work. For although the bull in the story was a composite of one down the road "that was always getting out and running his head through the fender of the truck" and the O'Connors' more pleasant Paleface, by the time Mrs. May is gored her bull is at least Zeus, the metamorphosing übergod of Greek myth, if not Christ, the horned unicorn of medieval tapestry: "the bull had buried his head in her lap, like a wild tormented lover, before her expression changed. One of his horns sank until it pierced her heart and the other curved around her side and held her in an unbreakable grip."

As Flannery was completing the story, she received news that she treated as if it were as much an epiphany as the quake of the bull's body against Mrs. May. Betty Hester informed her in January that she was going to be baptized. "I'm never prepared for anything," Flannery quickly reacted. "All voluntary baptisms are a miracle to me and stop my mouth as much as if I had just seen Lazarus walk out of the tomb." Overlooking her six months' worth of arguments for faith, from Aquinas, Maritain, and Guardini, she adopted the posture of someone who had been holding back, not wanting "to stuff the Church down your throat." In honor of her March 31 baptism, Flannery sent a finished copy of "Greenleaf," just accepted by John Crowe Ransom at *Kenyon Review,* to be published in the Summer 1956 issue, and to earn her a first "1st Prize" O. Henry Award, chosen that year by Paul Engle and Constance Urdang.

Finished by the start of April 1956, as well, was her talk on literary freaks, for the American Association of University Women in Lansing, Michigan. So three weeks later Flannery set off again on the crutches she was calling her "flying buttresses." The trip involved a plane to Detroit, where she was met by her hosts, Alta Lee and Rumsey Haynes at ten thirty p.m., and taken to their home as a guest for four nights. Finding that she had a talent for such "intellectual vaudeville," she had already delivered addresses locally: in Macon, for a Women's Book Review Group; in Atlanta, at a Pen Women tea and for the Georgia Council of Teachers of English. But this trip marked the first of the out-of-state appearances — often physically demanding — that she began making across the nation on a mission to explain her work in speeches painstakingly rewritten for each occasion.

Alta Lee Haynes was surprised by the modesty of her guest. "There she was, so young and smiling, and fresh despite the late hour and the long trip," she remembered. "Her crutches, we'd all worried about them, seemed to enhance, to set off her attractiveness. . . . Half way up the stairs I learned a lesson in etiquette. Rumsey was leading the way, Flannery was navigating expertly, and I was following — chattering friendly inanities. Each time I said a word Flannery would stop and turn completely around to face me. Finally I saw the light and stopped talking. . . . Her behavior was consistently gracious." In her talk at Eastern Lansing High School, O'Connor said that modern writers must often tell "perverse" stories to "shock" a morally blind world. "It requires considerable courage," she concluded, "not to turn away from the story-teller."

Soon after her return home, Betty Hester officially asked Flannery to serve as "sponsor" for her final step of acceptance into the Roman Catholic Church, her confirmation, scheduled for the following June, when she would take the Christian name "Gertrude," with the blessing of Father John Mulroy of the Cathedral of Christ the King in Atlanta. Flannery's participation, though, would be by proxy, as the two still had not met in person. Betty cryptically inquired whether she ought first to share some horrible details from her past. "I am highly pleased to be asked and to do it and as for your horrible history, that has nothing to do with it," Flannery wrote back decisively. "I'm interested in the history because it's you but not for this or any other occasion." As a confirmation gift, she sent *A Short Breviary* in a more "garish-looking" edition than her own. Betty, however, would wait six more months before revealing her secret.

Because Betty was going public with her conversion, and seemingly shuffling off the coil of Simone Weil's hesitancy about the Christian religion, Flannery felt empowered to invite her to participate more fully in the Church. As an act of Lenten "mortification," as well as tapping into a source of free copies of contemporary novels and works of theology, Flannery had begun writing one-page reviews for the *Bulletin*. A biweekly paper published by the Diocese of Atlanta — newly created that year as an independent diocese under Bishop Francis E. Hyland — the *Bulletin* ran about twelve of Flannery's articles a year over the next eight years. Her first review, which appeared in the February 1956 issue, treated an anthology of Catholic short fiction; as she wrote a friend, "I have just had the doubtful honor of reviewing *All Manner of Men* for the diocesan paper, yclept the *Bulletin*." So Flannery recommended

Betty to its editor, Eileen Hall, and she was quickly enlisted to write her own 200-word reviews. "The competition is at least not overpowering," Flannery promised.

Out of this nexus of the Atlanta diocese, the *Bulletin,* and Betty Hester, soon appeared William Sessions, a writer and instructor at West Georgia College. In his twenties, Sessions was likewise reviewing for the diocesan paper while still on the brink of conversion, having been brought up Southern Baptist. When Betty mentioned him in a letter, Flannery recalled admiring his review in the *Bulletin* of the newly translated English version of Guardini's *The Lord,* a book that she had already sent to Hester. She wrote to thank him for the review and to invite him to make a springtime visit to Andalusia, though she pretended to have second thoughts when Betty informed her that following graduation from the University of North Carolina and while pursuing an MA at Columbia, Sessions had spent time as a ballet dancer in Manhattan. "When forced to a program of it," Flannery proclaimed, "I am liable to twist hideously in my seat."

Sessions visited Andalusia on Ascension Day, a Thursday, in May 1956, beginning what would constitute a mutual, three-way friendship with Betty and Flannery. The connection was natural and Flannery read his stories, some of which she felt were ready to be sent out; prayed for his intentions before his own confirmation; and, in the fall, looked over his application for a Fulbright to study theology with Guardini at the University of Munich. But she could also make mean, funny remarks about him to Betty. In a hilarious account of his arrival at the farm, she reported that he talked his way up the steps "without pause, break, breath," until supper when he encountered "a little head wind" from Regina, "also a talker." If Flannery and Betty were sisters, "Billy" was the younger brother they liked to pick on. Flannery was fond of him, *and* he was her piñata. "I was basically treated as Billy the Idiot," Sessions has characterized the situation.

Finally, the fourth weekend in June, Betty agreed to visit Andalusia herself. Flannery solicitously tried to make the trip as painless as possible, sensing her guest's hesitation at venturing outside her narrow life in Atlanta, and, as far as their friendship, off the page. She promised an air-conditioned bus and a ride back Sunday evening with Uncle Louis; his young driver, named Franklyn; and their passenger, Betty Watkins, a government worker whose "conversation is limited to where she buys her shoes." Betty Hester declined both the offer to stay the night and the subsequent car ride, choosing instead to take the bus home, although she disliked air-conditioning. Flannery promised to meet her at the Andalusia gate, "me sitting on bumper waving crutch," and was quite surprised on first sight to find her guest prettier than she had been led to believe: "I always take people at their word and I was prepared for white hair, horn-rimmed spectacles, nose of eagle and shape of gingerbeer bottle. Seek the truth and pursue it: you ain't even passably ugly."

No sooner had Betty left than Flannery was coaxing her to stay longer next time, feeling that she had been "poised for flight — a lark with a jet engine." As she had not taken a meal, Regina was not "quite convinced that you exist on a plane with the rest of us." But their meaningful conversation kept Flannery pondering afterward. Of Betty's comment that she had evidently given up long ago thinking that anything could be worked out on the surface, Flannery expounded more fully in her next letter that she had come to a deeper understanding only in the last years, as a result of sickness and success: "I have never been anywhere but sick. In a sense sickness is a place more instructive than a long trip to Europe, and it's a place where there's no company, where nobody can follow. . . . Success is almost as isolating and nothing points out vanity as well."

As if such a coy attitude were more ladylike, Regina liked to say that Flannery did not seek out friends but waited until they came to her. Certainly after the publication of *A Good Man Is Hard to Find,* O'Connor was a target for lots of unsolicited attention. Betty Hester was her happiest connection. Others she simply made fun of. As she wrote Robie Macauley, "I seem to attract the lunatic fringe mainly," like Mr. Jimmie Crum of Hollywood who asked for an autographed picture for the wall of his rare coin and stamp shop, or two theological students who selected her as "their pin-up girl — the grimmest distinction to date." She helped Paul Curry Steele, a writer, who had a history in mental institutions, enter the Iowa Writers' Workshop, based solely on a story he mailed her, although she distanced herself when the tone of his lengthy letters turned angry.

Regina was forced to make sense of the cars driving up more and more during Flannery's downtime in the afternoons, often filled with strangers. Flannery told the Fitzgeralds that "Some Very Peculiar Types have beat a path to my door these last few years and it is always interesting to see my mother hostessing-it-up on these occasions." Typical of such a surprise visitor that year was Father James McCown, S.J., assistant pastor at St. Joseph's Catholic Church in Macon, who had read *A Good Man Is Hard to Find.* He commandeered a ride from Horace Ridley, an affable local whiskey salesman, to drive forty miles to seek out its author. In Milledgeville, the rumpled cleric asked directions from Father Toomey's mother, who replied, "Mary Flannery is a sweet girl. But I'm afraid to go near her. She might put me in one of her stories."

As Flannery told the Fitzgeralds, "a white Packard drove up to our humble yard and out jumped an unknown Jesuit." Yet Father McCown was as surprised by the author as she was by him. She appeared at the screen door in old jeans, long before they became modish, and a brown blouse, leaning on aluminum waist-high crutches and staring out for a disquieting few seconds until the priest explained that he liked her stories. "Proud you did," she said, smiling at last. "Wanna come in?" She told Betty that he was the first priest to say "turkey-dog to me about liking anything I wrote." When Alfred Kazin spoke that spring at Macon's Wesleyan College, McCown drove him out for a visit, along with Professors Tom and Louise Gossett. And McCown gradually became a spiritual adviser to Flannery, later characterizing her issues, such as whether to eat ham broth at Sanford House on a fast day, as "of the scope and seriousness of a convent-bred schoolgirl."

Stuck on the farm, Flannery depended on these random visitors for a wider social life; likewise she avidly relied on local events for fodder for her fiction. As she had told Erik when he accused her of parlaying their time together into "Good Country People": "Never let it be said that I don't make the most of experience and information, no matter how meager." By the summer of 1956, most noticeable to her was the encroachment of the modern world, as commercialism and industrialization transformed the landscape and Andalusia received its first telephone line — number 2-5335 — described by Flannery as "a great mother-saver." Georgia Power Company's Sinclair Dam on the Oconee River had created a high-power generating plant and a fifteen-thousand-acre lake north of town. And Milledgeville was annexing a five-hundred-acre wooded area just across Highway 441 for a housing subdivision.

Andalusia, five years after mother and daughter took up full-time residence, was now a fully operating dairy farm, with its overseer, Regina O'Connor, characterized by one friend as "very oriented towards making money." She was helped by the same crew of three or four full-time African American workers, as well as revolving white families, including the Stevenses, the Mays, and the Matysiaks, who departed, disgruntled, the next year, only to return two years later. Regina's main emphasis was still on herds of milk-producing cows, and artificial breeding was deployed to ensure top milk-producing calves. Shetland ponies were a secondary operation, with six-month-old colts sold at market around Christmastime. But Mrs. O'Connor had also begun considering selling off timber rights; within a few summers, Flannery watched through the screen door as Regina held a front-porch auction for some pinewood acreage, bargaining for twenty-five thousand dollars more than expected.

O'Connor sketched the dangers of such development for the farm surrounded by a line of black piney woods in "A View of the Woods," a story as political in its ecological implications as "The Displaced Person." Completed in September 1956, her tale of greedy Mr. Fortune and his nine-year-old granddaughter — in love with a lawn and view that her grandfather is willing to sell off to a future of "houses and stores and parking places" — accurately described the fate of the Eatonton Highway area. "The electric power company had built a dam on the river and flooded great areas of the surrounding country," she wrote in her story. "There was talk of their getting a telephone line. There was talk of paving the road that ran in front of the Fortune place." Left standing at its climax, as published the next fall in *Partisan Review,* in place of the bull of "Greenleaf," was a true "huge yellow monster," an earth-digger machine, "gorging itself on clay."

Of all Flannery's new friends, the one she most wished to see at Andalusia, of course, was the one most resistant to visiting. But that fall she finally convinced Betty to return, promising her a ride from Atlanta with "breathless" Bill Sessions, just back from San Francisco, where he had been studying German at Berlitz in anticipation of his Fulbright trip abroad. The two friends visited on Saturday, October 23, with Regina planning a meal around sweet potatoes. Flannery had much to share. She had finished a painting of her chukar quail. And she and her mother were the proud owners of a stainless-steel Hotpoint refrigerator, with an automatic ice-maker, bought with proceeds from the sale of "The Life You Save May Be Your Own" for a television adaptation. "While they make hash out of my story," she said, "she and me will make ice in the new refrigerator."

But in a letter immediately following the visit, Betty felt compelled to fill in Flannery on the details of what she called her "history of horror" before their friendship went any further. Hester had endured a particularly difficult childhood, as her father abandoned the family when she was young. At age thirteen, she watched her mother commit suicide while neighbors, believing her mother to be playacting, refused to call the police. Shipped off in the late 1930s to Young Harris Academy, she didn't fit in with most of her fellow Methodist students. Yet the avowed atheist, who disdained "men and men's ideas," had her admirers. "I thought she was the pussycat's whiskers," recalled her college roommate Anne Dunlap. "I have a vivid picture of her sitting cross-legged in the middle of her bed, smoking one cigarette right after another, expounding deep, dark philosophy."

The decisive event that she related to Flannery, though, occurred in Germany, where she was dishonorably discharged from the military for sexual indiscretion, having been intimately involved with another woman. Such incidents concerning lesbians were treated with special virulence in the Cold War period. Following wartime encouragement of enlistment as Waves or Wacs, women remaining in the military, rather than returning to motherhood, stood out as a deviant group stereotyped as lesbian, and often associated with Communism. Introductory lectures warned newly enlisted women about "confirmed" lesbians, and encouraged informing on them. In her coming-out letter to Flannery, Betty spoke of feeling "unbearably guilty" for her part in the incident, and offered to end their friendship to prevent scandal from being visited on the author.

Flannery's response to Betty's revelation was immediate and caring: "I can't write you fast enough and tell you that it doesn't make the slightest bit of difference in my opinion of you, which is the same as it was, and that is: based solidly on complete respect." As to Betty's point about scandal, Flannery argued, "I'm obscure enough. Nobody knows or cares who I see. If it created any tension in you that I don't understand, then use your own judgment, but understand that from my point of view, you are always wanted." Flannery did suggest that they not tell Regina as "she wouldn't understand." Given the nature of their friendship, she parsed the matter theologically, "Where you are wrong is in saying that you *are* a history of horror. The meaning of the Redemption is precisely that we do not have to *be* our history." She then invited Betty for Thanksgiving dinner.

When Betty declined the invitation to a goose dinner with Bill Sessions and Father McCown, she evidently questioned the premise of Flannery's theology: Did she mean that she was expected to change her nature by entering the Church? Flannery clarified: "I wish you could come but I respect your reasons. Perhaps what I should have said is that you are more than your history. I don't believe the fundamental nature changes but that it's put to a different use when a conversion occurs and of course it requires vigilance to put it to the proper use." Soon enough their friendship was back on track, with a shared secret. For Christmas, Betty sent the *Notebooks* of Simone Weil, and Flannery thanked her, for "Simone Weil but even more for your own letters." Within nine months, Betty began to visit Andalusia again, for a few longer stays. As with the Fitzgeralds, Flannery grew to think of her as one of her "adopted kin."

Yet Betty did have a crush on Flannery, and, in this case, was the unrequited partner. Forty years later, she wrote a fan letter to the Atlanta novelist Greg Johnson — as she had once written Flannery — and the subject of her "in some odd ways truly strangely innocent" friend took over their correspondence. She addressed Johnson's remark that he felt "speculating about her sexual feelings in print would no doubt have been extremely distasteful to her," by agreeing and adding that he might even be underestimating the distaste by limiting it to print alone. Betty confided that Flannery had once said to her, 'In my stories is where I live." In a tender confession, she concluded to Johnson, "As you must sense, I did love her *very*, very much — and, God knows, *do*."

᠅

IN THE FALL of 1956, Georgia State College for Women recruited a new president whose name alone would have qualified him for an executive post in many a Southern college: Robert E. Lee, nicknamed "Buzz." Although he fulfilled some of the expectations raised by his famous name, such as the flourish of ending a public talk with the supposed last words of the Confederate general — "Strike the Tent!" — Lee was actually a tall, handsome young man, in his midthirties, with moderate social views. He was hardly as liberal, though, as Guy Wells, president during O'Connor's college years, who once inspired a Klan cross-burning on the front lawn of the Governor's Mansion for holding an integrated meeting of college administrators. As Flannery told of the Wells incident, "The people who burned the cross couldn't have gone past the fourth grade but, for the time, they were mighty interested in education."

When Dr. Lee was appointed by the Regents, though, Flannery was far less involved in the day-to-day life of the college she used to refer to, in shorthand, to Betty Boyd, as "the institution of higher larning across the road." She kept up friendships with her teachers Hallie Smith and Helen Greene, and English Department chairwoman, Rosa Lee Walston, as well as the librarians who hosted her signing party. She had a nodding acquaintance with faculty who lunched at Sanford House. But the Governor's Mansion only truly returned to her ken when the new college president invited his sister, Mary Attaway Lee, or "Maryat" — quickly to become the least likely and most challenging of Flannery's new friends — and their mother, Grace Barbee Dyer Lee, of Covington, Kentucky, to visit him, his wife, and their three little children for Christmas 1956.

Thirty-three-year-old Maryat Lee had a compelling résumé. Having grown up in their Kentucky family home, presided over by her lawyer-businessman father, Dewitt Collins Lee, she attended National Cathedral School, in Washington, DC; studied acting at Northwestern University; and graduated, in 1945, from Wellesley College, majoring in Bible History. Moving to New York City, she worked for the anthropologist Margaret Mead and earned an MA at Union Theological Seminary, where Paul Tillich directed her thesis on the origins of drama in religion. Already an activist, Maryat put theory into practice in her 1951 production, *Dope!,* a street play in Harlem, covered by *Life,* and published in *Best Short Plays of 1952–53.* By the end of 1956 she was living a consummately unconventional life in a walk-up tenement, with a bathtub in the kitchen, at 192 Sixth Avenue in Greenwich Village, between Prince and Spring streets.

Unlike Flannery, who adopted in public the cover of a prim, Southern lady, camouflaging what everyone agreed were "highly unladylike" thoughts, Maryat's appearance was every bit as extreme as her thinking and writing. Nearly six feet tall, with a long face, strong "Lee chin," and hazel eyes, she strode the streets of Milledgeville outfitted in pants, boots, a black overcoat, and an imposing Russian lamb's wool hat. "Maryat was the ultimate bohemian aunt who would show up wearing these outrageous clothes in the middle of the night, carrying brown bags with cans of beer, which were illegal, as it was a dry county, and my father was not allowed to have any liquor in the house, as president," remembers her niece Mary Dean Lee. "Hers was a larger-than-life, charismatic personality. Whenever she visited, it was very exciting for me."

Feeling oppressed by the holiday season spent in the antebellum mansion, and beset by family dramas that she helped stir up, Maryat was longing, three days after Christmas, to return north. "I remember that I was feeling churlish," she recalled, "having been dined and 'punched' by my fun-loving sister-in-law for a solid week of parties — dinner parties, luncheon parties, even breakfast parties of forty people — and not having upset the apple cart by word, frown, or deed." Yet she received a note from Barbara ("Charlye") Wiggins Prescott, a poet at Macon's Wesleyan College, where Maryat had briefly taught speech and drama, telling of O'Connor in worshipful tones. On the same day, Flannery, also prodded by Prescott, telephoned Maryat to invite her to Andalusia.

Expecting the worst — "a local lady writer" — Maryat, having never read or heard of Flannery O'Connor, complied. When she arrived, dressed in pants and pink tennis shoes, Mrs. O'Connor called for her to come through the front way to avoid the peacock droppings. Looking down quickly at a hole in Maryat's sneaker, Regina hid her disapproval by politely remarking, "*My,* aren't you *smaht* to be prepared." She then unlocked the front door from a big ring of keys, commenting as she led her into the dining room that you can't be too careful these days with "the niggahs." But "Just as I opened my mouth to address myself to the inference that as Southerners we all accepted what the situation really was," recalled the outspoken and politically liberal Maryat, "Flannery made her entrance," preceded by "the soft long swinging crutch thud sound."

At first sight, Flannery did indeed look the part of a local lady writer, in her conservative dress, stockings, and shiny patent-leather shoes. "She was so awkward in her get-up that instead of leaving, I began to be curious." Maryat was especially conscious of the author's "astonishingly beautiful eyes" grazing over her, and quickly looking away when the glances were returned. Still irked at Regina's racist comment, Maryat announced that she was catching a ride in a few hours to the Atlanta airport with the family of Emmett Jones, the black gardener at the college — a blatant violation of the code that allowed blacks as chauffeurs, not friends. Sensing the shocked response of her mother, Flannery abruptly suggested a walk, and led them, swinging her crutches, through the house, as Regina called after, "Well, yawl watch out for that ole sun."

Pushing out the unlocked back door, and past Chinese geese, each of which Flannery called "Sister," as she stroked the orange bumps on their foreheads, and down their soft, stiff necks, the two women paused finally at a pasture fence. As Lee recalled the meeting two decades later, Flannery took the unusual step of sharing some details of her illness, and of her decision to move back home with her mother, as she pulled at the barbed wire in little tugs. The silence following her confidence was broken only by "the croupy cry of a goose, the random buzz of a winter fly." She then showed Maryat the henhouse that she dreamed of one day furnishing with two cane-bottomed chairs and a refrigerator, as a private office, admitting that "the parental presence never contributes to my articulateness." The two, of course, also discussed religion. As Lee recalled: "Her words had theological overtones. I asked if she were Catholic. 'Yes,' she answered quietly. 'Really into it?' 'Yes, I am.' 'Oh,' I said. Uh-oh, I said to myself."

Before Maryat left, Flannery handed her copies of a few stories, including "You Can't Be Any Poorer Than Dead," published in *New World Writing*. Fearing that she might not like the work, Maryat read one story before leaving for the airport. "I was excited, relieved, impressed — and mystified." She wrote of her discovery that "although metaphysics was central, there were simply no false moves." Immediately on returning to Manhattan, she wrote her reactions, and Flannery responded, starting a correspondence that would amount to more than 250 letters. (Maryat addressed one of her first, "In Care of the Henhouse.") Maryat soon took her place, too, in the world of O'Connor's fiction, both as a caricature and as a source of anecdotes and themes from current events. An odd couple of friends, Flannery joked of their "kinship between us, in spite of all the differences there are."

In the middle of January, "Buzz" Lee traveled to Philadelphia to interview potential faculty, and took time to pay a rare visit to his sister in New York. She sent him home with a copy of *Dope!* to deliver to Flannery, which he did, stopping by the farm on a Sunday evening. As Flannery wrote up the visit for Maryat, "I thought now this is a mighty nice man to come all the way out here to bring me a book, but by the time he left, I found myself engaged to talk in the GSCW chapel on the 7th of February. As I say, your brother will go far." Not a religious event as its name implied, Chapel, as in Flannery's day, was the weekly student convocation in Russell Auditorium for speakers and cultural events. Lee volunteered to introduce her, and glibly asserted that she had been "on and off the best seller lists." Flannery wrote Maryat, "I decided this was an innocent calumniation."

O'Connor's address at the Thursday assembly was titled "The Fiction Writer and His Country," a version of which she had delivered at Wesleyan College, in December. But this talk, with many moving parts she was forever rearranging, held special piquancy delivered in her hometown. Its theme was the local as a portal to the universal. O'Connor made her point with highly regional references to "the reek of Baldwin County." Its climax could easily have been a response to Maryat. When she read *Dope!*, Flannery had punned, on Lee's MA thesis on medieval morality plays, "a real morality play if I ever saw one and altogether powerful in spite of it." The "in spite of" was an inkling of the conclusion to her speech that morality for an artist meant conveying a vision, not a lesson: "If the writer is successful as artist, his moral judgment will coincide with his dramatic judgment. It will be inseparable from the very act of seeing."

While O'Connor's talk was not covered in the local papers, including the school newspaper, the half-hour teleplay of "The Life You Save May Be Your Own" caused more of a stir. Shown on CBS-TV's *Schlitz Playhouse of Stars,* which she mistakenly thought was produced "by Ronald Regan (?)," the program starred "a *tap-dancer* by the name of Gene Kelly" as Tom T. Shiftlet and was broadcast on Friday evening, March 1. The "idiot daughter," played by Janice Rule (and her mother, by Agnes Moorehead) is swept up at the story's revised end by a Shiftlet with a conscience, and driven off into a pleasant sunset. Flannery, "disliking it heartily," watched the production with her aunt Mary Cline, who deemed the ending improved. Reminiscent of Poe, shadowed by children flapping their arms like the Raven after the publication of his famous poem, Flannery told Maryat, "Children now point to me on the street. The city fathers think that I have arrived finally."

Though protesting that writing speeches was a distraction from her true vocation, Flannery spent much of the winter and spring of 1957 ignoring this "better judgment," including an appearance at Emory on "How the Writer Writes." When Granville Hicks asked for a copy of her GSCW address for his anthology, *The Living Novel: A Symposium,* including essays by Saul Bellow, Ralph Ellison, and Herbert Gold, Flannery complained, "I begin to feel like a displaced person myself, writing papers and not fiction." Yet rather than decline, she decided to recast the talk, "designed for a student audience," into a more publishable essay. Her excuse was an invitation from Robert Fitzgerald, who was spending a semester away from Italy as a visiting professor at Notre Dame, to address an audience of faculty and their wives, clergy, graduate students, and seminarians. For these "Cathlick interleckchuls" she felt she could unveil her Christian subtext.

Arriving on Sunday, April 14, at the Chicago airport, where Robert Fitzgerald met her to connect to a flight to South Bend, Flannery was happily reunited with one of her most important friends and mentors for the first time in nearly four years. "She seemed frail but steady, no longer disfigured by any swelling, and her hair had grown long again," he recalled. "She managed her light crutches with distaste but some dexterity." Her host put her up at the Morris Inn, the best accommodation in town, built of yellow Indiana stone, on the edge of campus. She visited with her Iowa City housemate Ruth Sullivan Finnegan, now married to a university professor, and met a new friend, Thomas Stritch, a "bachelor don," the nephew of Cardinal Stritch of Chicago, and another cradle Catholic publishing short stories, for whom she developed an "inordinate affection."

If Fitzgerald's motives in inviting Flannery had been purely self-serving — he simply wished to see her — he was pleasantly surprised on Monday evening to discover that she "had wonderful things to say as a public speaker." Her appearance before an audience of three hundred that she reckoned to Maryat was "25% Bumbling Boys, 25% skirted and beretta-ed simmernarians" proved successful enough for extra chairs to be moved into the hall. She read her paper, as Fitzgerald remembered, "intent upon it, hanging on her crutches at the lectern, courteous and earnest and dissolvent of nonsense." Arguing that she was not your stereotypical Southern gothic writer — "unhappy combinations of Poe and Erskine Caldwell" — O'Connor insisted that her own use of the grotesque was meant to convey a shocking Christian vision of original sin. "To the hard of hearing you shout," she said, "and for the almost blind you draw large and startling figures."

Fitzgerald rightly recognized that the "score" of talks she was beginning to give "brought her into the world again and gave her a whole new range of acquaintances." But her stories were touching enough readers that even when she stayed home her circle of friends and fans was expanding exponentially, belying the stereotyping of her in the press as a reclusive Emily Dickinson of Milledgeville. She had recently received a letter of praise from Robert Lowell's friend the poet Elizabeth Bishop. While the two never met, Bishop did telephone once from Savannah: "Quite soon a very collected, very southern voice answered and immediately invited me to 'Come on over.'" (Bishop later admitted to feeling a bit "intimidated" by O'Connor.) When the poet sent a teeny, carved cross in a bottle from Brazil, Flannery wrote back, "If I were mobile and limber and rich I would come to Brazil at once after one look at this bottle. . . . It's what I'm born to appreciate."

A highly informal letter arrived that spring from Cecil Dawkins, a young fiction writer from Alabama, teaching at Stephens College in Missouri. A friend lent Dawkins a copy of *A Good Man,* and she found the stories revelatory. "I sat down with a six pack of beer one night and I started reading this book and I got increasingly excited," she recalled, "and when I had finished, I wrote a note on just a yellow pad and said, 'You're really great. . . . You're terrific'; and I didn't know where to send it. I just sent it to Milledgeville and I didn't know if she'd ever get it. But I got an answer by return mail and we wrote until she died." Although they met only three times, Flannery recommended Dawkins to her agent, and to Yaddo; she also helped the Roman Catholic writer with her religious doubts. "She became my reader," said Dawkins. "Her reader was Caroline Gordon and Flannery read everything I wrote when I was finished."

The fourth or fifth visitor to become a truly close friend in less than a year was Louise Abbot, a lovely young woman trying to combine motherhood and writing, who lived with her lawyer-husband and small children in Louisville, Georgia, just sixty miles away. Abbot first encountered O'Connor's stories at St. Joseph's in Atlanta, where her husband was hospitalized: "I tried reading them aloud to my husband, but had to stop because it hurt him to laugh." Though a recognized writer, with a prize-winning story published in *Mademoiselle,* she confessed to almost trying to pass herself off as a journalist to meet O'Connor. "I am very glad that you have decided not to be a lady-journalist," Flannery wrote back, inviting her to Andalusia, "because I am deathly afraid of the tribe."

On the Thursday in late April 1957 when Louise Abbot was invited to Andalusia for the afternoon, her husband had earlier legal business in Milledgeville, so she killed time by taking in *Giant,* starring Elizabeth Taylor, at the local movie theater. Driving up the red clay road at precisely three thirty, she admitted in her own letter to Maryat Lee, years later, of her first meeting with O'Connor, that her reading of the stories had been so superficial that she imagined that "we would have a few beers together and enjoy some dark comedy about Southern small towns." Abbot wrongly expected that she was going to greet a fellow agnostic with whom she could disparage local manners and mores. She found herself greatly surprised, the first of many surprises being Flannery's crutches, as she propped open the screen door dressed in blue jeans, a long-tailed plaid shirt, and loafers. But, like Maryat, her visitor soon found herself absorbed instead by her "very expressive" light blue eyes.

As they sat rocking in the tall, high-backed chairs, Louise was sensitive enough to pick up on some of the tensions between Flannery and her mother. Unlike Maryat, she was able to chat with Mrs. O'Connor quite easily. Yet when Regina seemed about to make a condescending remark, as Louise described herself as "wanting" to write, Flannery interjected, "She's had a story published. She's a *professional* writer." Before disappearing into her room to fetch copies of *Wise Blood* and *Understanding Fiction,* Flannery startled Louise by turning and saying, "*You* stay here." Abbot noticed, "There was a quality in Flannery that forbade intimacy." At the suggestion that she was a "famous writer," Flannery scowled. "I believe in a good deal of Hell's fire on this earth, and if I thought of myself in such a way for a minute, I'd consign myself to it promptly."

Yet as they found common ground in shared Savannah girlhoods in the 1930s and a perverse love of "The Worry Clinic," the advice column of Dr. George W. Crane that ran almost daily on the comics page of the *Atlanta Constitution* until 1957, a friendship flowered: Flannery's favorite was Crane's counsel to a lethargic soul to donate a water cooler to his church because "where your treasure is, there will your heart be also." When Louise revealed that her family was Associate Reformed Presbyterian, Flannery asked, "What in the wurld-d is that?" Louise, in turn, was surprised to find that Flannery was Roman Catholic. "Yes, we believe . . . ," she began, and recited the entire Apostles' Creed, as nineteen peacocks high-stepped across the lawn. Walking together to her car, Louise admitted to being a bit lonely as a housewife-writer in Louisville. "Come back as often as you can," said Flannery. "I'm in the same position you are." Louise Abbot was soon returning often, invited to join Flannery and Regina for lunch in the combination sitting and dining room, or at Sanford House; she was one friend Flannery could trust not to judge her mother, or their relationship.

Over the spring and summer the letters between Flannery and her closer friend Betty Hester turned from theology to the carpentry of constructing a good story and gossip. The true zing in her correspondence that season, though, came from the irrepressible Maryat Lee, living a life of adventure that fulfilled her niece's characterization of her as Auntie Mame. Maryat had failed to mention that she was engaged to an Australian named David Foulkes-Taylor, whom she met while covering the coronation of Queen Elizabeth in 1952. When she finally broke the news of a summer wedding, Flannery wrote back, "The following is good Georgia advice: don't marry no foreigner. Even if his face is white, his heart is black."

The marriage did take place, on the freighter *Mukahuru Maru,* sailing from Long Beach, California, to Japan. But the union did not go off without a hitch. Along the way, Foulkes-Taylor met a man to whom he was attracted, while Maryat, in Tokyo, soon developed a one-sided crush on the film critic and well-known writer on Japanese culture Donald Richie, who remembers her "intense manner and big, square teeth." In the midst of such news, and plenty of light banter from Flannery about Chairman Mao, opium parlors, and saber-toothed tigers, Maryat sent a four-page letter in late May exclaiming that she loved her, too. While she did not label herself "bisexual" until the seventies, such free love was already part of Maryat's style. Yet Flannery might well have been surprised to have her confess, from eight thousand miles away, "Oh Flannery, I love you too. Did you know that? I almost said it when we were standing by a fence. . . . What would you have done if I had come up with it? Gone flippity flapping away on your crutches I bet."

As with Betty, Flannery did not blink, or "flippity flap" away, but she did transpose the discussion into a more spiritual key. "Everything has to be diluted with time and with matter, even that love of yours which has to come down on many of us to be able to come down on one," she carefully responded. "It is grace and it is the blood of Christ and I thought, after I had seen you once that you were full of it and didn't know what to do with it or perhaps even what it was. Even if you loved Faulkes and Ritche and me and Emmet and Emmet's brother and his girl friend equally and undividedly, it all has to be put somewhere finally." Maryat groused that her reply was full of pious clichés, not flesh and blood. The line went quiet between them for four months. When Maryat got back in touch, Flannery steadily reassured, "I am not to be got rid of by crusty letters."

Where Flannery truly diluted her friendship with Maryat, as with much of the time and matter of her life, was in her fiction. When Maryat sent the letter of rapprochement in October, Flannery was already at work on "The Enduring Chill," the story that treated her own fluctuating illness, but was also a trial sketch of

Maryat as a perfect life model for one of her favorite types, the egoistic artist-intellectual. While the character Asbury shared some of Flannery's symptoms, he was closer to Maryat: like her, he was a playwright living in a New York tenement walk-up with "a closet with a toilet in it"; his work in progress, "a play about Negroes," was a swipe at Maryat's performed in Harlem by an all-black cast; his forced integration, smoking a cigarette with black workers in the milk shed, captured the spirit of her taboo ride to the airport with Emmett.

The story was also a mulled response to Maryat's opinions on religion as spouted on their first meeting while Flannery, according to Maryat, "suffered my remarks with curious attention." The comment that stuck, as Flannery wrote her, concerned "the orthodoxy, which I remember you said was a ceiling you had come through." In "The Enduring Chill," the water stains "on the ceiling" above Asbury's bed transform into the Holy Spirit, surprisingly envisaged as a fierce bird of chill-inducing ice *descending,* in graceful revenge. "But — the last paragraph! You really seem to have busted a ceiling," Maryat joked when she read the story in *Harper's Bazaar.* "This is the closest I have seen you come to your mind's passion." She got its message about Asbury, as well: "the descent of the Holy Icicle, despite himself." When Maryat sent a gift subscription to the *Village Voice,* Flannery thanked her for the newspaper, which was founded in 1955 by Norman Mailer and Dan Wolf out of a downtown apartment: it "reminds me of my character, Asbury, and his life in the city." Maryat signed one of her next letters, "Wishing for an icicle to descend, M."

Flannery read "The Enduring Chill" aloud publicly just once, at what she called a "pseudo-literary&theological gathering," a weekly reading group held at Andalusia, instigated by William Kirkland, the local Episcopal minister, where Maryat read a play in progress that spring, too. Lasting from the fall of 1957 until 1960, the group began with a grand plan to discuss "theology in modern literature" and was made up of six to eight regulars, mostly GSCW professors, plus an air force sergeant and a psychiatrist from the mental hospital. Flannery was thankful when their reading list relaxed from Kierkegaard and Sartre to Lardner and Welty. On the evening she presented her new story in the smoke-filled dining room, Kirkland recalls that she played up the comic relationship of Asbury and his physician: "She really bore down with special emphasis on his comment, 'What's wrong with me goes *way* beyond Block.'"

Maryat's reading from her play *Kairos,* set in the South, took place while she was in town for the formal investiture of her brother as college president on April 3, 1958. She later remembered the group as "not particularly scintillating; everybody on good behavior. . . . It was a bit academic for me." Mary Barbara Tate, a high school English teacher at the time, and a member of the group, recalls, "Maryat read us a play one night that she had written. She was such a nut. She had such an ego. And yet there was something very warm and appealing about her. I liked her." Maryat's knack for scandal was accented by the presence of a companion, Jean "Poppy" Raymond, formerly a principal ballerina in an Australian dance company, whom she had met on the eventful Japanese freighter trip and was now living with in New York City; she and Foulkes-Taylor had parted company in Hong Kong, though they still remained married.

Alert to all the imagery from O'Connor's stories lurking in the landscape of the farm, established authors began arriving, as well. By the spring of 1958, Andalusia had become a known destination. The young poet James Dickey, later the author of *Deliverance,* stopped by in early March. Dickey told a friend that when he started writing, O'Connor was the only author in Georgia who "was doing anything." That day he identified himself mostly as an admirer of Robert Lowell. On a subsequent visit, O'Connor happily reported that he brought his son, "to show his little boy the ponies." "My father tempted me there with talk of Shetland ponies," concurs Christopher Dickey, who went on to become *Newsweek*'s Paris bureau chief. "I was horrified because I had never met anyone so sick and crippled. But, as a child, I kept one of her peacock plumes in my collection of treasures."

Katherine Anne Porter, at work for twenty-seven years on her novel *Ship of Fools,* arrived, too, for lunch after a late-March public reading in Macon; she was driven over by the Gossetts. Flannery was amused when she heard that Porter performed at the college wearing "a black halter type dress sans back, & long black gloves which interfered with her turning the pages. After each story, she made a kind of curtsy, which someone described as 'wobbly.'" Entertaining the "very pleasant and agreeable" Southern writer — her "Noon Wine" was an early influence at Iowa — Flannery noted that she "plowed all over the yard behind me in her spike-heeled shoes to see my various kinds of chickens." In a more lyrical account of the afternoon, Porter recalled her "gracious" hostess as "tenderly fresh-colored, young, smiling . . . balanced lightly on her aluminum crutches, whistling to her peacocks who came floating and rustling to her, calling in their rusty voices."

Chapter Nine

EVERYTHING THAT RISES

✺

Whenever Flannery talked about her upcoming trip to Lourdes, planned for three weeks in April and May 1958, she cast herself as an accidental pilgrim. This sole trip outside the United States, by the woman who had already decided that sickness was "more instructive than a long trip to Europe," was not of her own design. Hearing of the Lourdes Centennial Pilgrimage — organized as a package tour by the Diocese of Savannah, to the site of Bernadette Soubirous's vision of the Virgin Mary in the south of France — Cousin Katie Semmes immediately thought of Mary Flannery, and her worsening condition. Knowing the reputation of Bernadette's spring for physical cures, she insisted on paying the $1,050.40 per-person fee to send both mother and daughter.

Over the six-month lead-up to their departure, Flannery mined the imminent event for all its comic potential, though her barbs about the "holy exhaustion" anticipated with a dozen fellow pilgrims, mostly "fortress-footed Catholic females herded from holy place to holy place," belied true anxiety. She blamed the trip entirely on Cousin Katie's "will of iron." Her trepidation began to sound reasonable when a final itinerary was presented that included, within a time frame of seventeen days, stops in London, Dublin ("I bet that'll be real sickening," she told the Fitzgeralds), Paris, Lourdes, Barcelona, Rome, and Lisbon. According to her math, she concluded to Betty Hester, "7 into 17 is 2 and a fraction and if four days are devoted to Rome, I figure them other places will not see much of us. By my calculations we should see more airports than shrines."

A reprieve came in February, when Dr. Merrill advised canceling the trip because her X ray revealed hip deterioration that he now admitted was probably a side effect of the lupus. He suggested possible treatment at Warm Springs. Flannery received the news with secret relief — but not Cousin Katie, who then offered to fund a less taxing trip that would include Lourdes, but not all the other stops. Flannery was hardly eager to take in what she kept calling "Baloney Castle" — the Blarney Castle, in Killarney. But she had hoped to see the Fitzgerald family. So when Sally offered to put the O'Connors up at their home in Italy and accompany them to rejoin the other pilgrims in Paris, Flannery agreed. "Left for two minutes alone in foreign parts," she joked to Sally, "Regina and I would probably end up behind the Iron Curtain asking the way to Lourdes in sign language."

Yet for all her satire, Flannery was not entirely opposed to the trip. In the face of skeptics, this unlikely "church lady" could be far less sarcastic about it. Flannery was sincere about the upcoming pilgrimage with Katherine Anne Porter, who briefly converted to Catholicism in her youth, during a brush with tuberculosis. She told Betty that when Porter asked, during her March visit, "where we were going in Europe and I said Lourdes, a very strange expression came over her face, just a slight shock as if some sensitive spot had been touched. She said that she had always wanted to go to Lourdes." She conceded to the Fitzgeralds that "my cousin is certainly very good to give us this trip." While claiming to prefer to visit the Matisse Chapel, in Vence, just completed in 1951, a journey to the heart of a nearly medieval spirituality was hardly unthinkable.

Three days before departing she responsibly filed her "Last Will and Testament of Mary Flannery O'Connor," at the Baldwin County Court House, reflecting a sense at the time of European travel as a major undertaking, and belying her focus, perhaps even more than usual, on her certain mortality. "Item-One" of the will directed her executrix, Regina O'Connor, to "set aside the sum of $100.00 for the purpose to have masses said for the repose of my soul." Robert Fitzgerald, named literary executor, was assigned care for all unpublished manuscripts and the letters that had been preserved by her in carbon copies. Her books and paintings were to be consigned to the GSCW library. After the filing of the will, the remainder of preparation over the weekend consisted of packing, with much extra fussing by Regina. Flannery relayed one exchange to Betty: "She is reading the Lourds book and every now and then announces a fact, such as, 'It doesn't make any difference how much you beg and plead, they won't let you in.' 'Won't let you in where?' 'In Lourds with a short sleeved dress on or low cut.' 'I ain't got any low cut dress.'"

On Monday, April 21, Flannery and her mother, "like Mr. Head and Nelson facing Atlanta," she joked to Maryat, boarded a plane bound for Idlewild Airport in New York City. Unlike the other fourteen pilgrims, who took a bus to the Manger-Vanderbilt Hotel, at Park Avenue and 34th Street, Flannery and her mother were met by a limousine dispatched by Farrar, Straus and Cudahy, to transport her to a meeting with Mr. Straus and Miss Cudahy. Giroux's advice on an escape clause had proved to be prescient, as both Carver and Lindley did depart Harcourt, and Flannery and her agent decided that her novel should be with Mr. Giroux. "I am properly back where I started from," she said, with delight. The publisher Roger Straus telegrammed ahead to colleagues in Paris and Rome, informing them of the arrival of "our new important American author."

On the evening of April 22, O'Connor and her mother returned to the airport by bus, with the group, for a transatlantic flight aboard the TWA Constellation. Separating from the others at Shannon Airport, a leg of the trip that Flannery, still holding on to the anti-Irish fervor of her girlhood, was only too happy to miss, they traveled on to London. Early the next morning the pair flew to Milan, where they arrived shortly after noon, and were met by Robert Fitzgerald. Nearly a year after driving Flannery from Chicago to South Bend, he now took her and Regina on a prettier ride from Milan to Levanto, a coastal town on the Ligurian Sea, south of Genoa, at the end of a thickly wooded pine valley. There Flannery was reunited with Sally, and with her three girls and three boys, for whom Flannery brought *Uncle Remus* tales after promising pocketknives and snuff.

The four days spent at the Fitzgeralds' villa — built on several levels on a steep hill dotted with olive trees, and overlooking the light blue sea, where Robert had been translating *The Odyssey* — certainly fulfilled Dr. Merrill's orders for Flannery to rest between the strenuous beginning and middle of her trip. On spring days the trees below exploded with white and pink blossoms, the night air grew heavy, and, through open windows, the blond children could often be seen, or heard, playing in the courtyard. O'Connor reread the *Uncle Remus* tales that she brought as a gift, as well as Nabokov's *Pnin,* finding the comic novel about an absentminded professor of Russian literature "wonderful." Even so, as she reported to Ashley Brown, "The first cold germ I met on the other side moved in and stayed for the 17 days so most everything I saw was through a fog."

Arriving in Paris from Milan with Sally and Regina, Flannery was forced by her cold to recuperate inside the art deco Hotel Ambassador, near the Paris opera house, where she was visited by Gabrielle Rolin, a young French journalist and novelist. "Instead of seeing Paris I saw her," said Flannery. Although Rolin judged the novel "almost unreadable," she brought her, as a gift, Emile Zola's *Lourdes*. "Flannery's way of speaking reminded me of Donald Duck," recalls Rolin, "and her 'home made permanent,' Shirley Temple, but her eyes . . . perhaps she owed this interior light to her faith, this look so sharp and blue. 'I owe it to my Irish origins,' she said. But there was something more. The terrifying Mrs. O'Connor also had a keen eye but she didn't look beyond her interlocutor. Flannery saw farther, higher, elsewhere. . . . The amiable Mrs. Fitzgerald's smile was a comfort after having encountered the acid grin of the mother."

Reunited with the group from Savannah, the three women then traveled south from Paris to the Haut-Pyrenees region of Lourdes, near the border of Spain, long a medieval pilgrimage route on the way to Compostela. Crossing through France, during one phase of this trip, Sally and Flannery had a long, confidential conversation in a train compartment. "She said to me . . . that she had come to terms with her illness, with the crippling, the isolation, the constant danger of death," recalled Fitzgerald. "That, in fact, her only remaining fear was that her mother would die before she did. . . . She added, 'I don't know what I would do without her.'" Yet when Fitzgerald later passed on this remark to Caroline Gordon, who never liked Mrs. O'Connor, she flashed her black eyes at Sally, and snapped scornfully, "Yes! She would have lost her material."

Flannery had mixed feelings about going to Lourdes, as she was used to being an observer of, or writer about, religious enthusiasm boiling over into visions and healings, rather than a participant. Yet the village itself was a study in contrasts. The accommodation for the Savannah group, on the evenings of April 30 and May 1, was the nineteenth-century Grand Hotel de la Grotte, on the avenue Bernadette-Soubirous, the cream-colored epitome of *la vieille France,* with hanging eaves, wrought-iron balconies, and long white wooden shutters, situated on rocks overlooking a valley cut by the teal green Gave de Pau, and just below a medieval fortress castle. Though Flannery dubbed the place a "clip-joint," because of a forty-two-dollar bill for Sally's cot, the hotel was the first choice for American pilgrims, including a group of 350 led that spring by Francis Cardinal Spellman, during a Jubilee Year attracting more than 5 million visitors.

Lourdes had always been subject to commercialization, almost within months of reports, in 1858, of the healing of the paralyzed fingers of Catherine Latapie, when she plunged them into the spring discovered by her friend Bernadette, at the direction of the Virgin Mary — an apparition the fourteen-year-old at first simply called "Aquéro," or "that thing," in the local patois. In the early twentieth century the aesthete and Roman Catholic convert Joris-Karl Huysmans derided its many honky-tonk shops as "a hemorrhage of bad taste." Flannery enjoyed quoting Mauriac's remark that "the religious goods stores were the devil's answer there to the Virgin Mary." Such marketing had only escalated in the past decades with the appearance of a six-hundred-page historical novel, *Song of Bernadette,* by the Jewish novelist Franz Werfel, and its adaptation as a 1943 Academy Award–winning, black-and-white Hollywood movie, starring Jennifer Jones.

But all sales of religious souvenirs ceased at the large iron St. Michael's Gate at the foot of the boulevard de le Grotte, which marked the beginning of the Domain, a sort of medieval town arranged about various churches, squares, and shrines, and full of pilgrims, many as maimed and afflicted as O'Connor's characters. In this veritable open-air hospital, the critics of Lourdes often had a change of heart. No less a snob than Huysmans allowed that "nowhere have I seen such appalling illnesses, so much charity and so much good grace." For Mauriac, the grotto was a "heart that never stops beating." "The heavy hand of the prelate smacks down on this free enterprise at the gates of the grotto," Flannery wrote Ashley Brown. "This is always full of peasants milling around and of the sick being wheeled on stretchers." In a postcard to Katherine Anne Porter, O'Connor penned a single line: "The sight of Faith and affliction joined in prayer — very impressive."

Not only was Flannery in the company of her mother and Sally, but they were joined on their first day by William Sessions, who was on a Fulbright grant in Freiburg, Germany, attending the lectures of Martin Heidegger — Hulga's philosophical obsession in "Good Country People." Sessions arrived on May 1, the weather having turned warm and humid, in spite of breezes from nearby snowcapped mountains. "I joined them for lunch my first day, and it was the upstairs of their small hotel," he remembered. "I kept wondering how Flannery had managed with her crutches. . . . Sally and Regina were on one side of the table, and I slipped into the outside seat beside Flannery. While we were eating, and Sally and Regina were talking, Flannery leaned over to me and cast her eyes rather slowly about the dining room. 'Look,' she whispered to me, 'at all those Mauriac faces.'"

That afternoon, Flannery, Regina, and Sally sat at the back of the Grotto, the outcropping of rocks where Bernadette had experienced her visions, while Sessions braved the crowds of farmers descended from all over France for May Day, a holiday honoring the Virgin Mary. As they were marching ceaselessly up and down, he jostled to get to the spigots dispensing springwater above a basin, hoping to score just one gift bottle intended for Caroline Gordon. "In the pushing and shoving among the pilgrims for the holy water, I was knocked into the basin but not before I'd filled three bottles," wrote Sessions. "Sally and the O'Connors were laughing when I returned with soaked polyester trousers but handing them bottles." In the evening, Flannery and her mother looked on as Sally and Bill took part in the nightly candlelit procession in Rosary Square, beneath the basilica, singing the Lourdes Hymn to the Virgin and saying the Rosary, their entire group marching behind a "Savannah" banner.

Flannery had been clear about not wishing to take the baths, an immersion in the springwater believed to possess healing properties. She insisted that she was going as "a pilgrim, not a patient." She assured Betty Hester, before departing, "I am one of those people who could die for his religion sooner than take a bath for it." Her resolve was strengthened by Gabrielle Rolin, who had remarked in Paris that the only true miracle at Lourdes was the absence of any epidemics from the filthy water. Yet Sally felt sure that Mrs. Semmes would be disappointed if Flannery returned home without taking part in the essential ritual. Using her French, and his German, she and Bill managed to secure for their friend an appointment for early the next morning. Flannery complained that Sally had a "hyper-thyroid moral imagination" — "she was determined that I take it and gave me no peace" — but grudgingly acceded to her arrangements.

Before nine o'clock, she arrived at *les piscines,* actually a series of seventeen sunken marble pools — six for men, eleven for women — allowing some privacy, with only about forty people ahead of her in the stone waiting portico, so the waters appeared clean. She drank from a communal thermos bottle circulated among the *malades.* And she put on the sack robe she was handed, still damp from the previous woman, before passing behind a curtain and being lowered into the water. "At least there are no societal trappings along with the medieval hygiene," she wrote Elizabeth Bishop. "I saw nothing but peasants and was very conscious of the distinct odor of the crowd. The supernatural is a fact there but it displaces nothing natural; except maybe those germs." Nor did she report a mystical experience. "Nobody I am sure prays in that water," she told Betty.

In the evening, the group flew to Barcelona, where they stayed

Robert Fitzgerald, with his oldest daughter, in Redding, Connecticut, 1949.

Sally Fitzgerald and five of her children on the lawn of their Connecticut home.

O'Connor at the "Autograph Party" for *Wise Blood,* Georgia State College for Women, May 1952. (Courtesy of the Flannery O'Connor Collection, Georgia College and State University Library, Milledgeville, Georgia.)

The main house at Andalusia, present day. (Courtesy of Flannery O'Connor–Andalusia Foundation.)

Sacred Heart Church, North Jefferson Street, Milledgeville. (Courtesy of the Archdiocese of Atlanta Office of Archives and Records.)

Erik Langkjaer, next to the car he drove when he visited Flannery, 1952. (Courtesy of Erik Langkjaer.)

O'Connor visiting Cold Chimneys, the Cheney home, Smyrna, Tennessee, July 1955. (Courtesy of The Ralph Morrissey Collection, Vanderbilt University Special Collections.)

Maryat Lee, application photo for Union Theological Seminary, 1947. (Courtesy of The Burke Library Archives at Union Theological Seminary, New York.)

Robert Giroux, O'Connor's
editor and publisher. (Photograph by Arthur W. Wang.
Courtesy of Mary Ellen
Wang.)

O'Connor on the porch
swing of the Cline House,
Milledgeville, 1961.
(Courtesy of the Flannery
O'Connor Collection,
Georgia College and
State University Library,
Milledgeville, Georgia.)

With Katherine Anne Porter, Andalusia, March 27, 1958. (Photograph from the Thomas Gossett Papers located in the Duke University Special Collections Library.)

O'Connor seated beneath her *Self-Portrait with Pheasant Cock* in the living room at Andalusia, June 1962. (Photo by Joe McTyre/ *Atlanta Constitution*.)

O'Connor on the front steps of the main house, Andalusia, 1962. (Photo by Joe McTyre/*Atlanta Constitution*.)

In front of her walnut bookcases, back parlor, Andalusia, 1962. (Photo by Joe McTyre/*Atlanta Constitution*.)

Posing with a peacock on the front steps, Andalusia, 1962. (Photo by Joe McTyre/*Atlanta Constitution*.)

In the driveway, with peacocks, Andalusia, 1962. (Photo by Joe McTyre/*Atlanta Constitution*.)

overnight at the Hotel Colón. In the morning, at the Cathedral, Flannery purchased a tile for Betty. Hearing so much about her from Flannery and Bill, Sally purchased for Betty, too, a small plastic statue of the Spanish Black Virgin of Montserrat, to be toted back to Georgia. Two of the Savannah travelers, the spinster sisters Eleanor and Marie Bennett, of Augusta, recorded the events of the remainder of May 3 in their highly detailed pilgrimage diary: "After lunch we left Barcelona by plane for Rome. On our way, we dipped down in Nice for thirty minutes; also, at Milan for customs, on entering Italy. This was our longest plane ride on the Continent, something over five hours. Flying over the Alps, it was a beautiful sight to see the mountain peaks through the clouds."

The high point of Flannery's journey turned out to be Rome, having already been intrigued by a promise from Caroline Gordon that the eternal city would improve her prose. Skipping the general tourism, Flannery stayed shuttered in her room at the Regina — a hotel coincidentally sharing her mother's name — until the next day, when she crossed the Tiber River with the group to attend a general audience with Pope Pius XII at St. Peter's Basilica. In the company of Archbishop O'Hara of Savannah, all were ushered by a knight-chamberlain to front box seats. At noon, to roars of "Viva Papa!" the pope, in his first Sunday audience after a long illness, was borne to his throne on his *sedia gestatoria*. Following the audience, he walked down to greet the travelers, giving a special blessing to Flannery, on account of her crutches. Impressed, she hurriedly wrote Betty, from Rome: "There is a wonderful radiance and liveliness about the old man. He fairly springs up and down the little steps to his chair. Whatever the special superaliveness that holiness is, it is very apparent in him."

Staying long enough for a Monday evening dinner in honor of Archbishop O'Hara, given by the group at the Regina Hotel, Sally needed to bid farewell once again to her friend, a familiar event in their history, to return to Levanto. So for the rest of the trip Flannery trained her sights on her fellow pilgrims. She and her mother were now both under the weather, and remained in their room in the Hotel Florida, in Lisbon, the last stop, while the others took a hundred-mile bus trip to Fátima, yet another site of a Marian visitation, in 1917. "Shrines to the Virgin do not seem to increase my devotion to her and I was glad not to go," she wrote Sally. But she avidly reported on the progress of the "4 old ladies who are always getting lost from the rest, 4 priests, 2 little boys, 12 &14, 2 secretaries, & me and ma." Of a suggestion of Monsignor T. James McNamara that she "write up" the trip, she rightly observed, "I don't think he has thought this through."

Upon their return to Andalusia on May 9, while Regina "revived as soon as she hit the cow country," Flannery was indeed a victim of exhaustion, needing to cancel a speaking engagement on "The Freak in Modern Fiction," scheduled at the University of Missouri in two weeks. "My capacity for staying home is now 100%," she declared, with great finality, to Ashley Brown. Mimicking Nelson in "The Artificial Nigger," she added, "Of course, I'm glad I've went once." Quite startling to her, though, was word from Dr. Merrill of an X ray showing that her hip had unexpectedly begun to calcify. She was now free to walk about her room without crutches. Flannery happily shared this news with Katie Semmes shortly before her cousin's death, at the age of ninety, in November. At the requiem mass at the Savannah Cathedral, Archbishop O'Hara said to Regina, when told of Flannery's improvement, "Ah, seeing the Pope did her some good!"

Flannery never did fulfill her writing assignment on Lourdes for Monsignor McNamara, or for Katie Semmes, who presented her with a leather-bound travel diary before her departure. She typed up her mother's notes for their cousin instead. Floating the opinion that "experience is the greatest deterrent to fiction," she promised Maryat that she might one day write her own account, but only "when the reality has somewhat faded." Yet though

Lourdes — "a beautiful child with smallpox" — never fully appears in her work, the trip affected her writing, she would claim, in a more essential way. When Katherine Anne Porter had visited, she swore that if she ever went to Lourdes, she would make a novena to finish her novel. Flannery borrowed this attitude. Recalling her experience in the grotto, she later confided that "I prayed there for the novel I was working on, not for my bones, which I care about less."

❈

INSPIRED BY THE waters of Lourdes, as well as by a "much better contract" from Robert Giroux at Farrar, Straus, Flannery did return to her second novel in earnest as soon as she was able after the trip. Already, by the third week of May, she could brag to Cecil Dawkins, "The little vacation from the Opus Nauseous seems to have done me some creative good anyway as I am at it with something like vigor, or anyway, have been for the last two days or so." And within a month, she had finished nearly a hundred pages of a first draft that she conceived as needing only about fifty more pages. "Unfortunately not any 50 will do," she told Betty. "However I am much heartened." She was again set on creating a dark chamber piece rather than a symphony, almost a novella, enough for her to wonder if the work should be published within a larger collection of stories.

While Flannery had agonized fitfully over her short novel for six years, and went through sharp ups and downs in her responses to it, she had already settled on its final riddle of a title the summer before: *The Violent Bear It Away,* a phrase taken from Matthew 11:12. The page was marked by a paper clip in her Douay translation of the Bible — the translation from the Latin Vulgate preferred by the Roman Catholic Church. Jesus' words, in full, read, "From the days of John the Baptist until now, the kingdom of heaven suffereth violence, and the violent bear it away." For O'Connor the violence implied was interior. "You have to push as hard as the age that pushes against you," she explained to Betty. She also felt this spiritual struggle was against death itself, for she penciled in the title phrase next to a passage in her copy of *Personalism,* by the French philosopher Emmanuel Mounier: "Love is a struggle: life is a struggle against death."

Yet for many readers the title remained enigmatic. Beginning with Maryat: "I am the dense kind," she wrote, when she heard the phrase. "The violent bear goodness away? purity? love? creation? God? mercy? It's a very southern title." Maryat teased that she was now inspired to write something entitled "The violent bare it." Flannery swatted back at Maryat, who proposed that she saw her scripts in "colors . . . pink, light blue," by describing her own palette: "my novel is grey, bruised-black, and fire-colored." After its publication, though, Flannery loved telling of a lady in Texas who wrote that a friend went into a bookstore looking for a paperback copy of *A Good Man Is Hard to Find,* and the clerk replied, "We don't have that one but we have another one by that writer. It's called THE BEAR THAT RAN AWAY WITH IT."

While keeping a respectful distance from William Faulkner — "I keep clear of Faulkner so my own little boat won't get swamped," she insisted — this second novel was much more haunted by his richly clotted images, and plot twists, than any of O'Connor's other works. Perhaps he was particularly on her mind because his translator Maurice-Edgar Coindreau had recently begun working on *Wise Blood* for the French publisher Gallimard. (When Coindreau told him of the O'Connor project, Faulkner raised his head, pointed a forefinger at him, and stated emphatically, "*That's* good stuff.") Her second novel's unburied great-uncle strongly suggests the burial complications of Addie Bundren in Faulkner's *As I Lay Dying;* "innocent," seven-year-old Bishop is a close relation of Benjy, the idiot narrator in *The Sound and the Fury;* Tarwater's pyromania is pure Yoknapatawpha County; and the novel's closing paragraph is remarkably close to "Barn Burning."

The opening chapter of *The Violent Bear It Away,* and its last thirty pages, came as easily to Flannery as the characters of Enoch or Hulga. She was on familiar terrain. Like Nelson and his uncle Mr. Head in "The Artificial Nigger," Tarwater, his name borrowed from a quack cure-all, and his great-uncle share a cooked breakfast before his death, as the author weaves in and out of their thoughts in the "one-and-a-half point of view" that O'Connor told Louise Abbot she devised for the novel: "one part third-person narrator, one-half omniscient narrator." For Mr. Meeks, the salesman who drives the hitchhiking nephew to the big city, she was tickled to borrow from Dr. Crane's advice column; like Dr. Crane, Meeks feels "you couldn't sell a copper flue to a man you didn't love."

Similarly the novel's notoriously perverse penultimate scene, and its apocalyptic finale, fell neatly into place. As an embodiment of the devil himself, O'Connor chose a stock character. Giving Tarwater a lift back to Powderhead, Tennessee, is a homosexual predator whom she first imagined for *Wise Blood,* but dispensed with: in one draft, Haze was importuned by Mercy Weaver, a cruising homosexual. When the Fitzgeralds asked about the broadly stereotypical character in a lavender shirt and Panama hat, who rapes the teenage Tarwater in the woods, Flannery swore that she had seen one such, "with yellow hair and black eyelashes — you can't look anymore perverted than that." In her extreme theology, this pederast Satan triggers grace. "Tarwater's final vision could not have been brought off if he hadn't met the man in the lavender and cream-colored car," she later explained.

The problem was the middle section, concerning Tarwater's life with his schoolteacher-uncle Rayber and his retarded cousin Bishop in an Atlanta-like big city — a section Flannery spent most of the next year and a half actively rewriting. She felt that she never came to terms with Rayber, a liberal, atheist, do-gooder, spouting jargon from sociology textbooks but fighting the "horrifying love" he cannot help feeling for his maimed son, whose existence makes no sense in his calculations. She found him, with his hearing aid, signifying a Cartesian separation of head and heart, to be a "stumbling block," and feared that she was "out of my depth" and did not "really know Rayber or have the ear for him." Two years later, when the critic Richard Gilman visited Andalusia, Flannery worried aloud that she hadn't "gotten right" the intellectual Rayber. "I don't reckon he'd be very convincing to you folks in New York," she said.

To make a point about Rayber's sentimental utopianism, she tucked in a light parody of J. D. Salinger's *Catcher in the Rye*. Flannery was a fan of Holden Caulfield, the hard-boiled adolescent pointing out the "phoniness" of adults. When Salinger's novel first appeared in 1951, she had pored over the book so avidly that Regina warned she was going to "RUIN MY EYES reading all that in one afternoon." But, by the late fifties, the "Catcher Cult" was the very definition of "cool," and she felt free to poke fun. Illustrating the naivete of his savior complex, O'Connor swiped Holden's catcher-in-the-rye fantasy — catching "thousands of little kids" falling off a cliff — for Rayber, who imagined himself in a garden where he would "gather all the exploited children of the world and let the sunshine flood their minds."

Flannery, having reached the age of thirty-three, experienced much renewed strength during the summer of 1958. Besides facing down her novel again, she decided to address the fear expressed to Sally on their European train ride, brought on by Regina's hospitalization for a bruised kidney before their departure. Flannery resolved to learn to drive when she found herself dependent on Aunt Mary, who, she told Betty, "can drive me nuts in about two minutes." A slight setback occurred when she flunked her test on

June 25, plowing in the wrong gear onto the front lawn of a stranger. The attending state police officer advised, "Younglady, I think you need sommo practice." But two weeks later, she returned and passed. The "swan of old cars," as Robert Lowell once called her, was now licensed to drive the "hearse-like" black Chevrolet with automatic transmission that she and her mother had ordered, with Uncle Louis's help.

About the time of the delivery of this "rolling memento mori," from Atlanta, she was also visited by a fan of her work, who became identified in her mind with her volatile feelings about the psychologists Sigmund Freud and Carl Jung, and, particularly, theories of the role of dreams and the subconscious in literary production and religious expression. Ted Spivey, a writer on myth and literature, and a professor at Georgia State College, was soon classified by her as "my Jung friend," and, therefore, a source of mixed feelings. As Louise Abbot, who knew them separately, parsed Flannery's friendship with her far more extroverted, excitable friend, "She certainly found him an intelligent and good man. But she was not interested when he came to order his own life according to dream interpretations, especially when he started dreaming about her."

Spivey, just two years her junior, and briefly a student of Allen Tate's at the University of Minnesota, had completed a dissertation on George Eliot, launching him on a mission to find an American woman writer with the intellect of Eliot, or Virginia Woolf, another favorite. When he began reading O'Connor's fiction, he felt that he might well have found her and screwed up his courage to write, suggesting a meeting for August 15, when he would be driving from Atlanta to visit his parents in Swainsboro. Flannery assented, giving directions to show up at two p.m. "When I knocked on her door," he wrote, "she appeared in a light-colored, rather conservative dress and suggested that we sit in rocking chairs on her porch. She asked me a few questions about myself, and within five minutes we were talking about writers and about their connection, when they had any, with religion. The talk lasted about two hours and was intense."

Leaving Andalusia that afternoon, Spivey was unsure whether the meeting had been a success, as he "could sense certain deep and sometimes disturbing currents" running through the author he would later describe as "the most complex person I have ever met." He soon had his answer, though, as before he even had a chance to write a bread-and-butter note, Flannery sent him a letter at his parents' home. "I have just finished a book which I am sure you would find relevant to your train of thought," she began. "This is *Israel and Revelation* by Eric Voeglin. . . . It has to do with history as being existence under God, the 'leap in being,' etc." Spivey was touched that she had recommended a writer so attuned to his interests, who became a favorite after he borrowed her copy. He was even more encouraged by her closing: "I enjoyed your visit and hope that you will stop again if you find it convenient when you pass this way."

Spivey's second visit took place in November while he was visiting his parents at Thanksgiving. By then, he had sent Flannery a copy of Martin Buber's *Eclipse of God* and was eager to hear her reaction to the contemporary Jewish theologian. "Now on a first-name basis, she met me dressed informally in slacks," remembered Spivey. "Because the weather had turned cold, we sat in the living room under the gaze of her well-known self-portrait." He interpreted the bird in the painting as an archetype, "a representation of her inner prophetic spirit." Flannery was surprisingly excited about the "dialogic" Buber, even admitting that she found him a "good antidote to the prevailing tenor of Catholic philosophy." She began to look beyond the apologetic Thomism of her formative years, while noting the absence of an indwelling Christ in Buber's

God as Other. Of Spivey, she wrote Betty, "He has a very fine mind inspite of the apocalyptic tastes."

"Prophetic" and "apocalyptic" were catchwords in the conversations of Flannery and Ted Spivey that winter, as they were the through-line of the novel she was writing, especially as she completed its last few pages — Tarwater, his eyes singed from fire, like Jonah returning to Nineveh, sets off "toward the dark city, where the children of God lay sleeping." Anxious for closure, Flannery had been counting off the pages to her friends. On New Year's Day 1959, she promised the Fitzgeralds, "I only have to bear with the prophet Tarwater for about ten or twelve more pages." She told Betty, of her imminent accomplishment, "I must say I attribute this to Lourdes more than the recalcifying bone." By month's end she was able to type and send off the forty-three-thousand-word manuscript, as with all her manuscripts since *Wise Blood,* to Caroline Gordon.

Flannery took advantage of the turnaround time while Mrs. Tate "had her say" with the draft, preparing for two workshop classes and a public reading of "A Good Man Is Hard to Find," which she was giving at the University of Chicago, the week of February 9, as a replacement for Eudora Welty, who needed to cancel her engagement. She claimed the seven-hundred-dollar fee "persuadeth me." Yet the logistics of this trip proved her most difficult ever. Placing her suitcase in the car on a wintry morning, Louise, their household helper, said mournfully, "Miss Mary, I hopes we meet again." Flannery dryly replied, "I hopes so too." En route, a blizzard and ice storm forced her plane down in Louisville, Kentucky, and she was put on a bus for a nine-hour ride. As Richard G. Stern, director of the writing program, recalled, "I met her at two a.m. in the immense terminal building downtown. She was off the bus first, her aluminum crutches in complex negotiation with handrails, helping arms, steps. Tall, pale, spectacled, small-chinned, wearily piquant. I was to recognize her, she'd written, by the light of pure soul shining from her eyes. Fatigue, relief, wit-edged bile were more like it."

The requirements for the honorarium included the caveat of living for five nights in the guest room of a women's residence hall so that she might "confer with the young ladies as to how to attain their ideals — this being a clause in some old lady's will who is providing 2/7 of the money." The stilted arrangement went no better than expected, reaching a low point when one of the girls, at tea, wondered, "Miss O'Connor, what are Christmas customs in Georgia?" She asked Stern, "Do they think I'm from Russia?" She read a dozen student manuscripts, "all bad but two," and gave a sparsely attended public reading, her style, according to her host, "full of wry strength." But she was happy to be able to meet Cecil Dawkins, who traveled to town with her friend Betty Littleton expressly to meet her mentor, for the first time, at a Saturday morning breakfast.

Awaiting Flannery, on her return home, was confirmation of news that she had already heard from Henry Rago, the editor of *Poetry* magazine, at a cocktail party in Chicago: she was a recipient of an eight-thousand-dollar Ford Foundation fellowship, an honor shared that year by Robert Fitzgerald and eight others. "I hope you are accustoming yourself to the pressure of the grant," she wrote Fitzgerald. "I feel it myself." When she had received her earlier Kenyon grant, funded by the Rockefellers, she invested in real estate: a five-room house on East Montgomery Street, on the way to the waterworks. "The house is subject to termite and poor white trash," she told Tom Stritch, "but I get $55 a month for it." Now she planned to buy an electric typewriter, a comfortable chair, and, otherwise, make the grant, paid over two years, "stretch into ten."

The last week in February she finally heard back from Caroline Gordon, who returned her manuscript covered with "doodles, exclamation points, cheers, growls." While Flannery cherished

Gordon as a first reader, she was beginning to separate from her as sole critical authority. She worried that Gordon was overly "enthusiastic," and questioned whether her comments tended to the stylistic rather than the substantive. For second opinions, she sent drafts to the Cheneys, the Fitzgeralds, and Catharine Carver, now an editor at Viking. Brainard Cheney found some parts "obscure." Robert Fitzgerald corroborated her sense that Rayber was "too much a parody"; so she rewrote the middle section for him, inventing the dramatic episode of a girl revivalist. As she kept mailing her redone pages, she complained to Carver, "When the grim reaper comes to get me, he'll have to give me a few extra hours to revise my last words. No end to this."

Resolving to "work on Tarwater the rest of the summer," Flannery did manage to entertain a number of visitors crucial to her literary career and, between drafts, even took a few trips herself. In April, her translator Maurice-Edgar Coindreau, teaching French literature at Princeton, arrived for a three-day stay at Andalusia. While most famous for setting off a Faulkner craze in France, with his 1931 essay in *La Nouvelle Revue Française,* he had recently been translating William Goyen and Truman Capote. Flannery worried about entertaining "an elderly French gentleman" for several days, but he busied himself easily, filming her flock of peacocks with his movie camera, and working on an introduction to *La Sagesse dans le Sang* (1959), in which he gave a brief history of American revivalism, including sketches of Billy Sunday and Aimee Semple McPherson, setting the novel in the context of the *"monde tragicomique de ces évangélistes."*

Two weeks later Flannery stayed again for four days with the Cheneys in Nashville, participating in a literary symposium at Vanderbilt, where she read "A Good Man Is Hard to Find." Ted Spivey, who was in the audience, remembered her as "sort of uptight . . . but very intense about reading that story." The next morning she was interviewed by several of the university's English majors, along with a fellow panelist and guest at the Cheneys', Robert Penn Warren. She disliked the formalities. "Whoever invented the cocktail party should have been drawn and quartered," she groused, but she was in awe of "Red" Warren, one of the first established writers to recognize her talent at Iowa. "I found her witty, shrewd, and strangely serene," Warren later recalled the event, "for you had the sense that she loved the world and even forgave nonsense, none too tardily. Some time later she sent my little girl, whom she had never seen, a bright piece of a peacock's tail."

Soon after she returned home in May, Robert Giroux, on a scouting tour, including visiting "all my famous authors," fittingly stopped at Andalusia after spending time with Thomas Merton at the Abbey of Gethsemani in Kentucky. "Brother Louis," his Trappist name, had shown great interest in O'Connor, of whose work he later wrote, "When I read Flannery O'Connor, I don't think of Hemingway, or Katherine Anne Porter, or Sartre, but rather of someone like Sophocles." He peppered Giroux with questions about her life on the farm, and gave him a beautifully designed presentation copy of his *Prometheus: A Meditation* to bring to her. "The aura of aloneness surrounding each of them was not an accident," observed Giroux. "It was their métier, in which they refined and deepened their very different talents in a short span of time."

Giroux first stopped at the Monastery of the Holy Spirit, a daughter house of Gethsemani in Conyers, just outside Atlanta, where, by chance, he met Bill Sessions. Taking a bus from the monastery, he was then picked up at the gate of Andalusia by mother and daughter. "The car was going about five miles an hour up this road," remembered Giroux. "As we drove in she had about thirty peacocks strutting around. They're very beautiful, but very stupid, and their trains were trailing. They were so slow that the car would run over their trains." He immediately went upstairs to change into his loafers and a flannel shirt: "I tried to be as informal and relaxed as possible. I could see this was all of interest to her, how men behaved." Giroux thought that the O'Connors were "really putting on the dog for the editor from New York," as he was then a guest at a formal lunch at the Cline Mansion, replete with silverware and crystal, served by a black butler in white cotton gloves.

A tense moment occurred at breakfast the next morning when Mrs. O'Connor asked, over cornflakes, "Mister Giroux, can't you get Flannery to write about nice people?" Giroux said, "I started to laugh. But Flannery was sitting utterly deadpan. I thought, 'Uh, oh. This is serious to her.' Flannery never smiled, or raised her eyebrow, or gave me any clue." On his return to New York he told Lowell of the trip and the poet passed on the news, adding an even sharper edge. "Her life is what you might guess," he wrote Elizabeth Bishop. "A small, managing indomitable mother, complaining that no one helps her, more or less detesting Flannery's work, impressed however, wishing she would marry — Flannery silent in her presence. A tall ancient Aunt living next to the old State Capitol, the unwanted peacocks . . . her Mother forcing her to bathe at Lourdes, an improvement, announced as a miracle by the Mother, Flannery silent. Battles between the Mother and the Catholic priest about an unwished-for altar tapestry."

By the fall Flannery finished typing up her manuscript and enjoyed a brief spell of satisfaction. "I sit all day typing and grinning like the Cheshire cat," she wrote Maryat of the novel, now clearly organized around the drowning-baptism of Bishop by Tarwater. "Does it have symbolisms in it?" her mother asked. "You know when I was coming along, they didn't have symbolisms." Caroline Gordon chose to visit Andalusia in October, after the novel was completed. She was driven there by Ashley Brown, who was teaching at the University of South Carolina. Brown had recently finished his doctoral dissertation on Gordon's work, including a chapter on her 1956 novel, a roman à clef based loosely on Dorothy Day, which Flannery thought "the best thing I've read on *The Malefactors.*" As Caroline was in the throes of a painful divorce from Allen Tate, though, the weekend was difficult, intensified by a formidable antagonism between her and Mrs. O'Connor.

Everyone came away a bit weary. Having spotted a dog she decided was lost on the highway, Caroline importuned Ashley to drive back to look for the animal, which they luckily never found. "I was not ABOUT to have that dog spend the night in my car," Ashley told Regina. On Sunday morning, Caroline gave Flannery a two-hour lecture on the "seems" and "as if " constructions in her prose. "When she is doing something like that she is most nearly herself," Flannery said. More "nerve-wracking" was "keeping her and my mother's personalities from meeting headlong with a crash." A near collision occurred with Caroline's censure of the O'Connors for using artificial breeding with their cows, which she deemed antithetical to Catholic theology. After her departure, Regina sharply remarked that she understood "why that man would want to divorce her."

Flannery took advantage of a two-month lull before the novel's publication — "this is the best stage," she told Maryat, "before it is published and begins to be misunderstood." She returned to story writing, with "The Comforts of Home." Unusual in its casting of a widowed mother as a bleeding-heart liberal who takes in the caricature of a sex-starved "Nimpermaniac," Star Drake (real name, Sarah Ham), the story revolves around the widow's only son, Thomas, driven to matricide by the presence of the "little slut." Making him resemble his namesake, St. Thomas, in more than "large frame," O'Connor planted an inside joke: when he chases the girl from his bedroom door by "holding the chair in front of him like an animal trainer." So, too, had Aquinas been fabled to chase away a prostitute with a red-hot poker. "It would be fashionable today to be in sympathy with the woman," Flannery archly wrote Betty, "but I am in sympathy with St. Thomas."

"The Comforts of Home" afforded a glimpse of a Jansenist aspect of Flannery's character that she usually kept hidden in her stories, along with the topic of sex altogether. But when Robie Macauley, succeeding John Crowe Ransom as editor of *Kenyon Review,* published the story a year later, with an inch-high illustration of a naked Star Drake, Flannery fumed. "I was pretty disappointed and sick when I saw the illustration you stuck on my story," she angrily wrote him. "I don't know what you've gained by it but you've lost a contributor." By way of explanation of such outbursts, Betty Hester, writing to Greg Johnson, fell back on her sense of Flannery's intact innocence, her professed desire to remain twelve. She presumed Flannery was most likely "unaware of the strangely sexual undertones of . . . Thomas' murder of his mother" in 'The Comforts of Home."

Ted Spivey, too, quickly became mindful of what he called her "revulsion at the frankly sexual in literature." She was devastating on the subject of Thomas Wolfe, or of critical praise for D. H. Lawrence's *Lady Chatterley's Lover* ("pious slop"), as well as the openly homosexual writings of Tennessee Williams and Truman Capote. "Mr. Truman Capote makes me plumb sick, as does Mr. Tenn. Williams," she wrote Betty. When anyone detected a sexual undercurrent in her own stories, she could be as outsized in response as she had been with Macauley. Receiving a letter from an acquaintance, six years earlier, ascribing a lesbian subtext to "A Temple of the Holy Ghost," she protested, "As for lesbianism I regard that as any other form of uncleanness. Purity is the twentieth centuries dirty word but it is the most mysterious of the virtues."

But such were not her immediate concerns with *The Violent Bear It Away,* officially on sale on February 8, 1960, and doubtless her most difficult publication experience, its main themes not sexual but prophetic and apocalyptic, its cast of characters more often freaks than folks. Dedicated to Edward Francis O'Connor, with a cover illustration of a gaunt boy in a black hat peering through cornstalks against a violet background, which Flannery felt evoked "The School of Southern Degeneracy," and back-cover praise of her "Blakean vision" from Caroline Gordon, the novel received decidedly mixed notices. Orville Prescott in the *New York Times* gave O'Connor backhanded praise as a "literary white witch," but felt her "harsh" novel failed; in the Sunday *Book Review,* Donald Davidson warned of "strong medicine"; Granville Hicks described the novel's style as "Southern Gothic with a vengeance" in the *Saturday Review.*

The article that caused Flannery the most pain was titled "God-Intoxicated Hillbillies" and ran in *Time* magazine at the end of February. Using the review as a pretext for detective work on the mysterious author, the unnamed critic helped realize Flannery's greatest fear of having her life, and disease, exposed, while also getting his medical facts wrong. O'Connor was characterized as "a retiring, bookish spinster who dabbles in the variants of sin and salvation like some self-tutored backwoods theologian. . . . She suffers from lupus (a tuberculous disease of the skin and mucous membranes) that forces her to spend part of her life on crutches." Flannery wrote the Cheneys of feeling violated, like "having a dirty hand wiped across your face. They even bring in the lupus." To Maryat, she complained, "My lupus has no business in literary considerations."

Far more pleasing was an overlooked essay in *Catholic World,* by P. Albert Duhamel, fittingly enough, a professor of Medieval Studies at Boston College. Alerting Cecil Dawkins to the piece, while alluding to Ingmar Bergman's art-house favorite *The Seventh Seal* (1957), its hooded figure of Death as allegorical as her own whispering Satan in *The Violent Bear It Away,* O'Connor wrote, "Perhaps I have created a medieval study. Which reminds, have you seen any films by this man Ingmar Bergman? People tell me they are mighty fine & that I would like them. They too are apparently medieval." She appreciated, as well, Joan Didion's praise for her "hard intelligence" in the *National Review.* Unlikely acceptance came with an excerpt after publication of the novel in the April issue of *Vogue,* crediting Flannery as "a young writer with an uncompromising moral intelligence and a style that happily relies on verbs, few adjectives, and no inflationary details."

Reactions from friends tended to be equally split. Wholehearted in her first response to the novel was Elizabeth Bishop. "I received Flannery's new book last week," she wrote Lowell. "That first section that was published somewhere before still seems superb to me — like a poem. In fact she's a great loss to the art, don't you think? . . . There's an idiot child named for me, I think." Writing back that "I hadn't connected 'Bishop' with you," Lowell was cooler: "The fire is there — a terrifying ending, the grotesque beginning — a short story to which the rest was added. . . . I don't know whether this book is her best or just her most controlled." In her response, Bishop, modulating her tone, conceded, "Yes, the Flannery book is a bit disappointing, I'm afraid — one wishes she could get away from religious fanatics for awhile. But just the writing is so damned good compared to almost anything else one reads: economical, clear, horrifying, *real.*"

Sharing most intimately in Flannery's reactions as she received these responses — the critical successes usually marked by a telegram or phone call from Bob Giroux — was Maryat Lee, in Milledgeville through February, recovering from an operation at Piedmont Hospital in Atlanta. She spent most afternoons in Flannery's room, making oil paintings of Andalusia, as Flannery herself painted, or read books. Admitting in her diary a "wave of tenderness" toward her friend, "so unapproachable that I am inhibited," Maryat felt her affection returned in other ways by Flannery, who took to calling herself "Aunt Fannie." She witnessed Flannery's pose of being unfazed by a letter from a young protégé criticizing this novel as inferior to her first. Seeing that his remarks "really dug very cruelly at her innards," Maryat ripped the letter into pieces and tossed it into the wastebasket, to Flannery's shock and relief.

Almost certain to see matters from a contrary point of view, Maryat — lying one afternoon on an exercise couch set crosswise at the end of the bed — told Flannery of deeming Rayber the most successful character in her novel. ("I found Rayber a very sympathetic and moving character," she wrote in her diary, "and probably from her point of view, not unlike myself, although of course I had nothing to do with Rayber.") From that visit on, a bemused Flannery addressed letters to her liberal humanist friend, with whom she often found herself at an impasse on religion and politics, by variations on Rayber — Raybutter, Raybalm, Rayfish, Rayverberator — adding an occasional marginal doodle of skull and crossbones, or a smiling thistle. Maryat likewise invented nicknames for Flannery based on the novel's inflammatory boy prophet — Tarbabe, Tarsoul, Tarsquawk.

※

WHEN ROBERT GIROUX had visited the previous spring, Flannery was most excited to hear him speak of Pierre Teilhard de Chardin, a French Jesuit priest and philosopher, as well as a paleontologist, present at the discovery of Peking Man, in 1929, whose philosophical writings were denied publication by the Roman Holy Office during his lifetime. The inventor of such science-fiction terms as "noosphere" and "omega point," to describe phases of a cosmos he theorized as evolving both materially and spiritually toward a culminating Body of Christ, Teilhard had died in 1955 at the age of seventy-three in New York City. An "omnivorous reader," as Giroux described her, Flannery was now anticipating the appearance of Teilhard's books in English translation, and this personal connection only redoubled her interest. As she reported to Ted Spivey, "My editor from Farrer, Straus was down here to visit me last week and I was asking him about Chardin and it turned out he knew him for about a month in New York before he died. He said he was very impressive."

Giroux recalled, "I said I met Father de Chardin, and she said, 'You did, where? I didn't know that he was ever in America.'" Flannery's editor went on to recount,

> *I explained that Roger Straus's uncle, a Guggenheim, funded some research. She said, "What was he like?" I said he was very handsome in a masculine way, and he had asked me about Merton, and whether I thought both his feet were firmly planted on the ground. I said, "Yes they are," and he said, "I'm glad to hear that." I told her of remarking to Roger that I had a vague feeling I had seen that face before — in Houdin's bust of Voltaire in the Metropolitan Museum. Roger said, "Of course, Voltaire's name was Arouet, and Chardin belongs to the Arouet family." Well she loved that.*

Giroux also told of attending Teilhard's funeral at St. Ignatius Church on Park Avenue, with the Straus family and "about twenty or thirty Jesuits at the altar."

The publication of Teilhard's writings in America, beginning in 1959 with *The Phenomenon of Man* — his 1938 manuscript attempting to reconcile Christian faith with evolutionary theory — was perfectly timed to answer a burning intellectual need of Flannery's. In November 1958, she already longed for "a new synthesis," and complained to Betty Hester, "This is not an age of great Catholic theology. . . . What St. Thomas did for the new learning of the 13th century we are in bad need of someone to do for the 20th." Her immediate provocation was the feeling that she was at a disadvantage in theological debates with Ted Spivey. "Only crisis theologians seem to excite him," she told Betty; yet she had to concede that the "greatest of the Protestant theologians writing today . . . are much more alert and creative than their Catholic counterparts. We have very few thinkers to equal Barth and Tillich, perhaps none."

Her search for eminent twentieth-century Catholic thinkers had begun a few years earlier when she started reviewing for the *Bulletin* in 1956. The local Episcopal rector and Andalusia reading-group cofounder, William Kirkland, said that his friendship with Flannery was sealed in the midfifties, when she discovered that they both owned well-worn copies of *Letters to a Niece,* by Baron Friedrich von Hügel, a turn-of-the-century Catholic humanist whose support of Darwinian science drew him dangerously close to the "Modernists" who had been excommunicated by Pope Pius X. O'Connor admiringly quoted in the *Bulletin* Hügel's advice to his niece not to be "churchy." Likewise her beloved Guardini, a friend of Buber's, was developing a fluid and dialectical theology considered a departure from absolute Thomism, which she praised for its "total absence of pious cliché."

But these near-contemporary theologians, along with William Lynch, Erik Langkjaer's teacher at Fordham, whose concept of a "theology of creativity" O'Connor singled out in a review in the summer of 1959, or the neo-Thomism of Etienne Gilson, in *Painting and Reality,* were just bits and pieces of a vision she finally saw synthesized in the writings of Teilhard de Chardin. In her first mention of Teilhard, in a February 1960 review of *The Phenomenon of Man,* O'Connor announced to the small circulation of readers of the *Bulletin* that the name, which she spelled out phonetically for them, "Tay-ahr," was one that "future generations will know better than we do." She went on, "The scientist and the theologian will perhaps require a long time to sift his thought and accept it, but the poet, whose sight is essentially prophetic, will at once recognize in this immense vision his own." At the center of this vision, she explained, was "convergence."

A careful reviewer, O'Connor quickly and intuitively hit on a characterization of Teilhard as poet and visionary that kept her in good stead as his posthumous writings were attacked by both scientists, for ascribing consciousness to matter, and theologians, for ignoring original sin, or contradicting the creation story in Genesis. But at Christmastime 1959, she had come across a "lucky find" in a commentary on a passage of St. Thomas Aquinas. "St. T. says that prophetic vision is dependent on the *imagination* of the prophet, not his moral life," she wrote Betty. Not only did this discovery make official her own kinship with Tarwater, but she could apply these same terms to Teilhard. Like her, he was a writer tilling the fields of language and imagination, meant to be judged by the power of his "prophetic" vision, rather than specific moral or scientific ideas.

At the heart of Teilhard's vision were formulations that obviously spoke to Flannery and created a strong resonance for her with the content as well as the poetic style of his writings. Particularly appealing was *The Divine Milieu,* an intimate, personal meditation, the second of his books, published in America in 1960 and described by her in the *Bulletin* as "giving a new face to Christian spirituality." She drew marginal lines in her copy next to Teilhard's concept of the Incarnation as "a single event . . . developing in the world"; a cosmic presence in local material lay behind her own arguing for regional writing. But the quieter concept that she kept mulling and returning to privately was "passive diminishments," Teilhard's unusual term for significant suffering, which she obviously applied to her own disease. As she wrote a friend: "Pere Teilhard talks about 'passive diminishments' in THE DIVINE MILIEU. He means those afflictions that you can't get rid of and have to bear. Those that you can get rid of he believes you must bend every effort *to* get rid of. I think he was a very great man."

Flannery proselytized avidly for this "great mystic . . . if there were errors in his thought, there were none in his heart," recommending him to a long list of friends, including Ted Spivey, Betty Hester, the Cheneys, Cecil Dawkins, Robert Fitzgerald, and Father McCown. Spivey's response disappointed her, as he found in Teilhard merely a "Jesuit mind." She shot back, "Some of the severest criticism I have read about it has come from other Jesuits," and she even pandered to Spivey a bit, by detecting in their evolutionary views "parallels between Jung and Teilhard that are striking." More to her liking was Brainard Cheney's confirmation that "his work is, I think, the most important philosophical statement for Christianity since the *Summa.*" When the *American Scholar,* a periodical of the Phi Beta Kappa Society, canvassed leading authors on the most important book published between 1931 and 1961, Gore Vidal chose *Doctor Faustus;* Alfred Kazin, *Finnegans Wake.* O'Connor's selection was *The Phenomenon of Man.*

In opening up to Teilhard, and moving beyond while never abandoning an absolute Thomism that some felt "too straitjacket," or old-fashioned, Flannery was aligning herself, as well, with a more general mood shift in the Church, signaled by the papacy of John XXIII, who had succeeded Pius XII in October 1958, five months after her audience with the ailing pope. In 1957, the Vatican banned Teilhard's works from Catholic bookstores. But John XXIII was more encouraging, saying, when asked about Teilhard's books, "I am here to bless, not to condemn." When a 1962 *monitum,* or formal warning, was issued, which the pope later deemed "regrettable" and Flannery found "depressing at first," she did draw back, suggesting that the *Bulletin* find a clergyman to review Teilhard's subsequent books. But she never lost her conviction that the Frenchman might be "canonized yet." She assured Father McCown, "If they are good, they are dangerous."

Certainly, throughout the spring and summer of 1960, visitors to Andalusia and a wide range of friends received copies of or were encouraged to read Teilhard's books. At the end of May, two such visitors might well have landed on Flannery's "Very Peculiar Types" list, except that both "wore very well." De Vene Harrold, known as "Dean," diagnosed with lupus in 1959, had just returned from a honeymoon with her new husband, Robert Hood, a painter, when she saw the *Time* piece on O'Connor and wrote for advice in a panic. On the couple's first visit, from St. Augustine, Florida, Flannery and Regina took them on a tour that featured her favorite junk-car yard. "Looka there, look there, would you," Flannery excitedly called out as she pointed from the highway. Driving by antebellum mansions in their Chevrolet, she chided her mother, "They don't want to see THIS part of town," and she steered them instead toward the poorer, black section. She then mailed Dean a copy of Teilhard's book for her "edification."

A group more likely to entertain discussions of Teilhard was made up of five Dominican nuns, along with their Superior, Sister Evangelist, of Our Lady of Perpetual Help Free Cancer Home in Atlanta, who visited Andalusia in July 1960, wishing for help with a project. Since Giroux's brief stopover and word of Merton the previous year, Flannery and her mother had become regular communicants at the Trappist Monastery of the Holy Spirit, often heading north on Sundays to attend mass. They would then linger to visit with the monks, especially the abbot, Augustine More, and the bonsai expert and gardener Father Paul Bourne, also chief censor for the Trappist order in America and, so, Merton's bête noire. "Paul Bourne was strict on Merton," recalls one Conyers monk. "He was finicky about any sexual stuff, and said that he had gotten some 'whining and complaining letters' from Merton. He taught us Church history on Tuesday mornings, was a litterateur, not a liberal, and had read all of Flannery's stuff. I think she saw in him a kindred spirit."

Abbot More and Father Bourne became regulars at Andalusia, and, on that Monday in July, the abbot — a "giggler" — had driven the Atlanta sisters in a station wagon to discuss their request for help on a book project. Their subject was Mary Ann Long, a twelve-year-old girl with a cancerous tumor growing on one side of her face, whom they cared for until her death. When they first contacted her, Flannery's reaction was a visceral "no" to the notion of writing a novel about the saintly girl, but the photographs they sent haunted her. "What interests me in it is simply the mystery," she wrote Betty, "the agony that is given in strange ways to children." So she agreed to help edit a book and write an introduction, half hoping a finished manuscript would never arrive. Paul Bourne jokingly wondered which of her "murder stories" had prompted them to approach her.

What Flannery carried away from these first letters and meetings was not yet a sense of kinship with Mary Ann so much as with the founder of the Dominican order, Rose Hawthorne, and, by extension, her father, the New England author of dark, gothic, moral tales. She went to her bookshelf and took down Nathaniel Hawthorne's "The Birthmark," which was included in her college *Understanding Fiction* anthology, and drew a connection between the beautiful Georgiana, subjected by her scientist-husband to a vicious precursor of cosmetic surgery to make her even *more* perfect, and Mary Ann's "plainly grotesque" tumor. But she also made a connection between the author and his saintly Catholic-convert daughter. Ever anxious about covering any tracks of Faulkner, by September she could easily write Bill Sessions advertising her newly adopted literary stepfather: "Hawthorne said he didn't write novels, he wrote romances; I am one of his descendants."

During the remainder of the fall and winter of 1960, Flannery devoted herself to talks and essays and even her single foray into magazine feature writing, thriftily titled "The King of the Birds," a previously discarded title for "The Displaced Person." While this article on her peacocks showed her knack for prose at once stylish and talky enough for the pages of *Holiday,* a chic travel magazine that paid her $750, she tucked a tiny nightmare into its ending. Skewing the mood for any readers alert enough to catch the downshift, she injected some dark changes into the anecdote about the Pathe cameraman, which she used as her opener: "Lately I have had a recurrent dream: I am five years old and a peacock. A photographer has been sent from New York and a long table is laid in celebration. The meal is to be an exceptional one: myself. I scream, 'Help! Help!' and awaken."

Using all of these occasions as opportunities to think aloud about the intellectual concerns between the lines of her fiction, Flannery traveled to Minnesota in October to take part in a three-day fiction workshop devoted to her work at the College of St. Teresa in Winona, and to present a talk on "Some Thoughts on the Catholic Novelist" at St. Catherine's College in St. Paul — pleased that she "met no duds" at either Catholic school. While not speaking directly of Teilhard, she did knot together the terms she first used when writing about him to describe her "Catholic novelist": "The fiction writer should be characterized by his kind of vision. . . . His kind of vision is prophetic vision. Prophecy . . . is dependent on the imaginative and not the moral faculty. . . . The prophet is a realist of distances." She also read "A Good Man Is Hard to Find" at the University of Minnesota, where she felt at an advantage, as "I sound pretty much like the old lady."

She was back in Georgia just in time for another such engagement during the third week in October: a southern arts festival at Wesleyan College, in Macon, where she was being "paid (well) to swap clichés about Southern culture" with Caroline Gordon, Katherine Anne Porter, and Madison Jones, as well as to speak on "Some Aspects of the Grotesque in Southern Fiction." Putting less emphasis at this non-Catholic event on Teilhard, she went public instead for the first time about her kinship with Hawthorne:

"When Hawthorne said that he wrote romances, he was attempting, in effect, to keep for fiction some of its freedom from social determinism, and to steer it in the direction of poetry." In O'Connor's own stories, where Elizabeth Bishop, "green with envy," swore that she could "cram a whole poem-idea into a sentence," she was striving for similar poetic freedom.

Following the festival, a dinner was held at Andalusia, which included Katherine Anne Porter, the moderator Louis Rubin, Ashley Brown, and the "strenuous" Mrs. Tate, again staying over the weekend, as well as her friend with lupus, Dean Hood, who drove six hours, unannounced, from Florida for the conference. "I helped Regina in the kitchen with Louise," Dean recalled. "I was outta my league in the living room." Katherine Anne Porter exclaimed that night with great regret that it was too late to visit a chicken Flannery had shown her on her last visit. "I call that really having a talent for winning friends and influencing people," Flannery wrote Cecil Dawkins, "when you remember to inquire for a chicken you met two years before. She was so sorry that it was night and she wouldn't get to see him again as she had particularly wanted to. I call that social grace."

Soon afterward, Flannery discovered that she had lost a bet with the nuns. She had wagered a pair of peacocks that they would never find a publisher for their memoir. Robert Giroux was interested, though he admitted that his author's "Introduction" to *A Memoir of Mary Ann,* not the nuns' writing, finally swayed him. In this eloquent essay, as fine as her best stories, dated December 8, she seized an opportunity to weave together her feelings about the girl forever fixed at the age of twelve; the "mystery" of disease, hers and Mary Ann's; the long shadow of Hawthorne, to whose memory the book was dedicated; and the hope for meaning that she found spelled out so compellingly in Teilhard. Indeed she made Mary Ann a human face for Teilhard's meditation on illness: "She and the Sisters who had taught her had fashioned from her unfinished face the material of her death. The creative action of the Christian's life is to prepare his death in Christ. It is a continuous action in which this world's goods are utilized to the fullest, both positive gifts and what Père Teilhard de Chardin calls 'passive diminishments.'"

※

By the beginning of 1961, Flannery was at work on a new story for which she was using as a title yet another popular phrase of Teilhard's, "everything that rises must converge," which summed up the priest's notion of all life, from the geological to the human, converging toward an integration of the material and the spiritual, not to mention an integration of the scientific theory of evolution and the theological dogma of Incarnation, of God made man. Giroux remembered sending her a French anthology of Teilhard's writings, with a section titled *"Tout Ce Qui Monte Converge."* After Teilhard's death, the French mint struck a medallion in his honor, stamped with his aristocratic profile and this mystical axiom. Writing to Roslyn Barnes, a young Catholic convert at Iowa, to whom she sent a copy of Teilhard's *Divine Milieu,* Flannery mentioned her "story called 'Everything That Rises Must Converge,' which is a physical proposition that I found in Père Teilhard and am applying to a certain situation in the Southern States & indeed in all the world."

This "certain situation" was a coy reference to political events creating big headlines in early 1961, as forces of change loosely filed under the label "the sixties" took hold in the South, across America and the world, and indeed throughout the Roman Catholic Church. Dovetailing with *aggiornamento,* or the spirit of renewal, introduced by John XXIII, was the election and inauguration on January 20 of a young Roman Catholic president, John F. Kennedy, whose candidacy Flannery supported, judging that "I think

King Kong would be better than Nixon" and scorning JFK's opponents of "the secularist-Baptist combination, unholy alliance." She told Cecil Dawkins, "All the rich widows in M'ville are voting for Nixon, fearing lest Kennedy give their money to the niggers."

In the South, much politics was racial politics, and the "certain situation" O'Connor was addressing in lofty Teilhardian terms was the civil rights movement. In December 1955, Rosa Lee Parks had refused to give up her seat to a white man on a segregated bus in Montgomery, Alabama, her dramatic gesture helping to force an issue obviously overdue: within days of her nonviolent resistance, fifty thousand black citizens walked to work in Alabama's capital city in a bus boycott lasting 381 days, led by the young Baptist minister Martin Luther King, Jr. In the fall of 1957, nine black teenagers integrated Central High School in Little Rock, Arkansas, as thousands of National Guardsmen patrolled in the schoolyard. The first sit-in at a Woolworth's lunch counter had just occurred, in February 1960, in Greensboro, North Carolina.

Yet while her Teilhardian phrase rang with the obvious implication of integration, Flannery's own position had shifted from the shocking contrariness of the girl who wrote from the point of view of black characters in her high school stories and decried the segregated buses she rode to Atlanta as a graduate student, to one of complex ambivalence. She had returned to settle in a society predicated on segregation and had taken on its charged voices and manners as the setting of her fiction. Certainly her mother was given to sharp racial comments, enough for the Gossetts to remember Flannery warning guests not to bring up the race issue. William Sessions has recalled a Thanksgiving dinner where her uncle Louis angrily slammed down a copy of *Life* magazine, featuring a photograph of Richard Cardinal Cushing of Boston washing the feet of a black man during a Maundy Thursday service.

Throughout the late fifties, Flannery had not seemed especially interested in coverage of the civil rights movement in the *Atlanta*

Constitution and the *Atlanta Journal,* her main sources of news (she did not own a television set until March 1961, when the sisters gave her one as thanks for her work on *Mary Ann*). She rarely discussed related political events. Yet eventually she came face-to-face with such topical issues, beginning mostly at the Trappist Monastery of the Holy Spirit in Conyers, also a favorite retreat of Dorothy Day. Indeed Bill Sessions had driven Day from Conyers to the Atlanta train station, following her visit to Koinonia, an interracial community in Americus, Georgia, where in 1957 she had survived a drive-by shooting. The incident prompted Flannery to voice her mixed feelings to Betty: "All my thoughts on this subject are ugly and uncharitable — such as: that's a mighty long way to come to get shot at, etc. I admire her very much. I still think of the story about the Tennessee hillbilly who picked up his gun and said, 'I'm going to Texas to fight fuhmuh rights.' I hope that to be of two minds about some things is not to be neutral."

Another visitor to Conyers, and another befriended by Bill Sessions, was John Howard Griffin, a white journalist who darkened his skin and wrote an account of his experiences traveling for six weeks through the Deep South in *Black Like Me* (1961), a classic study of racism. A Roman Catholic convert, Griffin wrote in his book of meeting "a young college instructor of English — a born Southerner of great breadth of understanding. . . . We talked until midnight. He invited me to go with him to visit Flannery O'Connor the next day." Griffin declined, feeling that he should spend his few remaining hours in the monastery. Less charitably, telling Maryat of the near meeting, Flannery wrote, "If I had been one of them white ladies Griffin sat down by on the bus, I would have got up PDQ preferring to sit by a genuine Negro." She told Father McCown that she would be delighted to see Griffin at Andalusia, but "not in blackface."

Like the broader Catholic Church, the great old enemy of the Klan, which was dispensing teachings on racial justice, the monks at Conyers were supportive of the civil rights movement. Though generally conservative, Paul Bourne, educated at Yale, was certainly liberal on this issue. And so O'Connor's monk friends were alert to the paradoxes of her attitude. "I would call Flannery a cultural racist," says one Conyers monk. "It wasn't that she didn't know they were children of God redeemed by the blood of Christ. Of course she knew that. But the vocabulary she used was typical Southern white. Paul said so. I never heard her. Her mother was worse. Flannery tempered it some. She did not hate black people. But she did resent the whiteys from the North coming down and telling us how to handle our problems with the blacks."

Leonard Mayhew, then an Atlanta priest, who occasionally visited her, sometimes bringing along his sister, the New York editor Alice Mayhew, says, "She never said anything racist, but she was patronizing about blacks, treated them as children. When I was introduced to black workers on the farm, they would take off their hats. I was both a white man and a priest. So they were doing double duty." O'Connor's position basically fell close to William Faulkner's. Segregation was an evil, Faulkner stated; but if integration were forced upon the South he would resist (in one feverish moment, he even said he would take up arms). In his personal life, his behavior toward African Americans was always cordial and kindly, but as one writer has characterized it, it was also "patronizing: he belonged, after all, to a *patron* class."

Flannery's foil in this race business, and a prime motivator of "Everything That Rises Must Converge," the uncharacteristically "topical" story she decided to write and her fictional comment on racial politics in the South, was Maryat Lee. Maryat had been unflagging in trying to bring Flannery around to a more forward position, perhaps even to use her public stature to advance social justice. In April 1959, Maryat met James Baldwin on the street in Manhattan, prior to his leaving for a trip, without a car, through Alabama, Mississippi, and Georgia. She wondered if Flannery would welcome a visit from the author whose first novel, *Go Tell It on the Mountain,* a coming-of-age story about growing up in Harlem, had been published within a year of *Wise Blood.* Flannery responded politely enough, though quite firmly: "No I can't see James Baldwin in Georgia. It would cause the greatest trouble and disturbance and disunion. In New York it would be nice to meet him; here it would not. I observe the traditions of the society I feed on — it's only fair. Might as well expect a mule to fly as me to see James Baldwin in Georgia. I have read one of his stories and it was a good one."

In other letters to Maryat, Flannery was far less polite. In accordance with the name game they began after *The Violent Bear It Away,* Flannery signed off one of hers "Cheers, Tarklux"; she might well have signed a number of others similarly. For as the two began, comically, to goad each other on the race issue, their little drama escalated rapidly, with Maryat cast as the ultimate Northern liberal, and Flannery a bigoted Southern redneck. Unfortunately, in a number of these letters, many still unpublished, Flannery slipped into her role too easily, her mask fitting disconcertingly well. She turned out to be a connoisseur of racial jokes, regaling Maryat with offensive punch lines.

More productively for O'Connor's more nuanced fiction, Maryat included in their slapdash correspondence anecdotes of her own misadventures in the shifting world of political etiquette that lodged challengingly with her foil, a.k.a. "Tarconstructed." She wrote of sitting on the subway next to a "colored" man in an expensive suit who was reading Vance Packard's *Status Seekers,* a popular book on social stratification in America. And she recounted, at length, a bus trip north from Milledgeville after her recuperation, in April 1960, when a black woman in "her Easter hat which was purplish red" sat beside her as a political act. Rather than be offended, Maryat offered to save her seat after a rest stop, apparently to the woman's disappointment, as she soon removed herself to a back seat: "I waved to her to join me, but she looked out the window."

Flannery adored this cautionary tale about the deflation of puffed-up political idealism by petty human conflicts. If not its entire reason for being, the incident became a central ingredient in "Everything That Rises Must Converge," her story of priggish, liberal, college-educated Julian escorting his mother, in her "hideous hat" with "a purple velvet flap," to a weight-reducing class at the Y on the newly integrated buses. Like Maryat, Julian makes a point of seating himself next to a well-dressed Negro carrying a briefcase. And he experiences an inner yelp of pleasure when a Negro woman, wearing an identical "hideous hat" with "a purple velvet flap" seats herself, with her little boy, across from Julian's mother — an object lesson he makes every effort to force her to understand. An elaborate interracial ballet of seat shuffling by whites and blacks ensues.

At the College of St. Teresa in Minnesota, O'Connor told a student interviewer, of writing black characters, "I don't understand them the way I do white people. I don't feel capable of entering the mind of a Negro. In my stories they're seen from the outside." This tack, while it was a type of artistic racism, worked well for her; Alice Walker, for instance, felt that O'Connor's keeping her distance "from the inner workings of her black characters seems to me all to her credit," sparing the world more stereotypes. Certainly in "Everything That Rises," her "one-and-a-half point of view" is reserved for Julian and his mother. Yet in its treatment of a burning social issue, as well as Julian's acute heartbreak over his mother's stroke, after she is slugged by the irate black woman with her red pocketbook, the story was a departure. "The topical is poison," Flannery explained her choice. "I got away with it in 'Everything That Rises' but only because I say a plague on everybody's house as far as the race business goes."

By the time that "Everything That Rises Must Converge" appeared in *New World Writing* in October 1961, and won the

O. Henry Award the following year, Flannery was much further along in her views on the pace of integration. While never giving up playing "Tarfeather" to her "Raybutton," Flannery would write Maryat in November 1962, "I'm cheered you like the converging one. I guess my mama liked it all right. My stories usually put her to sleep. She's accepting all the changes in her stride." And, in 1963, well in advance of the passage of the Civil Rights Act of 1964, O'Connor wrote a friend, "I feel very good about those changes in the South that have been long overdue — the whole racial picture. I think it is improving by the minute, particularly in Georgia, and I don't see how anybody could feel otherwise than good about that."

In addition to taking her title phrase from Teilhard, Flannery identified with his habit of writing for the ages. "As long as he lived," she told Betty, "he was faithful to his Jesuit superiors but I think he must have figured that in death he would be a citizen of some other sphere and that the fate of his books with the Church would rest with the Lord." Likewise in her talks on the "Catholic Novelist," Flannery claimed that she would swap "a hundred readers now" for "one in a hundred years." As Teilhard wrote for a time when evolution would be universally accepted, so O'Connor wrote for a moment when she was sure the races would converge. No matter what routines she did privately, in her stories she always presented blacks with dignity; indeed, in *The Violent Bear It Away,* only "a Negro named Buford Munson" finally gives the uncle his Christian burial. In literature, as in life, she clearly believed "love to be efficacious in the loooong run."

Chapter Ten

"REVELATION"

During her next visit to Andalusia, in the summer of 1961, Caroline Gordon gave Flannery a jolt when they discussed, as they always did, her latest writings. As in most of their other visits, Caroline stayed in the left room on the second floor, and Ashley Brown, her "chauffeur," was assigned the "upstairs junk room." Because they were arriving on a Friday afternoon, when the O'Connors dined at Sanford House, Flannery left Louise instructions to let them in. Ashley, as usual, brought along a few bottles of sherry, much appreciated by Regina. "We got along right from the beginning," says Brown. "Regina was not given to having intellectual conversation at the dinner table. But she was a Southern lady of a certain generation I was extremely familiar with. Not too many people were permitted to wash dishes, as I was, after dinner. It was all very easygoing."

Ashley's task was to keep Mrs. O'Connor occupied while Caroline and Flannery went off to discuss theology and literature. Even Caroline was impressed by the depth and breadth of Flannery's growing collection of books. "Few people realized that she actually knew a lot of theology," she later reminisced to Robert Giroux. "I know I was astonished when I saw her library." On this trip, Flannery shared an early draft of a new story that she had begun working on, "The Lame Shall Enter First." Taken from snippets of *The Violent Bear It Away,* left lying about in her imagination, the story was another attempt to get right the triangle of a liberal widower, his "average or below" son, and a tormented, delinquent teenager. As she worked on the second novel in 1953, she had bragged to Robert Fitzgerald of "a nice gangster of 14 in it named Rufus Florida Johnson." Having decided to excise Rufus, she was now resuscitating him.

She had first come upon her title, six years earlier, in an elevator in Davison's department store, on Peachtree Street in downtown Atlanta. An elderly woman entered behind Flannery, who was navigating on her newly acquired crutches, and said in a pitying voice, "Bless you, darling!" As Flannery wrote Betty of the incident, the woman then "grabbed my arm and whispered (very loud) in my ear, 'Remember what they said to John at the gate, darling!' It was not my floor but I got off and I suppose the old lady was astounded at how quick I could get away on crutches. I have a one-legged friend and I asked her what they said to John at the gate. She said she reckoned they said, 'The lame shall enter first.' This may be because the lame will be able to knock everybody else aside with their crutches." The phrase aptly fit her character Rufus, with his "monstrous club foot."

But when Caroline read the new pages, she was not impressed. She found them "completely undramatic." Going beyond her usual criticism, Caroline pierced to the essence of O'Connor's fiction. As Flannery summed up her comments to Cecil Dawkins, "Caroline says I have been writing too many essays and it is affecting my style. Well I ain't going to write no more essays." While she did not keep her promise as far as talks were concerned, she did seem happy for any excuse not to write more magazine articles. She had found such writing paid well but was full of indignities. "I'm amused by the letter from *Holiday*," she wrote Elizabeth McKee. "The fellow obviously thinks it's a great accomplishment to write something for them." When the magazine requested another piece on a Southern town, she complained that doing so might "activate my lupus."

As soon as Caroline and Ashley departed, Flannery set to work redeeming her story. "She did think the structure was good and the situation," she told Betty of further comments from Gordon. "All I got to do is write the story." So she deepened the drama by borrowing from Hawthorne's allegory in "The Birthmark." Her social worker, Sheppard, with his "narrow brush halo" of prematurely white hair and wish to reform wayward boys, shares a penchant for human engineering with Hawthorne's mad scientist Aylmer. Like Aylmer's unwitting victim, his wife, Georgiana, who expires along with her blemish, Sheppard's son Norton, whom his father wishes to teach to be "good and unselfish," accidentally hangs himself while peering through an attic telescope for some sign of his dead mother. The stand-in for Aylmer's cloddish assistant, Aminadab, is Rufus, the very incarnation of fundamental evil in the guise of a young boy with a Hitlerian forelock.

Although her story was now moral and nearly allegorical, like Hawthorne's, rather than "topical," Flannery used current events and popular culture to update, and to camouflage, the original. In May 1961, Alan Shepard, "America's first space hero" — his name tantalizingly close to that of her own Sheppard, who buys Rufus a telescope to teach him the wonders of space travel — made a suborbital flight in *Freedom 7.* Flannery had been following the space race, her new symbol for human pride, on TV, and the next January reported to Betty, regarding the forthcoming televised space launch of John Glenn, "Tomorrow I am orbiting with Glenn." In July, *Wild in the Country,* a dramatic film about the "rehabilitation of a country boy from delinquency," starring Elvis Presley, showed in Milledgeville. So Flannery took great pleasure in having her own country boy, Rufus, shimmy down a hallway in Norton's dead mother's corset, belting out Presley's "Shake, Rattle and Roll."

A subtle shift in her fictional world was taking place, too, in the depictions of the ever-present mother figure. While matricide continued as a favorite climax, a softer approach was subtly introduced. In "Everything That Rises Must Converge," the fatal clobbering of Julian's mother is followed by his mournful keening as he discovers "the world of guilt and sorrow." While Norton's mother is deceased, her presence in "The Lame Shall Enter First" is benign. "The little boy wouldn't have been looking for his mother if she hadn't been a good one when she was alive," Flannery told Betty. Certainly acceptance of her own mother was a condition to which Flannery aspired, as she gradually shifted, during the 1960s, from using "I" to "we," when speaking of matters at home. As Maryat wrote, over a decade later, in one of her journals, "I'm convinced that she used Regina in some way as part of her worship. Regina was her cross. She was Regina's cross. It worked. They both basked now and then in the glow of it."

Yet crossbearing was an arduous daily discipline, and much tension remained. Having once accused her of getting "away with murder" for the shocking "likeness" to Regina in the gored Mrs. May of "Greenleaf" ("She don't read any of it," assured Flannery), Maryat did witness some difficult moments. She was quite startled one afternoon when Regina barged into Flannery's room, stormed over, and "smacked the windows open" to scream at Shot for some infraction. After she left, slamming the door behind her, Maryat said, "Surely she doesn't do that in the mornings!" Flannery nodded vigorously. "She does do it." Admittedly a girl at the time, Catherine Morai, a parishioner at Sacred Heart Church, felt that she routinely observed friction between them at early mass: "I have a very strong memory of Flannery struggling down the church steps with her crutches and her braces. The look on her mother's face was angry and annoyed."

Throughout the summer of 1961, Regina's all-consuming business project was the transformation of Andalusia from a dairy farm to a beef farm, while also expanding its timber sales. Some of the attraction of the new venture was having a business that would not require as many workers to operate the milk barn. "The staff is non compos mentis every weekend," Flannery wrote the Gossetts, "and she HAS HAD ENOUGH." By July, they had sold their dairy herd, bought a purebred shorthorn bull, and were now fully in the beef business. Bulls were enough of a presence by the fall that when talk turned to building a bomb shelter, Flannery claimed to dream nightly of "radiated bulls and peacocks and swans." Of the constant activity in a stretch of timberland, the critic Richard Gilman recalled, during his visit, "I could hear the dull whine of distant buzz-saws."

Flannery's own project was researching a hip operation that she hoped would allow her to walk freely again, without crutches. The Lourdes miracle, as humble as it was, had been short-lived, and she was seeking a more reliable improvement. Her closest confidante in these medical matters had become Maryat, and Flannery was surprisingly receptive as her friend began to explore experimental avenues of treatment; she was conferring especially with Dr. Henry Sprung, a lupus specialist in Providence, Rhode Island. In April, Flannery reported to Maryat that she had visited Dr. Merrill's office in Atlanta for injections of cortisone and Novocain in both hips to ease her sitting and standing; full relief lasted only about two weeks. In July, she shared her frustration that "Scientist Merrill" had nixed a surgical-steel hip-implant operation, approved by her bone doctor, because he was afraid of reactivating her lupus with a kidney flare or an infection.

Flannery was experiencing some disappointments, too, in her

important friendships. Chief among them was Betty Hester, for whom she had such tender feelings. While she had feigned some indifference to Betty's choice to be confirmed in the Roman Catholic Church five years earlier, the move was actually a source of great joy. She hoped Betty would find in religion the strength that she sensed the fragile young woman, who had such difficult setbacks in life, sorely needed. And so she suffered when Betty told her, shortly after a visit to Andalusia in September, that she had decided to leave the Church. As with her response to news of Erik's engagement, Flannery retreated into the protective plural, writing Betty that "I don't know anything that could grieve us here like this news." She deemed the turn of events "painful."

Flannery eventually came to blame this loss of faith on Iris Murdoch, the Dublin-born novelist who had been strongly influenced by Simone Weil, and by Wittgenstein, whose lectures she attended at Cambridge. Earlier in the year, Flannery had read two of Murdoch's novels, *The Flight from the Enchanter* and *A Severed Head,* finding them "completely hollow." But Betty grew infatuated with these works, which were full of ethical questions and sexual complications among the English upper class. "This conversion was achieved by Miss Iris Murdoch," Flannery wrote Cecil Dawkins of the weird literary battle for Betty's soul. "It's as plain as the nose on her face that now she's being Iris Murdoch, but it is only plain to me, not her." Flannery's misgivings were borne out by several bouts of depression suffered by Betty. Their friendship survived, but with less hopefulness on Flannery's part than in the first years. Betty went on to initiate a correspondence with Murdoch that lasted until her own death — by suicide, in 1998, when she was seventy-six.

Nonetheless, with a brief break in early November to address the cloistered nuns of Marillac College near St. Louis, Missouri, on "The Catholic Novelist in the Protestant South," Flannery did manage to finish "The Lame Shall Enter First" by year's end. Still angry at Robie Macauley for the illustration that she claimed was a misguided attempt to "compete with PLAYBOY," she submitted the story instead to her old teacher Andrew Lytle, now editor of the *Sewanee Review.* She never knew that Lytle had passed on reviewing *Wise Blood,* or, as Macauley later revealed, that at Iowa he "found her fiction rather uncouth." Yet, like many readers, Lytle was won over as her adult stories appeared; he even wrote for her 1956 Guggenheim reapplication that she was "immensely improved since I first taught her." Lytle not only accepted the story, but planned a special summer issue around O'Connor's fiction, with essays by Robert Fitzgerald and John Hawkes.

Flannery had actually known Lytle's intriguing choice, the young novelist John Hawkes, since the summer of 1958, when he and his wife stopped by on their way to Florida from Harvard, where he was teaching. He then mailed her two of his early novels, which she admired as "the grotesque with all stops out." When James Dickey visited, he surprisingly revealed that he, too, was an avid reader of Hawkes's dark, surrealist works. "You may state without fear of contradiction that you now have two fans in Georgia," she quickly wrote Hawkes. Three years later, in a rare blurb, she praised his 1961 novel, *The Lime Twig:* "You suffer *The Lime Twig* like a dream. It seems to be something that is happening to you, that you want to escape from but can't." Hawkes, likewise, championed O'Connor, shocking a Brandeis University audience by reading aloud, before its publication, the rape scene of Tarwater from her latest novel.

Yet the liveliest point of contention — and interest — between the two was Hawkes's main theory about O'Connor's writing: that hers was a "black," even "diabolical," authorial voice. Since he first read her fiction ten years earlier, at the prompting of Melville's granddaughter, Eleanor Melville Metcalf, in Cambridge, he had been developing this line of thought, much like William Blake's perverse reading of John Milton as "of the Devil's party." Flannery never sanctioned the notion, but neither was she completely dismissive. She even baited Hawkes a bit. When she learned he would be writing an essay accompanying "The Lame Shall Enter First," she sent him the story with a teasing note: "In this one, I'll admit that the devil's voice is my own." When Hawkes's "Flannery O'Connor's Devil" appeared in the summer of 1962, she wrote him, "I like the piece very very much." But, privately, to Ted Spivey, she refuted the essay as "off-center": "Jack Hawkes' view of the devil is not a theological one. His devil is an impeccable literary spirit whom he makes responsible for all good literature. Anything good he thinks must come from the devil. He is a good friend of mine and I have had this out with him many times, to no avail."

✳

FLANNERY TRIED UNSUCCESSFULLY to withdraw "The Lame Shall Enter First" in final page proofs, when she "decided that I don't like it." Over the next year and a half she often spoke of finding herself at a creative impasse. When Father McCown wrote, praising "Everything That Rises Must Converge," which appeared in *The Best American Short Stories 1962,* she answered vulnerably, "But pray that the Lord will send me some more. I've been writing for sixteen years and I have the sense of having exhausted my original potentiality and being now in need of the kind of grace that deepens perception, a new shot of life or something."

Such reappraising began as she approached her thirty-seventh birthday. Flannery had never marked her birthdays with any celebration. When Betty sent her a birthday card that year, she responded, "When I was a child I used to dread birthdays for fear R. would throw a surprise party for me. My idea of hell was the door bursting open and a flock of children pouring in yelling SURPRISE! Now I don't mind them. That danger is over." Yet she was obviously meditating during this Lenten season on a curious quiet in her usually noisy life of the imagination, as she struggled with the flu in her front room, which was thick with the scent of Vicks VapoRub. Her sense of being at a juncture was clearly borne out during the morning work hours: 1962 was remarkable as a year when she created no new stories. Instead she gave nearly a dozen public talks and readings.

In April, she made the first of these "powerful social" appearances by speaking at both Meredith College and North Carolina State College, "strictly a technical school," in Raleigh, on "The Grotesque in Southern Literature." Returning home for a week, she was then off again to Converse College, in Spartanburg, South Carolina, to take part in a literary festival with Eudora Welty, Cleanth Brooks, and Andrew Lytle. Exempting Welty from the scorn she often expressed for her fellow Southern writers — especially Carson McCullers, whose recent novel, *Clock Without Hands,* she derided as "the worst book I have ever read" — Flannery respected the older writer. "I really liked Eudora Welty," she confirmed to Cecil Dawkins. "No pretence whatsoever, just a real nice woman." She loved retelling Welty's anecdote of sending a love scene to Faulkner for criticism, and his replying, "Honey, it isn't the way I would do it, but you go right ahead."

She did find time, when she returned to Andalusia, to write a preface for a reissue of *Wise Blood,* to be published by Farrar, Straus and Cudahy. Her one-paragraph note, requested by Giroux, was mostly a technical requirement for lengthening copyright. She had resisted the assignment for several months, complaining to Betty that " 'Explanations' are repugnant to me" and feeling that future critics should simply read everything she had written, "even and particularly the Mary Ann piece." Nonetheless, she set to work constructing a note that she intended to be "light and oblique. No claims & very few assertions." The final result, though, was rather heavy, and blunt. Forever prevented from mistaking the novel as a satire on religion, readers opening this edition, with its red cover and imagery of blind eyes, were met with a disclaimer from the author stating that she had written "a comic novel about a Christian *malgre lui,* and as such, very serious."

Maryat was livid when she read the new preface, and shot off an impassioned complaint to her friend: "Now what did you go and put a PREFACE on it for you damn Jeswit, why it's a ruddy apologia." Giroux explained, "Flannery was a paradoxical person and a paradoxical writer. It's what fascinates us. It's a natural human reaction when a person is so contradictory." But the reaction among some of her more secular friends to this paradox was to begin to feel that she did not accept, and perhaps in some truly shuttered way did not even allow herself to understand, the implications of her writings. Like John Hawkes, Maryat simply decided to ignore Flannery's own pronouncements. "The writing is one thing and the thinking and speeches are another," she wrote a mutual friend. "Jekyl and Hyde if you will. Perhaps."

Praising to Betty the essential ingredients of "much liquor and male companionship, both of which I could stand more of more often," Flannery then visited the Notre Dame campus on May 4, after two days of her more usual fare of speaking on "The Catholic Novelist in the Protestant South" to the sisters of Rosary College, outside Chicago. Driving her from Rosary, including a stretch in the middle lane of Chicago's teeming Congress Street Expressway, flanked by "odiferous diesel trucks," Joel Wells has recalled her candor; when asked what she thought of the recently published sensation *To Kill a Mockingbird,* by Harper Lee, she replied, "It's a wonderful children's book." She then returned to South Bend, just a month later, to receive an honorary doctor of letters at St. Mary's College, the "sister college" of Notre Dame.

Between her first trip to the Midwest and her second, for collecting her hood, which her mother duly "wrapped up in newspaper against moths and put in the back reaches of the closet," she made an appearance at Emory to talk about "The South." When the critic Granville Hicks visited Andalusia in April, Flannery insisted, of her crutches, "They don't interfere with anything." Such certainly seemed to be the case with these demanding connections between cars, trains, and plane, as her mother met her at the Atlanta airport with a wheelchair. In the audience on the warm Sunday afternoon of May 20, for the Emory talk, given outside on the Quadrangle, was Alfred Corn, who went on to become a well-known poet and critic. Then a first-year student, studying *Wise Blood* in a Great Books course, he vividly remembers her "wearing a blue plaid skirt and a white blouse, buttoned at the top, of course, and unattractive pointed glasses."

While too nervous to walk up to speak with her afterward, as "she was that awesome creature, a *famous writer,*" Corn did screw up his courage to write, like Cecil Dawkins before him, putting as the address simply "Milledgeville." With early aspirations to the Christian ministry, Corn, from South Georgia, confessed to a crisis of faith upon entering college. Flannery carefully addressed these concerns in a handful of profound letters, in the genre of Hügel's *Letters to a Niece.* In response to his worries about the challenge of secular learning, she shared her own experience: "At one time, the clash of different world religions was a difficulty for me. Where you have absolute solutions, however, you have no need of faith." Instead she suggested a respect for "mystery," a term she first applied to illness, but which was increasingly key in her theology. As for the conundrum of predestination and God's punishment, she offered a literary answer: "Even if there were no Church to teach me this, writing two novels would do it. I think the more you write, the less inclined you will be to rely on theories like determinism. Mystery isn't something that is gradually evaporating. It grows along with knowledge."

That June a second of Flannery's friendships splintered, this time with her intellectual sparring partner Ted Spivey, who had added to the heat of their debates in recent years by defending the Beat writers Jack Kerouac and Allen Ginsberg, of whom she allowed, "There is a lot of ill-directed good in them." Spivey claims that a noticeable cooling occurred after he announced his engagement to Julia Douglass, a Georgia schoolteacher. When O'Connor "knew I was going to get married it made her real mad," says Spivey. "I had a feeling she wanted to marry me, as a matter of fact." Yet Flannery had already refuted this notion in a letter to Betty two years earlier, "My Jung friend is not a little bit in love with me but resents me rather thoroughly I think. Not that the two are mutually exclusive, I just don't think the first is so." As likely a cause for the rift was her growing exasperation with his significant dreams, which included Carson McCullers in her closet, Louise and Jim Abbot in her bed, and, most galling, dreams about Regina.

While speaking with students at Rosary College, Flannery had bemoaned that she had no new novel under way, as much as she wished she did, and so planned on "an awful lot of porch-settin'" on her return home. In June, she tried to put an end to this arid stretch by beginning work on a third novel, *Why Do the Heathen Rage?* Its title was taken from a conservative religious column printed on Saturdays in the *Atlanta Journal*. Having long expressed a wish to turn "The Enduring Chill" into the first chapter of a novel, she adopted much of the setup of its country farm: an intellectual son forced home by a bad heart; a snooty schoolteacher sister; a perpetually irate mother; and the addition of an invalid father. Instead of finding Heidegger, Walter's mother has to suffer the indignity of coming across her son's copy of *The Satiric Letters of St. Jerome.* When a section was published in *Esquire* in July 1963, an accompanying editorial note stated, "Flannery O'Connor's novel is as yet untitled, and she says it may be years before it's finished."

Yet the character jumping out from hundreds of pages of drafts, written over the next year, was not included in the excerpt, and may have been both the work's secret motor, and its roadblock. For while Walter, a bookish "secular contemplative," embodies a side of herself Flannery described as "hermit novelist," Sarah (sometimes called Oona) Gibbs is an outright satiric cartoon of Maryat Lee: she lives in an apartment on Second Avenue with other members of her commune, the Friendship Fellowship, a send-up of the Koinonia community in Georgia. In a letter, Sarah brags to Walter, "I have broken through the ceiling of a cramping religion." Yet most of the manuscripts trail off with the activist Sarah speeding southward in her little red car to meet Walter, who has passed himself off as a black man to trick her. As the O'Connor scholar Virginia Wray has plausibly written, "The depth of respect for and genuine warmth evidenced in O'Connor's letters to Maryat Lee during the 1960s may have led O'Connor to cease her satiric barrage, especially since during this period Lee was suffering from some serious health problems." (Maryat was having thyroid problems and could not find any helpful medication.)

Whatever the nature of the block that she was experiencing — not necessarily final for an author averaging seven years for a novel — the character Walter Tillman, dressed, like Flannery in her at-home outfit, in "plaid shirt and . . . jeans and moccasins," did reflect some of her intellectual interests at the time. A huge event to Flannery in the fall of 1962 was the October 11 convening of the Second Vatican Council, the first ecumenical council of the Roman Catholic Church in ninety-two years. "But it's so obviously the work of the Holy Spirit," she enthusiastically told Louise Abbot. Described in an article by John Kobler in the *Saturday Evening Post* as an attempt to "reflect the Teilhardian spirit," the pope's charge "to open the windows of the Church" encouraged wider scholarship. Like Walter's, Flannery's library now included an underlined copy of St. Jerome, the fourth-century "desert father" she was reading, meeting Thomas Merton halfway. The Trappist monk had recently published a book of sayings of the Eastern Desert Fathers.

In November she embarked on a Southern lecture swing, involving four talks in six days, beginning with East Texas State University, in Commerce, Texas. "Nobody can get me out now but Kruchev," she groaned before leaving home, referring to the recent standoff between the Russian premier and President Kennedy in the Cuban missile crisis. In and around Dallas, she picked up some tasteless jokes about race to relay back to Maryat. Most stimulating was New Orleans, where she arrived to give talks at the Catholic student Newman Club of the University of Southwest Louisiana in Lafayette; the University of Southeast Louisiana in Hammond; and Loyola. Her guide to the city was Richard Allen, once her double date in high school. This encounter was less of a fiasco, as Allen, now curator of a museum of jazz at Tulane, guided her past "a Negro nightclub called 'Baby Green's Evening in Paris,' which I might some day like to investigate." As she kidded with John Hawkes, "If I had to live in a city I think I would prefer New Orleans to any other — both Southern and Catholic and with indications that the Devil's existence is freely recognized."

On Sunday evening, November 18, she made her way to Marquette Hall to deliver her basic talk on "The Catholic Novelist in the Protestant South," freshened up with introductory quips about Walker Percy, whose recent success, *The Moviegoer,* had won a 1962 National Book Award and whose answer to newsmen, asking why there were so many good Southern writers — "because we lost the War" — pleased her no end. She planned to meet her fellow Catholic novelist — who also used Caroline Gordon as a first reader — and Percy had made his way over the causeway from Covington. By the time Flannery arrived at the second-floor reception, she was exhausted, having been carried up an unanticipated flight of exterior stairs, slung between Richard Allen and a teenage girl. Even Percy, who grew up in Alabama, found himself "thrown at first by her deep Georgia accent," until they managed some small talk about Katherine Anne Porter. Yet he always treasured a typescript of her speech, and modeled Val, an ex-nun in his novel *The Last Gentleman,* on O'Connor.

Although she was turning only thirty-eight in March, during 1963 O'Connor was often afforded the treatment of an elder statesman rather than a young woman writer. Her itinerary was full of special bookings: on March 8, at a symposium on religion and the arts, with the poet John Ciardi at Sweet Briar College in Virginia; on April 24, at Troy Stage College in Troy, Alabama; over the week of October 14, at Hollins College in Roanoke, Virginia; at the College of Notre Dame in Baltimore; and finally, at Georgetown University in Washington, DC. In June, she had been lauded with yet another honorary doctorate at graduation ceremonies at Smith College in Northampton, Massachusetts. It was an "oppressive" day, lightened for her only by the presence of Robert Fitzgerald. Her citation, she told Tom Stritch, was "something (fishy) about 'man's inhumanity to man.'"

Yet her struggle to discover a deeper mode of fiction — tantamount to an extended writer's block, or at least writer's puzzlement — continued to agitate beneath the surface of all these awards and honors. In May, clearly echoing concerns expressed fourteen months earlier to Father McCown, she wrote Sister Mariella Gable, a teaching nun she had met at Marillac, who was working on an essay about ecumenism in O'Connor's stories, "I appreciate and need your prayers. I've been writing eighteen years and I've reached the point where I can't do again what I know I can do well, and the larger things that I need to do now, I doubt my capacity for doing."

O'Connor's novel in progress was certainly not providing the solution. In September, she complained to John Hawkes, "I have been working all summer just like a squirril on a treadmill, trying to make something of Walter and his affairs and the other heathens that rage but I think this is maybe not my material (don't like that word)."

Early in the fall, the dry spell finally broke. Flannery had been suffering from increased fatigue, diagnosed as severe anemia, for which she was treated with an iron preparation. She was spending more of her afternoon hours in the waiting room of Dr. Fulghum's office a few blocks from Baldwin County Hospital, on the edge of Milledgeville. Here in his cramped, twelve-by-twelve reception room, with chairs set along the walls, and dominated by a sunburst wall clock, she began gathering impressions of country types and their small talk that felt like a story to her, about Mrs. Ruby Turpin, one of those "country women . . . who just sort of springs to life; you can't hold them down or shut their mouths." She later told Cecil Dawkins of her "reward for setting in the doctor's office. Mrs. Turpin I found in there last fall."

As the story she titled "Revelation" opens, an imposingly "stout" Ruby Turpin arrives with her "somewhat shorter" and compliant husband, Claud, at a doctor's office. He needs treatment for a leg ulcer, caused by a cow kick, and she sets him down beneath a sunburst clock. Taking in a roomful of all strata of white folk, Ruby busies herself with some demanding mental arithmetic about the relative social worth of "white-trash" versus "colored people who owned their homes and land," while studying a lineup of shoes that includes red high heels, bedroom slippers, and Girl Scout shoes with heavy socks. The wearer of the Girl Scout shoes turns out to be Mrs. Turpin's nemesis. For as she indulges in cliché-ridden chat, this college student, reading *Human Behavior,* beans her with the thick, blue textbook, lunges at her throat, and, while being wrestled down by a nurse, delivers the "revelation": "Go back to hell where you came from, you old wart hog."

In the character of this deranged girl, Flannery found a way to pencil in a private joke to Maryat that was not truly hurtful, because it was so exaggerated and comic in its bold outlines. Like her friend Mary "Maryat" Attaway, daughter of Grace Lee, the Mary Grace in "Revelation" is a Wellesley student; and as Flannery borrowed a funny anecdote from her as a trigger for "Everything That Rises," so a childhood memory of Maryat's provided the vehicle of violent grace in this story. Maryat had once greatly entertained Flannery by recounting "how in the 6th grade I threw a book ostensibly at a boy who ducked and it hit my detested teacher." Knowing full well Flannery's refractory method, Maryat was not at all put off by the satire. When her young niece Mary Dean Lee asked why Flannery "made Mary Grace so ugly," Maryat wisely answered, "Because Flannery loves her."

The stretching into new territory, or "larger things," occurs in the second part of "Revelation," when Claud and Ruby Turpin return home from the doctor's office. In a rare glimpse of marital intimacy, husband and wife take a nap together, while Ruby anguishes about why she had been "singled out for the message . . . a respectable, hard-working, church-going woman." Compared to Job, and in a letter to Maryat to "a country female Jacob," Ruby goes off to shout at God across a hog pen while she "scoots" down the pigs. Having been reading, over the summer, the Arden editions of Shakespeare's plays, ordered for a dollar apiece, O'Connor lets Ruby soliloquize, "How am I a hog and me both? How am I saved and from hell too?" And then, peering into the dusky sky, Ruby "gets the vision," a topsy-turvy correction of all she believed:

> *a vast horde of souls were rumbling toward heaven. There were whole companies of white-trash, clean for the first time in their lives, and bands of black niggers in white robes, and battalions of freaks and lunatics shouting and clapping and leaping like frogs. And bringing up the end of the procession was a tribe of people*

whom she recognized at once as those who, like herself and
Claud, had always had a little of everything and the God-given
wit to use it right.

Flannery completed "Revelation" within eight weeks, and, as with "Good Country People," her only other story written relatively quickly, her first reader, Caroline Gordon, was entirely impressed. "Caroline was crazy about my story," she wrote Betty. "She read it to her class and they laughed until they cried or so she reported." The only rewriting occurred when Catharine Carver interpreted the ending as her *"blackest"* and Ruby as "evil." Flannery understood that this story was a departure, with its celestial vision of racial convergence — a transposing of Martin Luther King's "I Have a Dream" speech, widely televised that August. But most innovative was the kinder, gentler fate of the big country woman, granted illumination. She wanted no mistaking Ruby as "just an evil Glad Annie." She told Maryat, "I like Mrs. Turpin as well as Mary Grace," awarding her friend "half interest in Mary Grace" and signing one letter to her as "Mrs. Turpin."

Although she could have sold "Revelation" to *Esquire* — where "Why Do the Heathen Rage?" appeared — for the grand sum of fifteen hundred dollars, Flannery chose to be paid substantially less to stay loyal to Andrew Lytle and the *Sewanee Review*. "I emulate my better characters," she wrote Betty, "and feel like Mr. Shiftlet that there should be some folks that some things mean more to them than money." Lytle was appreciative, judging both "The Lame Shall Enter First" and "Revelation" to have been "magnificent things." When her close friends read the story, they concurred. "The breath was pushed out of me by this story," Maryat wrote her. "You have done it. You have gone past them all. . . . The reception of Violent Bare has obviously not really touched your confidence — as it might have." Recalls Louise Abbot, "I felt

'Revelation' marked a turning point in Flannery's thinking, feeling, writing, everything. And that she had started in another direction."

❋

ON THE MONDAY before Christmas 1963, Flannery fainted, giving Regina a scare, and was immediately put to bed, where she remained for the next ten days. Her weakness was severe enough that this young woman who managed to get to church at seven o'clock most weekday mornings, on crutches, missed even the high festival of Christmas Day mass. "Not enough blood to run the engine or something," she scribbled a note, in longhand, to Betty. Warning signals had been mounting over the past month — she grew too weak to be "hitting this typewriter" the week following November 22, as she watched the "sad" events of John F. Kennedy's assassination and funeral on television; new tests revealed a lower blood count. In truth, she had begun the long, slow process of dying.

Flannery handled her latest medical downturn as she had all the others, by focusing on her writing. Using an electric typewriter to conserve energy, by Sunday, January 5, she took up her correspondence again and was able to return to mass for the first time. The weather cooperated, with ice storms that had frozen the plumbing giving way to near-spring days. Regina, in a red coat, was venturing out, "frisking" her small magnolia, and the peacocks had begun hollering. Flannery took advantage of a rising hemoglobin count — from 8.5 to 11.6, with 13 as normal — to write to Robert Giroux, on January 25, of her resolve to put together a second collection of stories, feeling that "Revelation" would "round it out," with seven others. Giroux wrote back, encouraging her to aim for the fall list, which would require a finished manuscript by May.

A recent addition to Andalusia that turned out to be an unpredicted pleasure to both Flannery and her mother that winter was an old record player, which the Sisters, recipients of a new machine, sent down with Louis from Atlanta. Flannery had been mulling over buying one, but instead invested in a new pair of swans to replace a beloved, now deceased, one-eyed female. Hearing of the gift, her friend Tom Stritch sent along a box of records from his basement. While Flannery claimed that "I have the Original Tin Ear," the music cast her back to Yaddo, where she had listened to classical records chosen by Robert Lowell. To try to understand why she preferred "straight up and down" Haydn, she asked Stritch to send some music reviews from *Ave Maria,* the Notre Dame weekly. As she wrote to Betty, "All I can say about it is that all classical music sounds alike to me and all the rest of it sounds like the Beatles."

Flannery had begun working on a story again, but more of her downtime was now given over to listening to records and watching television than her friends ever expected. TV satisfied a taste for the vulgarities of popular culture that used to be filled for her solely by newspaper coverage — of Roy Rogers's horse, Trigger, attending church in Pasadena, or a local beauty contest for "Miss North Georgia Chick." Now she was up on "Geritol, Pepto-Bismol, Anacin, Bufferin, any kind of soap or floor wax, etc. etc." A sports fan, her *aperçu* on the Kennedy assassination was that "all commercial television is stopped until after the funeral and even the football games called off, which is about the extremest sign of grief possible." She and Tom Stritch communicated about their mutual televised passions, stock-car races and track events. She even "postponed my work an hour" to catch W. C. Fields's 1941 comedy, *Never Give a Sucker an Even Break.*

In the third week of February, she received a verdict from her doctors that she would need to have a hysterectomy to remove an enlarged fibroid tumor, the cause of her severe anemia and fainting spells. Dr. Merrill was hesitant to allow any sort of surgery for fear of triggering a lupus flare and wished to have the operation take place in Atlanta. But Flannery refused to leave Milledgeville. Mary Cline had just been released from the hospital, and Regina, recovering from a week in bed with the flu, was caring for her. She did not want to impose the extra strain of an Atlanta hospitalization on her family, or herself. In preparation, she canceled readings scheduled that April for Boston College and Brown University, where John Hawkes was teaching, as well as for the University of Texas. In order to safeguard against reactivating the lupus, she was "loaded with cortisone."

Admitted to Baldwin County Hospital on Monday, February 24, 1964, Flannery spent the night before her operation correcting the galleys of "Revelation," which had just come in the mail from the *Sewanee Review*. As she reread the pages in the hospital light, the story suddenly "didn't seem so hot." For the operation the next day the local surgeon, Dr. Walker, enlisted five blood donors and briefly considered an artificial kidney. Over the three days following, she was kept on glucose and cortisone drips. While she shared such surgical details with Maryat, everyone else was treated to a lighter version of events. "One of my nurses was a dead ringer for Mrs. Turpin," she wrote Betty in a typical dispatch. "Her Claud was named Otis. . . . She didn't know she was funny and it was agony to laugh and I reckon she increased my pain about 100%."

The outcome of this operation, from which she returned home on March 5, was at first deemed positive. "It was all a howling success from their point of view," she wrote Robert Fitzgerald, "and one of them is going to write it up for a doctor magazine as you usually don't cut folks with lupus." Within two weeks, though, she was back in bed, "not doing any brain work but reading," while subject to postoperative infections and cystitis. Her physical reaction was dramatic enough that by the time of her thirty-ninth birthday, on March 25, she was no longer concealing her inkling that something was gravely wrong. "I suspect it has kicked up the lupus again," she wrote Betty three days later. "Anyway, I am full of kidney pus and am back on the steroids." She described for Betty a visit to the doctor's office the day before: "same scene as in 'Revelation.'"

A new friend and correspondent was Cudden Ward Dorrance, a sixty-year-old short story writer, and friend of Allen Tate's, whom she had met at a breakfast at Georgetown. Dorrance, himself dying of emphysema from smoking, sent her the two books she was closest to during this month. The first was C. S. Lewis's *Miracles,* the Anglican author's meditation on the transformative power of imagination. Flannery noted a correspondence between Lewis's Christian novels and hers: "we both want to locate our characters . . . right on the border of the natural & the supernatural." Then, for Easter 1964, Dorrance sent Lewis's *Letters to Malcolm: Chiefly on Prayer,* which she regarded "as being probably what I need worse personally." She confided to him an excess of "nervous energy," from being back on the steroids she had endured from 1951 to 1961, and requested that he "pray I don't have to stay on them long."

The turn of a month led to a return to the hospital, where Flannery found herself the third week in April for ten days. The antibiotics that Dr. Merrill suggested for treating kidney infection were insufficient to halt her careening physical problems. "Monday I woke up covered from head to foot with the lupus rash," she alerted Brainard Cheney. "A sign that things are as screwy inside as out so I headed for the hospital and here I am for an indefinite stay." In a conspiracy of improbabilities, Mary Cline was also in the hospital again, on the floor above Flannery's, having survived a nearly fatal heart attack. They both returned the same day to Andalusia, where her aunt was set up in a recent back-parlor addition. Her Florencourt cousin Catherine Firth soon arrived from Kansas City to help out at the farmhouse that Flannery nicknamed "Jolly Corners Rest Home."

Flannery's first instinct on her return home was to ensure that a second book of stories would be published, no matter what happened next. So on May 7 she wrote a highly detailed letter of instructions to Elizabeth McKee. Her initial plan had been to go back into the originals with her usual vengeance of rewriting and polishing. But under doctor's orders to spend the rest of the summer in bed and a prohibition on any typing outside of short business letters, she arrived at a more practical compromise. She simply asked her agent to round up copies of the stories as they had been printed in magazines, and assemble the book from these. "I think I'll be able to make any really necessary changes on the proofs," she promised. She then listed the eight stories she was envisioning, winding up with "Revelation." The book's title remained an open question.

Unable to sit for long at the typewriter, in May Flannery shifted to writing stories in her mind. Of one such purely conceptual creation, she told Charlotte Gafford, who had completed a thesis on her work at Birmingham-Southern College, and sent crystallized violets and a book of poems as get-well gifts, "I am writing me this story in my head and I hope by the time they let me up maybe I'll have it." Even such mental work, though, was made more difficult by sluggishness; once a week she visited the doctor for a blood transfusion, spiking her energy, and resulting in a few letters to friends. "I havent had it active since 1951 and it is something renewing acquaintance with it," she alluded to her lupus, in one such missive to the Gossetts. On good days, she worked for an hour. "My my I do like to work," she wrote Maryat. "I et up that one hour like it was filet mignon."

Flannery eventually heard from Robert Giroux with his approval of the plan to go ahead with the book, using stories in print. She had since decided, on looking over them, to withdraw "The Partridge Festival," as a "very sorry story." In its place, she mentioned, for the first time, one "that I have been working on off and

on for several years that I may be able to finish in time to include."
The intended story was "Judgment Day," a retelling of her first
published story from Iowa, "The Geranium." Roiling in her head
over the month was the notion to circle back to her beginnings and
redo her original successful story, revealing how far she had come.
As she began retooling the original, old man Tanner, in his daughter's New York apartment, is not just homesick, but actively plot-
ting his escape, even if in a box. The note he pins to his pocket
reads, "IF FOUND DEAD SHIP EXPRESS COLLECT TO
COLEMAN PARRUM, CORINTH, GEORGIA."

Yet every few weeks brought a new hardship. Toward the end
of May, the unfortunate news was a medical decision that O'Connor
would need to check back into Piedmont Hospital, the ultramod-
ern, 250-bed redbrick hospital in the Buckhead section of Atlanta,
where she had been given a series of bone tests in late 1960. Before
leaving for the hospital, she signed a contract for her collection,
with the title she had originally suggested: *Everything That Rises
Must Converge.* As she wrote Maryat on May 21, referring to her
Milledgeville Drs. Fulghum and Burrell, "Going to Piedmont tomorrow to let Arthur J. Merrill take over. F. & B. give up, more or
less, for the present anyways." She at least felt confident, with Dr.
Merrill, that "he knows what he's doing."

Her eye for irony unimpaired, Piedmont Hospital provided
much material; and as weak as she was, with visitors discouraged,
a number of friends managed to get past Regina, who guarded the
door by day and resided nearby with her sister Aunt Cleo at night.
The hospital included a nursing school, and among Flannery's favorite characters to pin to an imaginary wall were its student
nurses. As she wrote in an account to Maryat, signed "Excelsior,"
"Here the student nurses switch in with very starchy aprons and
beehive hairdos and say such things as 'What's bugging you, huh?'"
Flannery wrote to Betty, "By now, I know all the student nurses
who 'want to write,' — if they are sloppy & inefficient & can't make

up the bed, that's them — they want to write. 'Inspirational stuff I'm good at,' said one of them. 'I just get so taken up with it I forget what I'm writing.'"

The first of her friends to show up was Abbot Augustine More, met by Regina, who warned him he could stay only three minutes, though he stayed thirty. One weekend, Caroline Gordon "breezed in . . . her hair the color of funnytoor polish." Gordon later recalled, "After the nurse had left the room, Flannery pulled a notebook out from under her pillow, 'The doctor says I musn't do any work. But he says it's all right for me to write a little fiction.' She paused to grin at us." Louise Abbot, having received a note from Flannery — "I am sick of being sick" — hurried to her "fourth or fifth floor" hospital room, its bank of windows overlooking the tops of green trees. "Guess who's here?" Regina sang, as she ushered in Louise. "Flannery has just waked up, and she pushes herself up on one elbow and smiles," remembered Abbot. "The afternoon sunlight in the room and the dark blue of her pajamas make her eyes bluer than I have ever seen them."

The child psychiatrist and Harvard professor Robert Coles, author of *Flannery O'Connor's South,* met O'Connor only once, at her bedside at Piedmont. Involved with issues of race relations in the South, he and his wife had become acquainted with Ruth Anne Jackson, a six-foot, 250-pound, African American woman who worked as a nurse's aide at Piedmont. She told them of "Mizz O'Connor," her patient, a writer "who believed in God," who she wanted them to meet. "I met a woman who was dying," says Coles, knowing nothing then of her reputation. "Her face was inflamed as a consequence of steroid treatment." Flannery was "tickled" to discover that Coles was from Concord and preferred Emerson to Thoreau. "You will find here in rural Georgia fallen angels by the thousands," his wife remembered her telling them, with the thinnest of smiles.

Complaining of a bed table "too high so you can't write on it without breaking your arm," Flannery did manage to accomplish impressive work from her hospital bed. She had actually finished the bulk of her rewriting of "Judgment Day," which she had briefly been calling "Going Home," when she completed "Revelation." In the hospital she mostly concentrated hard, within her flickering imagination, to make out the curious images and plot of her next story, "Parker's Back." She wrote to Catharine Carver on June 17, warning her that when she returned home she would be sending her "Judgment Day" for her opinion. "I have another in the making," she added, "that I scratch on in longhand here at the hospital at night but that's not my idea of writing. How do those French ladies such as Madame Mallet-Joris write in cafes, for pitys sake?"

She had slowly been building "Parker's Back," layer by layer, over several years. Her first glimmer of the story came when she ordered George Burchett's *Memoirs of a Tattooist* from the Marboro bookstore list, which delighted her with its photograph of the old tattooist's wife covered in tattoos, "like fabric." Since at least 1960, she had been composing her story of O. E. Parker, a tattoo-covered young man and his disapproving wife, Sarah Ruth, daughter of a "Straight Gospel preacher." In her unfinished third novel, she briefly found a spot for a man whose body was covered in tattoos — Mr. Gunnels, the farm help, with the face of God tattooed upon his back. When Walter tries to take a picture of the haunting image, his hand trembles and the photo comes out blurry.

Often more intimate in letters than in person, Flannery, during her grave illness, shared some of her most vulnerable feelings with Cudden Ward Dorrance, whom she had met once, and Janet McKane, a schoolteacher from Manhattan, whom she had never met but who had written her a letter that touched off a flurry of responses, beginning in January 1963, often including childhood memories from Savannah, or her brief time in Manhattan. On April 2, McKane organized a high mass to be said for Flannery's recovery at a Byzantine rite church in Manhattan. "I read my Mass prayers this morning," Flannery wrote her on the day, "not Byzantine by any means but with much appreciation of what you were doing for me." So tucked into her story was a signal to McKane, like so many to Maryat, because she chose as the image for Parker's back a tattooed Byzantine Christ, done in "little blocks."

Flannery's hospital stay was marked by four blood transfusions and an endless series of tests. Her weight was down about twenty pounds. As days turned into weeks and finally, to her near disbelief, *"one month,"* the only new prescription by the doctors was a low-protein diet, since her kidneys were unable to refine toxins out of meat, eggs, and cheese. "I'm for medicare; otherwise I got few convictions and almost no blood," she wrote the Cheneys, as her lupus, and so her hospital bill, was not covered by insurance; she and her family had been paying most of the medicine and hospital bills. But a hint of resignation crept into her tone, amid all the comedy, when Dr. Merrill decided that she would not be helped by further hospitalization. "Dr. Fulghum is back in the driver's seat," she ominously informed Maryat, "& Dr. M. has checked out." When the volunteer ladies in pink smocks brought three letters from Janet McKane, she closed her reply with a heartbreaking couplet from Gerard Manley Hopkins:

> *Margaret, are you grieving*
> *Over Goldengrove unleaving? —.*

On Saturday, June 21, Flannery was once again home at Andalusia, where Regina set up a table and electric typewriter by her bedside. "I can get out & get at it," she wrote Cudden Ward Dorrance, "work an hour & rest an hour, etc. That's all I ask." Within these hour-long reprieves, she secured the last pieces of her book. "I look like a bull frog but I can work," she guaranteed Tom Stritch, thanking him for her favorite music of the month, liking "the 4-hand piano Chopin thing best; there is a point in it where the peafowls join in." Feeling tentatively emboldened, she arranged to push back the book's publication date until spring 1965, so that she could do some rewriting on "The Enduring Chill," decide whether to include "You Can't Be Any Poorer Than Dead," let "Judgment Day" sit "a few weeks longer," finish "Parker's Back." She counted nine or ten options for inclusion in the book.

The stories Flannery finished in this hospital-like setting shared with "Revelation" both maturity of tone and ambitious scope. In the midst of "Judgment Day," old Tanner remembers being down South, whittling a pair of eyeglasses from wood and fitting them onto the face of the black worker Coleman Parrum — Jim to his Huck Finn — while asking, "What you see through those glasses?" "See a man," answers Coleman. The point is their spiritual kinship. In "Parker's Back," when O. E. Parker unveils the image of God on his back to his pregnant wife, she beats the blasphemous tattoo bloody with a broom. The story ends in a flood of emotion, with Sarah, at dawn, peering through a window at her husband, "leaning against the tree, crying like a baby." As the O'Connor critic Frederick Asals has written, these last stories were growing somehow "mellower."

Her dosage of prednisone having been ordered cut in half by Dr. Merrill, at the beginning of July, due to a rise in the nitrogen content of her blood, Flannery was now deprived even of "nervous energy." Yet, as she reported to Maryat, she was at least not experiencing some of the more ethereal side effects she had recorded before the hospitalization and transfusions: "hearing the celestial chorus — 'Clementine' is what it renders when I am weak enough to hear it. Over & over. 'Wooden boxes without topses, They were shoes for Clementine.'" Punning on the Latin "lupus," she ruefully wrote Sister Mariella Gable of her disease, "The wolf, I'm afraid, is inside tearing up the place. I've been in the hospital

50 days already this year." In an attempt to restore some of her energy, the doctor adjusted her medication to more frequent but smaller doses of prednisone.

On July 8, Flannery wrote to Janet McKane, apologizing for the "fancy" stationery. She documented an amusing catalog of get-well cards, decorated with chickens, Bugs Bunny, and the "funny" kind with "Get the hell out of that bed" messages, and she bragged that while she tossed the cards in the trash, saying "a prayer for the soul of the sender," she economically kept any stationery to reuse. Included in this hilarious letter, though, was somber news, shared only with Janet, that when the priest brought her Communion the day before, "I also had him give me the now-called Sacrament of the Sick. Once known as Extreme Unction." Flannery knew that this sacrament of "final anointing," renamed by the Second Vatican Council, did not presume death. Yet her special request indicated that she saw herself as dangerously ill.

For the next three weeks, Flannery devoted every inch of her consciousness to her two stories, climbing out of bed "into the typewriter about 2 hours every morning." Catharine Carver returned "Judgment Day," with a few queries, but mainly praise for the story. So Flannery then sent "Parker's Back" to her, which she also mailed to Caroline Gordon and Betty Hester. This time around, her "first reader" advanced a very theological theory, suggesting that the story illustrated, in Sarah's puritanical horror at an iconic tattoo of Christ, the Docetist heresy that Jesus had only a spiritual body, not a physical one. She also sent a heady telegram: "Congratulations on having succeeded where the great Flaubert failed!" But Flannery grumbled to Betty, of "a lot of advice" she was ignoring from Gordon. "I did well to write it at all." She focused instead on well-timed news about "Revelation": "We can worry about the interpitations of Revelation but not its fortunes. I had a letter from the O. Henry prize people & it got first."

Although Flannery was now devoting twenty-two hours a day

to resting up for writing, over the last two weeks in July she was forced to return to the doctor's office and the Baldwin County Hospital several times. Having suffered three coronary arrests, Dr. Fulghum was no longer making house calls. When Flannery's symptoms of kidney infection returned, he put her on a double dose of antibiotics again and withdrew the cortisone. Bringing along a Günter Grass novel, *The Tin Drum,* sent by Maryat, O'Connor went once more to the hospital for a blood transfusion to lift her hemoglobin count, again below eight. "It's six of one and a half dozen of the other," she decided. As she had once written, "Sickness before death is a very appropriate thing and I think those who don't have it miss one of God's mercies." Among those mercies was evidently acceptance. "They expect me to improve," she had written Cecil Dawkins. "I expect anything that happens."

On July 28, Flannery penned her last letter, a card, in a shaky, nearly illegible hand, addressed to "Dear Raybat." Adopting a big-sister tone, she worried about an anonymous crank call that Maryat told her of receiving. "Cowards can be just as vicious as those who declare themselves — more so," Flannery warned. "Dont take any romantic attitude toward that call. Be properly scared and go on doing what you have to do, but take the necessary precautions. And call the police. That might be a lead for them." She then apologized, "Don't know when I'll send those stories. I've felt too bad to type them." Her sign-off: "Cheers, Tarfunk." When her mother discovered the card a few weeks later, left at the bedside, she sent it on to Maryat, with a note, "Mary Flannery enjoyed your visit to her and I'm so glad you came. The enclosed was on her table."

Mary Jo Thompson and Fannie White, of Sanford House, stopped by Andalusia on the evening of Saturday, July 25, on their way to dinner in Macon. They had brought with them some food from the restaurant to drop off with Regina. Over the past decade, the pair had continued to spend nights at the farm once a week; closer to Regina than to Flannery, they remained important members in the O'Connors' support network, made up mostly of single women. "We had not dreamed we would see Flannery," recalls Mary Jo Thompson. "But she told her mother to tell us not to leave. And she dressed, even though I know she didn't have the strength. She came out onto the porch and sat in the rocking chair and visited with us. And that was good-bye, because we never saw her again."

The following Wednesday, Flannery was once again extremely ill. Her cousin Catherine called an ambulance early in the morning, and she was rushed to the hospital. On Sunday, August 2, many of her close, local friends received calls, alerting them. "A friend, Mary Jo Thompson, has called to tell that Flannery is critically ill," remembered Louise Abbot. "The end could come at any moment. My impulse is to drive over there, but I'm told she would not know me." Flannery received the Eucharist, and at some point during a very hot, very still Sunday, as her kidneys began to fail, was administered last rites by Abbot Augustine More of Conyers. Shortly before midnight, she slipped into a coma, and was pronounced dead, at the age of thirty-nine, on August 3, at 12:40 a.m.

❋

A LOW REQUIEM funeral mass was held for Flannery O'Connor the following day, August 4, at 11:00 a.m., at Sacred Heart Church. It was a sunny Tuesday, with temperatures in the low nineties. A sizable number of cars were parked that morning on Hancock and Jefferson streets, bordering the little redbrick church that stood on land given by Flannery's great-grandmother. The building's brown shutters were closed against the August heat. "There was a lot of people there," recalls Alfred Matysiak, the son of the Polish farm worker. "It was a good crowd. I remember that." Louise Abbot, informed of the details by Uncle Louis, had driven to Milledgeville with a group of friends from Louisville, and remembered the sanctuary as "full but not crowded."

Music was playing on the small church organ as mourners filed in, including those nuns and priests who were scattered throughout the congregation. Among them was Monsignor Patrick O'Connor, a cousin from Savannah. Seated to the left of the altar, inside the rail, were Abbot Augustine, Father Paul Bourne, and Brother Pius, all from the Trappist monastery. Flannery's family members were seated to the left of the altar, at the front of the congregation. Her casket rested in the center aisle. The walls had recently been painted a color that Flannery ruefully described as "nursery pink," a decision of her rector, Father John Ware, which was rivaled in her disapproval only by his removal of painted statues of the Virgin and saints, given by the Cline family. But on this occasion, the celebrant was Monsignor Joseph Cassidy, pastor of the Cathedral of Christ the King in Atlanta.

Seated at the rear of the chapel, Louise Abbot found herself distracted from the somber atmosphere as she glanced out a nearby window at "a crape myrtle in full fuchsia bloom . . . tossing and blowing in a sudden breeze, catching the sunlight and sending shadows rippling down the louvered blinds." Her attention was captured, too, by the woman sitting in front of her, whom she believes was Betty Hester: "She sits like a child being punished, her head down as far as it will go, her shoulders sagging, her hands heavy on her lap. An aura of the solitary surrounds her. Her grief exerts an almost magnetic force. . . . During the service the monks have a look of joyous detachment. The woman in front of us shakes with sobs. She tries and is unable to control herself."

Although Monsignor Cassidy had been rector at Sacred Heart during Flannery's first year of college, when she was a member of the Newman Club that he advised, the family inexplicably requested that he give no eulogy. Chafing a bit under the restriction, he made a few general remarks in tribute, including the phrase, "When a person has been and has done what can never be forgotten . . ." At the conclusion, flanked by acolytes, he processed around the gray casket, an incense vessel swinging from his left hand, thick smoke swirling up in a large cloud. The casket was then moved slowly up the aisle. Regina rose, genuflected, and followed close behind, as she and her daughter had once walked behind Edward's casket. The rest of the family paused to allow her space before following. Privately, Regina spoke of not blaming God for her daughter's early death, but of being grateful for their extra years together. She had lived much longer than expected.

The burial service immediately afterward at Memory Hill Cemetery was brief. A prayer was offered by the elegant, white-haired orator Monsignor Patrick O'Connor, who was a stage actor before entering the seminary and whom Flannery had seen for the first time in thirty years at Conyers. She had been happy to know again this cousin of her father's, with whom she had a rapport, and they had talked enthusiastically of his memories of the family. The prayer that he offered at her graveside included the words "and if by reason of sin she may have forfeited eternal life in heaven," yet he rendered the word "may" with such lack of conviction as to make the phrase superfluous. Flannery O'Connor was then laid to rest beside her beloved father, the gravel spot eventually marked with a flat stone of Georgia marble, like the cover of a book, engraved with a cross.

BECAUSE THE FUNERAL had taken place within a single day of her dying, in her hometown, none of Flannery's friends up north had even a chance to attend. Most of them found out the news when they opened the *New York Times* that Tuesday morning and felt the shock of seeing her picture staring out at them, the obituary cautiously labeling her as "one of the nation's most promising writers." With *Everything That Rises Must Converge* still in piles on her editor's desk, the newspaper revived some of the controversies over

The Violent Bear It Away. For friends closer to home, the *Atlanta Constitution* told of a writer "most highly regarded in Europe . . . so quietly did she live among us."

Her old roommate from Iowa City, Barbara Tunnicliff Hamilton, did not learn of O'Connor's death until her eyes fell on the "Milestones" page of *Time* magazine the following week. "Flannery had made it," she wrote, of her first reaction. "The people who knew about such things valued her as those of us who lived with her and cared about her when she was young had hoped they would." As one of those who cared about her early on, as well as a prime example of "people who knew about such things," Robert Lowell wrote to Elizabeth Bishop immediately on hearing the news, "I think the cards seemed heavily stacked against her, and her fates must have felt that they had so thoroughly hemmed her in that they could forget, and all would [have] happened as planned, but really she did what she had decided on and was less passive and dependent than anyone I can think of."

The man most in a position to know just how independent from some extraordinarily constricting outward circumstances O'Connor could be was her editor Robert Giroux, now in possession of the completed manuscript for her final book. Like many others, though, he felt at loose ends about how to mark his personal grief. So he seized an opportunity when a postal card came in to the Farrar, Straus and Giroux offices, from an unknown friend of Flannery's, Janet McKane, announcing a memorial mass to be held in the Byzantine rite at a church on Third Avenue. "I went and found only two people present, myself and Miss McKane, and it was a *high* mass!" he reported to Caroline Gordon. "Behind the altar was a towering mosaic of Christ, and when I read Flannery's story, I realized that Parker's choice of tattoo was of course this figure. (Miss McKane told me afterwards that Flannery had always been fascinated by the Byzantine rite.)"

When *Everything That Rises Must Converge* was published the following April 1965, the response was more powerful, and uniform, than for any of O'Connor's other books. Playing into the fascination, of course, was the tragedy, as the simple white book cover carried only an epitaph on the back from Thomas Merton, "I write her name with honor, for all the truth and all the craft with which she shows man's fall and his dishonor." Flap copy described the book as a "worthy memorial," and began with a factual error, "The death of Flannery O'Connor at 38 marked the loss of one of America's most gifted contemporary writers at the height of her powers." Yet such public relations were backed up by general recognition of a vision that now looked full and coherent. The critic Charles Poore in the *Times* judged "her promise . . . fulfilled"; "the work of a master," said the *Newsweek* critic; and so on.

Attuned enough to O'Connor to have recognized her potential without reading a word, when she first walked into his office with Lowell, on a wintry afternoon in 1949, Giroux now wished to secure her literary rank. So he next put together a chronologically arranged collection of her short fiction, from her first published story, "The Geranium," through to its final, mature rendition, "Judgment Day." The strategy succeeded; many readers and critics recognized the sort of underlying pattern that Henry James once described as "the figure in the carpet." And *The Complete Stories* was awarded the 1972 National Book Award in Fiction, the prize she had lost to John O'Hara in 1956. Backstage at the awards ceremony, Giroux had a bit of a contretemps with a celebrated author who complained, "Do you really think Flannery O'Connor was a great writer? She's such a Roman Catholic." But Giroux said, "You can't pigeonhole her. That's just the point. I'm surprised at you, to misjudge her so completely. If she were here, she'd set you straight. She'd impress you. You'd have a hard time outtalking her."

Onstage, Giroux proved quite capable of advocating for her in a convincing way, setting the audience straight. The awards of 1972 were highly politicized, as the Vietnam War dragged on with no end in sight. Accepting the posthumous thousand-dollar prize, on behalf of Regina O'Connor, who was ill at home in Milledgeville, Giroux, "the soft-spoken vice president and editor of Farrar, Straus & Giroux," gave what the *Times* called "the sharpest indictment of literary and moral standards": "In an age of mendacity, duplicity and document-shredders, the clear vision of Flannery O'Connor not only burns brighter than ever but it burns through the masks of what she called 'blind wills and low dodges of the heart.' She once said, 'When I'm asked why Southern writers particularly have a penchant for writing about freaks, I say it's because we are still able to recognize one.'"

Yet such full-throated acclaim, and all the interest following, would have been impossible had Flannery not kept her eye, during her last six months, on "the pin point of light" that Mrs. Flood kept trying to make out at the end of *Wise Blood.* As O'Connor took pains to correct the galleys of "Revelation" the night before her operation in Baldwin County Hospital; or hid under her pillow, at Piedmont, the notebook in which she was scratching out "Parker's Back"; or worked, back home, making changes to "Judgment Day," on a bedside desk Maryat Lee remembered as "one of those flimsy tables from Woolworth's," she was intent on "going home," closing the circle, making a book, rigging the peacock's tail to unfurl. It was no accident that Haze had been stuck in a train berth, "like a coffin," or, O'Connor was anxious to conclude, that Tanner pops up from his, shouting, "Judgment Day!"

Flannery had spent her life making literary chickens walk backward. But she had also spent much of her adult writing life looking down the barrel of the Misfit's shotgun. Just as her friends had to discern the contours of true suffering between the lines of her funny vignettes of invalidism, so her stories included a coded spiritual autobiography. In her front room at Andalusia, rewriting some final words while "the grim reaper" waited, she stuck in a last wink and a smirk, not just to Caroline Gordon and Robert

Giroux, but to that one reader she claimed she would be happy with "in a hundred years." After old Tanner's daughter fulfills her father's wish to ship his body home to Georgia, Flannery — in the story's closing line, written mostly in quavering blue ink — endowed her with the hint of a resurrected body:

Now she rests well at night and her
good looks have mostly returned.

ACKNOWLEDGMENTS

I first stepped into the world of Flannery O'Connor in the late 1970s. She was my favorite fiction writer, and I would often read a few paragraphs of "The Artificial Nigger" or "Revelation" for inspiration while trying my hand at writing stories completely unlike hers. I was a graduate student at Columbia University at the time, too, with a concentration in Medieval and Renaissance Literature and, between the lines of her stories, I imagined that I detected qualities that struck me as "thirteenth-century" — ribald humor, gargoyled faces and bodies, frontal action, threats of violence, and, most of all, the subtle tug of a spiritual quest in a dark universe animated by grace and significance.

The timing of this literary infatuation proved lucky. While I was still under the sway of O'Connor's fiction, *The Habit of Being,* a collection of her letters, edited by her friend Sally Fitzgerald, appeared in 1979, accompanied by much press attention. I apparently wasn't the only one with a deep fascination with the mysterious woman behind the striking fiction. I did have an "aha!" experience while reading in the letters of the impact of the theology of Thomas Aquinas on her fiction. But such heady theories quickly became grounded in the even more compelling daily gossip. I would read a few letters and then turn to the back cover to study again the Joe McTyre 1962 photograph of O'Connor on her front steps, seemingly engaged in dialogue with a preening peacock.

Seized with the bright idea that I, and no one else, should attempt a biography of Flannery O'Connor — though I had so far published only a chapbook of poetry — I wrote to Sally Fitzgerald. I had heard somewhere that she was writing a memoir of O'Connor, and I wondered if she would approve my going forward. She responded on February 26, 1980, from the Mary Ingraham Bunting Institute of Radcliffe College, where she was a fellow, with the leveling news that she was writing a literary biography and that I would do well to find another subject. "In short," she wrote, "I am afraid that our projects *would* overlap in important ways." She let me down politely, though, kindly adding, "Should I ever feel the need of an assistant, I will certainly think of you and your proposal."

I awaited the appearance of Fitzgerald's book for over two decades. Early in 2003, an editor asked me if I had ever considered writing another biography, because I had since written about the poet Frank O'Hara. My first thought: Whatever happened to the biography of Flannery O'Connor? Sally Fitzgerald had died in June 2000, at the age of eighty-three, leaving behind an unfinished manuscript that has yet to appear. As my personal test for deciding on projects has always been to write the book that I want to read but cannot find on the shelf, I could think of no better choice. So I simply began with an exploratory trip to O'Connor's childhood home in Savannah, Georgia.

Of course the Flannery O'Connor of 2003 was a far more canonic figure than the Flannery O'Connor of 1980. With each passing year, her status as "minor" has been adjusted upward, as her stories have been anthologized, and more high school and college students discover her work. Among their professors, she has become a one-woman academic industry: as of 2008, the Modern Language Association catalogued 1,340 entries under O'Connor, including 195 doctoral dissertations and seventy book-length studies. The annual *Flannery O'Connor Bulletin* — now *Flannery O'Connor Review* — begun in 1972, is entirely devoted to critical reevaluations of her work. An important indicator of this shifting assessment was her inclusion as the first postwar woman writer in the Library of America series; her 1988 volume widely outsold Faulkner's, published three years earlier.

Most startling during my six years of writing this book has been the accompanying spike in interest in O'Connor in popular culture — formerly the domain, according to her, of Miss Watermelon of 1955. John Huston's 1979 adaptation of *Wise Blood* is a Netflix staple. Bruce Springsteen has credited O'Connor as the inspiration for his album *Nebraska*. On *The Charlie Rose Show,* Conan O'Brien, who wrote his senior thesis at Harvard on O'Connor, spoke of her as "one of the funniest, darkest writers in American history . . . I was drawn to her." (The actor Tommy Lee Jones, too, wrote a senior paper at Harvard on O'Connor.) Andalusia Farm is now a literary shrine, open to the public. O'Connor's books have been published in translation in more than forty countries: her fame has become global. My daily "Google Alert" for "Flannery O'Connor" attests that the phrase "like something out of Flannery O'Connor" is now accepted shorthand, like "Kafkaesque" before it, for nailing many a funny, dark, askew moment.

GIVING THE LIE to the stereotype of Flannery O'Connor as an eccentric recluse is the number of her friends, classmates, and relatives who shared anecdotes and lively memories with me throughout my research and writing. I found their voices touching, funny, and full of insight, and this book would have lacked much vital spirit without them. Making the following "list of credits" even longer is the inclusion of all the librarians, archivists, curators, scholars, experts, and admirers of various kinds who have devoted so much energy to further understanding, often without having ever met O'Connor, but having been drawn into her force field by stories read early on and never forgotten. To anyone I inadvertently left out, my apologies, and thanks.

In Savannah, I was greatly helped from the outset by the Flannery O'Connor Childhood Home Foundation, especially its directors and officers Rena Patton, Robert Strozier, Carl Weeks, and Bill Dawers, my trusty guide to contemporary Savannah. Mrs. Hugh R. Brown, diocesan archivist, opened to me the O'Connor family church records, and gave me access to an informative essay and panel interviews conducted by her late husband, Hugh R. Brown. I was pleased to speak with O'Connor's second cousin Patricia Persse and other Savannah childhood friends and acquaintances: Jane Harty Abbott, Alice Carr, Angela Dowling, Dan O'Leary, Newell Turner Parr, and Sister Jude Walsh. For historical background, I was given many materials by the Georgia Historical Society, and by Mark MacDonald at the Historic Savannah Foundation. I am grateful to Dale and Lila Critz, the current owners of Katie Semmes's home, for allowing me to visit; and for their hospitality, to Bobby Zarem, John and Ginger Duncan, Robert E. Jones, Walter and Connie Hartridge, and the Savannah College of Art and Design.

In each of many visits to Atlanta, I was shown extraordinary hospitality by the Emory University Professor of English Richard Rambuss and his partner, Charles O'Boyle, as well as by Virginia Spencer Carr. At Emory Special Collections, I received expert guidance to the Betty Hester letters, unsealed in 2007 after twenty years, from Director Steve Enniss, as well as from the O'Connor scholar and University Vice President and Secretary Rosemary Magee and University Archivist Virginia Cain, who led me on a tour of Emory University Hospital, where O'Connor was hospitalized in 1951. For background on Piedmont Hospital, where O'Connor was hospitalized in 1960, and again in 1964, I was given detailed information by the historian and archivist Diane Erdeljac. I was aided on many occasions by the Atlanta Historical Society, and for information on Peachtree Heights in the 1930s, I am indebted to Bill Bell. I was honored to be able to speak with two of O'Connor's Atlanta first cousins, Dr. Peter Cline and Jack Tarleton.

All roads in O'Connor research lead to Milledgeville, where Flannery lived most of her years, and where the bulk of her papers are deposited. Most knowledgeable in all things having to do with O'Connor's letters, manuscripts, and memorabilia is Nancy Davis-Bray, associate director for Special Collections at Georgia College and State University. My special thanks to the good-natured Marshall Bruce Gentry, professor of English at GSCU and editor of the *Flannery O'Connor Review,* for inviting me as keynote speaker at the 2006 "O'Connor and Other Georgia Writers" conference, and for publishing my talk in the journal in 2007; and to his predecessor, a walking repository of O'Connoriana, Sarah Gordon. For allowing me to remain as a guest in his rambling ranch house during stays that could go on for months, I am indebted to Dan Bauer, assistant professor of English; and for his friendship, to Michael Riley, associate professor of English. Robert J. Wilson III, professor of History, shared valuable historical information about Milledgeville, as did Craig Amason, executive director of the Andalusia Foundation, who facilitated, as well, my 2005 *Travel and Leisure* article, "House of Stories," on the opening of the farm to the public. My introduction to Milledgeville was a lovely picnic with Louise Florencourt, executor of Regina O'Connor's estate and cotrustee of the Mary Flannery O'Connor Charitable Trust, on the front porch of Andalusia. I was also a luncheon guest in Milledgeville of O'Connor's friend and biographer William Sessions.

For memories of Mary Flannery O'Connor during her childhood years in Milledgeville, I relied on conversations with Charlotte Conn Ferris, Dr. Floride Gardner, Martha Marion Kingery, Elizabeth Shreve Ryan, Frances Powell Binion Sibley, and John Thornton. I twice visited O'Connor's cousin Frances Florencourt at her home in Arlington, Massachusetts, where she shared clippings, photographs, and letters from the family archive; and I was pleased to be a guest speaker in March 2007 at her course on O'Connor at the Regis College Learning in Retirement program. I spoke, too, with her late brother-in-law, Dr. Robert Mann, husband of the late Margaret Florencourt, at his home in Lexington, Massachusetts. Many shared anecdotes about the adult O'Connor in Milledgeville: Dr. Zeb Burrell, Pete Dexter, Mary More Jones, Mary Dean Lee, Dr. Robert E. Lee, Kitty Martin, Alfred Matysiak, Sr., Catherine Morai, Dorrie Neligan, Carol Sirmans, Mary Barbara Tate, Mary Jo Thompson, and Margaret Uhler.

Most remarkable was the overwhelming response to a mailing to O'Connor's fellow alumnae of the Georgia State College for Women, through the Alumni Affairs Office; I received more than fifty replies. For their generous communications by either letter, telephone, or e-mail, I thank Virginia Wood Alexander, Louise Simmons Allen, Dr. Marion Barber, Irene Dysart Baugh, Merle Chason Bearden, Mary Elizabeth Anderson Bogle, Frances Foster Bowen, Catherine J. Boyce, Virginia B. Brannan, Anne Shipman Brennan, Nona Quinn Buntts, Dorothy Channell, Anna Logan Drvaric, Elizabeth Stokes Dunaway, Gertrude Ehrlich, Charmet Garrett, Elizabeth Wansley Gazdick, Zell Barnes Grant, Katherine D. Groves, Sunny Hancock Hammond, Mary Ann Hamrick, Lou Ann Hardigne, Elizabeth Harrington, Mary Emma Henderson, Harriet T. Hendricks, Martha Johnson, Ann Fitzpatrick

Klein, Helen Matthews Lewis, Ann Davis Lomax, Bee McCormack, Imogene McCue, Dr. Mary McEver, L. Leotus Morrison, Marion Peterman Page, Ana Pinkston Phillips, Jane Garrett Phillips, Frances Lane Poole, Frances Rackley, Jeanne Peterson Robinson, Peggy George Sammons, Carol Simpson, Bette Rhodes Smith, Jane Strozier Smith, Karen Owens Smith, Betty Spence, Marylee Kell Tillman, Elizabeth Williams Turner, Gladys Baldwin Wallace, Dorothy L. Warthen, Ophelia Page Wilkes, Aileen T. Williams, Jane Sparks Willingham, and Joan DeWitt Yoe.

Helping me to navigate the various manuscripts, archives, and records at the University of Iowa during my stay in Iowa City were Sidney F. Huttner, head of Special Collections; David McCartney, university archivist; Sarah Harris, registrar; and Margaret Lillard, Alumni Association records supervisor. At the Iowa Writers' Workshop, I was greatly helped by its human memory bank, Connie Brothers; Marilynne Robinson, acting director in 2005, connected me with Norma Hodges, who met with me and shared memories of being in the Workshop with O'Connor. Most helpful in giving me a sense of the Workshop at the time, in a volley of e-mails, was James B. Hall. Others kindly agreeing to communicate with me were Eugene Brown, Charles Embree, Bernie Halperin, Dr. James R. McConkey, W. D. Snodgrass, Mary Mudge Wiatt, Mel Wolfson, and Robert R. Yackshaw. Barbara Tunnicliff Hamilton not only recalled memories of O'Connor at Currier House, but sent along photographs of her housemate. Surprise sources were the writer-photographer John Gruen, and his wife, the painter Jane Wilson, who had also been friends of the subject of my last biography, Frank O'Hara.

I would have been happy under any circumstances for the chance to spend two weeks at Yaddo on a 2005 summer residency, but especially so as I worked during the time on researching O'Connor's own 1948–49 stay. I am thankful to the president of Yaddo, Elaina Richardson; and to the source of much archival information, Lesley M. Leduc, public affairs coordinator. For direction in finding my way through the Yaddo Records at the New York Public Library, I relied on the archivist Ben Alexander, who later sent me his dissertation, *Yaddo: A Creative History,* and Micki McGee, curator of the October 2008 Yaddo exhibition at the library. Sharing with me their memories of O'Connor at Yaddo were Frederick Morton and Jim Shannon, son of the late Jim and Nellie Shannon. Most incisive and illuminating about O'Connor at Yaddo and in Manhattan, as well about as her early writings and friendship with Robert Lowell, was the late Elizabeth Hardwick, whom I interviewed in her apartment in the fall of 2003. I wish to thank Saskia Hamilton, too, for advice in exploring Lowell's correspondence.

My extensive afternoon-long interview and several subsequent phone conversations with the late Robert Giroux were enormously helpful, not only for his memories of O'Connor's arrival in New York City in 1949, but for his perceptions about her writing and publishing throughout her lifetime. When in doubt, I found that I could turn to the transcript of his interview for wise and judicious opinions on many a topic. Janet August and Amy Atamian, the current owners of the Fitzgeralds' home at Seventy Acre Road, in Redding, Connecticut, showed great hospitality in allowing me to visit one Saturday afternoon in January 2007. They also introduced me to knowledgeable experts on the history of the area: Kay Abels, Ridgefield Historical Society; Brent Colley, Ridgefield online historian; Dan Cruson, Newton town historian; Lynn Hyson, reporter for the *Redding Pilot;* and Patty Miller Hancock, daughter of the previous resident, Virginia Miller.

For information pertaining to O'Connor's most productive years after her return south I am indebted to several research institutions and individuals. Research Librarian David Smith at the New York Public Library was indefatigable, locating numerous articles and books and answering nearly weekly pleas for help.

Other librarians, curators, and editors who contributed include Michael Carter, librarian at the Cloisters; Marvin J. Taylor, director, Fales Library and Special Collections, New York University; Stephen Crook, librarian, Berg Collection, New York Public Library; Sheri Young, archivist, National Book Foundation; David Bagnall, managing editor, Modern Language Association International Bibliography; Max Rudin, publisher, Library of America; Thomas P. Ford, reference assistant, Houghton Library, Harvard University; Margaret Sherry Rich, reference librarian and archivist, Rare Books and Special Collections, Princeton University Library; and Lynn Conway, Georgetown University archivist. I traveled to Lourdes, where I was helped by Agnès Baranger, Service Communication, Sanctuaires Notre-Dame de Lourdes; and to West Virginia University in Morgantown, West Virginia, where I was guided through the papers of Maryat Lee in the West Virginia Historical Manuscript and Archives Collection by Lori Hostuttler.

Among the most significant in bringing O'Connor to life, and providing memories and insights in interviews by phone and e-mail, as well as sharing unpublished correspondence, was Erik Langkjaer, now living with his wife, Mette, in Copenhagen. The word "gentleman" always springs to mind when I think of Erik. Others of O'Connor's close friends, who helped color in the picture for me were certainly Louise Abbot, whom I met in her home in Louisville, Georgia; Ashley Brown; and Dr. Ted Spivey. Valuable personal insights were also provided in interviews by Robert Coles, Alfred Corn, Christopher Dickey, Richard Giannone, Leonard Mayhew, and Gabrielle Rolin. For his patient clarification of the medical complications of lupus, I am indebted to Michael D. Lockshin, MD, professor at the Joan and Sanford Weill College of Medicine of Cornell University. I appreciate Martha Asbury, Fran Belin, William French, and Donald Richie for sharing their memories of Maryat Lee. For his unpublished correspondence with Betty Hester, I thank Greg Johnson; and for their memories of

Hester, Janet Rechtman and Judy McConnell. Other important assistance of many different kinds was given by Jean-Francois Anton, Neil Baldwin, Susan Balée, John Berendt, A. Scott Berg, Mark Bosco, S.J., Jean Cash, Michael Cunningham, Lisa E. Davis, PhD, Paul Elie, Bruce Fulton, Michael Gehl, Dr. Edwin Gleaves, Roger Harris, Edward Hirsch, Frances Kiernan, Gary Logue, Jon Jewett, Josh Milstein, Honor Moore, Jean Nathan, Georgia Newman, Christopher O'Hare, Padgett Powell, Patrick Samway, S.J., Michael Selleck, Ken Silverman, Gore Vidal, and Edmund White.

I could not have completed this project within six years without the support of a 2004 John Simon Guggenheim Memorial Foundation Fellowship in Biography; a 2007 National Endowment for the Humanities Fellowship, designated a "We the People Project," for "promoting knowledge and understanding of American history and culture"; and a 2006 Furthermore Grant in Publishing, a program of the J. M. Kaplan Fund. I had the boon during the spring semester of 2006 of the assistance of Michael McAllister, a Columbia University School of the Arts Hertog Fellow, through the excellent program administered by Patricia O'Toole. I received steady support as well from the William Paterson University of New Jersey, where I am a professor of English, and where I was generously granted an academic leave for my 2004–2005 Guggenheim year and a sabbatical leave for the 2006–2007 academic year, as well as release time for research throughout the duration of the project. I especially wish to thank the librarians of the Cheng Library for their assistance in securing scores of articles and dissertations through interlibrary loan, and my department chair, Linda Hamalian, and colleague and Gertrude Stein scholar Edward Burns. A former student, Michael Ptaszek, contributed in countless ways while working during all of these years as my personal assistant. For advice and comments on a presentation of my work in progress, I thank fellow members of the Biography Seminar at New York University, funded by the Whiting Foundation.

I especially wish to thank my tireless agent, Joy Harris, for finding just the right home for this project. And my editor at Little, Brown, Pat Strachan, rightly legendary for her hands-on engagement, adroit use of the editor's pen, and subtle guidance in a cool and reassuring tone; my own infatuation with O'Connor was more than matched by hers, as I often found her rereading stories for a second or third time to test out observations. This book could not exist in its present form without the help of my perceptive friend Barbara Heizer, who closely read each word, chapter by chapter, as I was writing, and gave sharp advice at every turn. The wise and urbane Joel Conarroe graduated from friend to literary saint in my estimation for his labor-intensive reading and comments on a first draft and galley pages. When I finally printed out the manuscript, my partner, Paul Raushenbush, the ultimate "good guy," asked brightly, after years of daily discussions, "What will we talk about now?" I'm confident that we'll find plenty of other topics to discuss, Paul, though nothing quite of the tenor of Flannery O'Connor.

Reprinted by permission of Farrar, Straus and Giroux, LLC: Excerpts from *The Complete Stories* by Flannery O'Connor. Copyright © 1971 by the Estate of Mary Flannery O'Connor. Excerpts from *The Habit of Being: Letters of Flannery O'Connor,* edited by Sally Fitzgerald. Copyright © 1979 by Regina O'Connor. Excerpts from "Introduction" by Flannery O'Connor from *A Memoir of Mary Ann* by the Dominican Nuns of Our Lady of Perpetual Help Home. "Introduction" copyright © 1961 by Flannery O'Connor. Copyright renewed 1989 by Regina O'Connor. Excerpts from *Mystery and Manners* by Flannery O'Connor, edited by Sally and Robert Fitzgerald. Reprinted by permission of Houghton Mifflin Harcourt Publishing Company: Excerpt from "A Circle in the Fire" in *A Good Man Is Hard to Find and Other Stories,* copyright 1948 by Flannery O'Connor and renewed 1976 by Mrs. Edward F. O'Connor. Excerpts from "A Late Encounter with the Enemy" and "The Life You Save May Be Your Own" in *A Good Man Is Hard to Find and Other Stories,* copyright 1953 by Flannery O'Connor and renewed 1981 by Regina O'Connor. Excerpts from "The Displaced Person" and "A Temple of the Holy Ghost" in *A Good Man Is Hard to Find and Other Stories,* copyright 1954 by Flannery O'Connor and renewed 1982 by Regina O'Connor. Excerpts from "The Artificial Nigger" and "Good Country People" in *A Good Man Is Hard to Find and Other Stories,* copyright © 1955 by Flannery O'Connor and renewed 1983 by Regina O'Connor.

Notes

✿

ABBREVIATIONS

PUBLISHED PRIMARY WORKS

CC   *Correspondence of Flannery O'Connor and the Brainard Cheneys*. Edited by C. Ralph Stephens. Jackson and London: University Press of Mississippi, 1986.

Con *Conversations with Flannery O'Connor*. Edited by Rosemary M. Magee. Jackson and London: University Press of Mississippi, 1986.

CW   *O'Connor: Collected Works*. Edited by Sally Fitzgerald. New York: Library of America, 1988.

HB   *The Habit of Being: Letters of Flannery O'Connor*. Edited by Sally Fitzgerald. New York: Farrar, Straus and Giroux, 1979.

MM   *Mystery and Manners: Occasional Prose*. Edited by Sally and Robert Fitzgerald. New York: Farrar, Straus and Giroux, 1969.

PG   *The Presence of Grace and Other Book Reviews*. Compiled by Leo J. Zuber and edited by Carter W. Martin. Athens: University of Georgia Press, 1983.

COLLECTIONS

Emory Flannery O'Connor Collection, Robert W. Woodruff Library, Emory University, Atlanta.

FSG   "Farrar, Straus & Giroux Inc. Records," New York Public Library, Astor, Lenox and Tilden Foundations.

GCSU   Flannery O'Connor Collection, Ina Dillard Russell Library, Georgia College and State University, Milledgeville.

Prince- Department of Rare Books and Special Collections, Firestone Library, Prince
ton   ton University.

UI   Records of the Iowa Writers' Workshop, Special Collections, University of Iowa.

UNC   "Dorrance Papers," Southern Historical Collection, University of North Carolina Library, Chapel Hill.

Yaddo   "Yaddo Records." Manuscripts and Archives Division, New York Public Library, Astor, Lenox and Tilden Foundations.

EPIGRAPH

ix "As for biographies": FOC to Betty Hester, July 5, 1958, *HB,* 290–91.

PROLOGUE: WALKING BACKWARD

3 "marked me for life": FOC, "The King of the Birds," *CW,* 832. Hilton Als retells the story as an example of "the first approval of her obsession with the grotesque" in "This Lonesome Place," *The New Yorker* (January 29, 2001): 83

3 "the New Yorker": "Notes," *CW,* 1270.

3 "Miss Katie": Loretta Feuger Hoynes, "We Remember Mary Flannery" panel, O'Connor Childhood Home, Savannah, Ga., November 2, 1990.

3–4 "Her fame had spread": *CW,* 832. A slew of such new items, edging on tall tales, dotted the newspapers of the day, including the *New York Times,* which ran a piece titled "Advent of Spring in Georgia, Weird Nature Tales," dateline "Savannah," about a chicken born to a farmer in Lee County, Georgia, with four legs that could "walk forward or backward": *New York Times* (May 30, 1930): E2.

4 "frizzled": Sally Fitzgerald, "Chronology," *CW,* 1238.

4 "the Pathé man": *CW,* 832.

4 "Odd fowl walks": "Unique Chicken Goes in Reverse," Pathe News Reel Series, 1931, GCSU.

5 "celebrity": FOC to Betty Hester, December 15, 1955, *HB,* 126.

5 "From that day": *CW,* 832.

6 "Now there are": Robert Lowell to Elizabeth Bishop, October 1, 1948, *The Letters of Robert Lowell,* edited by Saskia Hamilton (New York: Farrar, Straus and Giroux, 2005), 111.

7 "My quest": *CW,* 832.

8 "dance forward": Ibid., 835.

8 "dignified ferocity": "Notes," *CW,* 1270.

CHAPTER ONE: SAVANNAH

13 "element of ham": FOC to Maryat Lee, Ground Hog Day, 1958, *HB,* 265.

13 "The things we see, hear, smell": FOC, "The Catholic Novelist in the Protestant South," *CW,* 855.

14 "unsettled": *Savannah Morning News* (March 25, 1925): 1.

14 "Sinner Must Be Reborn": Ibid., 11.

15 "I never was one": FOC to Betty Hester, December 20, 1958, *HB,* 309.

16 "I was brought up": FOC to Janet McKane, July 25, 1963, *HB,* 531.

16 "inmates": Hugh R. Brown, "Flannery O'Connor, The Savannah Years," unpublished essay, 6, private collection.

17 "We had a black cook": Patricia Persse, in discussion with the author, September 15, 2004.

17 "I remember the square": Dan O'Leary, in discussion with the author, September 15, 2004.

18 "It was so Catholic": Brown, "Savannah Years," 5.

19 "My first memories": Katherine Groves, "We Remember Mary Flannery" panel, O'Connor Childhood Home, Savannah, Ga., February 4, 1990.

21 "I don't think mine": FOC to Betty Hester, February 25, 1956, *HB,* 141.

21 "Mass was first said": FOC to Janet McKane, May 17, 1963, *HB,* 520.

22 "a grand pyrotechnic display": "Looking Back: 1890," *Union-Recorder.*

22 "for the northern markets": "Thirty Years Ago in Baldwin," *Union-Recorder,* March 16, 1923.

22 "Little girl, what you got": Alice Carr, in discussion with the author, September 25, 2004.

22 "I don't know anybody": FOC to Father James H. McCown, April 3, 1956, *HB,* 142.

23 "interesting, quiet": undated newspaper clipping, private collection.

23 "put on his white": Sally Fitzgerald, "The Invisible Father," *Christianity and Literature* 47, no. 1 (Autumn 1997): 15.

23 "a robust, amused": Robert Fitzgerald, "Introduction," *Everything That Rises Must Converge* by Flannery O'Connor (New York: Farrar Straus and Giroux, 1965), x.

24 "The wedding will take place": *Savannah Morning News,* October 8, 1922; following the marriage in Milledgeville, a Savannah wedding reception was held at the home of William Jay Harty on Gwinnett Street.

25 "There seems little doubt": Sally Fitzgerald, "Invisible Father," 16.

26 "'umbled": Christopher O'Hare interview with Margaret Florencourt Mann. These interviews were conducted and transcribed by O'Hare for a Flannery O'Connor documentary that has yet to be released.

26 "beautifully cared for": Barbara McKenzie, *Flannery O'Connor's Georgia* (Athens: University of Georgia Press, 1980), xvi.

27 "Roll of the Female Orphanage Society": Brown, "Savannah Years," 24.

27 "King of Siam": Sally Fitzgerald, "Flannery O'Connor: Patterns of Friendship, Patterns of Love," *Georgia Review* 52, no. 3 (Fall 1998): 409.

27 "Hold your head up": Kathleen Feeley, S.S.N.D, "'Mine Is a Comic Art . . .' Flannery O'Connor," *Realist of Distances: Flannery O'Connor Revisited,* edited by Karl-Heinz Westarp and Jan Nordby Gretlund (Aarhus, Denmark: Aarhus University Press, 1987; New Brunswick, N.J.: 1972), 67.

27 "Ed would not have put": Sally Fitzgerald, "Invisible Father," 10.

28 "R.C.O'C.": Ibid., 9.

28 "All the mothers walked the little girls to school": Brown, "Savannah Years," 20.

29 *"every day":* Sally Fitzgerald, "Invisible Father," 16.

29 "novena-rosary tradition": FOC to John Lynch, February 19, 1956, *HB,* 139.

29 "big girls": Brown, "Savannah Years," 9–13.

30 "I delivered": Dan O'Leary, in discussion with the author, September 15, 2004.

30 "a pidgeon-toed": FOC, "Biography," GCSU.

31 "Tarso-Supernator-Proper Built": FOC, untitled story, GCSU.

31 "some sort of corrective": Patricia Persse, in discussion with the author, September 15, 2004.

31 "If I took off": "We Remember Mary Flannery" panel, November 2, 1990.

32 "I suppose my father": FOC to Betty Hester, July 28, 1956, *HB,* 167–68.

32 a pencil and blue crayon: Kelly Suzanne Gerald, "Flannery O'Connor: Toward a Visual Hermeneutics" (PhD dissertation, Auburn University, 2001), 7–8.

33 "She'd stand there": Brown, "Savannah Years," 16.

34 "When we were": "We Remember Mary Flannery" panel, February 11, 1990.

34 "backyard quail farm": "Quail Farm on Peachtree," *Atlanta Constitution*, Sunday edition, June 4, 1939.

34 "Nothing remarkable": Brown, "Savannah Years," 15.

34 "full of wire": Unidentified fragment, GCSU.

34 "pulled the rubber bands": Lillian Dowling Odom, "Flannery O'Connor Childhood Friend: Lost and Found," unpublished manuscript, 3, private collection.

35 "a very innocent speller": FOC to Ben Griffith, March 3, 1954, *CW,* 923.

35 "Mother, I made": Odom, "Childhood Friend," 19.

35 "smash an atom": FOC, *Wise Blood,* working draft, GCSU.

36 "A lot of them": FOC to Dr. T. R. Spivey, August 19, 1959, *CW,* 1104.

36 "taught by the sisters": FOC to Father James H. McCown, January 12, 1958, *CW,* 1061.

36 "hot house innocence": Brown, "Savannah Years," 11.

36 "a long standing avoider": FOC to Elizabeth Bishop, June 1, 1958, *CW,* 1073.

36 "From 8 to 12": FOC to Betty Hester, January 17, 1956, *CW,* 983.

36 "as natural to me": FOC to William Sessions, July 8, 1956, *HB,* 164.

37 "a very peculiar child": Patricia Persse, "We Remember Mary Flannery" panel, February 3, 1990.

37 turned a child away: Sister Jude Walsh, "Armstrong State College Panel on O'Connor," Savannah, Ga., May 1989: "Marguerite [Pinckney Knowland] told me that one day one of her playmates came with her and she came to the house with Marguerite but she was dispatched home by Mrs. O'Connor and made clear to Marguerite that she did not want her to bring any other children with her when she came to play."

37 *"Let's Pretend":* Information on the program was taken from: Arthur Anderson, *Let's Pretend and the Golden Age of Radio* (Boatsburg, Pa.: BearManor Media, 2004).

38 "How do we get": Cynthia Zarin, "Not Nice," *The New Yorker* (April 17, 2006): 38.

38 "Mrs. O'Connor was": Newell Turner Parr, "We Remember Mary Flannery" panel, February 10, 1990.

39 "She had pages and pages": Ibid.

39 "But then Marguerite": Sister Jude Walsh, in discussion with the author, June 5, 2006.

39 "No one was spared": Thea Jarvis, "Flannery — Georgia's Own," *Atlanta Journal and Constitution,* May 8, 1980. According to Kathleen Feeley, the short satiric descriptions of uncles and cousins were typed; another booklet of words and pictures was titled "Ladies and Gents, Meet the Three Mister Noseys." Under the appropriate faces were the captions "Mr. Long Nose; Mr. Sharp Nose; Mr. Snut Nose": Kathleen Feeley, S.S.N.D., " 'Mine Is a Comic Art . . . ,' " 67.

39 "I wrote a book": FOC to Maryat Lee, March 9, 1960, GCSU.

40 "We heard stories": Brown, "Savannah Years," 18.

40 "We were a rough": Ibid.

40 "the strictness of a certain nun": Jean Cash, *Flannery O'Connor: A Life* (Knoxville: University of Tennessee Press, 2002), 16.

41 "It reminded me": Sister Jude Walsh, in discussion with the author, June 5, 2006.

41 "They were strict": Patricia Persse, in discussion with the author, September 15, 2004.

41 "prissy": Sister Jude Walsh, "We Remember Mary Flannery" panel, February 11, 1990.

41 "genteel Victorian ladies": FOC to Cudden Ward Dorrance, March 29, 1964, UNC.

42 "Mary Flannery was at dancing": Odom, "Childhood Friend," 18.

43 "He was so tall": Kitty Smith, quoted in Alice Alexander, "The Memory of Milledgeville's Flannery O'Connor Is Still Green," *Atlanta Journal,* March 28, 1979.

43 "swept into office": "E. F. O'Connor, Jr. Commands Legion," *Savannah Morning News,* June 28, 1936.

43 "aloof": Cash, *Flannery O'Connor,* 9.

43 "I am never likely to romanticize": FOC to Betty Hester, July 28, 1956, *HB,* 168.

43 "More likely": Sally Fitzgerald, "Invisible Father," 11.

43 "He was quite an orator": Angela Ryan Dowling, in discussion with the author, October 12, 2004.

44 "Head of Legion": *Savannah Morning News,* November 11, 1936.

44 "in tones not usually": FOC to Betty Hester, July 1956, *HB,* 166.

44 "Last year I read": Ibid.

44 "My father wanted": Ibid., July 28, 1956, *HB,* 168.

44 "I suppose": Ibid., August 11, 1956, *HB,* 169.

45 "at that time": FOC to Elizabeth Hardwick and Robert Lowell, March 17, 1953, *CW,* 909.

45 "Oh I don't know": Sally Fitzgerald, "Invisible Father," 11.

45 "Tried to get in touch": Edward O'Connor to Erwin Sibley, December 23, 1937, GCSU.

46 "When I was twelve": FOC to Betty Hester, February 11, 1956, *CW,* 985.

46 "She never knew": Newell Turner Parr, "We Remember Mary Flannery" panel, February 11, 1990.

47 "MF": FOC, untitled story, GCSU.

47 "I know some folks": FOC, memorabilia, GCSU.

47 "First rate": Sally Fitzgerald, "Chronology," *CW,* 1238.

48 "read those books": MFOC to Helen Soul, undated letter, Emory.

48 "Awful": Sally Fitzgerald, "Chronology," *CW,* 1238.

48 "Peculiar but I never could": FOC to Betty Hester, June 14, 1958, *HB,* 288.

48 "wasn't a literary": Ibid., June 28, 1956, *HB,* 164.

48 "was stiff already": FOC, untitled fragment, GCSU.

49 "Can't tell you": Edward O'Connor to Erwin Sibley, January 4, 1938, GCSU.

49 "Cousin Katie": FOC to Sally and Robert Fitzgerald, February 15, 1959, *HB,* 318.

49 "My papa": FOC to Elizabeth Fenwick Way, August 4, 1957, *HB,* 233.

50 "I think you probably": FOC to Maryat Lee, February 24, 1957, *CW,* 1023.

CHAPTER TWO: MILLEDGEVILLE: "A BIRD SANCTUARY"

51 "the glad news": Nelle Womack Hines, ed., *A Treasure Album of Milledgeville and Baldwin County, Georgia* (Macon, Ga.: Press of J. W. Burke, 1949), 48.

52 "It was *well*": FOC to George Haslam, March 2, 1957, *CW,* 1023.

52 "Why don't you": FOC to Maryat Lee, May 20, 1960, *HB,* 396.

52 "Mrs. E. F. O'Connor": "Social and Society," *Union-Recorder,* July 1926.

52 "Mr. and Mrs. Ed O'Connor": "Social Highlights," *Union-Recorder,* November 11, 1937.

52 "a styling epicenter": Padgett Powell, "Andalusia Is Open," *Oxford American,* (July/August 2003): 30.

52 "We have a girls' college": FOC to Ben Griffith, February 13, 1954, *CW,* 919.

53 "A thing like this": Carson McCullers, *Clock Without Hands* (Boston and New York: Houghton Mifflin, 1961), 217.

53 "probably has the distinction": Hines, *Treasure Album,* 8.

53 "a town of columns": Cynthia Parks, "Flannery O'Connor," *Florida Times-Union and Journal,* September 2, 1984.

53 "Milledgeville Federal": Robert J. Wilson III, "A Brief Sketch of Milledgeville," unpublished essay, private collection.

53 "idealistic": Ted R. Spivey, *Flannery O'Connor: The Woman, the Thinker, the Visionary* (Macon, Ga.: Mercer University Press, 1955), 77.

53 "If war comes": "Milledgeville: 150th Birthday," *Union-Recorder,* April 1953.

54 "in public the rights": E. A. Houston, "Tribute to Mr. Peter J. Cline," *Union-Recorder,* March 7, 1916

54 "trouped through": FOC, working draft, GCSU.

54 "an austere nun": Betty Boyd Love, "Recollections of Flannery O'Connor," *Flannery O'Connor Bulletin* 14 (1985): 65.

54 "Sister was the first": Regina O'Connor marginal writing, Betty Boyd Love, "Recollection of Flannery O'Connor" manuscript, GCSU.

55 "Sister would always": Dr. Peter Cline, in discussion with the author, June 11, 2006.

55 "a strong resemblance": Love, "Recollections," 65.

56 "Infants, girls": Josephine Hendin, *The World of Flannery O'Connor* (Bloomington: Indiana University Press, 1972), 6.

56 "We'd have these big": Jack Tarleton, in discussion with the author, June 10, 2006.

56 "a speaking likeness": Christopher O'Hare interview with Sally Fitzgerald.

56 "alcoholic": Dr. Peter Cline, in discussion with the author, June 11, 2006.

57 "Mary Flannery needs to work": "Report of Mary Flannery O'Connor. Peabody Elementary School. 1937–1938," GCSU.

58 "Her mother handpicked": Jack Tarleton, in discussion with the author, June 10, 2006.

58 "gold-rimmed": unidentified fragment, GCSU.

58 "I remember sitting": Christopher O'Hare interview with Frances Florencourt.

58 "Oh, I've found Amelia Earhart": Jean Cash, *Flannery O'Connor: A Life* (Knoxville: University of Tennessee Press, 2002), 45.

58 "She would bring": Regina Sullivan, "Armstrong State College Panel on O'Connor," Armstrong College, Savannah, Ga., May 1989.

59 "I could sew": FOC, "The King of the Birds," *CW,* 832.

59 "They played better": Charlotte Conn Ferris, in discussion with the author, November 4, 2003.

59 "I was always interested": Elizabeth Shreve Ryan, in discussion with the author, February 10, 2004.

59 "I think the times": Cash, *Flannery O'Connor,* 47–48.

59 "We had a running": Dr. Peter Cline, in discussion with the author, June 11, 2006.

60 "the invisible man": Robert J. Wilson III, in discussion with the author, January 5, 2004.

60 "I remember sitting": Frances Florencourt, in discussion with the author, December 10, 2004.

60 "To this day": Jack Tarleton, in discussion with the author, June 10, 2006.

60 "wild horses": Cash, *Flannery O'Connor,* 48.

61 "Mary Flannery spent": Ibid.

61 "obligatory": Ibid.

61 "garden suburb": The description of Peachtree Heights is taken mostly from Bill Bell, *A History of Peachtree Heights East to 1950* (Atlanta: Gateway Publishing, 2000).

62 "Miss Mary": FOC to Cudden Ward Dorrance, April 9, 1964, UNC.

62 "My mother and I": Jack Tarleton, in discussion with the author, June 10, 2006.

63 "Mary Flannery and I": Dr. Peter Cline, in discussion with the author, June 11, 2006.

63 "She once described": Caroline Gordon, "Heresy in Dixie," *Sewanee Review* 76, no. 2 (Spring 1968): 263.

64 "Our uncle Bernard": Dr. Peter Cline, in discussion with the author, June 11, 2006.

64 "He's never mentioned": FOC to Betty Hester, May 17, 1964, *HB,* 578.

64 "Being an ex–Bell House": "Cupid Raids the Bell House," *Atlanta Journal Magazine* (February 3, 1929): 3.

64 "Bell House was musty": Jack Tarleton, in discussion with the author, June 10, 2006.

65 "Dr. Cline Hosts": undated clipping from *Atlanta Journal,* private collection.

65 "My idea about Atlanta": FOC to Dr. T. R. Spivey, March 12, 1964, *CW,* 1203.

65 "Regina and my mother": Dr. Peter Cline, in discussion with the author, June 11, 2006.

66 "I come from": FOC to Betty Hester, June 28, 1956, *CW,* 997–98.

66 "a cross between": Preston Russell and Barbara Hines, *Savannah: A History of Her People since 1733* (Savannah: Frederic C. Beil, 1992), 158.

66 "destitute": Susan Kessler Barnard, *Buckhead: A Place for All Time* (Athens, Ga.: Hill Street Press, 1996), 145.

66 "absurdist vision": Spivey, *Flannery O'Connor,* 114.

66 "We met her": FOC to Cecil Dawkins, November 8, 1960, *CW,* 1135.

68 "I sure am sick": FOC to Louise Abbot, January 13, 1961, *HB,* 426.

69 "which Flannery sputtered": De Vene Harrold, unpublished manuscript, GCSU.

69 "coming slow": FOC, untitled fragment, GCSU.

70 "following a two-week": *Atlanta Journal,* February 3, 1941.

70 "In recent months": *Union-Recorder,* February 6, 1941.

71 "I went to the funeral": Elizabeth Shreve Ryan, in discussion with the author, February 10, 2004.

71 "I think she did have": Christopher O'Hare interview with Louise Abbot.

71 "I've never spent much time": FOC to Betty Hester, February 11, 1956, *HB,* 136.

72 "The reality of death": Sally Fitzgerald, "Rooms with a View," *Flannery O'Connor Bulletin* 10 (1981): 17.

72 "I don't know how": Kelly Suzanne Gerald, "Flannery O'Connor: Toward a Visual Hermeneutics" (PhD dissertation, Auburn University, 2001), 11.

72 *One Result:* MFOC, cartoon, *Peabody Palladium,* October 28, 1940.

73 "single-frame satires": Gerald, "Visual Hermeneutics," 11.

73 "a female Ogden Nash": Nelle Womack Hines, "Flannery O'Connor Shows Talent as Cartoonist," *Union-Recorder,* June 17, 1943.

73 "His mind began to wander": FOC, "The First Book," GCSU.

73 "Fish oil": FOC, "Recollections on My Future Childhood," GCSU.

74 "the illustrations about a young": FOC to Brainard and Frances Neel Cheney, March 13, 1957, *CC,* 53.

74 "the rest of what I read": FOC to Betty Hester, August 28, 1955, *HB,* 98.

75 "We didn't have a lot": Elizabeth Hardwick, in discussion with the author, May 24, 2004.

75 "never opened it": FOC, "Recollections," GCSU.

75 "She wrote these books": Deedie Sibley, in discussion with the author, May 24, 2004.

75 "M.F. has finished": Gertrude Treanor to Agnes Florencourt, March 16, 1941, private collection.

76 "Herman's HENRIETTA": FOC, "Mistaken Identity," GCSU.

76 "Peabodite Reveals Strange Hobby": *Peabody Palladium* 5, no. 3 (December 16, 1941): 2.

76 "The Good": Alice Alexander, "The Memory of Milledgeville's Flannery O'Connor Is Still Green," *Atlanta Journal,* March 28, 1979.

76 "We were always told": Elizabeth Shreve Ryan, in discussion with the author, February 10, 2004.

76 "The teacher did run": Cash, *Flannery O'Connor,* 37.

76 "I went to a progressive": FOC to Betty Hester, August 28, 1955, *CW,* 950.

77 "Mr. English": FOC, fragment of an early version of *Wise Blood,* GCSU.

77 "hello": Georgia A. Newman, "A 'Contrary Kinship': The Correspondence of Flannery O'Connor and Maryat Lee — Early Years, 1957–1959" (PhD dissertation, University of South Florida), 7.

77 "I can see her plodding": Charlotte Conn Ferris, in discussion with the author, November 4, 2003.

77 "I am the only one": "Peabodite," *Peabody Palladium* (December 16, 1941): 2.

77 "the way the halls": Gerald E. Sherry, "An Interview with Flannery O'Connor," *Critic* 21 (June–July 1963): 29–31.

77 "Now next Wednesday": Barbara Beiswanger, "Flannery O'Connor," unpublished memoir, GCSU.

78 "The topical is poison": FOC to Betty Hester, September 1, 1963, *HB,* 537.

78 "Here, Adolph!" "Peabodite," *Peabody Palladium* (December 16, 1941): 2.

78 "From 15 to 18": FOC to Dr. T. R. Spivey, August 19, 1959, *CW,* 1103.

78 "Senior, Senior": MFOC, cartoon, *Peabody Palladium* (March 2, 1941): 2.

78 "In Hopes That a Jimmie": MFOC, cartoon, *Peabody Palladium* (December 14, 1941): 2.

79 "She just thought": Elizabeth Shreve Ryan, in discussion with the author, February 10, 2004.

79 "How she looked": William Ivey Hair, with James C. Bonner, Edward B. Dawson, and Robert J. Wilson III, *A Centennial History of Georgia College* (Milledgeville: Georgia College, 1979), 211.

79 "Being in a creative": Elizabeth Shreve Ryan, in discussion with the author, February 10, 2004.

80 "My dad-gum foot's": Cash, *Flannery O'Connor,* 47.

80 "integrate English": FOC, "The Teaching of Literature," *MM,* 127.

80 "At that time they said": Dr. Floride Gardner, in discussion with the author, June 16, 2006.

80 "terribly disappointed": Cash, *Flannery O'Connor,* 36.

80 "At Long Last": MFOC, cartoon, *Peabody Palladium* (May 23, 1941): 2.

80 "When our schooldays": Alexander, "Memory," *Atlanta Journal,* March 28, 1979.

81 "our mothers": Mary Virginia Harrison, "Mary Virginia Harrison Collection," GCSU.

81 party at the Cline Mansion: The description of the graduation party is taken mostly from the *Union-Recorder,* May 28, 1942.

81 "I recollect Mrs. O'Connor": Elizabeth Shreve Ryan, in discussion with the author, February 10, 2004.

CHAPTER THREE: "MFOC"

82 "Lucy Gains College": FOC, Folder 199-e, GCSU.

82 "the most progressive": FOC, Folder 15b, GCSU.

82 "I enjoyed college": FOC to Janet McKane, July 9, 1963, *HB,* 530.

83 "I first met Flannery": Betty Boyd Love, draft of "Recollections of Flannery O'Connor," GCSU.

83 "twining over": Betty Boyd, "Reflection," *Corinthian* (Fall 1942): 12.

83 "Some new, unheard-of ": M. F. O'Connor, "Pffft," *Corinthian* (Fall 1944): 16.

83 "pretty terrible poems": Love, "Recollections" draft, GCSU.

84 "have not written anything": FOC to Betty Boyd, November 5, 1949, *HB,* 19.

84 "horribly serious": Love, "Recollections" draft, GCSU.

84 "Betty Boyd was": Jane Sparks Willingham, in discussion with the author, November 29, 2004.

84 "the two people": Betty Boyd, "My First Impression of GSCW," *Corinthian* (Fall 1942): 8.

84 "a great many hours": Love, "Recollections" draft, GSCU.

84 "I soon became": Betty Boyd Love, "Recollections of Flannery O'Connor," *Flannery O'Connor Bulletin* 14 (1985): 65.

85 "Miss Mary was a businessman": Jean Cash, *Flannery O'Connor: A Life* (Knoxville: University of Tennessee Press, 2002) 28.

85 "Miss Mary . . . inherited": Helen I. Greene, "Mary Flannery O'Connor: One Teacher's Happy Memory," *Flannery O'Connor Bulletin* 19 (1990): 45.

85 "She and Dr. Boeson": Lou Ann Hardigne, in discussion with the author, November 1, 2004.

86 "When I sit down": FOC, "The Grotesque in Southern Fiction," GCSU, 9.

86 "poetic and romantic": "Miss Katherine Scott Reads Paper to D.A.R.," *Union-Recorder,* October 21, 1943.

86 "They would not have been": Mary Barbara Tate, in discussion with the author, March 6, 2004.

86 "They would start talking": Cash, *Flannery O'Connor,* 57.

87 "Even then, it was obvious": William Schemmel, "Southern Comfort," *Travel-Holiday* (June 1988): 72.

87 "I found my ideal": Boyd, "My First Impression."

87 "Girls were crying": Louise Simmons Allen, in discussion with the author, November 2, 2004.

88 "Sugar was scarce": Virginia Wood Alexander, e-mail to the author, October 23, 2005.

88 "This war is making us think": *Colonnade,* April 11, 1942.

88 "calling attention to the prejudice": *Colonnade,* April 18, 1932.

88 "foreign ideas": William Ivy Hair, with James Bonner, Edward B. Dawson, and Robert J. Wilson III, *A Centennial History of Georgia College* (Milledgeville: Georgia College, 1979), 201.

89 "Palace Beauty Salon": MFOC, "Two Fragments," GCSU.

89 "I grew up in Madison": Gladys Baldwin Wallace, letter to the author, October 22, 2004.

89 "People find it odd": Helen Matthews Lewis, in discussion with the author, January 29, 2004.

89 "older spinster-suffragette": Helen Matthews Lewis, "GSCW in the 1940s: Mary Flannery Was There Too," *Flannery O'Connor Review* 3 (2005): 50.

90 "Ours are girls": Ibid., 51.

90 "Most of the time": Zell Barnes Grant, letter to the author, October 25, 2004.

90 "They were so close": Jane Sparks Willingham, in discussion with the author, November 29, 2004.

91 "She was very fond": Cash, *Flannery O'Connor,* 55.

91 "Now let me see": FOC, unpublished portion of letter to Betty Boyd, November 5, 1949, GCSU.

91 "This should reassure": Ibid., November 17, 1949.

91 "shortly, probably asking": FOC to Betty Boyd Love, April 24, 1951, *HB,* 24.

91 "We kept trying": Helen Matthews Lewis, in discussion with the author, January 29, 2004.

91–92 "country bumpkin": Ibid.

92 "she did write": FOC to Betty Hester, November 25, 1955, *CW,* 972.

92 "kept ducks": Love, "Recollections" draft, GCSU.

92 "Flannery did not want": Harriet Thorp Hendricks, letter to the author, November 1, 2004.

93 "Connie Howell": *Colonnade,* November 9, 1943.

93 "I will not": Alice Alexander, "The Memory of Milledgeville's Flannery O'Connor Is Still Green," *Atlanta Journal,* March 28, 1979.

93 "Dr. Wynn was a gentleman": Cash, *Flannery O'Connor,* 58.

93 "He was a laughingstock": Mary Barbara Tate, in discussion with the author, March 6, 2004.

93 "A few days later": MFOC, "Going to the Dogs," *Corinthian* (Fall 1942): 14.

94 "Unusual Occupations": Kelly Suzanne Gerald, "Flannery O'Connor: Toward a Visual Hermeneutics" (PhD dissertation, Auburn University), footnote 14: 32.

94 "It may look like": Betty Boyd Love, "Recollections," *Flannery O'Connor Bulletin,* 66.

94 "The Immediate Results": MFOC, cartoon, *Colonnade* (October 9, 1942): 4.

95 "I thought of her then": Gertrude Ehrlich, e-mail to the author, October 6, 2004.

95 "Aw, nuts!": MFOC, cartoon, *Colonnade* (October 24, 1942): 4.

95 "It seemed to rain": Virginia Wood Alexander, e-mail to the author, October 23, 2005.

95 "I remember her being": Frances Lane Poole, letter to the author, October 17, 2004.

96 "Doggone": MFOC, cartoon, *Colonnade* (November 14, 1942): 4.

96 "fast making a name": Nelle Womack Hines, "Mary O'Connor Shows Talent as Cartoonist," *Macon Telegraph and News,* June 13, 1943.

97 Waves: The description of the Waves at GSCW is taken largely from Hair et al., *Centennial History,* 215–18.

97 "They'd get out every morning": Jane Sparks Willingham, in discussion with the author, November 29, 2004.

97 "We had very little contact": Hair et al., *Centennial History,* 216.

98 "They were always in the way": Helen Matthews Lewis, in discussion with the author, January 29, 2004.

98 "Officer or no officer": *Colonnade* (January 23, 1943): 4.

98 "When convoys passed": Charmet Garrett, letter to the author, November 10, 2004.

99 "two of the soldiers": Gertrude Treanor, letter to Agnes Florencourt, May 11, 1941, private collection.

99 "Miss Katie used to sit": Love, "Recollections" draft, GCSU.

99 "I can still remember": Johnny Marko, letter to Katherine Cline, undated, "Special Collections," GCSU.

99 "About this time of day": Jim Bird, letter to Katherine Cline, undated, "Special Collections," GCSU.

100 "a handsome Marine": Sally Fitzgerald, "Flannery O'Connor: Patterns of Friendship, Patterns of Love," *Georgia Review* 52, no. 3 (Fall 1998): 409.

100 "tin leg": FOC to Betty Hester, March 10, 1956, *HB,* 145.

100 "Oh, well": MFOC, cartoon, *Colonnade* (April 3, 1943): 2.

100 "a close comradeship": Sally Fitzgerald, "Patterns," 410.

101 priesthood: Sally Fitzgerald writes that "he asked her to continue to write to him, which she did until she apparently decided that it was inappropriate to continue, and they drifted out of contact." Sullivan eventually left the seminary to pursue a career in business and later married. "Patterns," 411.

102 "womanpower in this war": "D.A.R. Endorses Aid for Liberty," *Union-Recorder,* March 18, 1943.

102 "Miss Hallie required": Marion Peterman Page, letter to the author, October 17, 2004.

102 "a twang": Karen Owens Smith, letter to the author, November 3, 2004.

102 "six, tall grey": FOC, "Exercise A," GCSU.

102 "The other houses": James Joyce, "Araby," *Dubliners,* edited by Robert Scholes and A. Walton Litz (New York: Penguin Books, Viking Critical Library, 1996), 29.

102 "Nine out of Every Ten": FOC, Folder 4-b, GCSU.

103 "highly recommendable": MFOC, [Review of *The Story of Ferdinand* by Munro Leaf], *Corinthian* 18, no. 2 (Winter 1943): 14.

103 "translucent mush": FOC, "Five Titled Exercises," GCSU.

103 "loud-labeled tin cans": FOC, "Exercise," GCSU.

103 "tin cans": William Faulkner, "Barn Burning," *Selected Short Stories of William Faulkner* (New York: Modern Library, 1993), 1.

103 "Excellent": Folder 4-c, GCSU.

103 "plain looking": Karen Owens Smith, letter to the author, November 3, 2004.

103 "At the time it seemed": Marion Peterman Page, letter to the author, October 17, 2004.

103 "zuit-suited": FOC, "A Place of Action," GCSU.

104 "belligerent": MFOC, "Home of the Brave," *Corinthian* (Fall 1943): 5.

104 "When I went to Iowa": FOC to Betty Hester, August 28, 1955, *CW,* 950.

105 Alka-Seltzer: Alexander, "Memory," *Atlanta Journal.*

105 "I had a course": FOC to Betty Hester, August 3, 1963, *HB,* 533.

105 "Think twice": FOC, a draft of a speech delivered at GCSU; Frances Poole, letter to the author, October 17, 2004.

105 "In college I read works": FOC to Betty Hester, August 28, 1955, *CW,* 950.

105 "She was considered dangerous": Cash, *Flannery O'Connor,* 66.

105 "My introduction to her": Ana Pinkston Phillips, letter to the author, October 21, 2004.

106 "Could I interest": MFOC, cartoon, *Colonnade* (November 9, 1943): 2.

106 "I had 3": FOC to Janet McKane, January 27, 1964, *HB,* 564.

106 "I remember Flannery as outstanding": Jane Strozier Smith, e-mail to the author, October 28, 2004.

106 "Master of Rotating Tops": MFOC, "Doctors of Delinquency," *Corinthian* (Fall 1943): 13.

106 "Tums and Ex-Lax": MFOC, "Biologic Endeavor," *Corinthian* (Spring 1944): 7, 8.

106 "until students quit school": MFOC, "Education's Only Hope," *Corinthian* (Spring 1945): 15.

107 "old fashion wardrobe": Elizabeth Wansley Gazdick, letter to the author, October 22, 2004.

107 "I was an art major": Joan DeWitt Yoe, letter to the author, October 21, 2004.

107 "She was one of the most": Helen Matthews Lewis, in discussion with the author, January 29, 2004.

107 "Well I know": Mary Barbara Tate, "Flannery O'Connor: At Home in Milledgeville," *Studies in Literary Imagination* 20, no. 2 (1987): 34.

107 "the smartest woman": FOC to Betty Boyd, November 5, 1949, *HB,* 19.

107 "very carefully brought up": Cash, *Flannery O'Connor,* 65.

107–108 "My survey of European History": Helen I. Greene, "Mary Flannery O'Connor," 44.

108 "Elms form a stately avenue": *Spectrum,* 1943.

108 "Oh, what is so effervescent": MFOC, "Effervescence," *Corinthian* 18, no. 2 (Spring 1943): 16.

109 "My roommate and I": Mary Elizabeth Anderson Bogle, letter to the author, October 17, 2004.

109 "Although the majority": The Editor, "Excuse Us While We Don't Apologize," *Corinthian* (Fall 1944): 4.

110 "a lot of encouragin'": Jean Wylder, "Flannery O'Connor, A Reminiscence and Some Letters," *North American Review* 225, no. 1 (Spring 1970): 59.

110 "I thought then": Bee McCormack, e-mail to the author, March 3, 2005.

110 "I like cartoons": FOC to Janet McKane, August 27, 1963, *CW,* 1191.

110 "You can go jump": Robert Fitzgerald, "Introduction," *Everything That Rises Must Converge* (New York: Farrar, Straus and Giroux, 1965), xii.

110 "wonderful, merry cartoons": Margaret Inman Meaders, "Flannery O'Connor: 'Literary Witch,'" *Colorado Quarterly* 10, no. 4 (Spring 1962): 377.

111 "In the linoleum cuts": Robert Fitzgerald, "Introduction," *Everything That Rises,* xii.

111 "Mary Flannery decorated": Greene, "Mary Flannery O'Connor," 45–46.

111 "We were laughing": Peggy George Sammons, e-mail to the author, October 25, 2004.

112 "Your quoting of a poem": FOC to Janet McKane, December 13, 1963, *HB,* 554.

112 "a bit breathlessly": Meaders, Flannery O'Connor, 381. Betty Boyd Love remembers FOC asking the question, in her briefer account in her "Recollections" draft, GCSU.

113 "humanizing the machine": George W. Beiswanger, "The Dance and Today's Needs," *Theatre Arts Monthly* 19, no. 6 (June 1935): 440.

113 "I understand she says": MFOC, cartoon, *Colonnade* (February 7, 1945): 4.

113 *The Making of the Modern Mind:* The full title of this book by John Herman Randall, Jr., was *The Making of the Modern Mind: A Survey of the Intellectual Background of the Present Age* (Boston: Houghton, 1926).

113 "an academic best-seller": Cash, *Flannery O'Connor,* 67.

114 "What kept me a sceptic": FOC to Alfred Corn, May 30, 1962, *CW,* 1164–65.

114 "[He] is the one": FOC to Sally and Robert Fitzgerald, Tuesday [Summer 1952], *HB,* 41.

114 "Philosophy class": Helen Matthews Lewis, in discussion with the author, January 29, 2004.

114 "It was philosophical *modernism*": Cash, *Flannery O'Connor,* 67.

115 "the hope for lasting peace": "G.S.C. Graduates Hooded Monday," *Union-Recorder,* June 14, 1945.

116 "The usual bunk": Cash, *Flannery O'Connor,* 57.

116 "the realm of further study": *Colonnade* (June 6, 1945): 2.

116 "Humph!": Sally Fitzgerald, "Rooms with a View," *Flannery O'Connor Bulletin* 10 (1981): 12.

CHAPTER FOUR: IOWA

117 Iowa Writers' Workshop: The Workshop began in 1936, under the direction of Wilbur Schramm. Paul Engle assumed the directorship in 1941 and held it for twenty-five years.

117 "one of the most": The account of the meeting is drawn from two sources: Colman McCarthy, "Servant of Literature in the Heart of Iowa," *Washington Post,* March 27, 1983; and Paul Engle, letter to Robert Giroux, July 13, 1971, "Farrar, Straus & Giroux Inc. Records," New York Public Library, Astor, Lenox and Tilden Foundations. In the *Post* piece, Engle gives a slightly different version of the note as: "My name is Flannery O'Connor. I'm from Milledgeville, Georgia. I'm a writer."

118 State University of Iowa: The name of the university was shortened, in 1964, to the University of Iowa.

118 "naturally blank": FOC to Elizabeth Hardwick and Robert Lowell, March 17, 1953, *CW,* 910.

119 "Iowa City was a bustling place": John Gruen, in discussion with the author, October 5, 2006.

119 "hick": James B. Hall, e-mail to the author, September 14, 2006.

120 "a new Bohemia": James B. Hall, *Contemporary Authors: Autobiography Series* 12 (Detroit: Gale Research Series, 1990), 132; Hall went on to write about twenty books of fiction and nonfiction, and was the founding provost of the Arts College of the University of California at Santa Cruz.

120 "I did know what it meant": FOC to Maryat Lee, February 24, 1957, *CW,* 1023.

120 Currier House: O'Connor did form a friendship with one roommate, Louise Trovato.

120 "I went to St. Mary's": FOC to Roslyn Barnes, December 12, 1960, *HB,* 422.

121 "shom storrowies": James B. Hall, *Seems Like Old Times,* edited by Ed Dinger (Iowa City: Iowa Writers' Workshop, 1986), 13.

121 "Who was likely": Richard Gilman, "On Flannery O'Connor," *New York Review of Books* 13, no. 3 (August 21, 1969): 24.

121 "selling stories": Bob Fawcell, "William Porter's Writing Career — from Pulp to Post," *Daily Iowan,* January 26, 1946.

122 "You can get an M.A. degree": "Engle, Paul," *Current Biography 1942* (New York: H. W. Wilson, 1942), 249.

122 "was able to breathe": FOC to Betty Hester, December 29, 1956, *CW,* 1017.

123 "a man's realization": FOC, State University of Iowa examination blue book, November 28, 1945, GCSU.

123 "It was a plain little room": Jane Wilson, in discussion with the author, October 5, 2006. The original offices for the Writers' Workshop were in Calvin Hall, just up the hill from the Iowa Memorial Union on Jefferson Street.

123 "Each meeting consists": Paul Engle, "How Creative Writing Is Taught at the University of Iowa Workshop," *Des Moines Sunday Register,* December 28, 1947.

123 "Her voice was quiet": Mary Mudge Wiatt, in discussion with the author, October 1, 2006.

124 "dat coat": FOC, "The Coat," *DoubleTake* 2, no. 3 (Summer 1996): 39.

124 "What first stuns": FOC, "The Writer and the Graduate School," *Alumnae Journal* 13, no. 4 (Summer 1948): 4. She was more tart by the time she said in a later talk, "Everywhere I go I'm asked if I think the universities stifle writers. My opinion is they don't stifle enough of them." FOC, "The Nature and Aim of Fiction," *MM,* 84.

124 "of the right sort": James B. Hall, "Our Workshops Remembered: The Heroic Phase," unpublished essay, 6, private collection.

124 "It did spoil": Robie Macauley, *Esprit: Journal of Thought and Opinion* 8, no. 1 (University of Scranton, Scranton, Pa., Winter 1964): 34.

125 "Flannery was so cold": Norma Hodges, in discussion with the author, May 6, 2005.

125 "I couldn't though have written": FOC to Maryat Lee, February 24, 1957, *CW,* 1023.

126 "pitched himself": Norma Hodges, in discussion with the author, May 6, 2005.

126 "This scene of the attempted": McCarthy, "Servant of Literature," *Washington Post,* March 27, 1983.

126 "I was right young": Sally Fitzgerald, "A Master Class: From the Correspondence of Caroline Gordon and Flannery O'Connor," *Georgia Review* 33, no. 4. (Winter 1979): 845.

127 "When I went there": Katherine Fugin, Faye Rivard, and Margaret Sieh, "An Interview with Flannery O'Connor, *Censer* (College of St. Teresa, Winona, Minn., Fall 1960): 59.

127 "discarded subject": FOC, "The Crop," *The Complete Stories* (New York: Farrar, Straus and Giroux, 1971), 34.

127 "Although I reckon": Jean Wylder, "Flannery O'Connor, A Reminiscence and Some Letters," *North American Review* 225, no. 1 (Spring 1970): 59.

127 "Then I began to write": FOC interview with Harvey Breit, *Galley Proof,* WRCA-TV (NBC), New York, May 1955, *Con,* 6.

128 "When R. P. Warren": Hall, "Our Workshops Remembered," 6.

128 "Horgan never even knew": FOC to Betty Hester, August 9, 1957, *CW,* 1042.

128 "a sort of waif of the art of writing": Paul Horgan to Father Quinn, April 25, 1969, *HB.*

128 "I write only about two hours": FOC to Cecil Dawkins, September 22, 1957, *CW,* 1042.

129 "in a rather uncertain": Allen Maxwell to FOC, July 16, 1946, GCSU.

129 "an easier, freer childhood": Sally Fitzgerald, "Flannery O'Connor, Patterns of Friendship, Patterns of Love," *Georgia Review* 52, no. 3 (Fall 1998): 417.

129 "kindred spirits": Barbara Tunnicliff Hamilton, "Flannery in Iowa City," unpublished essay, 1, private collection.

129 "They would have house parties": Barbara Tunnicliff Hamilton, in discussion with the author, October 2, 2005.

130 "business woman": Hamilton, "Flannery in Iowa City," 2.

130 "I didn't bother her": Barbara Tunnicliff Hamilton, in discussion with the author, October 2, 2005.

130 "had to": Hamilton, "Flannery in Iowa City," 1.

130 "She was very serious": Barbara Tunnicliff Hamilton, in discussion with the author, October 2, 2005.

130 "With the door open": Barbara Tunnicliff Hamilton, e-mail to the author, September 30, 2006.

131 "When more than half": Doris Cone, "Writers' Workshop at Iowa U. Draws New York Publisher," *Cedar Rapids Gazette,* November 24, 1946.

131 "The Barber": The story was first published in *New Signatures: A Collection of College Writing,* edited by Alan Swallow (Prairie City, Ill.: James A. Decker, 1948), 113–24. For a discussion of the story's probable debt to Ring Lardner's "The Haircut," see Sarah Gordon, *Flannery O'Connor: The Obedient Imagination* (Atlanta: University of Georgia Press, 2000), 65.

131 "Flannery's answer": Jean Cash, "O'Connor in the Iowa Writers' Workshop," *Flannery O'Connor Bulletin* 24 (1995–96): 71.

132 "She once said to my wife": James B. Hall, e-mail to the author, September 6, 2006.

132 "I see I should ride": FOC to Betty Hester, November 16, 1957, *CW,* 1050.

132 black woman: Ralph C. Wood, *Flannery O'Connor and the Christ-Haunted South* (Grand Rapids, Mich.: Wm. B. Eerdmans, 2004), 102.

132 "Iowa Barber School": FOC to Robie Macauley, October 13, 1953, *CW,* 914.

133 "like Billy Grahme": Folder 17, GCSU.

133 "He thought of Bing Crosby": Ibid. Actually O'Connor was confusing *Boys Town,* starring Spencer Tracy, with two films in which Bing Crosby played a priest — *Going My Way* (1944) and *The Bells of St. Mary's* (1945).

133 "Now, Miss O'Connor": Jean Cash, *Flannery O'Connor: A Life* (Knoxville: University of Tennessee Press, 2002), 95.

133 "I didn't really start": FOC to Betty Hester, August 28, 1955, *CW,* 950–51.

134 "It started when": Paul Levine, "The Soul of the Grotesque," *Minor American Novelists,* edited by Charles Alva Hoyt (Carbondale and Edwardsville: Southern Illinois University Press, 1970), 107.

134 "a journey that never impressed": FOC to Betty Hester, January 31, 1959, *HB,* 317.

134 Dixie Limited: In her talk "Some Aspects of the Grotesque in Southern Fiction," O'Connor compared Faulkner to the Dixie Limited: "The presence alone of Faulkner in our midst makes a great difference in what the writer can and cannot permit himself to do. Nobody wants his mule and wagon stalled on the same track the Dixie Limited is roaring down," *CW,* 818.

134 "the dilapidated station": "1 p. working draft," GCSU.

134 "I sat down next to": FOC to Maryat Lee, April 28, 1960, *HB,* 392–93.

135 "the Oedipus complex": "Look for Their Names on the Bindings," *Cedar Rapids Gazette,* June 10, 1948.

135 "a thump of recognition": FOC, "*Wise Blood,* working draft," GCSU.

136 "pizen snake": Andrew Nelson Lytle, "The Hind Tit," *I'll Take My Stand: The South and the Agrarian Tradition,* by Twelve Southerners (Baton Rouge: Louisiana State University Press, 1977), 234.

136 "I was told later": Andrew Lytle, *Esprit: Journal of Thought and Opinion* 8, no. 1 (University of Scranton, Pa., Winter 1964): 33.

136 "make a federal case": Hall, "Our Workshops Remembered," 11.

136 "She would put a man in bed": Carl H. Griffin, "Andrew Lytle at DeKalb College, a Return Engagement," *Chattahoochee Review* 8, no. 4 (Summer 1988): 98.

136 "sink the theme": FOC to Betty Hester, January 28, 1957, Emory.

136 "a bale of cotton": James B. Hall, e-mail to the author, September 6, 2006.

136 "She was a lovely girl": Griffin, "Andrew Lytle," 97–98.

136 "Why, she can just walk": James B. Hall, e-mail to the author, July 14, 2005.

137 "People who were favored": Eugene Brown, in discussion with the author, October 6, 2006.

137 "It comes to us all": "Look for Their Names on the Bindings," *Cedar Rapids Gazette,* June 10, 1948.

137 "She paid me for doing": Hamilton, "Flannery in Iowa City," 3.

137 "Her magnified eyes": Norma Hodges, "Flannery," *River King Poetry Supplement* 2, no. 3 (Autumn 1996): 4.

137 T. S. Eliot's: O'Connor's adult library contained twelve of Eliot's books. For a discussion of Eliot's influence on O'Connor, see: Sally Fitzgerald, "The Owl and the Nightingale," *Flannery O'Connor Bulletin* 13 (Autumn 1984): 44–58.

137 "His search for a physical home": FOC, "SYNOPSIS: (after first four chapters)," GCSU.

138 "typed": "Flannery O'Connor Wins Rinehart-Iowa Award for Novel," *Daily Iowan,* May 29, 1947.

138 "We had dinner there": Cash, *Flannery O'Connor,* 93.

139 "She was a loner": Charles Embree, in discussion with the author, October 3, 2006.

139 "It was wholly typical": Paul Engle to Robert Giroux, July 13, 1971, FSG.

139 "In spring, it was as though": Hall, "Our Workshops Remembered," 8.

139 "Andrew was talking": James B. Hall, e-mail to the author, July 14, 2005.

139 "I was in Milledgeville": Frances Florencourt, e-mail to the author, October 26, 2006.

140 Old Dental Building: In a letter to the author, dated October 29, 2006, Robert Yackshaw wrote, "I have spent time with her at the Student Union. And at the Library. And much more at The Old Dental Building next to University Hall: the place where graduate assistants had offices with lower members of the English faculty."

140 "was most a hundred": FOC to Roslyn Barnes, September 29, 1960, *HB,* 410.

140 "Mrs. Guzeman was not very fond": FOC to Jean Williams Wylder, December 28, 1952, quoted in Wylder, "Flannery O'Connor," 60.

140 "Flannery was sitting alone": Ibid., 58.

141 "I doubt if Flannery": Ibid., 59.

141 "He was a brilliant": Bernie Halperin, in discussion with the author, June 25, 2005.

141 "entirely original": Thomas E. Kennedy, "A Last Conversation with Robie Macauley," *Agni* 45 (Boston College: 1997): 182.

141 "I used to date": Robie Macauley to Steve Wilbers, April 16, 1976, UI.

142 "We ate in a big": Cash, *Flannery O'Connor,* 100.

142 "Robie took care": Ibid., 99.

142 "Flannery and I": Ibid.

142 "party man . . . soul mate": Ibid.

143 "So I reckon": Wylder, "Flannery O'Connor," 59.

143 "tame and friendly": Robert Lowell to Allen Tate, March 15, 1950, Princeton.

143 "He was so sensitive": James B. Hall, "Our Workshops Remembered," 7.

143 "simple, austere": FOC to Mary Virginia Harrison, "Tuesday," GSCU.

143 "When it was gone": Hank Messick to Stephen Wilbers, July 21, 1976, UI.

144 "right nice": Wylder, "Flannery O'Connor," 59.

144 "two black bears": FOC, *Complete Stories,* 90; in "The Heart of the Park," Hazel's last name is Weaver.

144 "completely absorbed": Wylder, "Flannery O'Connor," 60.

144 "two indifferent bears": FOC to Elizabeth Hardwick and Robert Lowell, March 17, 1953, *CW.* The two lions once in City Park had reportedly been brought back from Africa by Harry Bremer, who kept them in his carriage house before giving them to the zoo: Gerald Mansheim, *Iowa City: An Illustrated History* (Norfolk, Va.: Donning Company Publishers, 1989), 164.

144 "barbarous Georgia accent": FOC to Carl Hartman, March 2, 1954, *CW,* 922.

145 "Flannery's novel is sure": Paul Griffiths to Paul Engle, February 16, 1948, "Papers of Paul Engle," UI.

145 "Flannery, in spite of all": Hansford Martin to Paul Engle, February 22, 1948, "Papers of Paul Engle," UI.

145 "We would invite": John Gruen, in discussion with the author, October 5, 2006.

145 "demon rewriter": Kennedy, "A Last Conversation," *Agni,* 182.

145 "Woman on the Stairs": *Tomorrow* 8, no. 12 (August): 40–44. *Tomorrow* was published in New York by Garrett Publications between September 1941 and August 1951. Retitled "A Stroke of Good Fortune," this story appeared in the Spring 1953 edition of *Shenandoah,* and as the fourth story in *A Good Man Is Hard to Find.*

145 "She read the story": Jane Wilson, in discussion with the author, October 5, 2006.

146 "She had this air": Norma Hodges, in discussion with the author, May 6, 2005.

146 "a personally shy": Austin Warren to Elizabeth Ames, February 20, 1948, Yaddo.

146 "as much promise as anyone": Andrew Lytle to Elizabeth Ames, February 24, 1948, Yaddo.

146 "one of the best young writers": Paul Engle to Elizabeth Ames, April 2, 1949, Yaddo.

146 "Flannery seems happiest": Hansford Martin to Paul Engle, April 24, 1948, "Papers of Paul Engle," UI.

146 "I'd say the description": Wylder, "Flannery O'Connor," 58.

146 "flat, nasal drawl": Gene Brzenk to Jean Wylder, December 26, 1972, UI.

147 "For once there was not": Wylder, "Flannery O'Connor," 62.

CHAPTER FIVE: UP NORTH

148 "It did not take Georgia": FOC to Elizabeth Ames, August 17, 1948, Yaddo.

149 "shadow": Marjorie Peabody Waite, *Yaddo: Yesterday and Today* (Albany, N.Y.: Argus Press, 1933), 21.

149 "creating, creating, creating": Ibid., 26.

149 "more distinguished activity": John Cheever, statement included in the minutes of the meeting of The Corporation of Yaddo at Yaddo, September 7, 1968, Yaddo.

150 "and Flannery O'Connor": Clifford Wright, "Diary," June 8, 1948, Yaddo.

150 "very quiet": Patricia Highsmith to Ronald Blythe, September 3, 1967; quoted in Andrew Wilson, *Beautiful Shadow* (New York: Bloomsbury, 2003), 141.

150 "I really think": FOC to Cecil Dawkins, December 10, 1959, *HB,* 362.

151 "She is like a well-meaning": Robert Lowell to George Santayana, November 14, 1948, *The Letters of Robert Lowell,* edited by Saskia Hamilton (New York: Farrar, Straus and Giroux, 2005), 115.

151 "There was the same laughter": Frederick Morton, in discussion with the author, November 19, 2006.

151 "ALL the time": FOC to Paul Engle, April 7, 1949, *CW,* 883.

151 "I would have been happier": FOC to Cecil Dawkins, July 19, 1962, *HB,* 483.

151 Hillside Studio: Cecil Dawkins worked in Meadow Studio, in 1962; in a letter of August 1, 1962 (ibid.), O'Connor writes to Dawkins, of her own 1948 studio, "Might well have been the one you have now"; O'Connor's description of her studio and her letter to Dawkins indicate that her studio was not on North Farm, used in 1948; of the three possible studios on the property, including Meadow, only Hillside had a "fireplace."

152 "a long single room": Ibid.

152 "greenpeaish": FOC, "The Peeler," unpublished manuscript, 6, Yaddo. In *Wise Blood,* Enoch's tie is "the color of green peas," *CW,* 23.

152 "In my whole time": FOC to Betty Hester, September 21, 1957, *HB,* 241.

152 "arty": FOC to Betty Hester, August 4, 1962, *CW,* 1171.

152 "At the breakfast table": FOC to Cecil Dawkins, December 23, 1959, *CW,* 1115.

153 "Miss Highsmith": Wright, "Diary," March 28, 1948.

153 "between those two stools": Patricia Highsmith to Ronald Blythe, September 3, 1967; quoted in Wilson, *Beautiful Shadow,* 141.

153 "in any collection": FOC to Cecil Dawkins, December 23, 1959, *CW,* 1115.

153 "Dad had been a ragpicker": Jim Shannon, in discussion with the author, May 25, 2005.

153 "all well over forty": FOC to Cecil Dawkins, December 23, 1959, *CW,* 1114.

154 "I remember she was": Frederick Morton, in discussion with the author, November 19, 2006.

154 "She lives by a kind": FOC to Betty Hester, March 19, 1960, *HB,* 383–84.

154 "an accomplished pianist": Elizabeth Ames, "Paul Moor file," Yaddo.

154 "Elizabeth McKee was": Robert Giroux, in discussion with the author, November 13, 2003.

154 "in my vague": FOC to Elizabeth McKee, June 19, 1948, *HB,* 5.

154 "Your work sounds very": Elizabeth McKee to FOC, June 23, 1948, GCSU.

155 "I don't have my novel": FOC to Elizabeth McKee, July 13, 1948, *HB,* 5.

155 "after a few weeks": FOC to Betty Hester, August 4, 1962, *CW,* 1171–72.

155 "a real Yaddo ringer": Robert Lowell to Elizabeth Bishop, January 5, 1949, *Letters,* 122.

156 "By the way": Edward Maisel to Elizabeth Ames, "O'Connor Guest File," Yaddo.

156 "She was completely": Robert Giroux, in discussion with the author, November 13, 2003.

156 "Do not make the absurd": Jacques Maritain, *Art and Scholasticism: With Other Essays (Art et Scolastique),* translated by J. F. Scanlan (New York: Charles Scribner's Sons, 1930), 54.

156 "Then you may count on": Elizabeth Ames to FOC, July 26, 1948, "O'Connor Guest File," Yaddo.

156 "I have worked with much": FOC to Elizabeth Ames, July 27, 1948, "O'Connor Guest File," Yaddo.

156 "Dear Flannery": Wright, "Diary," July 30, 1948.

156 "Dear Elizabeth": FOC to Elizabeth Ames, August 17, 1948, "O'Connor Guest File," Yaddo.

157 "I sleep in my coffin": FOC to Paul Engle, August 25, 1948, "Papers of Paul Engle," UI.

157 "It's too hot": FOC to Elizabeth Ames, August 17, 1948, "O'Connor Guest File," Yaddo.

157 "ancient wealthy": FOC to Clifford Wright, August 10, 1948, Wright, "Diary."

157 "She was a brilliant": Frederick Morton, in discussion with the author, November 19, 2006.

157 "My love to you": Elizabeth Ames to Elizabeth Hardwick, November 23, 1948, "Hardwick Guest File," Yaddo.

157 "She seems to have": Malcolm Cowley, "O'Connor Guest File," Yaddo.

157 "hard to like": Newton Arvin, ibid.

158 *On Native Grounds:* Published by Harcourt, Brace in 1942.

158 "a thorny mysterious return": Alfred Kazin, *New York Jew* (New York: Vintage Books, 1979), 312.

158 "It is beautiful": FOC to Cecil Dawkins, September 6, 1962, *CW,* 1174.

158 "I cannot really believe": FOC to Elizabeth McKee, July 21, 1948, *HB,* 6.

159 "Yaddo is a sort of": Robert Lowell to Ezra Pound, [n.d., fall 1948], *Letters,* 114.

159 "pleasant": Robert Lowell to Elizabeth Bishop, December 18, 1948, *Letters,* 120.

159 "an introverted and extroverted": Ibid., October 1, 1948, *Letters,* 111.

159 "the friend of Moscow": Malcolm Cowley, *A Century at Yaddo* (Saratoga Springs, N.Y.: Corporation of Yaddo, 2000), 18.

159 "acute and silent": Robert Lowell to Elizabeth Bishop, [n.d., fall 1948], *Letters,* 699.

159 "There's a girl": Robert Lowell to Caroline Gordon, [n.d. November 1948], *Letters,* 116.

160 "She fell for him": Sally Fitzgerald, "Flannery O'Connor: Patterns of Friendship, Patterns of Love," *Georgia Review* 52, no. 3 (Fall 1998): 415.

160 "I lost her": Ibid.

160 "She wasn't in love": Robert Giroux, in discussion with the author, November 13, 2003.

160 "I feel almost too much": FOC to Betty Hester, April 21, 1956, *CW,* 992.

160 "I think one of the best": Robert Lowell to Elizabeth Bishop, January 14, 1949, *Letters,* 704.

160 "I watched him that winter": FOC to Betty Hester, April 21, 1956, *CW,* 992.

160 "Christ-haunted": FOC, "The Catholic Novelist in the Protestant South," *CW,* 861; in *Wise Blood,* O'Connor writes, of Haze, "Later he saw Jesus move from tree to tree in the back of his mind, a wild ragged figure motioning him to turn around and come off into the dark," *CW,* 11.

160 "Cal Lowell says": Caroline Gordon to Brainard Cheney, February 4, 1953, Frances and Brainard Cheney Collection, Jean and Alexander Heard Library, Vanderbilt University, Nashville.

160 "It seems such a short time": Robert Lowell to Elizabeth Bishop, August 10, 1964, *Letters,* 452–53.

161 "She's run through the local": Robert Lowell to Robie Macauley, [n.d., fall 1948], *Letters,* 699–700.

161 "I read it about ten": FOC to Betty Hester, August 24, 1957, *HB,* 237.

162 "habit of the practical": Maritain, *Art and Scholasticism,* 9.

162 "The pure artist": Ibid., 13.

162 "you don't have to be good": FOC to Betty Hester, September 15, 1955, *CW,* 955.

162 "Guggenheiming it": Wright, "Diary," November 19, 1948.

162 "enGuggenheimed": Ibid., December 27, 1948.

162 "sentence by sentence": Robert Lowell, Recommendation for Flannery O'Connor, Fiction Category, [n.d., fall 1948], Archive of the J. S. Guggenheim Foundation.

163 "I introduced him to": Robert Lowell to T. S. Eliot, January 18, 1949, *Letters,* 130.

163 "It was not gin": FOC to Robert Lowell, December 28, 1958, *CW,* 1086.

163 "high moral tone": Wright, "Diary," December 5, 1948.

163 "ingeniously funny": Ibid., December 27, 1948.

163 "perfect": Ibid., December 21, 1948.

163 "grotesque": Ibid., January 27, 1949.

163 "My suggestion": Robert Lowell to Elizabeth Bishop, December 8, 1948, *Letters,* 120.

163 "aloud to the two": Ibid., December 24, 1948, *Letters,* 122.

163 "It would be nice": Jean Wylder, "Flannery O'Connor, A Reminiscence and Some Letters," *North American Review* 225, no. 1 (Spring 1970): 62.

164 "please show": FOC to Elizabeth McKee, January 20, 1949, *HB,* 8.

164 "a pretty straight": John Selby to FOC, February 16, 1949, GCSU.

164 "He too thought": FOC to Paul Engle, April 7, 1949, *CW,* 882.

164 "Send me, please": Paul Engle to FOC, May 16, 1949, GCSU.

164 "Please tell me": FOC to Elizabeth McKee, February 17, 1949, *CW,* 880.

164 "kind of aloneness": John Selby to FOC, February 16, 1949, GCSU.

164 "I am not writing": FOC to John Selby, February 18, 1949, *CW,* 881.

164 "the hardening of the arteries": John Selby to Paul Engle, May 9, 1949, GCSU.

165 "seemed to be attending": Kazin, *New York Jew,* 314.

165 "dimpled agreeable": Wright, "Diary," December 5, 1948.

165 "Lizzie Hardwick": Ibid., January 27, 1949.

165 "Lowell and Elizabeth Hardwick": Kazin, *New York Jew,* 313.

165 "Most of all": Elizabeth Hardwick, "Flannery O'Connor, 1925–1964," *New York Review of Books* (October 8, 1964): 21.

165 "She was a plain": Elizabeth Hardwick, in discussion with the author, October 31, 2003.

166 "pious": Robert Lowell to Peter Taylor, October 22, 1948, *Letters,* 113.

166 "It was a gloomy": Kazin, *New York Jew,* 312.

166 "the agrarian–little magazine": Wright, "Diary," January 27, 1949.

167 Agnes Smedley: Her most recent biographer, Ruth Price, discovered, to her dismay, through recently released papers in Soviet archives that Smedley was indeed "as cunning and crafty an operator as her detractors on the right ever alleged." "Introduction," *The Lives of Agnes Smedley* (Oxford, New York: Oxford University Press, 2005), 9.

167 "She idolized": Jim Shannon, in discussion with the author, May 25, 2005.

167 "fantastic idea": Wright, "Diary," February 14, 1949.

167 "I had refused": James Ross to Elizabeth Ames, July 16, 1949, "James Ross Guest File," Yaddo.

168 "I shall compare": Robert Lowell, "Minutes of Special Meeting of the Directors of the Corporation of Yaddo," February 26, 1949, 15, Yaddo.

168 "Molotov cocktails": Elizabeth Hardwick, "Minutes," 28.

168 "They frequently came": Elizabeth Ames, "Minutes," 57.

168 "some of the excitement": Edward Stonequist, "Minutes," 5.

168 "very pleasant": FOC, "Minutes," 31.

169 "It wasn't as much": Elizabeth Hardwick, in discussion with the author, October 31, 2003.

169 "When I look at my birds": FOC to Elizabeth Ames, February 9, 1958, Yaddo.

169 "The guests departed": Malcolm Cowley to Louis Kronenberger, March 8, 1949, "Malcolm Cowley Papers," Newberry Library; quoted in Ian Hamilton, *Robert Lowell* (New York: Random House, 1982), 148.

169 "We have been very upset": FOC to Elizabeth McKee, February 24, 1949, *HB*, 11.

169 "There's too many people": FOC, "The Peeler," *The Complete Stories* (New York: Farrar, Straus and Giroux, 1971), 69.

170 "There is one advantage": FOC to Betty Boyd, November 5, 1949, *HB*, 19.

170 "very nice girl": FOC to Betty Hester, April 21, 1956, *HB*, 152.

170 "I think Elizabeth is a lot": Ibid., January 12, 1957, *HB*, 196.

170 "But mine was upper": Elizabeth Hardwick, in discussion with the author, October 31, 2003.

170 "an unopened Bible": FOC to Jean Wylder, March 1949, quoted in Cash, *Flannery O'Connor: A Life* (Knoxville: University of Tennessee Press, 2002), 123.

170 "very good co-op cafeteria": FOC to Betty Hester, September 8, 1962, *HB*, 491.

171 "to become an intellectual": Ibid., June 1, 1956, 161.

171 "shooting sparks": Ian Hamilton, *Robert Lowell* (New York: Random House, 1982), 149.

171 "She did this with some difficulty": Robert Fitzgerald, "Introduction," *Everything That Rises Must Converge* (New York: Farrar, Straus and Giroux, 1965), xii.

172 "how this affable": Beth Dawkins Bassett, "Converging Lives," *Emory Magazine* 50, no. 4 (April 1982): 18.

172 "shapes black-spinning": FOC, "The Train," *Complete Stories,* 56.

172 "Mrs. Fitzgerald is 5 feet 2": FOC to Betty Hester, June 1, 1956, *HB*, 161.

172 "unusual": Robert Giroux, in discussion with the author, November 13, 2003.

173 "my good editor": FOC to Betty Hester, May 16, 1959, *CW,* 1096.

173 "received the shock": Ian Hamilton, *Lowell,* 149–50.

174 "Let me right now correct": FOC to Betty Hester, May 14, 1960, *HB*, 395.

174 "a Big Intellectual": FOC to Betty Hester, December 16, 1955, *CW,* 976.

174 "It did become famous": Elizabeth Hardwick, in discussion with the author, October 31, 2003.

175 "a frame of mind": "Petition in support of Elizabeth Ames," March 21, 1949, Newberry Library, Chicago. Quoted in Ian Hamilton, *Lowell,* 151.

175 "a poet and a Roman Catholic": "Panel Discussions of the Cultural Conference Delegates Cover a Wide Range of Subjects," *New York Times,* March 27, 1949.

175 "But you are a woman": Ian Hamilton, *Lowell,* 156.

175 "to take with her": Giroux, "Introduction," *Complete Stories,* ix.

175 "I didn't get any": FOC to Paul Engle, April 7, 1949, *CW,* 883.

176 "blew our lids": Robert Lowell to Anthony Ostroff, August 23, 1957, *Letters,* 291.

176 "Why didn't you teach": Helen Greene, "Mary Flannery O'Connor: One Teacher's Happy Memory," *Flannery O'Connor Bulletin* 19 (1990): 46.

176 "On one side we see communism": James Carroll, "What We Can Learn from Our Reaction to Billy Graham's Crusades," *Boston Globe,* June 28, 2005.

176 "Our action": FOC to Betty Boyd, June 8, 1949, GCSU.

176 "much worse than Georgia": FOC to Janet McKane, July 7, 1963, *HB,* 530.

177 "I liked riding": Ibid., June 5, 1963, *HB,* 522.

177 "All the women": FOC to Betty Boyd, June 22, 1949, GCSU.

177 "uptown": FOC to Janet McKane, July 20, 1963, *HB,* 530.

177 "I didn't see much": FOC to Janet McKane, June 19, 1963, *CW,* 1188.

177 "not overly talkative": Virginia Wray, "Flannery O'Connor on the West Side: Dr. Lyman Fulton's Recollections of a Short Acquaintance," *English Language Notes* 39, no. 1 (September 2001): 73.

177 "goat's milk cheese": FOC to Mary Virginia Harrison [Mrs. John A. Mills], March 12, 1950, GCSU.

178 "I do remember": Wray, "Flannery O'Conor on the West Side," 75.

178 "An Easter Attraction": *New York Times,* April 17, 1949.

178 "a pipe smoker": "Vows of the Peacock," *The New Yorker* (July 16, 1949): 12.

178 "laughing": FOC to Janet McKane, June 5, 1963, *HB,* 523; the most likely candidate for the statue is an early fourteenth-century, forty-eight-inch-high walnut *Enthroned Virgin and Child,* from the Île-de-France, painted in polychrome, gilded ocher, accession number 25.120.290. Although O'Connor claimed her statue "wasn't colored," Michael Carter, Cloisters librarian, says, "the color is often so faded on medieval statuary that someone might remember it as unpainted." Michael Carter, in discussion with the author, February 9, 2006. McKane turned up a photo in a *Metropolitan Museum of Art Bulletin* that O'Connor agreed was the one; the June 1963 edition of the *Bulletin* includes a photo of the statue on page 331.

178 "the Child had a face": Ibid., July 9, 1963, *HB,* 529.

179 "about a baboon": *Wise Blood, CW,* 79. The scene was included in newspaper ad copy as a thrill: "Rescues children from the big blaze," *New York Times,* August 21, 1949; Jon Lance Bacon noted the connection in *Flannery O'Connor and Cold War Culture* (Cambridge: Cambridge University Press, 1993), 122.

179 "I don't think New York City": Wray, "Flannery O'Connor on the West Side," 74.

179 "culture fog": FOC to Betty Boyd, October 17, 1949, *HB,* 16.

179 "comes in there August 15": FOC to Brainard Cheney, August 13, 1957, *CC,* 59.

179 "Me and Enoch": FOC to Robie Macauley, [n.d.], *CW,* 886.

180 "miles from anything": FOC to Betty Boyd, [n.d.], *CW,* 883.

180 Redding: The Fitzgeralds, and O'Connor, used a Ridgefield mailing address — R.D.4/Ridgefield, Conn. — because rural delivery to that portion of Redding was handled at the time by the Ridgefield post office.

180 "hurt their feet": Robert Fitzgerald, "Introduction," *Everything That Rises,* xiii.

180 "which I find": FOC to Betty Boyd, October 17, 1949, *HB,* 16.

180 "looking slender": Robert Fitzgerald, "Introduction," *Everything That Rises,* xiv.

180 "Flannery would lie": "Panel Discussion: GCSU, April 3, 1977," *Flannery O'Connor Bulletin* 6 (1977): 79.

181 "while the dinner": FOC to Betty Hester, June 1, 1956, *HB,* 161.

181 *Miss Lonelyhearts:* West's influence shows up in drafts of *Wise Blood,* as "Shrike," the newspaper editor in *Miss Lonelyhearts,* is used as the name for two different characters, and remains, as an allusion, in Sabbath's correspondence with a newspaper advice columnist; Elizabeth Hardwick described West's novels as "morality plays . . . classified as comedies" and "funny as a crutch." Elizabeth Hardwick, "Funny as a Crutch," *New York Review of Books* (November 6, 2003): 24. O'Connor later claimed that West was an influence "stylistically" in her early twenties, but she was "disappointed" upon rereading him: "Miss Lonely Hearts seemed a sentimental Christ figure which is a contradiction in terms." FOC to Marcus Smith, July 12, 1976, *CW,* 1215.

181 "They were our movies": Robert Fitzgerald, "Introduction," *Everything That Rises,* xiv.

181 "gewgaws": Sally Fitzgerald, "Patterns of Friendship," 417.

181 "my adopted kin": FOC to Sally Fitzgerald, December 26, 1954, *CW,* 927.

181 "master of the house": Sally Fitzgerald, "Rooms with a View," *Flannery O'Connor Bulletin* 10 (1981): 13.

181–182 "Well I can't sustain": Sally Fitzgerald, "Panel Discussion," *Flannery O'Connor Bulletin* 6 (1977): 78.

182 "due to criticism": Christopher O'Hare interview with Sally Fitzgerald.

182 "The novel is going": FOC to Elizabeth McKee, October 26, 1949, *HB,* 17.

182 "unethical": Ibid.

182 "malicious": FOC to Mavis McIntosh, October 31, 1949, *CW,* 884.

182 "a writer on my own": Alice Alexander, "The Memory of Milledgeville's Flannery O'Connor Is Still Green," *Atlanta Journal,* March 28, 1979.

182 "outside": FOC to Mary Virginia Harrison, October 15, 1949, GCSU.

182 "Marriages are always a shock": FOC to Betty Boyd, November 17, 1949, *HB,* 19.

182 "She *did* husband": Beth Dawkins Bassett, "Converging Lives," *Emory Magazine* 58, no. 4 (April 1982): 19.

182 "We spent an hour": Robert Lowell to Robert Fitzgerald, [n.d., December 1949], *Letters,* 150–51.

183 "I won't see you": FOC to Elizabeth Hardwick and Robert Lowell, [n.d.], *CW,* 886.

183 "having a kidney": FOC to Elizabeth McKee, December 30, 1949, GCSU.

183 "She wrote to me": Wray, "Flannery O'Connor on the West Side," 76.

183 "radical cure": FOC to Elizabeth McKee, February 13, 1950, *CW,* 887.

183 "We worked on at our jobs": Robert Fitzgerald, "Introduction," *Everything That Rises,* xvi.

183 "I noted what good spirits": Giroux, "Introduction," *Complete Stories,* xi.

184 "She was now one of": Robert Fitzgerald, "Introduction," *Everything That Rises,* xvi.

184 "typing arms": Ibid.

184 "I am wondering": FOC to Betty Hester, March 5, 1960, *CW,* 1123–24.

184 "ran from one end": FOC to Maryat Lee, October 9, 1962, *HB,* 495.

185 "smiling perhaps": "Editor's Note," *HB,* 21.

185 "a shriveled old": Ibid., 22.

185 "a state of complete": Christopher O'Hare interview with Sally Fitzgerald.

CHAPTER SIX: THE LIFE YOU SAVE

189 "any story I reveal": FOC to Betty Hester, September 24, 1955, *CW,* 957.

189 "I know for a fact": Robert Fitzgerald, "Introduction," *Everything That Rises Must Converge* (New York: Farrar, Straus and Giroux, 1965) xiv. O'Connor assured him that the description was based on a visit to the Manhattan "cold-water flat" of her *Mademoiselle* editor, and Guggenheim recommender, George Davis. FOC to Sally and Robert Fitzgerald, February 11, 1958, *HB,* 267.

190 "Borne home": FOC to Maryat Lee, October 9, 1962, *HB,* 495.

190 "full of old rain crows": FOC to Betty Boyd Love, December 23, 1950, *CW,* 888.

191 "He was a little fella": Margaret Uhler, in discussion with the author, July 20, 2004.

191 "Internal medicine": Dr. Zeb Burrell, in discussion with the author, October 1, 2004.

191 "Am in the hospital": FOC to Elizabeth McKee, December 19, 1950, GCSU.

191 "Scientist Merrill": FOC to Maryat Lee, March 27, 1962, GCSU.

191 "the Scientist": FOC to Frances Neel Cheney, August 3, 1955, *CC,* 20.

192 "I stayed there a month": FOC to Betty Boyd Love, April 24, 1951, *HB,* 24.

192 "She was already weak": Christopher O'Hare interview with Sally Fitzgerald.

192 SLE: While women are ten times more likely to develop SLE than men, and black women three times more likely than white women, "kinship patterns" of lupus shared by family members, including father-daughter, are not uncommon. Dr. Michael Lockshin, Joan and Sanford Weill College of Medicine of Cornell University, e-mail to author, March 12, 2007.

192 "it comes and goes": FOC to Elizabeth Hardwick and Robert Lowell, March 17, 1953, *CW,* 910.

192 "I have not had the rash": FOC to Elizabeth Fenwick Way, May 2, 1957, *HB,* 217.

192 "When I was nearly dead": FOC to Maryat Lee, August 2, 1961, *HB,* 448.

193 "In '51": FOC to Maryat Lee, May 15, 1964, *CW,* 1208.

193 "I owe my existence": Ibid., February 11, 1958, *CW,* 1063.

193 "I was an intern": Robert Coles, in discussion with the author, January 2, 2004.

193 "moon-like": FOC to Janet McKane, April 2, 1964, *HB,* 572.

193 "I was five years writing": FOC to Betty Hester, November 25, 1955, *CW,* 970.

194 "the large doses of ACTH": FOC to Sally and Robert Fitzgerald, September 20, 1951, *CW,* 890.

194 "during this time": FOC to Betty Hester, November 2, 1955, *CW,* 970.

194 "a subtle parody": "Frustrated Preacher," *Newsweek* (May 19, 1952): 115.

194 "I just unfortunately": FOC to Carl Hartman, March 2, 1954, *CW,* 922.

195 "I have finished my opus": FOC to Betty Boyd Love, April 24, 1951, *HB,* 24.

195 "Me & maw": FOC to Sally and Robert Fitzgerald, September 20, 1951, *CW,* 890.

196 "You could, literally": Robert Strozier, in discussion with the author, September 14, 2004.

197 "Regina was very petite": Christopher O'Hare interview with Mary Jo Thompson.

197 "With me, Flannery tended": Jean Cash, *Flannery O'Connor: A Life* (Knoxville, University of Tennessee Press, 2002), 171.

197 "the cows are fat": "Andalusia Farm Has Milk Production Plus a Varied Assortment of Stock," *Union-Recorder,* June 19, 1958.

198 "Would you check": FOC to Elizabeth McKee, April 24, 1951, *HB,* 24.

198 "I thought, Wow": Robert Giroux, in discussion with the author, November 13, 2003.

198 "mighty pleased": FOC to Mavis McIntosh, June 8, 1951, *HB,* 25.

198 "renascence": "The aspirations for a Catholic 'renascence' were expressed in the journal of that title." Paul Elie, *The Life You Save May Be Your Own* (New York: Farrar, Straus and Giroux, 2003), 496.

198 "It is no accident": Caroline Gordon to Brainard Cheney, December 31, 1951. Quoted in Cash, *Flannery O'Connor,* 207.

198 "This girl is a real": Sally Fitzgerald, "A Master Class: From the Correspondence of Caroline Gordon and Flannery O'Connor," *Georgia Review* 33, no. 4 (Winter 1979): 828.

199 "almost my mother": Robert Lowell to Caroline Gordon, [n.d., fall 1945], *The Letters of Robert Lowell,* edited by Saskia Hamilton (New York: Farrar, Straus and Giroux, 2005), 49.

199 "She presented herself": Kenneth Silverman, in discussion with the author, March 8, 2007.

199 "vague": FOC to Elizabeth McKee, February 17, 1949, *CW,* 880.

199 "a lady around here": FOC to Sally and Robert Fitzgerald, September 20, 1951, *CW,* 890.

199 "spending the day": Ibid., [n.d.] "Tuesday," *CW,* 891.

199 "stout stake": Gordon's letter is printed in full in Sally Fitzgerald's "A Master Class."

200 "Johnsonian English": Ibid., 838.

200 "All these comments": FOC to Caroline Gordon, quoted in Ibid., 845.

201 "autobiographical": Sally Fitzgerald, "Rooms with a View," *Flannery O'Connor Bulletin* 10 (1981): 16.

201 "freaks": Caroline Gordon to FOC, quoted in "A Master Class," 831: "Robert Fitzgerald reported to me something that you said that interested me very much, that your first novel was about freaks, but that your next book would be about folks."

201 "I have twenty-one": FOC to Sally and Robert Fitzgerald, September 20, 1951, *CW,* 890.

201 "He was sort of like": Alfred Matysiak, in discussion with the author, July 27, 2004.

201 "I have just discovered": FOC to Sally and Robert Fitzgerald, [n.d.] "Tuesday," *CW,* 891.

202 "She always tells us": FOC to Brainard and Frances Neel Cheney, December 15, 1953, *CC,* 10–11.

202 "She says she ain't": FOC to Sally Fitzgerald," [n.d. "Friday," Summer 1953], *HB,* 62.

202 "gleaned many": Carter W. Martin, "Introduction," *The Presence of Grace and Other Book Reviews by Flannery O'Connor* (Athens: University of Georgia Press, 1983), 3.

202 "Want to Win": *Union-Recorder,* September 14, 1950.

202 "dashing": "Confederate Vet to See Wife Get Degree at GSCW," *Union-Recorder,* August 23, 1951; August 30, 1951.

203 "The local High Dining": FOC to Maryat Lee, November 10, 1957, GCSU.

203 "It seems like the O'Connors": Mary Jo Thompson, in discussion with the author, May 25, 2004.

203 "If it opened at twelve": Christopher O'Hare interview with Frances Florencourt.

203 "Flannery mostly ate": Dorrie Neligan, in discussion with the author, June 3, 2004.

203 *Wise Blood:* The dedication read, simply, "For Regina."

204 "very pretty": FOC to Sally and Robert Fitzgerald, [n.d.] "Wednesday," *CW,* 895.

204 "distressed": FOC to Helen Greene, May 23, 1952, *CW,* 897.

205 "One reason I like": Betsy Lochridge, "An Afternoon with Flannery O'Connor," *Atlanta Journal and Constitution Magazine* (November 1, 1959): 40.

205 "he was a mystic": FOC to Betty Hester, November 10, 1955, *CW,* 968.

206 "that man owes a lot": FOC to Sally and Robert Fitzgerald, [n.d.] "Saturday," *CW,* 892.

206 "I can tell you": Christopher O'Hare interview with Robert Giroux.

206 "I was disappointed": Robert Giroux, "Introduction," FOC, *The Complete Stories* (New York: Farrar, Straus and Giroux, 1971), xii.

206 "odd": Milton S. Byam, *Library Journal* 77 (May 15, 1952): 894; *Kirkus Reviews* likewise faulted the novel's "Capoted cosmos": "A grotesque for the more zealous avant-gardists; for others, a deep anaesthesia." *Kirkus Reviews* 19, no. 9 (May 1, 1952): 252.

206 "a writer of power": William Goyen, "Unending Vengeance," *New York Times Book Review* (May 18, 1952): 4.

206 "arty": "Southern Dissonance," *Time* (June 9, 1952): 108, 110.

206 "if the struggle": *The New Yorker* (June 14, 1952): 106.

206 "sheer monotony": Oliver LaFarge, "Manic Gloom," *Saturday Review* 35, no. 21 (May 24, 1952): 22.

206 "I am steeling": FOC to Robert Giroux, May 24, 1952, *HB,* 37.

207 "Flannery O'Connor, in her first": Sylvia Stallings, "Young Writer with a Bizarre Tale to Tell," *New York Herald Tribune Book Review* (May 18, 1952): 3.

207 "ancestral mansion": "Frustrated Preacher," *Newsweek* (May 19, 1952): 114.

207 "a remarkably accomplished": John W. Simons, "A Case of Possession," *Commonweal* 56, no. 12 (June 27, 1952): 297.

207 "My mother said she": FOC to Sally and Robert Fitzgerald," [n.d.] "Tuesday," *CW,* 891.

207 "My current literary": Ibid., [n.d.] "Wednesday," *CW,* 895.

208 "Mrs. Semmes went to bed": Patricia Persse, "Armstrong State College Panel on O'Connor," Savannah, Ga., May 1989.

208 "Wherever did she learn": Hugh Brown, "Savannah Landmark," *Flannery O'Connor Bulletin* 18 (1989): 43.

208 "I can see her right now": Charlotte Conn Ferris, in discussion with the author, November 4, 2003.

208 "I wish you could": Robert Fitzgerald, "Introduction," *Everything That Rises,* xix.

208 "I also had an 83-year-old": FOC to John Lynch, February 19, 1956, *HB,* 138.

208 "When I read her first novel": William Schemmel, "Southern Comfort," *Travel-Holiday* (June 1988): 72.

208–209 "I read *Wise Blood*": Mary More Jones, in discussion with the author, May 26, 2004.

209 "I enjoyed it": James H. McCown, "Remembering Flannery O'Connor," *America* (September 8, 1979): 87.

209 "spotting inconsistencies": Charles Claffy, "She Returned to Milledgeville and Then She Began Her Work," *Boston Globe* (July 2, 1981): 2.

209 "I hope you won't": FOC to Robie Macauley, May 2, 1952, *HB,* 35.

210 "Autograph Party": "Autograph Party Is Planned for Miss O'Connor," *Union-Recorder,* May 8, 1952; "Flannery O'Connor to Be Honored at Library Today," *Union-Recorder,* May 15, 1952; "Autograph Party Given at Library for Miss O'Connor," *Union-Recorder,* May 22, 1952.

210 "Cocktails were not served": FOC to Betty Boyd Love, postmarked May 23, 1952, *HB,* 36.

210 "most brave": FOC to Miss Satterfield and the library staff, May 17, 1952, GCSU.

210 "I have rarely enjoyed": Margaret Inman Meaders, "Flannery O'Connor: 'Literary Witch,'" *Colorado Quarterly,* 10, no. 4 (Spring 1962): 380.

210 "an old dame": FOC to Sally and Robert Fitzgerald, [n.d.] "Wednesday," *CW,* 896.

211 "I have been told": Mary Barbara Tate, "Flannery O'Connor at Home in Milledgeville," *Studies in Literary Imagination* 20, no. 2 (1987): 34.

211 "When I was through": Robert Lowell to Flannery O'Connor," [n.d., late May or early June 1952], *Letters,* 187.

211 "now goes about enraging": Ibid., December 1953, Iowa City, *Letters,* 203.

211 "a Protestant saint": FOC to Carl Hartman, March 2, 1954, *CW,* 919.

211 "I think she left": Andrew Lytle to Thomas H. Carter, June 24, 1952, Thomas Carter Papers, University Library, Washington and Lee University, Lexington, Va.

212 "I still can't read Flannel Mouth": Robert Lowell to FOC, March 24, [1954], *Letters,* 226.

212 "Thank you for sending": Quoted in Elie, *The Life You Save,* 501.

212 "Evalin Wow": FOC to Robert and Sally Fitzgerald, [n.d.] "Wednesday," *CW,* 897.

212 "Does he suppose": FOC to Robert Lowell, May 2, 1952, *CW,* 896.

212 "writes of an insane": Isaac Rosenfeld, "To Win by Default," *New Republic,* 127 no. 1 (July 7, 1952): 19–20.

212 "in a pallid light": FOC to Robert Fitzgerald, [n.d.] "Tuesday," *CW,* 899.

213 "But Rosenfeld": Robert Fitzgerald, "Introduction," *Everything That Rises,* xviii.

213 "looking ravaged": Ibid., xix.

213 "climbed in the car": FOC to Caroline Gordon, September 10, 1952, *CW,* 900.

214 "after being helpful": Robert Fitzgerald, "Introduction," *Everything That Rises,* xix.

214 "allergic": FOC to Robert Fitzgerald, [n.d.] "Tuesday," *CW,* 899.

214 "slum child": Robert Fitzgerald, "Introduction," *Everything That Rises,* xix.

214 "had to stay": FOC to Robert Fitzgerald, [n.d.] "Tuesday," *CW,* 898.

214 "pure Georgia rhetoric": Robert Fitzgerald, "Introduction," *Everything That Rises,* xix.

215 "Flannery, you don't have": The account is taken from Christopher O'Hare's interview with Sally Fitzgerald.

216 "You always overdo!" Rosemary Magee and Emily Wright, "The Good Guide: A Final Conversation with Sally Fitzgerald," *Flannery O'Connor Review* 3 (2005): 22.

216 "She was a very nice-looking": FOC to Sally Fitzgerald, [n.d.] "Tuesday," July 1952, *HB,* 38.

216 "It was a great boon": FOC to Robert Fitzgerald, [n.d.] "Tuesday," *CW,* 899.

217 "a kind of Guggenheim": FOC to Sally Fitzgerald, [n.d.], Summer 1952, *HB,* 40.

217 "I know now that it is": FOC to Robert Fitzgerald, [n.d.] "Tuesday," *CW,* 899.

217 "over the phone": FOC to Sally Fitzgerald, [n.d.] Summer 1952, *HB,* 40.

218 "a gret place": FOC to Sally and Robert Fitzgerald, [n.d., Summer 1952], "Sunday," *HB,* 40.

218 "I'm going to order": FOC, "The King of the Birds," *CW,* 833.

219 "my one-cylander": FOC to John Hawkes, July 27, 1958, *CW,* 1075: "I braved the Faulkner, without tragic results. Probably the real reason I don't read him is because he makes me feel that with my one-cylander syntax I should quit writing and raise chickens altogether."

220 "Someone said you had something": Robert Lowell to Flannery O'Connor, [n.d.] December 1953, *Letters,* 203.

220 "I did have one in *Harper's*": FOC to Robert Lowell, January 1, [1954], *HB,* 65.

220 Shiftlet: "Harry Shiftlet Now with Airborne Artillery Battalion," *Union-Recorder,* May 12, 1955.

220 "a triumph": Robert Fitzgerald, "Introduction," *Everything That Rises,* xx.

221 *Kenyon Review* fiction fellowship: The *Kenyon Review* Fellowship in Fiction was funded by the Rockefeller Foundation. The two other 1953 fellows were Irving Howe, in Criticism; and Edwin Watkins, in poetry.

221 "The Life You Save May Be Your Own": The story was published in *Kenyon Review* 15, Spring 1953; reprinted in *Prize Stories 1954: The O. Henry Awards,* edited by Paul Engle and Hansford Martin; and as the third story in *A Good Man Is Hard to Find.*

CHAPTER SEVEN: THE "BIBLE" SALESMAN

222 "Like all good farm folk": FOC to Louise and Tom Gossett, April 10, 1961, *HB,* 438.

222 "routine is a condition": FOC to Betty Hester, February 10, 1962, *HB,* 465.

222 "14th century man": Thomas Merton, *The Journals of Thomas Merton: Volume Four, 1960–1963,* edited by Victor A. Kramer (San Francisco: Harper, 1997): "March 11 1961" entry, 98.

223 "hermit novelist": FOC to Maryat Lee, June 28, 1957, *CW,* 1036.

223 *A Short Breviary:* O'Connor picked up from the Fitzgeralds the practice of reading from this collection of daily hymns, offices, and prayers for the canonical hours, used especially by monks, nuns, and priests.

223 "Flannery sat in the *fifth*": Elizabeth Horne, quoted in George A. Kilcourse, Jr., *Flannery O'Connor's Religious Imagination* (New York: Paulist Press, 2001), 2.

223 "I like to go": FOC to Brainard Cheney, November 29, 1953, *CC,* 10.

223 "Nobody lays a hand": FOC to Betty Hester, August 3, 1963, *HB,* 533.

223 "She didn't want to come back": Christopher O'Hare interview with Margaret Florencourt Mann.

223 "My round uncle": FOC to William Sessions, September 1, 1955, *HB,* 240.

224 "Get that scoundrel": FOC, "The King of the Birds," *CW,* 840.

224 "That was our weekend": Mary Jo Thompson, in discussion with the author, May 25, 2004.

224 "the colored milker": FOC to Brainard and Frances Neel Cheney, December 10, 1957, *CC,* 63.

224 "blundering around": FOC to Thomas Stritch, January 22, 1964, *CW,* 1196.

224–225 "around here": FOC to Betty Hester, January 11, 1958, *CW,* 1059.

225 "Wormless they did not": FOC to Mrs. Rumsey Haynes, July 18, 1956, GSCU.

225 "set time": FOC to Cecil Dawkins, September 22, 1957, *CW,* 1043.

225 "But I may tear it": Betsy Lochridge, "An Afternoon with Flannery O'Connor," *Atlanta Journal and Constitution Magazine* (November 1, 1959): 40.

225 "I have a large ugly": FOC to Betty Hester, June 1, 1956, *HB,* 161.

225 "rat's nest": Ibid., October 12, 1955, *HB,* 109.

225 "You Can't Be Any Poorer Than Dead" was published in *New World Writing* 8, October 1955, and revised and rewritten as the opening chapter of *The Violent Bear It Away.* Its original title, when first submitted to *NWW,* was "When the Plague Beckons."

226 "The River" was published in *Sewanee Review* 61, Summer 1953, and as the second story in *A Good Man Is Hard to Find.*

226 "Evy eye": FOC to Sally and Robert Fitzgerald, [n.d.] "Thursday," *CW,* 904.

226 "A Good Man Is Hard to Find" was published in *The Avon Book of Modern Writing I,* edited by William Phillips and Philip Rahv, 1953, including stories by

Colette, Diana Trilling, Irving Howe, Isaac Rosenfeld; reprinted in 1960 in *The House of Fiction,* edited by Caroline Gordon and Allen Tate; and was the opening story in the collection of the same title.

226 "The Misfit": "'The Misfit' Robs Office, Escapes with $150," *Atlanta Constitution* (November 6, 1952): 29.

226 Bessie Smith's: Sally Fitzgerald, "Happy Endings," *Image: A Journal of the Arts and Religion* 16 (Summer 1977): 77.

226 "It was no coincidence": Christopher O'Hare interview with Sally Fitzgerald.

227 "Catie would read": Robert Giroux, in discussion with the author, November 13, 2003.

227 "I remember one day": Christopher O'Hare interview with Robert Giroux.

227 "Both the baptizing": Robert Lowell to FOC, [n.d.] December 1953, *Letters,* 203.

227 "a fresh mind": FOC to Cecil Dawkins, September 22, 1957, *CW,* 1043.

227 "receiving on the front": FOC to Maryat Lee, [n.d.] "Thursday," *HB,* 447.

227 "I work in the mornings": FOC to Louise Abbot, February 27, 1957, *HB,* 205.

227 "One of the few signs": Christopher O'Hare interview with Louise Abbot.

227–228 "None of my paintings": FOC to Sally and Robert Fitzgerald, [n.d.] "Friday," *CW,* 912.

228 "Never saw such long": FOC, "The King of the Birds," *CW,* 837.

228 "I go to bed at nine": FOC to Betty Hester, August 9, 1957, *CW,* 1042.

228 "I read it for about twenty": Ibid., August 9, 1955, *CW,* 945.

228 "I read a lot of theology": FOC to Cudden Ward, March 29, 1964, UNC.

229 "I can with one eye": FOC to Elizabeth Hardwick and Robert Lowell, March 17, 1953, *CW,* 910.

229 "I stayed away": FOC to Cecil Dawkins, July 16, 1957, *CW,* 1037.

229 "a Dane": Ann Waldron, *Close Connections: Caroline Gordon and the Southern Renaissance* (New York: G. P. Putnam's Sons, 1987): 350.

229 "After checking out": Helen I. Greene, "My Flannery O'Connor," *Flannery O'Connor Bulletin* 19 (1990): 47.

229 "She was sure that Flannery": Christopher O'Hare interview with Erik Langkjaer.

230 "He and Mary Flannery": Greene, "My Flannery O'Connor," 47.

231 "I never heard of *Conversations*": FOC to Sally and Robert Fitzgerald, May 7, 1953, *HB,* 58.

231 Danish-British accent: Some of the background details of the account are taken from a personal interview with Erik Langkjaer, on May 7, 2007, as well as several e-mail exchanges.

231 "that I had come to the U.S.": Christopher O'Hare interview with Erik Langkjaer.

232 "You wonder how anybody": FOC to Erik Langkjaer, April 1, 1955, private collection.

232 "practically bald-headed": FOC to Sally and Robert Fitzgerald, January 25, 1953, *CW,* 907.

232 "a little bloated": Christopher O'Hare interview with Erik Langkjaer.

232 "the saint everyone": Ibid.

233 "Was he ever handsome": Mary Jo Thompson, in discussion with the author, May 25, 2004.

233 "I used to go with her nephew": FOC to Betty Hester, August 28, 1955, *CW,* 949.

234 "the most melodramatic": FOC to Maryat Lee, October 14, 1959, *CW,* 1113.

234 "I remember there were cowbells": Pete Dexter, in discussion with the author, January 21, 2005.

234 "The Partridge Festival" was published in the *Critic* 19, March 1961.

235 "my mother still didn't": FOC to Cecil Dawkins, August 10, 1960, *HB,* 405.

235 "Quincy State Hospital": FOC to John Hawkes, June 22, 1961, *CW,* 1151.

235 "She liked to point it out": Erik Langkjaer, in discussion with the author, May 7, 2007.

235 "The Cheneys said": FOC to Sally and Robert Fitzgerald, May 7, 1953, *HB,* 58.

235 "theologically weighted symbolism": Brainard Cheney, review of *Wise Blood, Shenandoah* 3 (Autumn 1952): 57.

235 "eventful": FOC to Betty Boyd Love, October 18, 1951, *HB,* 29.

236 "Mrs. C.": FOC to Sally and Robert Fitzgerald, May 7, 1953, *HB,* 58.

236 "the petit cercle": Caroline Gordon to Sue Jenkins, [n.d., mid-January 1958], quoted in Ashley Brown, "An Unwritten Drama: Sue Jenkins Brown and Flannery O'Connor," *Southern Review* 22 (Autumn 1986): 729.

236 "Cleanth Brooks and others": Ashley Brown, "Flannery O'Connor: A Literary Memoir," *Realist of Distances,* 19.

237 "At that stage": Christopher O'Hare interview with Ashley Brown.

237 "I'm no Georgia Kafka": FOC to Ashley Brown, May 22, 1953, *CW,* 911.

237 "She was intelligent": Ashley Brown, in discussion with the author, April 30, 2007.

237 "Whatever do you want": Brown, "Flannery O'Connor," 23.

237 "I consider Caroline": Brainard Cheney to FOC, March 2, 1953, *CC,* 5.

237 "We just hit it off": Jean Cash, *Flannery O'Connor: A Life* (Knoxville: University of Tennessee Press, 2002), 212.

238 "She seems a very solid": Brainard Cheney to Robert Penn Warren, August 24, 1953, *CC,* 8.

238 "This seems to me her": Brown, "Flannery O'Connor," 22.

239 "I heard a lot of Tennessee": FOC to Robie Macauley, October 13, 1953, *CW,* 914.

239 "most agreeable": FOC to Sally and Robert Fitzgerald, [n.d.] August 1953, *HB,* 62.

239 "we liked to read": Cash, *Flannery O'Connor,* 212.

239 "I asked the steward": FOC to Sally and Robert Fitzgerald, [n.d.] August 1953, *HB,* 62.

239 "the D.P.": FOC to Brainard and Frances Cheney, June 8, 1954, *CC,* 17.

239 "They had what were called": Al Matysiak, in discussion with the author, July 27, 2004.

240 "The boys in white": "Sacred Heart School News," *Union-Recorder,* November 5, 1953.

240 "In the American and British": "DP's," *Life,* July 30, 1945, 13.

240 "subversives": *Permitting Admission of 400 Displaced Persons into the United States. Hearings Before Subcommittee on Immigration and Naturalization on the Judiciary. HR 2910,* 80th Congress, 1st sess., Washington, DC, 1947, 405–6.

240 "It is our Christian": Ibid., 190–91.

240 "Displaced Family": Polly Brennan, "Displaced Family Arrives on Farm from Poland," *Union-Recorder,* July 21, 1949.

241 "who has no teeth": FOC to Sally and Robert Fitzgerald, [n.d.,] "Thursday," *CW,* 894.

241 "Miss O'Connor could not believe": Al Matysiak, in discussion with the author, July 27, 2004.

241 "They need much less": Rudolf Heberle and Dudley S. Hall, *New Americans: A Study of Displaced Persons in Louisiana and Mississippi* (Baton Rouge: Displaced Persons Commission, 1951), 3–4.

241 "If I talked with her": Alfred Matysiak, in discussion with the author, July 27, 2004.

242 "We did speak about faith": Christopher O'Hare interview with Erik Langkjaer.

243 "long-legged": FOC, "The Displaced Person," *Sewanee Review* 62, no. 4 (October–December 1954): 634.

243 "perfectly round": Ibid., 637.

243 "The two colored people": FOC to Betty Hester, May 19, 1956, *HB,* 159.

243 "endlessly": Alice Walker, "Beyond the Peacock: The Reconstruction of Flannery O'Connor," *In Search of Our Mothers' Gardens* (New York: Harcourt, 1983), 42.

243 "Her mother was probably": Christopher O'Hare interview with Erik Langkjaer.

244 "I remember standing": Kitty Martin, in discussion with the author, January 30, 2005.

244 "What to Do": The information on the *March of Time* newsreels is taken from Leonard M. Olschner, "Annotations on History and Society in Flannery O'Connor's 'The Displaced Person,'" *Flannery O'Connor Bulletin* 16 (1987): 63–64.

244 "suspicion": FOC to Sally and Robert Fitzgerald, [n.d.] "Wednesday," *CW,* 895.

245 "following my nose": FOC to Cecil Dawkins, October 27, 1957, *CW,* 1046.

245 "O Raphael": FOC to Janet McKane, July 14, 1964, *HB,* 592.

245 "He leads you": FOC to Janet McKane, July 1, 1964, *CW,* 1214.

245 "The prayer had some imagery": FOC to Betty Hester, January 17, 1956, *CW,* 983–84.

245 "frightened by the grey": FOC, "The Displaced Person," 654.

245 "The Displaced Person" was published in *Sewanee Review* 62, October 1954, and was the final story in *A Good Man Is Hard to Find.*

246 "novella": FOC to Caroline Gordon, November 14, 1954, *CW,* 926.

246 "The Atlantic": FOC to Brainard and Frances Neel Cheney, April 11, 1954, *CC,* 15.

246 "self-portrait with a pheasant": FOC to Sally and Robert Fitzgerald, [n.d.] "Friday," *HB,* 61.

246 "He has horns": FOC to Janet McKane, June 19, 1963, *CW,* 1187.

246 "stunned": Louise Abbot, e-mail to author, June 11, 2007.

246 "I praised it": Christopher O'Hare interview with Erik Langkjaer.

247 "her kinsman": FOC to Betty Hester, June 15, 1957, *HB,* 226.

247 "She loved to talk about": Christopher O'Hare interview with Erik Langkjaer.

247 "rather careful in her movements": Christopher O'Hare interview with Ashley Brown.

247 "She was using a stick": Christopher O'Hare interview with Erik Langkjaer.

247 "I am doing very well": FOC to Caroline Gordon, November 14, 1954, *CW,* 926.

248 "A Circle in the Fire" was published in *Kenyon Review* 16, Spring 1954; was reprinted in *Prize Stories 1955: The O. Henry Awards,* edited by Paul Engle and Hansford Martin, and in *The Best American Short Stories 1955,* edited by Martha Foley; and was the seventh story in *A Good Man Is Hard to Find.*

248 "Baby Born": *Atlanta Journal,* November 14, 1952.

248 "He remarked that in these stories": FOC to Betty Hester, November 25, 1955, *CW,* 971–72.

249 "passion": Ibid., December 8, 1955, *CW,* 973.

249 "Baldwin Faces Forest": *Union-Recorder,* September 27, 1951.

249 "The reformatory": FOC to Maryat Lee, July 5, 1959, *HB,* 339.

249 18.23: *Statistical Abstract of the United States* 1952 (Washington, DC, U.S. Dept. of Commerce, 1953), 142.

249 "A Temple of the Holy Ghost" was published in *Harper's Bazaar* 88, May 1954; and was the fifth story in *A Good Man Is Hard to Find.*

249 "dislike intensely": FOC to Janet McKane, November 28, 1963, *CW,* 1195.

250 "I did read enough": Virginia Spencer Carr, *The Lonely Hunter* (Athens and London: University of Georgia Press, 2003): 433.

250 "a memorable addition": Carmel Snow, "The Editor's Guest Book," *Harper's Bazaar* 88 (May 1954): 54.

250 "The weekend I planned": FOC to Brainard and Frances Neel Cheney, June 8, 1954, *CC,* 16.

250 "certainly distressed": Ibid., May 20, 1954.

251 "barring mortal": FOC to Frances Neel Cheney, [n.d.] "1945, Sunday," *CC,* 17.

251 "We drove through the countryside": Christopher O'Hare interview with Erik Langkjaer.

252 "I haven't seen any dirt roads": FOC to Erik Langkjaer, June 13, 1954, private collection.

252 "Thank you": Ibid., July 18, 1954.

253 "researches into the ways": FOC to Sally and Robert Fitzgerald, December 20, 1952, *CW,* 905.

253 "Well you go": "An Interview with Flannery O'Connor and Robert Penn Warren: *Vagabond* / 23 April 1959," *Con,* 20–21.

253 "nigger statuary": FOC to Betty Hester, September 6, 1955, *CW,* 954.

253 "I hate to insult": Sally Fitzgerald, "Letters to the Editor," *Flannery O'Connor Bulletin* 23 (1994–95): 180.

253 "the redemptive quality": FOC to Ben Griffith, May 4, 1955, *CW,* 931.

253 "the story as a whole": Sally Fitzgerald, "Letters to the Editor," 181.

254 "Mr. Ransom took": FOC to Caroline Gordon, November 14, 1954, *CW,* 926.

254 "to gain some altitude": FOC to Ben Griffith, May 4, 1955, *CW,* 931.

254 "In those last two paragraphs": Ibid.

254 "my favorite and probably the best": FOC to Maryat Lee, March 10, 1957, *CW,* 1027.

254 "Without yr kind permission": FOC to Sally Fitzgerald, December 26, 1954, *CW,* 927.

254 "in about four days": FOC to Betty Hester, June 1, 1956, *HB,* 160.

254 "less conscious technical": FOC to Betty Hester, August 24, 1956, *CW,* 1000.

255 "Before I realized it": FOC, "Writing Short Stories," *MM,* 100.

255 "the Om. Nar.": Caroline Gordon to FOC, February 19, 1955, GCSU.

255 "It is without exception": Allen Tate to FOC, February 22, 1955, GCSU.

256 "lady Ph.D.": FOC, "Writing Short Stories," *MM,* 98.

256 "Write me an unintelligible": FOC to Erik Langkjaer, January 9, 1955, private collection.

256 "Do you think Erik": FOC to Erik Langkjaer, April 1, 1955, private collection.

257 "Yes, she did": Christopher O'Hare interview with Sally Fitzgerald.

257 "We are glad that you plan": FOC to Erik Langkjaer, May 3, 1955, *CW,* 936.

257 "Good Country People": The story was published in *Harper's Bazaar* in June 1955, and was included as the ninth story in *A Good Man Is Hard to Find.* The editor Robert Henderson at *The New Yorker* rejected "Good Country People" on April 6, 1955, claiming in a letter to Elizabeth McKee, "It's an interesting story with a great many good things in it, but I'm afraid we're not quite persuaded by the tour-de-force ending." *The New Yorker* (editor C. M Newman) had previously rejected an O'Connor story titled "Running," on February 28, 1952; "A Late Encounter with the Enemy" (editor Henderson) on April 30, 1952; and "The River" (editor Newman) on December 22, 1952.

257 "very hot story": FOC to Sally and Robert Fitzgerald, April 1, 1955, *HB,* 76.

257 "in some sort of disguise": Christopher O'Hare interview with Erik Langkjaer.

257 "Dear boy": FOC to Erik Langkjaer, April 29, 1956, private collection.

258 "bezerk": FOC to Erik Langkjaer, February 26, 1958, private collection.

258 "Eric": FOC to Roslyn Barnes, June 29, 1962, *HB,* 482.

258 "I just by the grace": FOC to Caroline Gordon and Allen Tate, March 1, 1955, GCSU.

258 "a wooden part": FOC, "Writing Short Stories," *MM,* 99; Sally Fitzgerald in an interview with Christopher O'Hare remarked that "I feel that it was a story about losing a kind of emotional woodenness that Flannery had developed, a protective woodenness."

CHAPTER EIGHT: FREAKS AND FOLKS

259 "I will be real glad": FOC to Robie Macauley, May 18, 1955, *CW,* 934.

260 "*Galley Proof* is an attempt": Harvey Breit, "Galley Proof: *A Good Man Is Hard to Find,*" in *Con,* 5–6.

260 "I don't know what she": FOC to Fred Darsey, May 25, 1955, Emory.

260 "Well I thought": Breit "Galley Proof," *Con,* 6.

260 "quietly": Harvey Breit, "In and Out of Books," *New York Times Book Review* (June 12, 1955): 8.

260 "I don't see much of it": Breit, "Galley Proof," 6.

260 "When you're a Southerner": Ibid., 8.

261 "very tired": FOC to Fred Darsey, June 8, 1955, Emory.

261 "nursemaid": Ibid., May 25, 1955.

261 "did all the work": FOC to Catharine Carver, April 2, 1955, *HB,* 76.

261 "The atmosphere at Harcourt Brace": FOC to Sally and Robert Fitzgerald, June 10, 1955, *CW,* 940.

262 "I like it fine": FOC to Catharine Carver, May 8, 1955, *HB,* 79.

262 "I think it will do justice": FOC to Robert Giroux, January 22, 1955, *HB,* 75.

262 "I had interviews": FOC to Sally and Robert Fitzgerald, June 10, 1955, *CW,* 940.

262 "melodramatic": Rebekah Poller, memoir, GCSU.

262 "I thought I could do": FOC to Elizabeth McKee, June 29, 1955, *HB,* 88.

263 "When you have a friend": FOC to Fred Darsey, April 11, 1955, Emory.

263 "I just love to sit": Ibid., May 25, 1955.

263 "There was a lot of his stuff": FOC to Betty Hester, March 29, 1956, *CW,* 990.

263 "Dear old Van Wyke": FOC to Sally and Robert Fitzgerald, June 10, 1955, *CW,* 940.

263 "It was interesting to see the guffaws": Caroline Gordon to Frances Cheney, [n.d.]. Quoted in Ann Waldron, *Close Connections: Caroline Gordon and the Southern Renaissance* (New York: G. P. Putnam's Sons, 1987), 322.

264 "a horror story": FOC to Sally and Robert Fitzgerald, June 10, 1955, *CW,* 940.

264 "alien to the American": Caroline Gordon to Andrew and Eleanor Lytle, June 15, 1955. Quoted in Waldron, *Close Connections,* 322.

264 "Malcolm was very polite": FOC to Sally and Robert Fitzgerald, June 10, 1955, *CW,* 940.

264 "about the best book": Caroline Gordon to Andrew and Eleanor Lytle, June 15, 1955. Quoted in Waldron, *Close Connections,* 321.

264 "She felt left out": Caroline Gordon to Allen Tate, St. Stephen's Day, 1955. Quoted in Waldron, *Close Connections,* 322.

264 "Dear Ferocious": FOC to Catharine Carver, June 9, 1955, GCSU.

264 "I think I am about as ferocious": FOC to Fred Darsey, June 8, 1955, Emory.

264 "I am fast getting a reputation": FOC to Erik Langkjaer, May 23, 1955, *CW,* 936.

265 "to a high rank": Orville Prescott, *New York Times,* June 10, 1955.

265 "the artful brevity": Caroline Gordon, "With a Glitter of Evil," *New York Times Book Review* (June 12, 1955): 5.

265 "there is brutality": *The New Yorker* (June 18, 1955): 93.

265 "Did you see the nice": FOC to Catharine Carver, June 27, 1955, *HB,* 88.

265 "was terrible, nearly gave me": FOC to Ben Griffith, July 9, 1955, *CW,* 941.

265 "highly unladylike": "Such Nice People," *Time* (June 6, 1955): 114.

266 "horrible pictures of me": FOC to Betty Hester, August 17, 1963, *HB,* 534.

266 "unusual reticence": Sylvia Stallings, *New York Herald Tribune Book Review* (June 5, 1955): 1.

266 "The effect, though 'glamorous'": Ashley Brown, *Realist of Distances,* 20.

266 "You should see Hazel Motes": FOC to Frances Cheney, September 7, 1955, *CC,* 22.

267 "from the American South": *Times Literary Supplement* (September 2, 1955): 505.

267 "This book is getting much": FOC to Sally and Robert Fitzgerald, June 10, 1955, *CW,* 940.

267 "Doesn't say much": FOC to Ben Griffith, June 9, 1955, *CW,* 941.

267 *Ten North Frederick:* The fiction judges for the 1956 National Book Award were Carlos Baker, John Brooks, Granville Hicks, Saunders Redding, and Mark Schorer.

267 "about God": Sally Fitzgerald, "Flannery O'Connor: Patterns of Friendship, Patterns of Love," *Georgia Review* 52, no. 3 (Fall 1998): 421.

267 "Dear Miss Hester": FOC to Betty Hester, July 20, 1955, *CW,* 942.

268 "Betty was very shy": William Sessions, "Screening and Discussion of Film Interview with Flannery O'Connor: *Galley Proof,*" Georgia College and State University, Milledgeville, March 30, 2006.

269 "my own work": FOC to Betty Hester, August 2, 1955, *CW,* 944.

269 "a generation of wingless": Ibid., July 20, 1955, *CW,* 942.

269 "disappointed look": FOC to Fred Darsey, June 8, 1955, Emory.

270 "I have thought of Simone Weil": FOC to Betty Hester, August 9, 1955, *CW,* 945.

270 "and what is more comic": Ibid., September 24, 1955, *CW,* 957–58.

270 "I have read almost 200": Ibid., August 21, 1955, *CW,* 947.

270 osteonecrosis: E-mail from Michael Lockshin, MD, to author, August 3, 2007.

270 "I am learning to walk": FOC to Betty Hester, September 24, 1955, *CW,* 956.

271 "It occurs to me": FOC to Betty Hester, October 12, 1955, *HB,* 109.

271 "Humpty Dumpty": FOC to Betty Hester, October 20, 1955, *CW,* 962.

272 "She was no beaut": Victor Judge, Vanderbilt Divinity School, e-mail message to the author, April 25, 2007.

272 "Cheap and nasty": Russell Kirk, "Memoir by Humpty Dumpty," *Flannery O'Connor Bulletin* 8 (1979): 14.

272 "quite horrified": Ibid, 16.

272 "I hope you won't let": Caroline Gordon to FOC, February 19, 1955, GCSU.

272 "Which is the way I feel": FOC to Robie Macauley, May 18, 1955, *CW,* 934.

272 "The Freak in Modern Fiction": FOC to Betty Hester, August 9, 1955, *CW,* 946.

272 "I get so sick of my novel": FOC to Brainard and Frances Neel Cheney, February 18, 1956, *CC,* 32.

273 "Miss Regina always": Alfred Matysiak, in discussion with the author, July 27, 2004.

273 "Greenleaf": The story was published in *Kenyon Review* 18 (Summer 1956); reprinted as the first-prize story in *Prize Stories 1957: The O. Henry Awards,* edited by Paul Engle and Constance Urdang; in *First-Prize Stories, 1919–1957,* edited by Harry Hansen; in *The Best American Short Stories 1957,* edited by Martha Foley; and in *First-Prize Stories, 1919–1963,* edited by Harry Hansen. It is the second story in *Everything That Rises Must Converge.*

273 "Stories of Gifted Writer": Ben Griffith, Jr., *Savannah Morning News,* June 5, 1955.

273 "brought out a lot of points": FOC to Ben Griffith, June 8, 1955, *CW,* 937.

273 "that was always getting out": FOC to Frances Neel Cheney, July 26, 1956, *CC,* 40.

273 "I'm never prepared": FOC to Betty Hester, January 17, 1956, *CW,* 982.

274 "to stuff the Church": FOC to Betty Hester, June 30, 1956, *HB,* 134.

274 "flying buttresses": Ibid., March 24, 1956, *HB,* 151.

274 "intellectual vaudeville": FOC to Sally and Robert Fitzgerald, May 8, 1955, *CW,* 933.

274 "There she was, so young": Alta Lee Haynes, "Flannery O'Connor Remembered, March 4, 1966," GCSU.

275 "perverse": "Modern Fiction Aspects Told by Novelist Flannery O'Connor," *State Journal* (Lansing, Mich.), April 25, 1956.

275 "I am highly pleased": FOC to Betty Hester, May 5, 1956, *CW,* 994.

275 "mortification": FOC to Betty Hester, February 25, 1956, *HB,* 140.

275 "I have just had the doubtful": FOC to John Lynch, February 19, 1956, *HB,* 138.

276 "The competition is at least": FOC to Betty Hester, May 19, 1956, Emory.

276 "When forced to a program": Ibid., February 25, 1956.

276 "without pause, break, breath": Ibid., May 19, 1956.

276 "I was basically treated as": William Sessions, GCSU, March 30, 2006.

277 "conversation is limited": FOC to Betty Hester, June 16, 1956, Emory.

277 "I always take people": FOC to Betty Hester, June 28, 1956, *CW,* 997.

278 "I seem to attract": FOC to Robie Macauley, May 18, 1955, *CW,* 935.

278 "Some Very Peculiar Types": FOC to Sally and Robert Fitzgerald, May 8, 1955, *CW,* 933.

278 "Mary Flannery is a sweet": James H. McCown, "Remembering Flannery O'Connor," *America* (September 8, 1979): 86.

278 "a white Packard": FOC to Sally and Robert Fitzgerald, January 22, 1956, *HB,* 133.

278 "Proud you did": McCown, "Remembering Flannery O'Connor," 86.

279 "turkey-dog": FOC to Betty Hester, February 11, 1956, *CW,* 986.

279 "of the scope and seriousness": McCown, "Remembering Flannery O'Connor," 88.

279 "Never let it be said": FOC to Erik Langkjaer, April 29, 1956, private collection.

279 "a great mother-saver": FOC to Betty Hester, August 11, 1956, *HB,* 169.

279 "very oriented towards making": Rosa Lee Walston, quoted in Jean Cash, *Flannery O'Connor: A Life* (Knoxville: University of Tennessee Press, 2002), 161.

280 "A View of the Woods": The story was published in *Partisan Review* 24 (Fall 1957), reprinted in *Prize Stories 1959: The O. Henry Awards,* edited by Paul Engle and Constance Urdang, and in *The Best American Short Stories 1958,* edited by Martha Foley. It is the third story in *Everything That Rises Must Converge.*

280 "breathless": FOC to Betty Hester, October 20, 1956, Emory.

280–281 "While they make hash": FOC to Betty Hester, September 8, 1956, *CW,* 1004.

281 "history of horror": FOC to Betty Hester, October 31, 1956, Emory.

281 "men and men's ideas": Bo Emerson, "The Secret Life of Betty Hester," *Atlanta Journal-Constitution,* March 28, 1999.

281 "confirmed": Allan Berube, *Coming Out Under Fire: The History of Gay Men and Women in World War Two* (New York: Free Press, 1990), 263.

281 "unbearably guilty": FOC to Betty Hester, October 31, 1956, Emory.

281 "I can't write you fast enough": Ibid.

282 "I wish you could come": FOC to Betty Hester, November 18, 1956, *CW,* 1007.

282 "Simone Weil but even more": Ibid., December 28, 1956, *CW,* 1017.

282 "in some odd ways": Betty Hester to Greg Johnson, November 20, 1996, private collection.

283 "Strike the Tent!": "GSCW President Is Speaker for R. E. Lee Program," *Union-Recorder,* January 24, 1957.

283 "The people who burned the cross": FOC to Maryat Lee, January 9, 1957, *CW,* 1019.

283 "the institution of higher": FOC to Betty Boyd Love, [n.d., postmarked September 20, 1952], *HB,* 44.

284 "Maryat was the ultimate bohemian": Mary Dean Lee, in discussion with the author, January 18, 2005.

285 "I remember that I was feeling": Maryat Lee, "Flannery, 1957," *Flannery O'Connor Bulletin* 5 (1976): 39.

285 "My, aren't you *smaht*": Maryat Lee, unpublished memoir, private collection.

285 "Just as I opened": Lee, "Flannery, 1957," 40.

285 "the soft long swinging": Lee, unpublished memoir, private collection.

285 "She was so awkward": Ibid.

286 "the croupy cry": Lee, "Flannery, 1957," 41.

286 "The parental presence": FOC to Maryat Lee, January 9, 1957, *CW,* 1020.

286 "Her words had theological": Lee, "Flannery, 1957," 43.

286 "I was excited": Ibid., 44.

286 "In Care of the Henhouse": Georgia A. Newman, "A 'Contrary Kinship': The Correspondence of Flannery O'Connor and Maryat Lee — Early Years, 1957–1959 (PhD dissertation, University of South Florida, 1999), 35; Lee never sent the letter so addressed.

287 "kinship between us": FOC to Maryat Lee, May 24, 1960, *HB,* 398.

287 "I thought now this is a mighty": Ibid., January 31, 1957, *HB,* 200.

287 "on and off": FOC to Maryat Lee, February 24, 1957, *CW,* 1022.

287 "the reek of Baldwin County": FOC, unpublished version of "The Fiction Writer and His Country," delivered at GSCW, "FOC Collection," GCSU; included in file of correspondence with Mrs. Rebekah Poller, daughter of the GSCW social science professor Herbert Massey; Poller attended the lecture, and recommended the talk to her friend Granville Hicks.

287 "a real morality play": FOC to Maryat Lee, January 31, 1957, *HB*, 200.

287 "If the writer is successful": FOC, unpublished version of "The Fiction Writer and His Country," GCSU.

288 "by Ronald Regan": FOC to Betty Hester, September 8, 1956, *CW*, 1004.

288 "a *tap-dancer*": FOC to Sally and Robert Fitzgerald, December 10, 1956, *CW*, 1009.

288 "disliking it heartily": FOC to Denver Lindley, March 6, 1957, *HB*, 206.

288 "Children now point": FOC to Maryat Lee, March 10, 1957, *CW*, 1027.

288 "better judgment": FOC to Granville Hicks, March 3, 1957, *HB*, 205.

288 "I begin to feel": Ibid., 206.

288 "designed for a student audience": Ibid., February 24, 1957, *HB*, 202.

288 "Cathlick": FOC to Brainard and Frances Neel Cheney, March 5, 1957, *CC*, 52.

288–289 "She seemed frail": Robert Fitzgerald, "Introduction," *Everything That Rises Must Converge,* xxiii.

289 "inordinate affection": FOC to Betty Hester, May 5, 1962, *CW*, 1162.

289 "had wonderful things to say": Robert Fitzgerald, "Introduction," *Everything That Rises,* xxiii.

289 "25% Bumbling Boys": FOC to Maryat Lee, April 17, 1957, *HB*, 215.

289 "intent upon it": Robert Fitzgerald, "Introduction," *Everything That Rises,* xxiii.

289 "unhappy combinations": FOC, "The Fiction Writer and His Country," *CW*, 802.

289 "To the hard of hearing": Ibid., 806.

289 "score": Robert Fitzgerald, "Introduction," *Everything That Rises,* xxiii.

290 "Quite soon": Elizabeth Bishop, "Flannery O'Connor, 1925–1964," *New York Review of Books* 3, no. 4 (October 8, 1964): 21.

290 "I sat down with a six pack": Cash, *Flannery O'Connor,* 240.

290 "I tried reading them aloud": Louise H. Abbot, "Remembering Flannery," *Flannery O'Connor Bulletin* 23 (1994–95): 61.

290 "I am very glad": FOC to Louise Abbot, February 27, 1957, *HB*, 205.

291 "we would have a few beers": Louise Abbot to Maryat Lee, January 19, 1977, private collection.

291 "very expressive": Abbot, "Remembering Flannery," 63.

291 "*You* stay here": Ibid., 65.

291 "famous writer": Ibid., 63.

292 "where your treasure": Ibid., 65.

292 "What in the wurld-d": Ibid., 66.

292 "The following is good": FOC to Maryat Lee, March 10, 1957, *CW*, 1027.

293 "intense manner": Donald Richie, letter to the author, October 15, 2007.

293 "bisexual": Robert E. Lee, in discussion with the author, May 2, 2004; Fran Belin, in discussion with the author, November 12, 2004.

293 "Oh Flannery": Maryat Lee to FOC [n.d., late May 1957], copies in FOC Collection, GCSU.

293 "Everything has to be diluted": FOC to Maryat Lee, June 9, 1957, *HB*, 225.

293 "I am not to be got rid of": FOC to Maryat Lee, October 8, 1957, *CW*, 1045.

293 "The Enduring Chill": The story was published in *Harper's Bazaar* 91, July 1958, and was the fourth story in *Everything That Rises Must Converge.*

294 "a closet with a toilet": FOC, "The Enduring Chill," *CW,* 552.

294 "a play about Negroes": Ibid., 551.

294 "suffered my remarks": Lee, "Flannery, 1957," 43.

294 "the orthodoxy": FOC to Maryat Lee, January 9, 1957, *CW,* 1020.

294 "But — the last paragraph": Maryat Lee to FOC, July 9, 1958, GCSU.

294 "reminds me of my character": FOC to Maryat Lee, May 6, 1959, *HB,* 331.

294 "Wishing for an icicle": Maryat Lee to FOC, August 22, 1958, GCSU.

294 "the pseudo-literary&theological": FOC to Betty Hester, March 7, 1958, *HB,* 271.

295 "theology in modern literature": FOC to Father James H. McCown, December 29, 1957, *CW,* 1057.

295 "She really bore down": Jean Cash, "Milledgeville 1957–1960: O'Connor's 'Pseudo-Literary & Theological Gatherings," *Flannery O'Connor Bulletin* 18 (1989): 25.

295 "not particularly scintillating": Cash, "Milledgeville 1957–1960," 20–21.

295 "Maryat read us a play": Mary Barbara Tate, in discussion with the author, June 3, 2004.

295 "was doing anything": Ted R. Spivey, *Flannery O'Connor: The Woman, the Thinker, the Visionary* (Macon, Ga.: Mercer University Press, 1955), 84.

295 "to show his little boy": FOC to John Hawkes, July 27, 1958, *CW,* 1075.

296 "My father tempted me": Christopher Dickey, e-mail to the author, January 17, 2005.

296 "a black halter": FOC to Cecil Dawkins, April 14, 1958, *CW,* 1069.

296 "plowed all over the yard": Ibid., 1068.

296 "gracious": Katherine Anne Porter, "Gracious Greatness," *Esprit: Journal of Thought and Opinion* 8, no. 1 (University of Scranton, Scranton, Pa., Winter 1964): 50.

CHAPTER NINE: EVERYTHING THAT RISES

297 "holy exhaustion": FOC to Sally and Robert Fitzgerald, November 4, 1957, *CW,* 1048.

297 "will of iron": Ibid., February 26, 1958, *CW,* 1064.

298 "I bet that'll be real": Ibid., November 4, 1957, *CW,* 1048.

298 "7 into 17": FOC to Betty Hester, December 14, 1957, *CW,* 1056.

298 "Baloney Castle": FOC to Ashley Brown, April 14, 1958, *HB,* 277.

298 "Left for two minutes": FOC to Sally and Robert Fitzgerald, February 26, 1958, *CW,* 1064.

298 "where we were going": FOC to Betty Hester, April 4, 1958, *CW,* 1067.

298 "my cousin is certainly": FOC to Sally and Robert Fitzgerald, November 4, 1957, *CW,* 1048.

299 "Last Will": "Last Will and Testament of Mary Flannery O'Connor," April 18, 1958, GCSU.

299 "She is reading the Lourds": FOC to Betty Hester, November 16, 1957, *CW,* 1049–50.

299 "like Mr. Head and Nelson": FOC to Maryat Lee, November 10, 1957, GCSU.

299 "I am properly back": FOC to Robert Giroux, April 17, 1958, *HB,* 278.

300 "our new important": Roger Straus to Silvio Senigallia, April 22, 1958, FSG.

300 On spring days: The description of the Fitzgerald villa is taken from W. A. Sessions, "Sally Fitzgerald 1916–2000: The Gratitude Is Ours," *Cheers!* 8, no. 1 (Spring/Summer 2000).

300 "wonderful": FOC to Ashley Brown, May 26, 1958, *CW,* 1072.

300–301 "Instead of seeing": Ibid.

301 "almost unreadable": Gabrielle Rolin, letter to author, September 26, 2007.

301 "She said to me": Sally Fitzgerald, "The Invisible Father," *Christianity and Litera-ture* 47, no. 1 (Autumn 1997): 7.

302 "clip-joint": FOC to William Sessions, May 15, 1958, *CW,* 1071.

302 "Aquéro": Ruth Harris, *Lourdes: Body and Spirit in the Secular Age* (New York: Viking, 1999), 5.

302 "a hemorrhage of bad taste": Ibid., 173.

302 "the religious goods stores": FOC to Ashley Brown, May 26, 1958, *CW,* 1072.

302 "nowhere have I seen": Harris, *Lourdes,* 339.

302 "heart that never stops": *The Official Guide of the Sanctuary,* Sanctuaires Notre-Dame de Lourdes, 18.

302 "The heavy hand of the prelate": FOC to Ashley Brown, May 26, 1958, *CW,* 1072.

303 "The sight of Faith": Katherine Anne Porter, "Gracious Greatness," *Esprit* 8, no. 1 (University of Scranton, Scranton, Pa., Winter 1964): 56.

303 "I joined them for lunch": W. A. Sessions, "Sally Fitzgerald 1916–2000," 4.

304 as "a pilgrim": FOC to Betty Hester, December 14, 1957, *CW,* 1056.

304 "hyper-thyroid": FOC to Betty Hester, May 17, 1958, *HB,* 282.

304 *les piscines:* The seventeen marble baths and stone portico were built in 1955.

304 "At least there are no societal": FOC to Elizabeth Bishop, June 1, 1958, *CW,* 1073.

304 "Nobody I am sure": FOC to Betty Hester, May 17, 1958, *HB,* 282.

305 "After lunch we left Barcelona": "Diary of Eleanor and Marie Bennett," Archives, Diocese of Savannah.

305 "There is a wonderful radiance": FOC to Betty Hester, "Monday" [May 5, 1958], *HB,* 280.

306 "Shrines to the Virgin": FOC to Sally and Robert Fitzgerald, May 11, 1958, *CW,* 1069.

306 "4 old ladies": FOC to Betty Hester, April 19, 1958, *HB,* 280.

306 "write up": FOC to Sally and Robert Fitzgerald, February 26, 1958, *CW,* 1064.

306 "revived as soon as": Ibid., May 11, 1958, *CW,* 1069.

306 "The Freak in Modern Fiction": A draft of the lecture intended for May 1958 is kept in the "FOC Collection," GCSU, along with a draft of the variant lecture she gave on "The Freak in Southern Fiction" at Birmingham-Southern College on November 25, 1958.

306 "My capacity for staying home": FOC to Ashley Brown, May 16, 1958, *CW,* 1071.

306 "Ah, seeing the Pope": FOC to Brainard and Frances Neel Cheney, December 2, 1958, *CC,* 81.

306 "experience is the greatest": FOC to Maryat Lee, May 20, 1958, *HB,* 284.

307 "a beautiful child": Sally Fitzgerald, "Chronology," *CW,* 1251.

307 "I prayed there for the novel": FOC to Janet McKane, February 25, 1963, *CW,* 1179.

307 "much better contract": FOC to Betty Hester, April 19, 1958, *HB,* 280.

307 "The little vacation": FOC to Cecil Dawkins, May 22, 1958, *HB,* 284.

307 "Unfortunately not any 50": FOC to Betty Hester, June 14, 1958, *HB,* 288.

308 "You have to push": Ibid., July 12, 1957, *HB,* 229.

308 "Love is a struggle": *Flannery O'Connor's Library: Resources of Being,* edited by Arthur F. Kinney (Athens: University of Georgia Press, 1985), 19.

308 "I am the dense kind": Maryat Lee to FOC, February 20, 1959, GCSU.

308 "colors": FOC to Maryat Lee, March 15, 1959, GCSU.

308 "We don't have that one": FOC to John Hawkes, November 28, 1961, *CW,* 1157.

308 "I keep clear of Faulkner": FOC to Betty Hester, March 20, 1958, *HB,* 273.

308 *"That's* good stuff": Sally Fitzgerald, "Flannery O'Connor: Patterns of Friendship, Patterns of Love," *Georgia Review* 52, no. 3 (Fall 1998): 419.

309 "one-and-a-half": Louise H. Abbot, "Remembering Flannery," *Flannery O'Connor Bulletin* 23 (1994–95), 77.

309 "with yellow hair": FOC to Sally and Robert Fitzgerald, April 20, 1959, *HB,* 329.

309 "Tarwater's final vision": FOC, "On Her Own Work," *MM,* 117.

310 "stumbling block": FOC to John Hawkes, October 6, 1959, *CW,* 1109.

310 "gotten right": Richard Gilman, "On Flannery O'Connor," *New York Review of Books* 13, no. 3 (August 21, 1969): 26.

310 "RUIN MY EYES": FOC to Sally and Robert Fitzgerald, [n.d., "Saturday," 1951], *CW,* 892.

310 "thousands of little kids": J. D. Salinger, *The Catcher in the Rye* (New York: Little, Brown, 1951), 173.

310 "can drive me nuts": FOC to Betty Hester, April 4, 1958, *CW,* 1066.

311 "Younglady": FOC to Rebekah Poller, June 27, 1958, *Flannery O'Connor Bulletin* 12 (1983): 70.

311 "swan of old cars": Robert Lowell to FOC, [n.d., December 1953], *The Letters of Robert Lowell,* edited by Saskia Hamilton (New York: Farrar, Straus and Giroux, 2005), 203.

311 "hearse-like": FOC to Betty Hester, August 30, 1958, *HB,* 294.

311 "my Jung friend": Ibid., April 30, 1960, *HB,* 394.

311 "She certainly found him": Louise Abbot, in discussion with the author, June 2, 2004.

311 "When I knocked": Ted R. Spivey, *Flannery O'Connor: The Woman, the Thinker, the Visionary* (Macon, Ga.: Mercer University Press, 1955), 15.

312 "could sense certain deep": Ibid., 16.

312 "I have just finished": FOC to Dr. T. R. Spivey, September 9, 1958, *HB,* 294.

312 "Now on a first-name basis": Spivey, *Flannery O'Connor,* 24.

312 "dialogic": FOC to Dr. T. R. Spivey, November 16, 1958, *CW,* 1079.

313 "He has a very fine mind": FOC to Betty Hester, November 8, 1958, *CW,* 1078.

313 "I only have to bear": FOC to Sally and Robert Fitzgerald, January 1, 1959, *HB,* 315.

313 "I must say I attribute": FOC to Betty Hester, January 3, 1959, *CW,* 1088.

313 "had her say": FOC to Betty Hester, January 31, 1959, *HB,* 317.

313 "persuadeth me": FOC to Brainard Cheney, [n.d., "Friday," February 1959], *CC,* 82.

313 "Miss Mary": FOC to Betty Hester, February 15, 1959, Emory.

313 "I met her at two a.m.": Richard Stern, "Flannery O'Connor: A Remembrance and Some Letters," *Shenandoah* 16, no. 2 (Winter 1965): 6.

314 "confer with the young ladies": FOC to Cecil Dawkins, January 14, 1959, *HB,* 316.

314 "Miss O'Connor, what are": FOC to Elizabeth Bishop, April 9, 1959, *CW,* 1093.

314 "Do they think": Stern, "Flannery O'Connor," 6.

314 "all bad but two": FOC to Louise Abbot, March 30, 1959, *CW,* 1091.

314 "full of wry strength": Stern, "Flannery O'Connor," 6.

314 "I hope you are accustoming": FOC to Sally and Robert Fitzgerald, March 24, 1959, *CW,* 1090.

314 "The house is subject to termite": FOC to Thomas Stritch, March 28, 1959, *CW,* 1091.

314 "doodles, exclamation points": FOC to Betty Hester, February 28, 1959, *CW,* 1088.

315 "enthusiastic": FOC to Sally and Robert Fitzgerald, February 15, 1959, *HB,* 318.

315 "obscure": Brainard Cheney to FOC, [n.d., late July? 1959], *CC,* 91.

315 "too much a parody": FOC to Catharine Carver, April 18, 1959, *CW,* 1094.

315 "When the grim reaper": Ibid., March 27, 1959, *CW,* 1090.

315 "work on Tarwater": FOC to Betty Hester, May 16, 1959, *CW,* 1096.

315 "an elderly French gentleman": FOC to Maryat Lee, March 29, 1959, *HB,* 325.

315 *"monde tragicomique"*: Melvin J. Friedman, "Flannery O'Connor in France: An Interim Report," *Critical Essays on Flannery O'Connor,* edited by Melvin J. Friedman and Beverly Lyon Clark (Boston: G. K. Hall, 1985), 132.

315 "sort of uptight": Jean Cash, *Flannery O'Connor: A Life* (Knoxville: University of Tennessee Press, 2002), 280.

316 "Whoever invented": FOC to Maryat Lee, April 25, 1959, *CW,* 1095.

316 "I found her witty": Robert Penn Warren, *Esprit: Journal of Thought and Opinion* 8, no. 1 (University of Scranton, Scranton, Pa., Winter 1964): 49.

316 "all my famous authors": Robert Giroux, in discussion with the author, November 13, 2003.

316 "When I read Flannery": Thomas Merton, "Flannery O'Connor," *Jubilee* 12, no. 7 (November 1964): 52.

316 "The aura of aloneness": Robert Giroux, "Introduction," *The Complete Stories* (New York: Farrar, Straus and Giroux, 1971): xiii.

316 "The car was going": Christopher O'Hare interview with Robert Giroux.

317 "Her life is what you": Robert Lowell to Elizabeth Bishop, February 24, 1960, *Words in the Air: The Complete Correspondence Between Elizabeth Bishop and Robert Lowell,* edited by Thomas Traviso with Saskia Hamilton (New York: Farrar, Straus and Giroux, 2008), 312. In this letter, Lowell expresses disappointment that their nomination of O'Connor for membership in the American Academy of Arts and Letters was unsuccessful that year. Among those admitted were Richard Eberhart, Harry Levin, and Willem de Kooning.

317 "I sit all day": FOC to Maryat Lee, July 5, 1959, *HB,* 339.

317 "Does it have symbolisms": FOC to Betty Hester, July 25, 1959, *CW,* 1101–102.

318 "the best thing I've read": FOC to Caroline Gordon, May 10, 1959, *HB,* 332.

318 "I was not ABOUT": FOC to Betty Hester, October 31, 1959, Emory.

318 "this is the best stage": FOC to Maryat Lee, July 5, 1959, *HB,* 339.

318 "The Comforts of Home": The story was published in *Kenyon Review* 22, Fall 1960, and was the fifth story in *Everything That Rises Must Converge.*

318–319 "It would be fashionable": FOC to Betty Hester, August 9, 1955, *CW,* 946.

319 "I was pretty disappointed": FOC to Robie Macauley, January 2, 1961, GCSU.

319 "unaware of the strangely sexual": Betty Hester to Greg Johnson, November 20 [1996], private collection.

319 "revulsion at the frankly sexual": Spivey, *Flannery O'Connor,* 31.

319 "pious slop": FOC to Betty Hester, April 30, 1960, *HB,* 394.

319 "Mr. Truman Capote": FOC to Betty Hester, December 8, 1955, *CW,* 973.

319 "As for lesbianism": FOC to Beverly Brunson, September 13, 1954, *CW,* 925.

320 "The School of Southern Degeneracy": FOC to Betty Hester, December 19, 1959, *HB,* 363.

320 "literary white witch": Orville Prescott, *New York Times* (February 24, 1960).

320 "strong medicine": Donald Davidson, "A Prophet Went Forth," *New York Times Book Review* (February 28, 1960): 4.

320 "Southern Gothic": Granville Hicks, "Southern Gothic with a Vengeance," *Saturday Review* (February 27, 1960): 18.

320 "a retiring, bookish": "God-Intoxicated Hillbillies," *Time* (February 29, 1960): 118.

320 "having a dirty hand": FOC to Brainard Cheney, February 26, 1960, *CC,* 108.

320 "My lupus has no business": FOC to Maryat Lee, March 5, 1960, *HB,* 380.

320 "Perhaps I have created": FOC to Cecil Dawkins, February 28, 1960, *HB,* 377.

321 "hard intelligence": Joan Didion, *National Review* 8, no. 15 (April 9, 1960): 240.

321 "a young writer": *Vogue,* April 1, 1960.

321 "I received Flannery's new book": Elizabeth Bishop to Robert Lowell, February 15, 1960, *Words in the Air,* 309.

321 "I hadn't connected 'Bishop'": Robert Lowell to Elizabeth Bishop, February 24, 1960, ibid., 312.

321 "Yes, the Flannery book": Elizabeth Bishop to Robert Lowell, April 22, 1960, ibid., 315.

321 "wave of tenderness": Maryat Lee, unpublished memoir, private collection.

322 "omnivorous reader": Christopher O'Hare interview with Robert Giroux.

323 "My editor from Farrer": FOC to Dr. T. R. Spivey, May 25, 1959, *CW,* 1097.

323 "I said I met the Father": Christopher O'Hare interview with Robert Giroux.

323 "a new synthesis": FOC to Betty Hester, November 22, 1958, *CW,* 1082.

323–324 "Only crisis theologians": Ibid., November 8, 1958, *CW,* 1078.

324 "greatest of the Protestant": Ibid., 1082.

324 "churchy": FOC, review of *Letters from Baron Friedrich von Hügel to a Niece,* edited by Gwendolen Greene, *Bulletin,* June 23, 1956; *PG,* 21.

324 "total absence": FOC, review of *The Rosary of Our Lady,* by Romano Guardini, *Bulletin,* April 28, 1955; *PG,* 16.

324 "theology of creativity": FOC, review of *The Image Industries,* by William Lynch, S.J., *Bulletin,* August 8, 1959; *PG,* 75.

324 *Painting and Reality:* FOC, review of *Painting and Reality,* by Etienne Gilson, *Bulletin,* May 3, 1958; *PG,* 56–57.

324 "Tay-ahr": FOC, review of *The Phenomenon of Man,* by Pierre Teilhard de Chardin, *Bulletin,* February 20, 1960; *PG,* 86–88.

325 "lucky find": FOC to Betty Hester, December 25, 1959, *HB,* 367.

325 "giving a new face": FOC, review of *The Divine Milieu,* by Pierre Teilhard de Chardin, *Bulletin,* February 4, 1961; *PG,* 108.

325 "Pere Teilhard talks": FOC to Janet McKane, February 25, 1963, *CW,* 1179.

326 "great mystic": FOC to Betty Hester, February 4, 1961, *CW,* 1144.

326 "Jesuit mind": FOC to Dr. T. R. Spivey, November 30, 1959, *CW,* 1114.

326 "parallels between Jung": FOC to Dr. T. R. Spivey, March 16, 1960, *HB,* 383.

326 "his work is": Brainard Cheney to FOC, October 7, 1962, *CC,* 157.

326 *American Scholar:* "Outstanding Books, 1931–1961," *American Scholar* 30, no. 4 (Autumn 1961): 618.

326 "too straitjacket": Robert Giroux, in discussion with the author, November 13, 2003.

326 "I am here to bless": John Kobler, "The Priest Who Haunts the Catholic World," *Saturday Evening Post* 236 (October 12, 1963): 45.

326 "regrettable": Ibid.

326 "depressing at first": FOC to Roslyn Barnes, August 4, 1962, *CW,* 1171.

326 "canonized yet": FOC to Brainard Cheney, October 31, 1963, *CC,* 181.

326 "If they are good": FOC to Father James H. McCown, March 21, 1964, *CW,* 1204.

327 "Looka there": De Vene Harrold, unpublished memoir, 1, "FOC Collection," GCSU.

327 "He was finicky": A Conyers monk, in discussion with the author, August 8, 2004.

327 "giggler": FOC to Betty Hester, May 14, 1960, Emory.

328 "What interests me": FOC to Betty Hester, April 30, 1960, *HB,* 394.

328 "murder stories": FOC to Robert Giroux, September 29, 1960, *CW,* 1133.

328 "plainly grotesque": FOC, "Introduction to a Memoir of Mary Ann," *CW,* 824.

328 "Hawthorne said he didn't write": FOC to William Sessions, September 13, 1960, *CW,* 1131.

329 "Lately I have had a recurrent": FOC, "The King of the Birds," *CW,* 842.

329 "Some Thoughts on the Catholic Novelist": The talk was published as "The Role of the Catholic Novelist," *Greyfriar* 7 (1964): 9.

329 "met no duds": FOC to Betty Hester, October 27, 1960, *HB,* 414.

329 "I sound pretty much like": FOC to John Hawkes, October 9, 1960, *CW,* 1134.

330 "When Hawthorne said": FOC, "Some Aspects of the Grotesque in Southern Fiction," *CW,* 818.

330 "green with envy": Elizabeth Bishop to Robert Lowell, May 5, 1959, *Words in the Air,* 300.

330 "strenuous": FOC to Cecil Dawkins, November 8, 1960, *CW,* 1135.

330 "I helped Regina in the kitchen": De Vene Harrold, unpublished memoir, 3.

330 "I call that really having": FOC to Cecil Dawkins, November 8, 1960, *CW,* 1135.

330 "She and the Sisters": FOC, "A Memoir of Mary Ann," *CW,* 828.

331 *"Tout Ce Qui Monte Converge":* Giroux, "Introduction," *Collected Stories,* xv.

331 "story called 'Everything'": FOC to Roslyn Barnes, March 29, 1961, *HB,* 438.

332 "King Kong": FOC to Betty Hester, July 23, 1960, *CW,* 1130.

332 "the secularist-Baptist": FOC to Maryat Lee, September 23, 1960, GCSU.

332 "All the rich widows": FOC to Cecil Dawkins, November 8, 1960, *CW,* 1135.

332 Gossetts: Ralph C. Wood, *Flannery O'Connor and the Christ-Haunted South* (Grand Rapids, Mich.: William B. Eerdmans Publishing, 2004), 117.

332 Sessions has recalled a Thanksgiving: Ibid., 113.

333 "All my thoughts": FOC to Betty Hester, May 4, 1957, *HB,* 218.

333 "a young college instructor": John Howard Griffin, *Black Like Me* (New York: Signet Books, 1962), 134.

333 "If I had been one of them white": FOC to Maryat Lee, May 21, 1964, *CW,* 1208.

333 "not in blackface": FOC to Father James H. McCown, October 28, 1960, *HB,* 414.

334 "I would call Flannery": A Conyers monk, in discussion with the author, August 8, 2004.

334 "She never said anything racist": Leonard Mayhew, in discussion with the author, December 15, 2004.

334 "patronizing: he belonged": J. M. Coetzee, "The Making of William Faulkner," *New York Review of Books* 52, no. 6 (April 7, 2005): 22.

335 "No I can't see James Baldwin": FOC to Maryat Lee, April 25, 1959, *CW,* 1094–95.

335 "Cheers, Tarklux": FOC to Maryat Lee, August 17, 1962, GCSU.

335 "Tarconstructed": Ibid., October 31, 1963.

335 "colored": Maryat Lee to FOC, March 16, 1960, GCSU.

335 "her Easter hat": Ibid., April 24, 1960.

336 "I don't understand them": Katherine Fugin, Faye Rivard, and Margaret Sieh, "An Interview with Flannery O'Connor," *Con* (Fall 1960): 59.

336 "from the inner workings": Alice Walker, "Beyond the Peacock: The Reconstruction of Flannery O'Connor," *In Search of Our Mothers' Gardens* (New York: Harcourt), 52.

336 "The topical is poison": FOC to Betty Hester, September 1, 1963, *HB,* 537.

336 "Everything That Rises Must Converge": The story was published in *New World Writing* 19, edited by Theodore Solotaroff, 1961; reprinted in *The Best American Short Stories 1962,* edited by Martha Foley and David Burnett; as the first-prize story in *Prize Stories 1963: The O. Henry Awards,* edited by Richard Poirier; and in *First-Prize Stories, 1919–1963,* edited by Harry Hansen. It is the opening story in the collection *Everything That Rises Must Converge.*

337 "Tarfeather": FOC to Maryat Lee, August 22, 1960, GCSU.

337 "Raybutton": Ibid., March 24, 1960.

337 "I'm cheered you like": FOC to Maryat Lee, November 9, 1962, *HB,* 499.

337 "I feel very good": Wood, *Flannery O'Connor and the Christ-Haunted South,* 103.

337 "As long as he lived": FOC to Betty Hester, February 4, 1961, *CW,* 1143–44.

337 "a hundred readers now": FOC, "Catholic Novelists and Their Readers," *MM,* 187; O'Connor was agreeing with a similar statement made by Arthur Koestler.

337 "love to be efficacious": FOC to Betty Hester, August 28, 1955, *CW,* 948.

CHAPTER TEN: "REVELATION"

338 "chauffeur": FOC to Ashley Brown, July 5, 1961, Princeton.

338 "upstairs junk room": Ibid., July 10, 1961.

338 "We got along": Ashley Brown, in discussion with the author, April 30, 2007.

338 "Few people realized": Caroline Gordon to Robert Giroux, October 13, 1964, FSG.

339 "a nice gangster": FOC to Sally and Robert Fitzgerald, February 1, 1953, *CW,* 908.

339 "Bless you, darling!": FOC to Betty Hester, November 10, 1955, *CW,* 969.

339 "completely undramatic": FOC to Cecil Dawkins, July 17, 1961, *HB,* 445.

340 "I'm amused by the letter": FOC to Elizabeth McKee, September 28, 1960, *HB,* 408.

340 "She did think the structure": FOC to Betty Hester, July 22, 1961, *HB,* 446.

340 "Tomorrow I am orbiting": FOC to Betty Hester, January 26, 1962, Emory.

340–341 "rehabilitation of a country boy": "Tender Drama of Rebellious Youth Stars Elvis, Hope and Tuesday," *Union-Recorder,* July 13, 1961.

341 "The little boy": FOC to Betty Hester, November 3, 1962, *HB,* 498.

341 "I'm convinced that she used": Maryat Lee, October 4, 1975, journal entry, private collection.

341 "away with murder": Maryat Lee to Robert Giroux, March 22, 1976, FSG.

341 "smacked the windows": Maryat Lee, draft of a letter to Rosa Lee Walston, private collection.

341–342 "I have a very strong": Catherine Morai, in discussion with the author, September 26, 2004.

342 "The staff is non compos mentis": FOC to Louise and Tom Gossett, April 10, 1961, *HB*, 438.

342 "radiated bulls": FOC to Thomas Stritch, September 14, 1961, *CW*, 1152.

342 "I could hear the dull whine": Richard Gilman, "On Flannery O'Connor," *New York Review of Books* 13, no. 3 (August 21, 1969): 26.

343 "I don't know anything": FOC to Betty Hester, October 28, 1961, *CW*, 1152.

343 "completely hollow": FOC to Betty Hester, May 13, 1961, *HB*, 439.

343 "This conversion was achieved": FOC to Cecil Dawkins, January 10, 1962, *HB*, 459–60.

344 "compete with PLAYBOY": FOC to Robie Macauley, January 2, 1961, GCSU.

344 "found her fiction": Jean Cash, *Flannery O'Connor: A Life* (Knoxville: University of Tennessee Press, 2002), 87.

344 "immensely improved": Andrew Lytle, Reference Letter for Flannery O'Connor's 1956 Reapplication for a Fellowship, Archives of the J. S. Guggenheim Foundation.

344 "the grotesque": FOC to Betty Hester, July 19, 1958, *HB*, 291.

344 "You may state without fear": FOC to John Hawkes, July 27, 1958, *CW*, 1075.

344 "You suffer *The Lime Twig*": John Hawkes's *The Lime Twig* (New York: New Directions, 1961), excerpt of O'Connor's book jacket praise.

344 "black": John Hawkes, "Flannery O'Connor's Devil," *Sewanee Review* 70, no. 3 (Summer 1962): 400.

345 "In this one, I'll admit": FOC to John Hawkes, February 6, 1962, *CW*, 1157.

345 "I like the piece very much": Ibid., April 5, 1962, *CW*, 1159.

345 "off-center": FOC to Dr. T. R. Spivey, January 27, 1963, *HB*, 507.

345 "decided that I don't like": FOC to Elizabeth McKee, May 28, 1962, *HB*, 475.

345 "But pray that the Lord": FOC to Father James H. McCown, March 24, 1962, *HB*, 468.

345 "When I was a child": FOC to Betty Hester, March 24, 1962, Emory.

346 "powerful social": FOC to Cecil Dawkins, April 25, 1962, *CW*, 1161.

346 "the worst book": FOC to Betty Hester, July 22, 1961, *HB*, 446.

346 "I really liked Eudora": FOC to Cecil Dawkins, April 25, 1962, *CW*, 1161.

346 "'Explanations' are repugnant": FOC to Betty Hester, June 10, 1961, *HB*, 442.

347 "a comic novel": FOC, *Wise Blood*, "Author's Note to the Second Edition" (New York: Farrar, Straus and Cudahy, 1962), 5.

347 "Now what did you go": Maryat Lee to FOC, August 15, 1962, GCSU.

347 "Flannery was a paradoxical": Robert Giroux, in discussion with the author, November 13, 2003.

347 "the writing is one thing": Maryat Lee, draft of a letter to Rosa Lee Walston, private collection.

347 "much liquor": FOC to Betty Hester, May 5, 1962, *CW*, 1162.

347 "odiferous diesel": Joel Wells, "Off the Cuff," *Critic* 21 (August/September 1962): 4.

347 "wrapped up in newspaper": FOC to Betty Hester, June 9, 1962, *HB*, 478.

348 "They don't interfere": Granville Hicks, "A Writer at Home with Her Heritage," *Saturday Review* 45 (May 12, 1962): 22.

348 "wearing a blue plaid": Alfred Corn, in discussion with the author, March 10, 2005; in an e-mail of the same day, Corn wrote, "The more I think about it the more it seems that the unspoken undercurrent of my exchange with FO'C had to do with my

being gay: 'How can I believe in a religion that says God will punish me for being who I am, even though I didn't choose my sexuality?'"

348 "she was that awesome": Alfred Corn, "An Encounter with O'Connor and 'Parker's Back,'" *Flannery O'Connor Bulletin* 24 (1995–96): 106.

348 "At one time": FOC to Alfred Corn, May 30, 1962, *CW,* 1164.

348 "Even if there were no Church": Ibid., August 12, 1962, *CW,* 1173–74.

349 "There is a lot of ill-directed": FOC to Dr. T. R. Spivey, June 21, 1959, *CW,* 1098.

349 "knew I was going to get married": Ted R. Spivey, in discussion with the author, June 23, 2005.

349 "My Jung friend": FOC to Betty Hester, April 30, 1960, *HB,* 394.

349 "an awful lot of porch-settin'": Wells, "Off the Cuff," *Critic,* 72.

349 "Flannery O'Connor's novel": FOC, *The Complete Stories* (New York: Farrar, Straus and Giroux, 1971): 554–55.

350 "secular contemplative": FOC, manuscript of "Why Do the Heathen Rage?" File 226b, GCSU.

350 "hermit novelist": FOC to Maryat Lee, June 28, 1957, *CW,* 1036.

350 "I have broken through the ceiling": FOC, manuscript of "Why Do the Heathen Rage?" File 218a, GCSU.

350 "The depth of respect": Virginia Wray, "Flannery O'Connor's *Why Do the Heathen Rage?* And the Quotidian 'Larger Things,'" *Flannery O'Connor Bulletin* 23 (1994–95): 25.

350 "plaid shirt": FOC, manuscript of "Why Do the Heathen Rage?" File 216, GCSU.

350 "But it's so obviously": Louise H. Abbot, "Remembering Flannery," *Flannery O'Connor Bulletin* 23 (1994–95): 75.

350 "reflect the Teilhardian": John Kobler, "The Priest Who Haunts the Catholic World," *Saturday Evening Post* 236 (October 12, 1963): 42.

351 Thomas Merton: Thomas Merton, *The Wisdom of the Desert* (New York: New Directions, 1960).

351 "Nobody can get me out": FOC to Ashley Brown, October 28, 1962, Princeton.

351 "a Negro nightclub": FOC to John Hawkes, November 24, 1962, *HB,* 500.

351 "because we lost the War": FOC, "The Regional Writer," *MM,* 59.

352 "thrown at first by her deep": Jay Tolson, *Pilgrim in the Ruins* (New York: Simon and Schuster, 1992): 307; Tolson is quoting from a letter by Walter Percy to Phinizy Spalding, March 1, 1963.

352 "oppressive": FOC to Betty Hester, May 11, 1963, *HB,* 518.

352 "something (fishy)": FOC to Thomas Stritch, June 14, 1963, *CW,* 1185.

352 "I appreciate and need": FOC to Sister Mariella Gable, May 4, 1963, 1184.

352–353 "I have been working all summer": FOC to John Hawkes, September 10, 1963, *HB,* 537.

353 "country women": FOC to Cecil Dawkins, November 5, 1963, *HB,* 546.

353 "reward for setting": Ibid., May 19, 1964, *HB,* 579.

354 "how in the 6th grade": Maryat Lee, draft of letter to Rosa Lee Walston, private collection.

354 "made Mary Grace": FOC to Betty Hester, May 17, 1964, *HB,* 578.

354 "a country female Jacob": FOC to Maryat Lee, May 15, 1964, *CW,* 1207.

354 "How am I a hog": *CW,* 652; I owe the insight about the connection between O'Connor's reading of Shakespeare and Mrs. Turpin's soliloquy to Paul Elie, *The Life You Save May Be Your Own* (New York: Farrar, Straus and Giroux, 2003), 353.

354 "gets the vision": FOC to Maryat Lee, May 17, 1964, *CW,* 1207.

355 "Caroline was crazy about": FOC to Betty Hester, January 25, 1964, *CW,* 1199.

355 *"blackest":* FOC to Betty Hester, December 25, 1963, *HB,* 554.

355 "I like Mrs. Turpin": FOC to Maryat Lee, May 15, 1964, *CW,* 1207.

355 "half interest": Ibid., May 21, 1964, *CW,* 1209.

355 "I emulate my better characters": FOC to Betty Hester, January 25, 1964, *CW,* 1199.

355 "magnificent things": Jean W. Cash, "The Flannery O'Connor–Andrew Lytle Connection," *Flannery O'Connor Bulletin* 25 (1996–97): 191.

355 "The breath was pushed out": Maryat Lee to FOC, April 20, 1964, GCSU.

355–356 "I felt 'Revelation' marked": Louise Abbot, in discussion with the author, June 2, 2004.

356 "Not enough blood": FOC to Betty Hester, December 25, 1963, *HB,* 554.

356 "hitting this typewriter": Ibid., November 23, 1963, *HB,* 549.

356 "frisking": FOC to Cudden Ward Dorrance, January 5, 1964, UNC.

356 "round it out": FOC to Robert Giroux, January 25, 1964, *HB,* 563.

357 "I have the Original Tin Ear": FOC to Betty Hester, January 25, 1964, *CW,* 1200.

357 "straight up and down": FOC to Thomas Stritch, February 11, 1964, *CW,* 1200.

357 "All I can say": FOC to Betty Hester, February 14, 1964, *HB,* 566.

357 "Geritol": FOC to Cecil Dawkins, March 22, 1961, *HB,* 435.

357 "All commercial television": FOC to Sally and Robert Fitzgerald, November 23, 1963, *HB,* 550.

357 "postponed my work": FOC to Betty Hester, April 13, 1963, *HB,* 513.

358 "loaded with cortisone": FOC to John Hawkes, February 20, 1964, *HB,* 567.

358 "didn't seem so hot": FOC to Betty Hester, March 14, 1964, *CW,* 1203.

358 "It was all a howling": FOC to Robert Fitzgerald, March 8, 1964, *HB,* 568.

358 "not doing any brain work": FOC to Maryat Lee, March 21, 1964, GCSU.

358 "I suspect it has kicked": FOC to Betty Hester, March 28, 1964, *HB,* 571.

359 "we both want to locate": FOC to Cudden Ward Dorrance, Easter, March 24, 1964, UNC.

359 "Monday I woke up": FOC to Brainard Cheney, April 22, 1964, *CC,* 187.

359 "Jolly Corners": FOC to Maryat Lee, May 3, 1964, GCSU.

360 "I think I'll be able": FOC to Elizabeth McKee, May 7, 1964, *HB,* 575.

360 "I am writing me this story": FOC to Charlotte Gafford, May 10, 1964, *HB,* 576.

360 "I havent had it active": FOC to Louise and Tom Gossett, May 12, 1964, *HB,* 576.

360 "My my I do like": FOC to Maryat Lee, May 15, 1964, *CW,* 1207.

360 "very sorry story": FOC to Robert Giroux, May 21, 1964, *HB,* 579.

361 "Going to Piedmont": FOC to Maryat Lee, May 21, 1964, *CW,* 1209.

361 "he knows what he's doing": FOC to Maryat Lee, May 26, 1964, GCSU.

361 "By now, I know": FOC to Betty Hester, June 10, 1964, *HB,* 583.

362 "breezed in": FOC to Ashley Brown, June 15, 1964, *HB,* 584.

362 "After the nurse had left": Caroline Gordon, "Heresy in Dixie," *Sewanee Review* 76, no. 2 (Spring 1968): 266.

362 "I am sick of being sick": FOC to Louise Abbot, May 28, 1964, *CW,* 1210.

362 "fourth or fifth": Abbot, "Remembering Flannery," 79.

362 "Mizz O'Connor": Robert Coles, in discussion with the author, January 2, 2004.

362 "You will find here": Robert Coles, "Introduction," *Flannery O'Connor's South* (Athens and London: Brown Thrasher Books/University of Georgia Press, 1993), xviii.

362 "too high so you can't write": FOC to Cudden Ward Dorrance, June 2, 1964, UNC.

363 "I have another in the making": FOC to Catharine Carver, June 17, 1964, *CW,* 1210.

363 "like fabric": FOC to Betty Hester, July 17, 1964, *CW,* 1217.

363–364 "I read my Mass prayers": FOC to Janet McKane, April 2, 1964, *HB,* 572.

364 "little blocks": FOC, "Parker's Back," *CW,* 667. Possible sources for this visual detail are: Betty Hester, as a 1962 Christmas gift, sent O'Connor André Malraux's *Voices of Silence,* with an illustration of the ninth-century *Christ in Glory* from the Cathedral of Santa Sophia in Constantinople; William Sessions and his wife, Jenny, also sent a postcard with a Byzantine Christ from Greece in the summer of 1961.

364 *"one month":* FOC to Brainard and Frances Neel Cheney, June 19, 1964, *CC,* 191.

364 "Dr. Fulghum is back": FOC to Maryat Lee, June 23, 1964, *CW,* 1211–12.

364 "Margaret": FOC to Janet McKane, June 19, 1964, *CW,* 1211.

364 "I can get out": FOC to Cudden Ward Dorrance, June 24, 1964, UNC.

364 "I look like a bull frog": FOC to Thomas Stritch, June 28, 1964, *CW,* 1213.

365 "a few weeks longer": FOC to Robert Giroux, June 28, 1964, *HB,* 589.

365 "mellower": Frederick Asals, *Flannery O'Connor: The Imagination of Extremity* (Athens: University of Georgia Press, 1982), 141.

365 "hearing the celestial chorus": FOC to Maryat Lee, May 15, 1964, *CW,* 1208.

365 "The wolf": FOC to Sister Mariella Gable, July 5, 1964, *HB,* 591.

366 "fancy": FOC to Janet McKane, July 8, 1964, *CW,* 1214.

366 "into the typewriter": FOC to Catharine Carver, July 15, 1964, *CW,* 1216.

366 "Congratulations": Gordon, "Heresy in Dixie," 266.

366 "a lot of advice": FOC to Betty Hester, July 25, 1964, *CW,* 1218.

367 "It's six of one": FOC to Maryat Lee, July 26, 1964, *CW,* 1219.

367 "Sickness before death": FOC to Betty Hester, June 28, 1956, *CW,* 997.

367 "They expect me to improve": FOC to Cecil Dawkins, June 24, 1964, *HB,* 587.

367 "Dear Raybat": FOC to Maryat Lee, July 28, 1964, *CW,* 1220.

367 "Mary Flannery enjoyed": Regina O'Connor to Maryat Lee, August 17, 1964, GCSU.

368 "We had not dreamed": Mary Jo Thompson, in discussion with the author, May 25, 2004.

368 "A friend": Abbot, "Remembering Flannery," 79–81; much of the account of O'Connor's funeral is based on Abbot's memoir.

368 Abbot Augustine More: Georgia A. Newman, "A 'Contrary Kinship'": The Correspondence of Flannery O'Connor and Maryat Lee — Early Years, 1957–1959 (PhD dissertation, University of South Florida, 1999), 209.

368 "There was a lot of people": Alfred Matysiak, in discussion with the author, July 27, 2004.

369 "nursery pink": FOC to James Farnham, May 18, 1964, *Flannery O'Connor Bulletin* 12 (1983): 66.

370 Privately: Regina O'Connor to Mrs. Rumsey Haynes, September 12, 1964, GCSU.

370 "one of the nation's": "Flannery O'Connor Dead at 39," *New York Times,* August 4, 1964.

371 "most highly regarded": "Flannery O'Connor Leaves Inspiration," *Atlanta Constitution,* August 4, 1964.

371 "Flannery had made it": Barbara Tunnicliff Hamilton, "Flannery in Iowa City," 4, private collection.

371 "I think the cards": Robert Lowell to Elizabeth Bishop, August 10, 1964, *The Letters of Robert Lowell,* edited by Saskia Hamilton (New York: Farrar, Straus and Giroux, 2005), 453.

371 "I went and found only two": Robert Giroux to Caroline Gordon, October 8, 1964, FSG. Giroux mistakenly refers to McKane as "Miss McClune" in the original letter.

372 "her promise": Charles Poore, "The Wonderful Stories of Flannery O'Connor," *New York Times,* May 27, 1965.

372 "The work of a master": "Grace Through Nature," *Newsweek* (May 31, 1965): 86.

372 "Do you really think": Robert Giroux, in discussion with the author, November 13, 2003.

373 "the soft-spoken": Henry Raymont, "Notes of Concern Mark Book Awards Ceremony," *New York Times,* April 14, 1972.

373 "one of those flimsy": Maryat Lee, draft of a letter to Rosa Lee Walston, private collection.

374 "Now she rests": FOC, "Judgment Day," *CW,* 695; I am grateful to Paul Elie's detailed description of the late revisions to the typescript, "observed firsthand in the Farrar, Straus and Giroux offices," in Elie, *The Life You Save May Be Your Own,* 375.

INDEX

✹

Farrar, Straus and Cudahy, 299, 346
Faulkner, William: and Coindreau, 315;
O'Connor's reading of, 104, 209, 308–
309, 328; on race, 334; Rosenfeld on, 212;
and Welty, 346
Faulkner, William, works: *As I Lay Dying,*
181, 308; "Barn Burning," 103, 309; "A
Rose for Emily," 123, 219; *The Sound and
the Fury,* 308; "That Evening Sun," 104,
129
feminism, 89–92, 97–98, 216
Fenwick, Elizabeth, 153–154, 175–176
Ferris, Charlotte Conn, 59, 77, 208
Finnegan, Ruth Sullivan, 130–131, 289
Firth, Catherine, 359, 368
Fitzgerald, Robert: on cold winters, 189;
and Ford Foundation fellowship, 314; in
Italy, 237; and Robert Lowell, 171–172,
173, 174, 182–183; on Edward
O'Connor, 23; and O'Connor on dis-
placed persons, 241; and O'Connor on
Langkjaer, 230–231, 235; and O'Connor
on Lourdes trip, 298; and O'Connor on
Teilhard de Chardin, 326; and
O'Connor on visitors, 278; on
O'Connor's cartoons, 111; and
O'Connor's *A Good Man Is Hard to Find,*
254, 262, 267; and O'Connor's hysterec-
tomy, 358; and O'Connor's impression
of Virgin and Child statue, 178; and
O'Connor's "The Lame Shall Enter
First," 339; and O'Connor's lecture at
Notre Dame, 288–289; and O'Connor's
"The Life You Save My Be Your Own,"
220–221; O'Connor's relationship with,
181, 195, 200, 201, 210, 217, 228;
O'Connor staying at Connecticut home
of, 179–180, 181, 183–184, 213–216, 225;
and O'Connor's *The Violent Bear It
Away,* 309, 313, 315; and O'Connor's visit
to Italy, 300; and O'Connor's will, 299;
and O'Connor's *Wise Blood,* 198, 201,
204, 207–208, 213; and *Sewanee Review,*
344
Fitzgerald, Sally: on Gordon, 199; and
Hester, 305; in Italy, 237; on Langkjaer,
257; and Lourdes trip, 301–305; and
Robert Lowell, 160, 171; on Edward
O'Connor, 43; on Regina O'Connor, 25;
and O'Connor on displaced persons,
241; and O'Connor on Langkjaer, 230–
231, 235; and O'Connor on Lourdes trip,
298; and O'Connor on visitors, 278; on
O'Connor's "A Good Man Is Hard to

Find," 226; and O'Connor's *A Good
Man Is Hard to Find,* 254, 262, 267; on
O'Connor's illness, 185, 192, 214–216,
301; O'Connor's relationship with, 181,
195, 200, 201, 210, 214–216, 217, 228;
O'Connor staying at Connecticut home
of, 179–180, 181, 183–184, 213–216, 225;
on O'Connor's "The Train," 172, 182;
and O'Connor's *The Violent Bear It
Away,* 309, 313, 315; and O'Connor's visit
to Italy, 300–301; and O'Connor's *Wise
Blood,* 198, 204, 207–208; on John Sul-
livan, 100
Flannery, John, 15, 18–19
Flannery, Mary Ellen, 15, 19
Flaubert, Gustave, 199, 366
Florencourt, Agnes Cline, 59, 62, 75, 99
Florencourt, Catherine, 59, 62, 65
Florencourt, Frances, 58–60, 62, 65, 140,
203
Florencourt, Frank, 59
Florencourt, Louise, 59, 62, 65, 177
Florencourt, Margaret, 59, 62, 65, 223
Ford Foundation fellowship, 314
Foulkes-Taylor, David, 292–293, 295
Freud, Sigmund, 269, 311
Fugitive poets, 136, 137, 143, 236
Fulghum, Charles, 71, 190–191, 353, 361,
364, 367
Fulton, Lyman, 177–178, 179, 183

Galley Proof (television show), 259–261,
264, 266
Gallop, Mary Boyd, 90–91, 210
Georgia Military College, 52, 53, 79, 89, 99
Georgia State College for Women: and
"Jessies," 19, 88–89, 90, 93, 97; Robert E.
Lee as president of, 283, 287, 295; and
O'Connor's books and paintings, 299;
and O'Connor's cartoons, 94–96, 98, 100,
101, 106, 110–111, 248; O'Connor's
classes at, 85–87, 101–107, 112–115;
O'Connor's enrollment in, 82–83, 84; in
O'Connor's fiction, 82; O'Connor's
graduation from, 115–116; O'Connor's
lecture for, 86, 287–288; Peabody Elementary as lab school for, 57; professors of, 51, 52; and Rat Day, 92–93; and
Waves, 97–99, 108, 111; Wells as president of, 283; and World War II, 87–89,
96–97, 98, 108–109; and YWCA, 89–90,
91
Georgia State Training School for Boys, 52,
249